Puritanism

Puritanism

Transatlantic Perspectives
on a Seventeenth-Century
Anglo-American Faith

Francis J. Bremer

EDITOR

Distributed by
Northeastern
University
Press

1993

Boston

Massachusetts Historical Society

Library of Congress Cataloging-in-Publication Data
PURITANISM: Transatlantic perspectives on a
seventeenth-century Anglo-American faith / Francis J.
Bremer, editor.
    p.   cm.—(Massachusetts Historical Society studies
in American history and culture ; no. 3)
    Includes bibliographical references and index.
    ISBN 0-934909-34-2
    1. Puritans—England.   2. Puritans—New
England.   3. England—Church history—16th
century.   4. England—Church history—17th
century.   5. New England—Church history.   I. Bremer,
Francis J.   II. Series.
BX9322.T73   1993
285'.9'09—dc20   93-14428
                                                   CIP

Designed by David Ford

papers from the 1991 Millersville University Conference
on Puritanism in Old and New England
Sponsored by the
Massachusetts Historical Society
Millersville University and
the Institute of Early American History and Culture

Massachusetts Historical Society Studies
in American History and Culture, No. 3

for Kristin

Contents

Contents   **viii**

Part Four: Contrasting Communities

Part Five: The Legacy

Contributors

FRANCIS J. BREMER is Professor of History at Millersville University of Pennsylvania and Editor of the Winthrop Papers for the Massachusetts Historical Society. He is the author of *Congregational Communion, Shaping New Englands, The Puritan Experiment,* and other books and articles on Anglo-American Puritanism.

SARGENT BUSH JR. is Professor of English at the University of Wisconsin at Madison. He is the author of *The Writings of Thomas Hooker: Spiritual Adventures in Two Worlds* and numerous articles on English and American literature. He is currently editing the correspondence of John Cotton.

CHARLES L. COHEN is Associate Professor of History at the University of Wisconsin at Madison. He is the author of *God's Caress: The Psychology of Puritan Religious Experience* and other studies of Puritan spirituality.

PATRICK COLLINSON is Regius Professor of Modern History at the University of Cambridge. He is the author of *The Birthpangs of Protestant England, The Elizabethan Puritan Movement, The Religion of Protestants,* and numerous other works on Tudor-Stuart religion and society.

STEPHEN FOSTER is Presidential Research Professor at Northern Illinois University. He is the author of *The Long Argument: English Puritanism and the Shaping of New England Culture, Notes from the Caroline Underground, Their Solitary Way,* and other studies of seventeenth-century English and American Puritanism.

CHARLES HAMBRICK-STOWE is pastor of the Church of the Apostles, United Church of Christ, in Lancaster, Pennsylvania and a member of the faculty of Lancaster Theological Seminary. He is the author of *The Practice of Piety: Puritan Devotional Disciplines in Seventeenth-Century New England* and editor of *Early New England Meditative Poetry: Anne Bradstreet and Edward Taylor.*

Contributors

ANN HUGHES is Senior Lecturer at the University of Manchester. She is the author of *Politics, Society and Civil War: Warwickshire 1620-1660*, *The Causes of the English Civil War*, and other studies of seventeenth-century England.

JOHN R. KNOTT is Professor of English at the University of Michigan. He is the author of *Milton's Pastoral Vision*, *The Sword of the Spirit*, *Discourses of Martyrdom in English Literature, 1563-1694*, and other works on seventeenth-century English literature.

PETER LAKE is Professor of History at Princeton University. He is the author of *Moderate Puritans and the Elizabethan Church*, *Anglicans and Puritans?* and numerous other studies on the religious life of Tudor and Stuart England.

CAROL G. SCHNEIDER is Executive Vice-President of the Association of American Colleges. Her Harvard doctoral thesis was on the subject of "Godly Order in a Church Half-Reformed: The Disciplinarian Legacy, 1570-1641."

KEITH STAVELY is the author of *Puritan Legacies: Paradise Lost and the New England Tradition, 1630–1890*, *The Politics of Milton's Prose Style*, and various other studies of seventeenth-century literature.

MARGO TODD is Professor of History at Vanderbilt University. She is the author of *Christian Humanism and the Puritan Social Order*, and various articles on seventeenth-century England.

Introduction

Puritan Studies: The Case

for an Atlantic Approach

Francis J. Bremer

THIS COLLECTION of essays is part of an ongoing effort to suggest a new way of looking at the Puritans, their faith, and their world. For quite a while I have believed that it is inappropriate to constrict the lives of men such as John Davenport or women such as Anne Hutchinson to interpretive categories implied by labels such as "American" or "English." The mental world of John Cotton was altered but not fundamentally changed by his move from Boston, Lincolnshire, to Boston, Massachusetts. Not only did such individuals continue to think much as they had before emigration, but those who remained in America continued to follow the news from their homeland and tried to shape events there. New England letters, books, and even some colonists regularly flowed eastward, the colonial loop being but one episode in the personal stories of temporary emigrants such as Hugh Peter who began and ended their lives in England. While it would be as much an error to approach the colonies as no more than additional English counties as it is to see them as truly a new world, efforts to integrate the Puritan experiment into the mainstream of English history may provide many benefits for Americanists and students of England's century of revolution.

To test this view, in 1975 I organized a conference at Thomas More College in Kentucky on "Puritanism in Old and New England." Authorities on English history such as Christopher Hill, Richard

Greaves, Paul Christianson, and Robert Zaller joined with Americanists such as Michael McGiffert, Sacvan Bercovitch, Robert Pope, and Chadwick Hansen to share in formal and informal exchanges. After a long hiatus, another such gathering convened in April 1991 at Millersville University of Pennsylvania, which sponsored the program in conjunction with the Massachusetts Historical Society and the Institute of Early American History and Culture. Each of the essays in this collection was originally presented at that meeting. Other papers of considerable interest were also delivered but have not been included either because their authors reserved them or they could not be fit into the format of this volume. We hope that all of them will eventually appear in print elsewhere.

Both conferences were intended to promote a new transatlantic understanding of Puritanism among the participants. English historians customarily view the colonies as a sideshow, and Americanists seek mainly to mine the ore of British history for the specific elements of background which will shed light on their colonial concerns. Each group, in short, views the interests of the other as a distinct, separate, and less compelling field. Yet those who attended the conference and most who will read this collection agree that Puritanism is an important part of English history and of the history of North America—even if they cannot agree on what Puritanism was! The assumption behind this collection is that what made men and women Puritans was more important than what made them East Anglians or New Englanders. The Puritan experience in one place—whether it be London, New Haven, or Arnhem in the Netherlands—illumines Puritanism wherever we find it. The work of Patrick Collinson and Peter Lake on the Elizabethan church is essential to understand the religion of New England's settlers, a point Stephen Foster has effectively demonstrated in *The Long Argument*. As Ann Hughes argues in her essay here, David Hall's examination of colonial popular belief in *World of Wonder, Days of Judgment* can suggest new perspectives on English Puritanism of the Interregnum period. The differences between the two societies were real, but by examining how the same movement evolved in different settings we are alerted to elements of Puritanism that we might otherwise overlook.

In addition to the transatlantic perspective, another trend in Puritan studies characterizes this volume, and that is the focus on religious feelings. In the 1970s scholars such as William K. B. Stoever and E. Brooks Holifield succeeded in restoring attention to the development of Puritan theology. Now other dimensions of Puritan

faith are being explored. The essays in this collection all deal with.
religion, but they seldom focus on doctrinal matters. Without ne-
glecting the life of the mind, scholars such as Charles Cohen and
Charles Hambrick-Stowe have directed attention to the life of the
heart. In their account, the experience of piety was the glue that ce-
mented Puritans together in godly communion and the boundary
across which it was difficult for native Americans to move.

While there have been some exceptions, American historians have
tended to take Puritanism for granted, accepting that the colonists
who came to New England were Puritans and that what they believed was Puritanism. English historians—faced with a far more
complex and fluid religious situation in the sixteenth and seventeenth centuries—have not been able to take that easy path and have
been immersed in heated arguments over the meaning of Puritanism.
In his essay on "Defining Puritanism—again?," Peter Lake reviews
some of this controversy and offers suggestions that focus our attention on a Puritan style of piety and divinity, largely nurtured in voluntary gatherings of saints. His approach acknowledges the importance of ecclesiastical structure but also explains why for much of the
Elizabethan and early Stuart period this was not a defining concern
of the movement. One of the themes that English historians are currently exploring is whether Puritanism was a divisive force. Lake in
his essay here and Patrick Collinson in a number of recent works
have suggested that "nonseparating" Puritans were concerned to
shun the "ungodly" and "ungodly practices" in their everyday lives,
and that this generated a fatal split in communities. Yet examination
of the New England experience may lead us to question this perspective, or at least refine it. Many of the elements which Lake finds central to Puritanism are the same that Stephen Foster found in the life
of the colonial layman Thomas Minor. But while in the colonies only
visible saints were allowed church membership, the remainder of the
community was not shunned by the godly. There was no simple bi-
polar division of saints and sinners. Men and women were regenerate
and elect, elect but not yet regenerate, or unregenerate—those who
were not yet born again might be in the middle category and yet be
chosen. New England's Puritans were willing to give the latter the
benefit of the doubt even though they did not welcome them to communion. The world of Thomas Minor seems not to have generated
the divisions which some see in England.

Lake and Foster both point to the pietistic style of the Puritan and the development and definition of that outlook and character are explored by Margo Todd and John Knott. Borrowing from the innovative literary studies of Stephen Greenblatt, Todd discusses the self-fashioning of Samuel Ward. While he drew upon historical models, Ward was heavily influenced by the community of the godly which he encountered at Cambridge. Social relations were at the heart of Puritan voluntary religion. Friendship was significant not only in shaping Puritan consciousness but also in sustaining the Puritan on a pilgrimage that was known to involve suffering. Ward's recognition that his path would entail being labeled "a madman" and being called "slanderous names, as names of puritans and precisians," is reminiscent of John Winthrop's similar expectation of abuse for taking the road he had chosen—that one would "be despised, pointed at, hated of the world, made a byword, reviled, slandered, rebuked, made a grazing stock, called Puritans, nice fools, hypocrites, hairbrained fellows, rash, indiscreet, vainglorious, and all that is nought."

The use that Puritans made of their experience of verbal abuse and other forms of suffering is brilliantly drawn out by John Knott in his study of John Bunyan. In the post-Reformation era when Bunyan lingered in prison, New England Puritans also suffered, challenged by growing political pressures on their holy commonwealths and most notably threatened during the time of King Philip's War. The pilgrimages of Indian captives such as Mary Rowlandson are evocative of the trials of Bunyan's Christians, pointing to their place in a broader Puritan tradition. And, on a different point, Knott's recognition of the growing stress placed by Bunyan on the role of the nonconformist pastor in guiding and nurturing the faithful parallels the growing assertion of clerical authority which Foster sees occurring in New England.

Another theme that runs through this entire collection is the importance of godly communion in the world of the Puritans. While the voluntary elements in Puritanism could have exerted a centrifugal force leading to diversity, conference among the saints helped them to strain towards symmetry and unity. Ward, Minor, Bunyan's Christiana—all rely on the help of faithful friends to shape their piety. In his essay, Sargent Bush explores some of the ways in which this was accomplished, focusing on the counseling efforts of John Cotton. Because Puritan Congregationalists eschewed the granting of ecclesiastical authority to any power above the gathered church, there were no formal mechanisms for imposing uniformity throughout the community of the faithful. Informal means of counsel, communion, and correspondence served to preserve the integrity of the movement, and respected clergymen such as Cotton played central roles in facilitating such contact.

Patrick Collinson, Carol Schneider, and Ann Hughes all address the question of the relationship among Puritans and seek to identify the reasons for the eventual breakdown of their communion and the formation of distinct sectarian communities. Collinson's essay explores the dynamics of the left wing of the movement, where orthodoxy shaded towards sectarianism. He examines how Puritan authors sought to define themselves in relation to both the established church and those who had separated from it. Schneider directs attention to the opposite end of the spectrum, where Presbyterians emphasized a concern for order. Hughes looks at tensions within Puritanism not so much along the breadth of the spectrum but as they existed between the learned elite of the movement and the less formally educated lay believers. Each scholar in turn emphasizes the striving towards unity by nonconformists who nevertheless eventually fragmented. Recent scholarship on the Puritans—particularly dealing with New England—has stressed the diversity of the movement. Philip Gura in particular has demonstrated the many "radical" views that circulated in the transatlantic community. Yet such work has had two unfortunate tendencies. On the one hand it has led to an implicit (and unintentional) reaffirmation of a "Puritan orthodoxy" against which the radicals reacted. And it has also tended to categorize the orthodox as conservative. Collinson, Hughes, and Schneider help us to recognize the danger of drawing lines too firmly along a spectrum of Puritan beliefs. Those who came to differ shared much in common, those who stayed together differed among themselves on some points, and "orthodox" as well as "radicals" retained an evangelical zeal that impelled them to reach out with their message to the ordinary men and women of their time.

Sometimes the nature of a movement or a system is most clearly highlighted in its failures. And the nature of the faith of the Puritans can perhaps be better apprehended when we look at their contact with non-Christian cultures in the wilderness of America. Certainly the mission to the Indians commanded the attention of Englishmen as well as New Englanders. Charles Cohen, in exploring the religious experience of the Massachusetts Amerindians, sheds light not only on the missions but on the importance of apprehending divine love in Puritan spirituality. In a field that has been dominated by arguments over Puritan intent in Indian relations, Cohen raises questions about the cultural transferability of basic notions of Puritan faith and whether it was possible for an Amerindian to experience grace as the Englishman did, or at least to understand that experience as the white Puritan did. By focusing on what is missing in Indian conversion narratives he also makes us more aware of key aspects in the English narratives. Keith Stavely uses Roger Williams's views to examine roads taken and those not taken as Puritans tried to define their identity as a community. Stavely illustrates Williams's views on the nature of New England society by examining the Rhode Islander's observations on the region's natives and also seeks to place Williams in a broader perspective by comparing his thoughts on society to those of his fellow radical John Milton. His focus on what made Roger Williams different tells us about the way others followed as well as the path taken by the Rhode Island rebel and demonstrates as well some of the common concerns that united Puritans on both sides of the Atlantic.

When does Puritanism come to an end? That, of course, depends on how one defines Puritanism. Traditionally, English historians end their tale with the Restoration and leave it to students of "Nonconformity" and "Dissent" to take the story further while colonialists have trouble pointing to any dramatic terminal point. But the emphasis on a style of Puritan piety, on a Puritan temperament, which runs through these essays makes it more likely that we will all come to focus more on Puritan continuities that lead into the eighteenth century and the revivals of that time. Charles Hambrick-Stowe, in the concluding essay, demonstrates that those who were born again in the fires of the Great Awakening saw themselves linked to the tradition of Cotton and Shepard, of Perkins and Owen. He examines the republication of seventeenth-century works in the time of the eighteenth-century revivals and the extent to which the proponents of the Awakening consciously drew on the piety of the old Puritans. The New Lights identified themselves with a Puritan tradition that continued to live, and a tradition that included those whose careers had ended in England as well as those who lived and labored in the colonies.

It is a commonplace to write and speak of the abundance of works on Puritanism and to ask whether there can possibly be justification for yet another study. But every time one is tempted to close the door on the field a new window is opened and a new angle of vision proposed that opens up unanticipated perspectives. There are few historical subjects that are capable of rewarding such intense attention. The essays that follow are evidence of the richness of the Puritan world and testimony to the imagination of the scholars that have been attracted to the field.

Part One: Defining Puritanism

Defining Puritanism—again?

Peter Lake

THE DEFINITION of Puritanism is an issue which has been both addressed and avoided to great profit by many great scholars. The result is that it is not a subject upon which there is anything very new to say. We can all rehearse the various positions and arguments that have been adduced to deal with this subject. Despite this I want to begin, boringly, by summarizing what I take to be the various responses to the problem of "Puritanism" made available by the more recent historiography on English religion in the period between roughly 1560 and 1640.

The first position is the equation of Puritanism with something like the Puritan movement as Patrick Collinson has described it.[1] On this view Puritanism involves a commitment to further reformation in the government or liturgy of the church. Where evidence of ceremonial non-conformity or attachment to a variety of schemes to alter the government of the church (ranging from various modes of modified episcopacy to presbyterianism and other varieties of radical Puritan ecclesiology) is present there is Puritanism, where it is not, there is the absence of Puritanism. The advantage of this approach is clarity of definition; on this view we know what we mean and what we are looking for in calling someone or something "Puritan."[2] The drawback is that in practice the prevalence of such formal signs of disaffection with the English church was a function of attendant political circumstance and in connection with non-conformity, of the

---

[1] Patrick Collinson, *The Elizabethan Puritan Movement* (London, 1967), passim.
[2] This is very much the approach adopted by Nicholas Tyacke in his seminal article "Puritanism, Arminianism and Counter-Revolution" in C. Russell, ed., *The Origins of the English Civil War* (London, 1973), now significantly modified by his important Dr. Williams Lecture, *The Fortunes of English Puritanism, 1603-40* (London, 1989).

3

promiscuous ways in which conformity was enforced by both local and national authorities. Puritanism could therefore appear and reappear like the smile on the face of the Cheshire cat, according to the circumstances of local and national politics. Such an approach also ignores the internal, emotional aspects of Puritan piety and practical divinity.

To avoid these drawbacks it is possible to define Puritanism as a style of piety, an emotional and ideological style, producing distinctive structures of meaning whereby both the world and the self could be construed, interpreted, and acted upon. Within this approach there seem to me to be two dominant tendencies. The first is centered on separating out distinctively, even exclusively, Puritan approaches or positions on any number of subjects, ranging from sabbath observance, household worship, the companionate marriage to overtly theological issues like covenant theology, experimental predestinarianism, particular styles of providentialism.[3]

The second largely eschews this search for a core of definitively Puritan notions or opinions and seeks to define the Puritan style as a distinctively zealous or intense subset of a larger body of reformed or protestant doctrines and positions. On this view the point is not so much to identify any one opinion or position as Puritan in the sense that only Puritans held it but to describe the totality of relations, the internal articulations and interconnections between the individual tenets and tendencies which made up the Puritan style. The nature of that style and its constituent parts is to be identified through the examination of the life and thought of those zealous English protestants labeled Puritans by their enemies and equated by themselves with "the godly" or the elect saints of God and marked off from their lukewarm contemporaries by the private forms of collective piety (the conventicles, repetitions of the heads of sermons, fasts and prayer sessions) rendered so familiar through the godly lives collected by Samuel Clarke and the more recent researches of Professor Collinson. Puritans defined under this rubric had an asymmetrical relationship to Puritanism defined as self-conscious disaffection with the structures and practices of the national church; crudely all or nearly all Puritans covered by that definition were also carriers of all or large parts of the Puritan style of piety and divinity, but all

[3] For such an attempt see R. Greaves, *Society and Religion in Elizabethan England* (Minneapolis, 1981).

denizens of that style were not necessarily non-conformists or opponents of episcopacy.[4]

A third approach or solution to the problem of Puritanism first systematically canvassed by the Georges and more recently generated or spun out of this last approach holds that so close are the constituent parts of the Puritan style to wider bodies of reformed or protestant thought, that residual notions of Puritanism as a free-standing view of the world are best jettisoned. Contemporaries' use of the word Puritan and deployment of images or characters of the archetypal Puritan are now best seen as exercises in literary game playing and polemical maneuver, rather than as references to any very stable or coherent Puritan position existing in the world independent of those literary types and stereo-types. I at least think that I can discern a subtle and playful version of this position within the recent writings of Professor Collinson.[5]

All these versions of "Puritanism" have been developed during a period when the ancient polarity or opposition between "Anglicans" and Puritans, an opposition which rendered the nature and existence of both poles unproblematic, even natural, has come under sharp attack. Here, as almost everywhere in this field, the way has been led by Professor Collinson who started to discover at the very center of the Elizabethan establishment the presence of core protestant and evangelical protestant attitudes of precisely the type that underlay "Puritanism." That was a process that started in the *Elizabethan Puritan Movement,* accelerated in his study of Grindal, and reached its apogee in the *Religion of Protestants,* where "Puritanism" all but disappeared inside a wider English reformed tradition, a tradition now established in a position of ideological hegemony through a myriad of local accommodations between godly magistrate and learned preacher and at the center by a similar alliance between a Calvinist or Calvinizing godly prince and a learned and evangelically concerned bench of bishops. The ideological cement for this vision of the early Stuart church was, of course, provided by Dr. Tyacke's

---

[4]For a defense of such an approach see Peter Lake, "Puritan Identities," *Journal of Ecclesiastical History* 35(1984): 112-123 and for an attempt to apply such an approach to a specific group see my *Moderate Puritans and the Elizabethan Church* (Cambridge, 1982).

[5]C. H. and K. George, *The Protestant Mind of the English Reformation* (Princeton, 1961); Patrick Collinson, *The Puritan Character: Polemics and Polarities* (Los Angeles, 1989); for a still more extreme statement of the same position see M. G. Finlayson, *Historians, Puritanism and the English Revolution* (Toronto, 1983) and more recently J. C. Davis, "Puritanism and Revolution: Themes, Categories, Methods and Conclusions," *Historical Journal* 34(1991): 479-490.

work on what he took to be the essentially adversarial relationship
between English Arminianism and the position or positions on predestination which passed for orthodox amongst educated protestants
under Elizabeth and James. Now instead of a binary opposition between Anglicans and Puritans we had an equally stark opposition
between Calvinists and Arminians, the terms of which were designed
to subvert or call into radical question the old Anglican/Puritan dichotomy. Now, instead of two opposing religious styles, we had
something like a unitary reformed tradition, intermittently disrupted
by discreet disputes over ceremonies or church government. Anglicanism instead of a unitary view of the world, a distinctive religious
style, became a series of rhetorics and polemical choices rendered
necessary to defend the structure and practices of the Church of
England from Puritan attack, and Puritanism shrank from a similar
status to being a subset of more general protestant or reformed attitudes of the type discussed above.[6]

My own position on the issue of Puritanism is an amalgam of the
second and third approaches. That is to say, I would wish to see Puritanism as a distinctive style of piety and divinity, made up not so
much of distinctively Puritan component parts, the mere presence of
which in a person's thought or practice rendered them definitively a
Puritan, as a synthesis made of strands most or many of which taken
individually could be found in non-Puritan as well as Puritan contexts, but which taken together formed a distinctively Puritan synthesis or style. This is not to rule out the possibility of our identifying
distinctively Puritan attitudes and opinions on a whole series of issues. (To take the example of sabbatarianism, even Dr. Parker admits
the existence of such Puritan shibboleths even as he marginalizes
their significance by labeling those issues upon which the Puritans
differed from his sabbatarian mainstream as "peripheral.") But it is
to argue that our concern should not be so much to list and delimit
a group of telltale Puritan opinions as to pull together a sense of the
central core of a Puritan style or tradition or world view.[7]

If we take this approach we avoid the drawbacks inherent in the

[6]Patrick Collinson, *Archbishop Grindal, 1519-1583: The Struggle for a Reformed Church*
(London, 1979); *idem.*, *The Religion of Protestants* (Oxford, 1982); Nicholas Tyacke, "Puritanism, Arminianism and Counter-revolution" and now see his *Anti-Calvinists: The Rise
of English Arminianism, c 1590-1640* (Oxford, 1987).

[7]K. Parker, *The English Sabbath* (Cambridge, 1988), esp. chaps. 4, 5 and 6; for a rather
different perspective now see J. H. Primus, *Holy Time: Moderate Puritanism and the Sabbath*
(Macon, Ga., 1989), esp. chaps. 7 and 8; for some more general remarks on this approach
see Lake, "Puritan Identities."

first response to the problem of definition outlined above; that is the appearance and disappearance of "Puritanism" (defined simply as nonconformity or support for some sort of further reformation) according to the exigencies of political circumstance and the attitudes towards conformity of the authorities in church and state. But arguably what is gained in stability of focus is lost again in terms of clarity or precision of definition. For this approach is almost inevitably going to generate a certain number of marginal cases, where the decision of whether to call someone a Puritan or when in the course of a long and well rewarded career someone stops being a Puritan and becomes something else is difficult, perhaps even impossible, to make and, therefore, almost by definition not worth making. Again, the "oppositionist" overtones which have always attended the usage of contemporaries and later historians when discussing Puritanism might seem to be called into question by this approach. For as Professor Collinson and others have pointed out carriers of what one might term a Puritan view of the world often constructed themselves and were accepted by others as pillars of the establishment, models of moderation and defenders of order and orthodoxy. Thus when Laudian anti-Puritans in the 1630s set out to reduce the church to what they took to be order, they often found themselves in conflict with local Puritan establishments, establishments as convinced of their own orthodoxy and rectitude as defenders of order in their counties as were the Laudians of their status as guardians of hierarchy, order, and degree in church and state. Similarly, in St. John's College in Cambridge in the 1590s it was the Puritan master William Whitaker who took his stand on the issue of obedience, order, and the defense of orthodoxy against dissident fellows out to cast him or his clique as favorers of "Puritanism."[8]

Professor Collinson has made much of this, and in the context of a debate with the likes of Michael Walzer about the inherent "radicalism" of "Puritanism," concluded that there was really very little "radical" at all about the alliance between godly magistrate and godly minister that came increasingly to dominate whole counties of Eng-

[8]For examples of Puritan pillars of the establishment see, for instance, C. Cross, *The Puritan Earl* (London, 1966); Jacqueline Eales, *Puritans and Roundheads: The Harleys and the Outbreak of the English Civil War* (Cambridge, 1990); for clerical membership of the establishment in Cambridge university under Elizabeth see Lake, *Moderate Puritans,* esp. chap. 8 on William Whitaker's period as master of St. John's; for a case study of a local Puritan establishment closing ranks against an intrusive Laudianism in the 1630s see Ann Hughes, "Thomas Dugard and his Circle in the 1630s: a Parliamentary-Puritan Connection?," *Historical Journal* 29(1986): 771-793; also see Peter Lake, "Puritanism, Arminian-

land from the 1570s on. Where, then, on this view, does "Puritanism" end and the establishment, against which Puritanism has always traditionally been defined, start?[9]

Following the thrust of two interlinked processes of political and cultural change Professor Collinson and Dr. Tyacke (in his earlier incarnation) have blurred that line, at times until it has become almost indistinguishable. On the one hand, viewing the early Jacobean church from the perspective of the Elizabethan Puritan movement, Professor Collinson has been understandably impressed by the relative absence of the peaks and troughs of political, public agitation for further reformation during the later period—at least after an initial flurry of activity either side of the Hampton Court conference. In the absence of public collisions between the Puritan conscience and the demands of authority of the sort which fatally disturbed the initial Grindalian moment, it was natural to assume that the same ideological and social forces that prompted that first experiment in incorporation and consensus would again come into play—hence the picture of the Jacobean church in *The Religion of Protestants* as the church of Grindal redivivus.[10]

That vision was confirmed by the logic of a second cultural process, the gradual but distinct protestantization of English culture and society in the period after 1570. In a series of brilliant studies Collinson has shown the ways in which the protestant impulse became integrated into the fabric of national and provincial life, both institutionally through the generation of lectures by combination, culturally through the spread of rather harsh iconophobic attitudes to the printed or painted image, and socially by demonstrating the ways in which supposedly "Puritan" or harshly protestant attitudes to social regulation in fact keyed in with the wider social concerns of local elites. The result is his compelling picture of Puritanism as a form of voluntary religion, largely contained within and enriching rather than seeking to overturn or remake the institutional and liturgical frameworks provided by the national church.[11]

On some readings this would seem to call into question the whole

---

ism and a Shropshire Axe-murder," *Midland History* 15(1990): 37-64 and more generally J. T. Cliffe, *The Puritan Gentry* (London, 1984), esp. chaps. 8, 9 and 10.

[9] Collinson, *Religion of Protestants,* chap. 4 and more generally "Towards a Broader Understanding of the Dissenting Tradition" in Patrick Collinson, *Godly People* (London, 1983).

[10] Collinson, *Religion of Protestants,* passim.

[11] Patrick Collinson, *The Birthpangs of Protestant England* (London, 1988), esp. chapter 4; also see his "Cranbrook and the Fletchers" and "Lectures by Combination: Structures

value of the concept or label Puritan and certainly to cast serious doubt on the status of anything one might call Puritanism as a coherent or freestanding view of the world. I have no desire directly to challenge or reject this position. Indeed, it would be doubly absurd for someone whose own early research was concerned to show the ways in which "Puritanism" or Puritans could penetrate inside "the establishment" to object too strenuously to the analysis summarized here. However, in *Moderate Puritans* and various attendant articles I was concerned to have my cake and eat it; that is to say, to examine and explore Puritan penetration of the establishment and thus to call into question, or in the current jargon to problematize the simple dichotomy between "Anglican mainstream" and "Puritan opposition" while at the same time insisting on the existence of an identifiable Puritan tradition of thought and feeling, a style of subjectivity and way of looking at the world, running throughout the period.[12] I still want to do both those things, and in order to defend the propriety of that desire I want to supplement and develop the position that I have attributed to Professor Collinson above.

I want to do that in a number of ways. Crudely, I want to suggest that the processes of protestantization described by Professor Collinson served both to integrate impulses and attitudes best described as Puritan into the establishment or rather parts of the establishments of Jacobean England and to render the strands of thought and feeling labeled Puritan by historians and some contemporaries more rather than less distinctive. In making this case, I will in part be simply mobilizing or juxtaposing parts of Collinson's oeuvre against other parts, appealing, if you like, from the last two chapters of *The Religion of Protestants* and "Cranbrook and the Fletchers" to the last chapter of the *Birthpangs of Protestant England* and "the English conventicle."[13]

---

and Characteristics of Church Life in 17th Century England," both in Collinson, *Godly People;* Collinson, *Religion of Protestants,* chaps. 5 and 6; also on the spread of protestant attitudes amongst the populace see David Cressy, *Bonfires and Bells* (London, 1989) and T. Watt, *Cheap Print and Popular Piety, 1560-1640* (Cambridge, 1991).

[12]Lake, *Moderate Puritans,* passim but especially chap. 7 on the emergence in the late sixteenth century of a distinctive Puritan style of piety or religious subjectivity; also see my "The Dilemma of the Establishment Puritan: The Cambridge Heads and the Case of Francis Johnson and Cuthbert Bainbrigg," *Journal of Ecclesiastical History* 29(1978): 23-35; "Robert Some and the Ambiguities of Moderation," *Archiv für Reformationsgeschichte* 71(1980): 254-278; "The Significance of the Elizabethan Identification of the Pope as Antichrist," *Journal of Ecclesiastical History* 31(1980).

[13]Patrick Collinson, "The English Conventicle" in D. Wood and W. J. Sheils, eds., *Voluntary Religion* (Oxford, 1986), *Studies in Church History,* vol. 24.

Let us start with the Puritan impulse toward incorporation within the various establishments of early Stuart England. There was clearly a strong drive toward power, status, and social and intellectual respectability at work among many Elizabethan hot protestants and Puritans. There was however more at stake here that the personal ambitions and aspirations of individual ministers or magistrates. Ideological considerations were also at work, for it was only from within the power structure that such men could effectively propagate and if necessary impose the values of true religion on their less enthusiastic countrymen. Thus, the other side of the coin of Puritan moderation and respectability was a social activism and religious zeal which to many contemporaries did not seem moderate at all.[14]

Now such Puritan activism is very often discussed under the rubric of the "reformation of manners." Too often the concern to effect such a reformation is regarded as a Puritan monopoly. However, as both Martin Ingram and Patrick Collinson have argued, concern about the issues of the vagrant poor, drunkenness, sexual promiscuity and bastardy, unlicensed ale houses, all issues that lay at the center of the reformation of manners, was scarcely a distinctive feature peculiar to the godly. In a period of population growth, intermittent trade depression, and harvest failure a concern with the problem of social order—the threats to it and the means to preserve it—was natural for the whole ruling class and many of the more prosperous groups of farmers, merchants, and artisans immediately below the gentry in the social hierarchy. In this context, the drive to regulate alehouses, particularly in time of dearth when grain was scarce, to control sexual license and keep the bastardy rate down, to do something about the poor and indigent united large sections of the social order. Moreover, as Professor Todd has pointed out, even at the level of ideas many of the notions about work in one's calling, wealth, and welfare, sometimes associated with Puritanism, in fact long predated Elizabeth's reign and by that period had come to form part of a common stock of notions about the social order shared by a large cross section of the educated classes.

Having said all that, it remains the case that very often the leading actors in moves toward the achievement of a reformation of manners were Puritans.[15] This was not because the notions of reform and control which underlay that reformation were Puritan monopolies, but

---

[14]Collinson, *Elizabethan Puritan Movement*, 248; Lake, *Moderate Puritans*, 46-54, 243-261.

[15]M. J. Ingram, *Church Courts, Sex and Marriage in England. 1570-1640* (Oxford, 1987), esp. chap. 3; Collinson, "Cranbrook and the Fletchers" and *Religion of Protestants*, chap.

because it was the godly who felt most keenly the need to express their religious calling, to validate their individual spiritual condition in a stream of other-directed works of charity and reform, and to protect the nation, through the repression and punishment of sin, from the providential visitations of a God provoked beyond endurance by that sin. We have, therefore, a relatively dynamic and decentralized vision of the social order in which true order was to be achieved through the autonomous response of many consciences to the dictates of the word and the demands of the common good. Neither that vision nor many of the nostrums about what constituted the common good were exclusively Puritan or even protestant, nor were they limited in their appeal to the godly. Yet within the conceptual limits set by this, in Professor Todd's terms "humanist," vision of the social order there operated a distinctly protestant and in its most developed and intense forms a Puritan zeal. That zeal was predicated ultimately on experimental predestinarian ideas about the nature of true belief and elect sainthood and often associated with notions of a covenant between protestant England and a loving yet demanding God. This covenant demanded, in return for the blessings of the gospel and continued protection from foreign invasion, war, and pestilence that England live up to the ideal of the godly commonwealth held before her by hot protestant preachers since the reign of Edward VI.[16]

Given the propensity (in the eyes of the godly at least) toward sin, irreligion, and ignorance of many of the English, this was a covenant which placed a peculiar obligation on the elect remnant within the population to be active in the cause of true religion. Only thus could they stave off the wrath of God from the nation as a whole. It was their sensitivity to concerns like these, in short their zeal, which

---

5; also see Margaret Spufford, "Puritanism and Social Control?" in A. Fletcher and J. Stevenson, eds., *Order and Disorder in Early Modern England* (Cambridge, 1985); M. Todd, *Christian Humanism and the Puritan Social Order* (Cambridge, 1987), passim. D. Underdown, *Fire from Heaven* (London, 1992), 102, 108; for a recent attempt to distinguish between the general impulse toward order and discipline in the face of social change and economic crisis and the particular in-put of Puritanism see Robert von Friedeberg, "Reformation of Manners and the Social Composition of Offenders in an East Anglian Cloth Village: Earls Colne, Essex, 1531-1642," *Journal of British Studies* 29(1990): 347-385.

[16] For this general point see Peter Lake, "The Impact of Early Modern Protestantism," *Journal of British Studies* 28(1989): 293-303; on protestant and Puritan notions of the covenant and of England as a nation in covenant with God see the articles by C. Davies, J. Facey and Peter Lake in Peter Lake and M. Dowling, eds., *Protestantism and the National Church* (London, 1987) and Collinson, *Birthpangs*, chap. 1; for a slightly later period see Michael McGiffert, "God's Controversy with Jacobean England," *American Historical Review*, 88(1983): 1151-1174; for a brilliant study of the impact of these attitudes on one English town see Underdown, *Fire from Heaven*.

prompted Puritans, both ministers and magistrates, justices of the peace, parliament men, and town governors to take the lead in the pursuit of the reformation of manners. But in so doing they were often acting as leaders of or spokesmen for wider bodies of opinion; in their own eyes and those of many of their contemporaries, they were public servants, commonwealthsmen, in the charged language of the 1620s, "patriots," serving values and aims common to wider bodies of opinion than can usefully be termed Puritan. Thus as Hassell Smith has shown it would scarcely be possible to understand the innerness of Nathaniel Bacon's stentorian efforts to ensure local order and good government in Norfolk without reference to his Puritan profession of authentic protestant values. And yet the forms which many of those efforts took—regulating the grain trade, representing the county's grievances to the Privy Council, maintaining the common peace both in and out of sessions, resisting the nefarious attempts of Sir Arthur Heveningham to make money out of the transaction of the crown's business in Norfolk—were scarcely in themselves distinctively Puritan activities. Much of the prominence of the godly as local governors in counties like Norfolk and Suffolk, while at first often caused (as Dr. MacCullough has argued for Suffolk) by the central government's need to rely on zealously protestant and Puritan local agents in the face of the popish threat, may well ultimately have rested on the propensity of other well-intentioned but lazy and lukewarm members of the bench to let their more driven and godly colleagues get on with the work. J. C. Davis's plea for a control group against which the distinctiveness of the godly gentry could be measured might legitimately be met by a study of the inactive and conventionally acquiescent members of the magisterial class.[17]

If all this means that their zeal in the pursuit of a certain view of order served to integrate Puritans into wider bodies of opinion, it also means that the roots of their distinctive zeal must be sought not in their class position or interests but within the religious culture of the godly. In the debate among historians about the social provenance and meaning of Puritanism this is to come down rather more on the side of Professor Collinson and Dr. Ingram than on that of Professor Underdown, Professor Hunt, and Dr. Wrightson. Building on the insights of Christopher Hill this last group has tended to see

[17]Hassell Smith, *County and Court* (Oxford, 1974); Diarmaid MacCullough, "Catholic and Puritan in Elizabethan Suffolk: A County Community Divides," *Archiv für Reformationsgeschichte* 72(1981): 232-289; Davis, "Puritanism and Revolution."

Puritanism as the ideology of the godly middling sort, and their allies amongst the clergy and gentry. On this view Puritanism was, amongst other things, an expression of these groups' urge to distinguish themselves from the groups below them in the social hierarchy and to exercise a certain control over those groups, a control in part legitimated by religion and in part, insofar as it was internalized and accepted as legitimate by the controlled, constituted by it. As such Puritanism was the ideological accomplice of certain processes of social differentiation taking place in the English village during this period. Because of population growth, parishes filled up from the bottom with poor people. Simultaneously, land holding tended to become concentrated in fewer and fewer hands. Compounded by other cultural changes, like the growth of literacy, Puritanism became the expression of the self image and class interests of this emergent middling sort, the ideology of hundreds of village oligarchies all over England. Professor Underdown has taken up this view of Puritanism and tried to give it yet more precise socio-cultural provenance by seeking to establish positive correlations between certain types of farming region and manorial structure and the spread of Puritanism, on the one hand, and the retention of more traditional forms of festive culture on the other. On this view, Puritanism became a leading agent of the separation between a traditional popular culture, centered on various festivals, sports, and recreations, many of them associated with the great feasts of the traditional liturgical year and the new literate, word-centered culture of the godly. Just as the old festive culture was both an expression of and a means of sustaining social unity so this new culture was both a product and an agent of social division or differentiation.[18]

For Collinson and Ingram all this is a little too cut and dried. According to Professor Collinson, Wrightson "in his influential study of the Essex village of Terling is in danger of confusing Puritanism with the officious, responsible respectability of the dozen or so local farmers of substance who sat in the vestry and ran the parish." Puritanism proper, defined as the religious culture of the self-consciously godly, may have enjoyed, even in Terling, a rather more tangential relationship to the center of power. As Collinson observes, "after the

---

[18]K. Wrightson, *Poverty and Piety in an English Village: Terling, 1525-1700* (London, 1979); W. Hunt, *The Puritan Moment* (Cambridge, Mass., 1983); D. Underdown, *Riot, Revel and Rebellion* (Oxford, 1985); for Collinson and Ingram's critique of this position see Ingram, *Church Courts*, chap. 3 and Collinson, *Religion of Protestants*, chaps. 5 and 6 and his "Cranbrook and the Fletchers"; also see Spufford, "Puritanism and Social Control?"

departure of their pastor, Thomas Weld, for New England they held conventicles in the house of the schoolmaster's widow."[19] Here then is the essence of the critique of visions of Puritanism centered on social control. At the heart of Puritanism were the forms of voluntary religion, religious sociability, the conventicles, private fasts, exercises, market day lectures around which the godly organized their devotional and social lives. These had no necessary relationship either to social control or the reformation of manners; the groups defined by this social and pietistic round were not necessarily members of only one social group, always drawn from the middling sort that made up the village oligarchies of rural England and the resulting division between the self professed godly and the profane was a distinction which cut across, rather than ran between, social boundaries.

So far so good, but even accepting all this it remains the case that Puritanism could be and often was divisive and polarizing in its social and ideological effects. Puritan zeal was undoubtedly often apprehended by those on the receiving end as a fit subject for resentment, however conventional the social values within which that zeal operated.[20] Even where the ends of order and discipline pursued by the godly were in themselves uncontroversial, the intensity with which they pursued those ends was not. Nor were Puritan attitudes and values always merely conventional. On a number of issues the godly possessed their own rationales for social activism, rationales which might sometimes operate alongside and reinforce conventional opinion but which were not merely coterminous with it. To take a couple of examples, Dr. Parker has undoubtedly demonstrated that the enforcement of sabbath observance was an object of widespread agreement amongst Elizabethan and Jacobean protestants. However, it remains the case that on a number of issues, most notably the status of the sabbath relative to the other holy days of the church, the extent to which any recreations were lawful on the sabbath and the relative seriousness of the sin involved in failing to keep the sabbath according to the highest standards of Puritan principle, the godly did indeed differ from their more lukewarm contemporaries. On the issue of drunkenness and the licensing of alehouses, as Dr. Wrightson has pointed out, there were all sorts of secular arguments ranging

---

[19] Collinson, *Birthpangs*, 153.

[20] Underdown, *Fire from Heaven*, chap. 4 for the general point and pp. 27-32 for evidence of local tensions created by Puritan religion; also see Ingram, *Church Courts*, 120-123, for another example of anti-Puritan feeling expressed in the form of a popular libel.

from the wasting of grain in time of dearth to the simple preservation of order which might unite Puritan thinking on the subject with that of their contemporaries, but the godly felt with peculiar intensity that the real threat from the demon drink stemmed from its capacity to undermine, indeed almost to efface, the divine image in humankind. Again while to many magistrates the drunkenness and disorder attached to various popular festivities might be a cause for concern, only the godly magistrate would see in those festivities the remnants of a pagan and idolatrous past, still embedded in the irreligious, ignorant and potentially popish culture of the populace.[21]

Again even some of the central elements of the culture of the godly, the forms of voluntary religion and sociability which really did distinguish the godly from their contemporaries, could prove divisive. If the godly themselves in no sense intended their meetings, exercises, and conventicles as the first step toward a formal act of separation, those meetings did indeed serve to distinguish the godly from their less enthusiastic or more profane fellows and were intended to do so. The groups of godly professors, gathered together in the house of the minister or some other parishioner to repeat the heads of the minister's last sermon, to fast and pray together resembled nothing so much as a church within a church. On occasion the godly of a particular parish even formed themselves into covenanted groups. Even where such semi-formal acts of self-recognition were absent there can be little doubt that in their own minds at least such people represented the godly leaven that leavened the whole lump of the national church.[22]

If that was the view from the inside looking out, there is also considerable evidence that such people appeared to their less zealous contemporaries as Puritans, self-righteous and self-selecting groups whose high opinion of themselves made them the object of a good deal of ill feeling and satirical humor. Thus ridiculed as Puritans, pharisaical hypocrites, the godly simply reversed the labeling process and insisted that anyone who used the word "Puritan" to attack true religion and godly conversation must *ipso facto* be a member of the ungodly and profane multitude, amongst whom God's elect were

---

[21] Parker, *English Sabbath*, chaps. 4, 5, and 6; K. Wrightson, "The Puritan Reformation of Manners, with Special Reference to the Counties of Lancashire and Essex, 1640-60" (Cambridge Ph.D. thesis, 1974), chap. 4 on "drink and drunkeness"; for such Puritan scruples against May games see T. Hall, *Funebria Floræ* (London, 1660).

[22] Compare the rather different accounts of the social impact of Puritan "voluntary religion" in Collinson, *Religion of Protestants*, chap. 6, *Birthpangs*, chap. 5 and in his "The English Conventicle."

doomed to live out their earthly existence. The end product of this process arrived when certain Puritans came to accept the term Puritan as a self description. As Jacqueline Eales has shown, Sir Robert Harley, for one, ironically inverted the literary character of a Puritan to describe the sort of honest protestant and patriot he took himself to be.[23]

The extent to which these divisions between the godly and the profane, or Puritans and their defamers, left the realm of ideology, of polemically constructed and literarily conditioned images, and invaded the world of social reality is still a vexed question. Professor Collinson has gone so far as to suggest that the lot of godly members of the national church imposed more existential strain and was hence more socially divisive than the situation of members of gathered churches. The latter having established their difference from the profane multitude by a formal act of separation, found it easier to relax in their day to day social relationships with the profane. The godly members of the national church, denied the existential release of such a definitive announcement of apartness, were forced to assert their separation from the delights, sins, and temptations of the world through processes of social shunning carried out in the course of their everyday lives, processes which must surely have caused offence amongst the shunned. It is equally clear that Puritans were aware of a certain obligation to preserve, as far as godly principle would allow, social peace with their neighbors, just as they were aware of the dangers of spiritual pride and pharisaical zeal. Thus William Bradshaw was at pains to enjoin his auditory to shun the sin not the sinner. It must have been difficult in practice to avoid confusing the one with the other, but just how far the godly indulged their propensity to shun and separate themselves from the profane and the ungodly in the course of their everyday lives is very difficult to establish.[24]

On the one hand, Puritan authors were quick to assert that, for would be saints, the godly were the proper object of charity, friendship, and even loans. We know too that some godly gentlemen like Sir Robert Harley were anxious to employ godly servants, when they

---

[23] See Lake, *Moderate Puritans,* 132; C. Dent, *Protestant Reformers in Elizabethan Oxford* (Oxford, 1983), 195 and 205, for examples of Robert Bolton and Henry Airay respectively inverting the conventional use of Puritan as a term of abuse and equating Puritanism with obedience to the dictates of divine law and conscience; Jacqueline Eales, "Sir Robert Harley K.B. (1579-1656) and the 'Character' of a Puritan," *British Library Journal* 15(1989): 134-157.
[24] Patrick Collinson, "The Cohabitation of the Faithful with the Unfaithful," in O. P. Grell, J. I. Israel, and Nicholas Tyacke, eds., *From Persecution to Toleration* (Oxford, 1991);

could be found. But we also know that men like Harley were able to maintain perfectly affable, indeed quite close social relations with other local gentry families like the Crofts, not noted for their Puritan affiliations. In Herefordshire the Harleys were quite abnormally godly and yet that abnormality did not prevent his fellow gentry from selecting Sir Robert more than once as a knight of the shire. Given the prominence as parliament men of many of the Puritan gentry described by Dr. Cliffe, it seems that this was a fairly general phenomenon and perhaps another example of Puritan zeal to serve the commonwealth keying in with broader definitions of what an active governor and patriot should look like, a fit which allowed the godly a prominence in both local and national politics somewhat out of proportion to their numerical strength. Given the numerous clashes between the claims of godly principle and the norms of upper class behavior over matters like the theater, fashionable clothing, or horseracing, detailed by Dr. Cliffe, it may be that the strains and conflicts induced by the pursuit of godliness were experienced quite as much within the consciences and consciousness of individual Puritans as they were expressed in their actual social relations. Certainly, as John Fielding has shown in the case of Robert Woodford, the Puritan steward of Northampton, Puritan principle might lead not so much to the avoidance of doubtful company or the demon drink as to fits of bad conscience and repentance experienced in the immediate aftermath of such encounters.[25]

It would be a mistake to conclude from this that Puritanism was merely a matter of polemical or literary images, or of the affective states of individuals whose conduct in the world was far more conventional than their rather lurid or overdrawn self images might lead us to expect. It is worth remembering that in discussing the subject of Puritanism at all we are, in part, seeking to enter the half-lit world of individual identity formation and consciousness and in that world the use of certain divisions and dichotomies between the profane and the godly, the internalization of certain standards of behavior and belief was an identifying mark of the godly, whether or not those dichotomies and divisions always found direct expression in social reality. To paraphrase a remark of J. G. A. Pocock, the categories and

---

Peter Lake, "William Bradshaw, Antichrist and the Community of the Godly," *Journal of Ecclesiastical History* 36(1985): 570-589.

[25]Jacqueline Eales, *Cavaliers and Roundheads*, passim; Cliffe, *Puritan Gentry*, esp. chaps. 3, 4, 5, 6, and 7; John Fielding, "Opposition to the Personal Rule of Charles I: the Diary of Robert Woodford, 1637-41," *Historical Journal* 31(1988):769-788.

divisions devised and adopted by contemporaries to structure reality were also part of the reality they structured. It is a mistake therefore in analyzing both the linguistic usages and conceptual categories of the godly (and the polemical images devised by their enemies to denounce them) to posit too sharp a division between the artifice and artificiality of the merely literary and the supposed reality of the social.

Moreover, it is clear that in many cases these attitudes and stereotypes were joined with behavioral forms which both the godly and their enemies regarded as distinctive and which could clearly in certain circumstances lead to division and disagreement. This is not to paint a picture of general social or ideological conflict between the godly and their enemies wherever Puritan styles of godliness raised their head. On the contrary, the incidence and nature of the disruption and division caused by the Puritan style would surely have depended on a whole series of variables. Of these the most simple and obvious could be the personality of an individual minister or magistrate. There is no reason to suppose that a personally moderate and pastorally sensitive Puritan minister could not service a community made up of many of Dr. Haigh's parish anglicans, humble Christians anxious to receive the sacrament and the rites of passage but unmoved by the strenuous message of Puritan pietism. By the same token, there can be no doubt that educated Puritan ministers found such a ministry existentially distressing nor that their vision of the world and of their own role as ministers almost invited them to challenge the assumptions and attitudes of their flock. The nature of that challenge would determine the nature of the response. It was all very well to listen to generalized denunciations of sin or even of particular sins; that after all was what a decent preacher was for. But if the minister got down to naming individual sinners, either directly or by broad hints that was a different matter. Omitting the sign of the cross from baptism at times or on demand was one thing, refusing to baptize with the sign of the cross at all was quite another.[26]

Of course, in the period before the early 1640s the multi-various compromises forced on the godly by their failure to capture the heights of ecclesiastical power and impose further reformation on the

---

[26]For an instance of the divisive impact of naming particular sinners in the pulpit see a case involving Richard Bernard described in M. Stieg, *Laud's Laboratory* (London, 1982), 202-203; for examples of anti-Puritan parishioners "sacrament gadding," see C. Haigh, "The Church of England, the Catholics and the People," in C. Haigh, ed., *The Reign of Elizabeth I* (London, 1984), esp. 217-218.

church under Elizabeth ensured that many of these tensions remained if not under control then at least contained within certain
fairly constricting limits. It was the essence of moderate Puritanism
that further reformation and the cause of the gospel should be fur-
thered within the institutional and liturgical structures provided by
the English church and from positions of cultural influence and political power secured within the various hierarchies that constituted
the contemporary status quo. That placed certain limits on, for instance, the severity with which the "profane" could be excluded from
the sacraments. After the outbreak of the civil war, of course, such
constraints were quickly removed, the religious atmosphere rapidly
polarized, and the myriad implicit compacts and compromises between the Puritan impulse and the demands of social and political
order established in the period before 1640 were called into question
and repeatedly renegotiated. As a variety of scholars have pointed
out, this had serious consequences both for the popularity of the
protestant cause and the ideological coherence of Puritanism itself.[27]

While it is impossible to describe these processes without reference
to tensions and traditions of thought and feeling from the period
before 1640, tensions and traditions for which the word Puritan still
provides a useful, indeed a necessary, shorthand term, the task
of getting the balance between continuity and discontinuity right in
describing the transition from what used to be called pre- to post-
revolutionary England remains perhaps the most important and
difficult assignment bequeathed by revisionist writers to their post-
revisionist progeny.[28] It was also, of course, the very different relationship between "the Puritan impulse" and the structures of cultural authority and political power in Old and New England that

[27]On the popular anti-Puritan backlash provoked by the renewed Puritan quest both
for formal reformation of the church and liturgy and newly ferocious versions of moral
and spiritual reformation see J. S. Morrill, "The Church in England, 1642-9" in J. S.
Morrill, ed., *Reactions to the English Civil War* (London, 1982); also see Derek Hirst, "The
Failure of Godly Rule in the English Republic," *Past and Present* 132(1991): 33-66; for a
rather more optimistic and balanced view see the important article by Ann Hughes, "The
Frustrations of the Godly" in J. S. Morrill, *From Regicide to Restoration* (London, 1992).

[28]It is primarily to these difficulties that J. C. Davies speaks in his "Puritanism and
Revolution." The best study of both the continuity and transformation of the Puritan
tradition in the revolutionary decades is still Geoffrey Nuttall's seminal *The Holy Spirit in
Puritan Faith and Experience* (Oxford, 1946). I have addressed some of these issues more
fully in a historiographical preface to a reprinted edition of Professor Nuttall's book (Chicago, 1992). For a very suggestive study of the ways in which the relationship between
"Puritanism" and "the people," far from being rendered stably oppositional by the war
and revolution, became, if anything, even more volatile and subject to renegotiation and
maneuver, see the article by Ann Hughes in this volume.

renders analyses of Puritanism that encompass those two locales so difficult to sustain.[29]

Again in the period before 1640 structural features could affect the impact of Puritanism. The ecclesiastical geography of a town or region, resultant tensions induced between neighboring ministers or between parish clergy and lecturers over sermon gadding might produce conflict. The social impact of Puritanism would presumably vary between parishes, like Terling, in which on Dr. Wrightson's account at least, the godly group was coterminous with the ruling elite and other parishes, like Dr. Ingram's Keevil, where it was not. Again the social impact of Puritan zeal might turn on the extent to which godly principle fell in with or cut across other more conventional impulses toward social order and that too could be a question of personality or circumstance. After all not all Puritan magistrates were like the awesomely severe Ignatius Jordan, as the somewhat frivolous response of the 1628 parliament to his furious zeal in the matter of adultery testifies. Again, if Essex in the 1620s and 1630s was as subject to social crisis as Dr. Hunt maintains, then the coherent response to that crisis adumbrated by Hunt's Puritan gentry might well have commanded the assent of a good many other gentry less committed to godly principle but no less committed to the cause of order. Essex, of course, was a county where the values of perfect protestantism had bitten relatively deep by the 1620s. In other areas things were rather different. Thus the prominent role played by popular anti-Puritanism in the emergence of a royalist party in Herefordshire, noted by Dr. Eales, may well have been a function of the fairly recent arrival in the area of Puritan religion.[30]

The picture I am trying to suggest is thus not one of generalized social or cultural conflict, but rather of certain distinctive and potentially divisive tendencies which in conjunction with a whole series of

[29]For a groundbreaking attempt to bring what have remained two frustratingly distinct historiographies together see Stephen Foster, *The Long Argument: English Puritanism and the Shaping of New England Culture, 1570-1700* (Chapel Hill, 1991).

[30]For an example of tension between a Puritan lecturer, Julines Herring, in Shrewsbury and a local conformist clergyman, Peter Studley, see Lake, "Puritanism, Arminianism and a Shropshire Axe-murder"; on the comparison between Terling and Keevil see M. J. Ingram, "Religion, Communities and Moral Discipline in Late Sixteenth and Early Seventeenth Century England: Case Studies," in K. von Greyerz, ed., *Religion and Society in Early Modern Europe* (London, 1984); for Ignatius Jordan's comeuppance in the 1628 parliament, see C. Russell, *Parliaments and English Politics* (London, 1979), 29; Hunt, *Puritan Moment*, chaps. 3, 4, 5, and 6; for the relative (in protestant terms) "backwardness" of early Stuart Herefordshire—resembling "more 'civil' counties fifty years earlier"—see Collinson, *Religion of Protestants*, 132; on the Harleys, see Eales, *Cavaliers and Roundheads*, esp. chaps. 3 and 4.

variables could and sometimes did produce tension, division and ill feeling. These were tensions and divisions which certain individuals and groups took up and integrated into a coherent pattern or picture of a divisive and/or subversive Puritanism in conflict with an otherwise unified or potentially unified social order and the festive culture which both expressed and perpetuated that unity. The extent to which the resulting picture of merry England had ever corresponded to reality is and was, in many ways, beside the point. Certainly by the early seventeenth century some of the most famous examples of this attitude, like the Cotswold games presided over by Sir Robert Dover, involved the self-conscious revival of country customs otherwise in danger of extinction. This festive antiquarianism, coupled with the fact in many areas of the country that the church ales and wakes located by Professor Underdown at the center both of traditional festive culture and of Puritan attempts to reform that culture had enjoyed a fairly exiguous and intermittent existence in the period prior to their suppression, might be taken to cast doubt on the healthiness of the country customs so beloved of the likes of Dover or the Laudian divine and poet Robert Herrick. Be that as it may, for the likes of Herrick and Dover such sports and pastimes betokened an organic and relatively friction-free society, a society now under threat from the divisive activities of the godly. In this, they represented the secular or profane equivalent of the rhythms and ceremonial norms of public worship established by the national church, which likewise served to maintain social unity and obedience to authority and were likewise subject to Puritan attack and subversion.[31]

By the 1620s and 1630s the result of these tensions amongst Laudians and committed conformists was a stereotype of Puritan deviance and subversion; word centered, sermon obsessed, and sermon gadding, at best indifferent and at worst hostile to the rites and ceremonies of the church and the demands of the beauty of holiness, sacrilegious in its attitude to the physical site and possessions of the church and the rights and tithes of the clergy, obsessed with their own status as elect saints, semi-separatist in their addiction to their own conventicles and meetings, bizarrely superstitious on the matter of the sabbath. Here was the defining other of the Laudian project, the threat against which the Laudian vision of order and unity in church and state was constructed. Stripped of its pejorative rhetoric there was a

---

[31] L. Marcus, *The Politics of Mirth* (Chicago, 1986), chaps. 1–5, esp. chap. 5 on Herrick; Underdown, *Riot, Revel and Rebellion,* chaps. 2-5; F. Heal, *Hospitality in Early Modern England* (Oxford, 1990), 358-365; Ingram, *Church Courts,* 101.

remarkable fit between the characteristics attributed to the godly by Laudian anti-Puritans and the distinctive forms of Puritan voluntary religion described in Clarke's lives and analyzed by Professor Collinson and others. Viewed both from inside and outside, then, there was considerable agreement about what Puritan godliness looked like, accompanied, of course, by complete disagreement about what it meant. From the inside looking out, Puritanism was in Patrick Collinson's words, about 'as factious and subversive as the homily of obedience.' From the outside looking in, in the eyes of many contemporaries it represented an alternately laughable and sinister threat to order and obedience. On the one hand, the area of agreement about what constituted the defining marks of the godly seems to me to provide telling evidence of the existence of a stable entity, style, or position which we can legitimately call Puritan. On the other, the very different versions of what it meant serve as a crucial index of just how divisive that Puritan style could be.[32]

Now this process of labeling and stereotyping, while it reached its apogee in Laudian writings of the 1630s was neither peculiar to the Personal Rule nor limited to Laudians. Rather the Laudian vision of Puritanism was comprised of many strands developed by various anti-Puritan and conformist authors, both popular and elite, since the 1570s. That fact serves to introduce a second process or tendency running through the early seventeenth century which also rendered the Puritan style of piety more rather than less distinctive. It is a process which I want to label, rather cumbersomely perhaps, as one of conformist differentiation. It was a process in its way as central to the protestantization of England as the emergence of the forms of voluntary religion described by Professor Collinson. It involved the generation of a distinctive religious style by conformists, by which term I mean here those members of the national church most concerned to defend and assert the ecclesiastical status quo against what they took to be Puritan subversion and attack. At the most general level it was a process produced by the clash between the values of perfect protestantism and the realities—institutional and structural as well as ideological—of an inclusive national church.

In origin the Puritan style was a product of the application of the central theoretical insights of the English reformed tradition to the

[32]For a case study of Laudian anti-Puritanism which seemingly very accurately reflected the activities of the godly, albeit described in unrelievedly lurid language, see Lake, "Puritanism, Arminianism and a Shropshire Axe-murder"; for the Collinson quote see *Religion of Protestants*, 177.

practical situation of the most zealous and self-consciously protestant elements in England. Initially, even the most austerely conformist opponents of Puritanism defined as a movement of dissent and reform also subscribed to versions of what best may be termed the Elizabethan reformed synthesis. This meant that the polemical engagement with presbyterianism and non-conformity was conducted within a formal doctrinal consensus acknowledged by both sides. It also meant that the exchanges took place within certain limits of practical assumption about, for instance, the centrality of the word to any properly protestant church and the dangers of attributing directly religious value or efficacy to outward humanly devised ceremonies. Here basic features of the protestant rejection of Rome served to limit the range of polemical options open to conformist defenders of the status quo. All this placed real constraints on the development of distinctively conformist styles of piety or divinity and initially the polemical engagement with "Puritanism" (defined as a movement for the reform of the liturgical and governing structure of the church) was organized around considerations of order, obedience, things indifferent, and the specific scriptural arguments adduced by the Puritans for their view of church government and the more general arguments about Christian liberty and the offence of the godly and the weak in faith with which they sought to defend their attitude to conformity. However, the debate about presbyterianism was not and could not be limited to these discrete issues. Ultimately, it raised the question of the nature and extent of the Christian community, the relationship of that community to the visible church and to the cause of secular order. In the course of addressing these issues conformist writers found themselves committed to far broader definitions of the Christian community and far less stringent definitions of what constituted true religion than their Puritan opponents. They found themselves heavily constrained in infusing the resulting vision of the church and Christian community with any very positive religious content by their shared commitment to the central insights of the English reformed tradition. I have made this case at length elsewhere and do not want to repeat it here in detail. Suffice it to say that various conformists attempted to transcend the limits imposed on their defence of the status quo by the evangelical and word-centered priorities of their own protestantism. John Bridges pushed hardest against those limits, while divines like Matthew Sutcliffe and Richard Bancroft largely ignored them, preferring the pleasures of caricaturing and denouncing the subversive consequences of the presbyterian platform. Only in the 1590s with the thought of Richard Hooker did conformist thought achieve a religiously powerful and emotionally compelling rendering of the status quo and a repudiation of Puritanism defined not merely as a series of positions on the structure of the church but also as a style of piety.[33]

As I have argued briefly at the end of *Anglicans and Puritans* and at greater length elsewhere there were considerable continuities between the position staked out by Hooker and Laudianism. But Laudianism was but the most extreme and coherent element in a more general process of conformist differentiation, whereby various individuals and groups reacting against what they took to be the divisive or potentially divisive aspects of Puritan piety modified or broke with central elements in the high Elizabethan reformed synthesis. The internal dynamics of this process are complex. As the brilliant research of Anthony Milton has revealed, the anti-Puritan polemical context was not the only or even the main motive force behind the gradual decomposition of what passed for orthodoxy amongst educated Elizabethan protestants. His study of early Stuart anti-papal polemic shows clearly the way in which a whole series of considerations—the opinions and political preferences of James I, the internal logic and dialectical nature of the engagement with Rome, as well as other considerations concerning the historical basis of the Church of England—contributed to the gradual modification and erosion of the certainties of the Foxeian rejection of popery. The changes here were subtle, not necessarily involving the abandonment of central positions or arguments but rather their combination with new and sometimes incompatible assertions and argumentative moves.[34]

However, one central element in all this was the presence of a Puritan, experimental predestinarian position, centered on the capacity of the godly to recognize one another in this life, the practical equation of the godly with the elect, and the apparently disruptive effects of certain forms of Puritan voluntary religion. In a case study of Robert Sanderson I argued that it was precisely Sanderson's geographical proximity to and ideological distaste for the congregation of John

---

[33]I summarize here the argument of my *Anglicans and Puritans?* (London, 1988).

[34]Peter Lake, "Lancelot Andrewes, John Buckeridge and Avant Garde Conformity at the Court of James I," in L. L. Peck, ed., *The Mental World of the Jacobean Court* (Cambridge, 1991) and Peter Lake, "The Laudian Style: Order, Uniformity and the Pursuit of the Beauty of Holiness in the 1630s," in K. Fincham, ed., *The Early Stuart Church* (London, 1993); A. Milton, *Catholic and Reformed: The Roman and Protestant Churches in English Protestant Thought, 1600-1640* (forthcoming from Cambridge University Press). For a shorter statement see Dr. Milton's article in Fincham, ed., *The Early Stuart Church.* I

Cotton that lay behind not only his adoption of a stridently anti-Puritan rhetoric but also various modifications in his style of divinity. Those shifts of emphasis and nuance were centered on the visibility of the visibly godly and the need for and nature of assurance in the truly elect. One can see similar processes of conformist peel back in the careers of other divines. John Downe was a product of Emmanuel and an associate of Joseph Hall, whose style of divinity was sufficiently "Puritan" to allow Professor von Rohr to include him in his excellent study of Puritan covenant theology. Yet Downe adopted a virulently anti-Puritan tone and preached visitation sermons sufficiently severe to win the admiration of Richard Montague. Again he too adjusted his style of divinity, again on the crucial issue of assurance, reacting against a preacher in Bristol who by claiming that every truly elect saint could and should reach a settled assurance of salvation plunged many of his auditory into deep crises of faith and confidence. At a more elevated and abstruse theological level, it may not be going too far to see the modified Calvinism of Arthur Lake, Joseph Hall, Samuel Ward, and John Davenant as not only a response to the theological debates in the Low Countries but also as modifications to previous Calvinist orthodoxy on the extent of the atonement, perseverance and assurance, and later the nature and efficacy of sacramental grace designed to render reformed orthodoxy as they understood it more compatible with the demands of an inclusive national church and to undercut the exclusivist rigidities of certain Puritan styles of divinity.[35]

Certainly, by the 1620s on a whole series of issues ranging from the theology of grace, to the grounds of the protestant rejection of popery, the status of episcopacy as a form of church government by divine right and sabbatarianism the old certainties of the high Elizabethan synthesis were being undercut and modified. In part those modifications had been prompted by a reaction against the perceived astringencies and extremities of Puritan attitudes to the church of Rome, experimental predestinarianism, or the sabbath, attitudes which in themselves were extensions or developments of core protes-

should like to thank Dr. Milton for many discussions of these issues and for allowing me to read the typescript of his forthcoming book.

[35] Peter Lake, "Serving God and the Times: The Calvinist Conformity of Robert Sanderson," *Journal of British Studies* 27(1988): 81-116; J. von Rohr, *The Covenant of Grace in Puritan Thought* (Atlanta, Ga., 1986), 66, 157, 168; John Downe, *Certain Treatises* (Oxford, 1633), 55-56 for his links to Hall. For his dispute with the Puritan minister in Bristol, see Downe's *A Treatise of the Nature and Definition of Justifying Faith,* printed and separately paginated in *Certain Treatises;* for the hypothetical universalism of the English delegation

tant notions. We are dealing here with an almost classically dialectical process. The result was that the positions occupied by the godly on these issues—their experimental predestinarianism, their hard line sabbatarianism, their limited acceptance of episcopacy as a human institution, their Foxeian attitude to the church of Rome—were all rendered more rather than less distinctive. As Kenneth Fincham has recently argued, even where a common sense of evangelical mission and protestant identity continued to unite a bishop like Arthur Lake with conforming Puritan ministers like Richard Bernard or William Sclater, it is clear that their opinions on many issues were very far from the same.[36]

Laudianism needs to be set in this context as but the most coherent and extreme element in a far more widespread ideological movement of conformist peel back or differentiation, in which the demands of an inclusive national church and the broad bottomed view of the Christian community which went with it, were brought into creative tension with the word centered, potentially exclusivist vision of the community of the godly that dominated high Elizabethan protestantism. The wider phenomenon of conformist differentiation, the subtle transformation and modification of the reformed tradition, ensured that when Laudianism seized the heights of ecclesiastical power in the late 1620s and 1630s many conformist divines who were neither Arminians nor Laudians sided with the Laudians in the face of what looked like a radical Puritan challenge to order. For their part, many of the godly came increasingly to regard divines like Hall as fatally tainted with the new counsels of Laudianism. Here the classic example is Burton's assault on Hall's book *The Old Religion*. Hall claimed to be merely defending what had come to be commonplaces of the Jacobean case against Rome, while Burton, newly sensitized by the threat to orthodoxy represented by Arminianism, denounced Hall as selling the pass to Montague and behind him to the papists.[37]

I am not arguing that while Puritanism remained static, an intellectual throwback to Elizabeth's reign, conformist thought shifted and the world changed. Clearly, there was a dynamism, an internal logic or logics at work within Puritan thought at this time as recent

at Dort, see Peter Lake, "Calvinism and the English Church, 1570-1635," *Past and Present* 114(1987): 51-60 and Nicholas Tyacke, *Anti-Calvinists*, chap. 4.

[36]K. Fincham, *Prelate as Pastor* (Oxford, 1990), 260-261, 300-301.

[37]J. Hall, *The Old Religion* (London, 1628) and the two replies by Henry Burton, *The Seven Vials* (London, 1628) and *Babel No Bethel* (London, 1629). I should like to thank Anthony Milton for bringing the importance of this exchange to my attention. Dr. Milton is preparing an article locating the debate about Hall's book in its full contemporary context.

monographs on covenant theology, experimental predestinarianism, the Puritan route to Arminianism, and the psychology of conversion, not to mention Professor Nuttall's classic study of the doctrine of the Holy Spirit, have all made clear.[38] My point is only that under a variety of pressures, polemical (anti-catholic and anti-Puritan), structural (the demands of an inclusive national church), and political (the need to resist the alleged "popularity" of the Puritans) conformist thought did shift in this period. Those shifts were not limited to the emergence of "Arminianism" or Laudianism, but occurred over a wider range of issues and on a broader ideological front than those terms would allow. The effect of that process was to render the style of piety and divinity labeled Puritan here—aggressively word centered, dominated by the division between the godly and the ungodly, a division underwritten by the doctrines of predestination, perseverance, and election and given practical expression in the forms of Puritan voluntary religion; centered on the three scriptural ordinances of the word preached, the sacraments, and the sabbath; prepared to accept the rest of the liturgy, observances, and government of the church at best only as things inherently indifferent and required by human authority and obsessed by the threat of an antichristian popery—more rather than less distinctive. It must be admitted that in the recent literature on the early Stuart church Puritanism has had rather a hard time of it. At present we are confronted with two opposed but structurally very similar interpretations of the period both concerned to stress consensus over conflict and to relegate the agents of conflict when it broke out to the margins of the picture. On the one hand, we have an account which starting with the godly's view of themselves as pillars of order and stability, and noting their integration in various parts of various contemporary establishments, secular and ecclesiastical, local and national, stresses protestant unity and accord and casts the rise of Laudianism as the intrusive fly in the otherwise fragrant and rather stable ointment of the early Stuart church.[39] On the other side, in the work of Dr. Bernard, Dr. Sharpe,

[38] See von Rohr, *Covenant of Grace;* R. T. Kendal, *Calvin and English Calvinism to 1649* (Oxford, 1979); Charles Cohen, *God's Caress* (New York, 1986); in more general terms as William Lamont has suggested there was an internal dynamic and debate within puritan divinity that led towards a challenge to Calvinist orthodoxy generated by the increasing voluntarism of Puritan preparationism. On this see Kendall's account of the shifts in John Cotton's position in *Calvin and English Calvinism,* 110-117 and 167-183. Also see Ellen More, "John Goodwin and the Origins of the New Arminianism," *Journal of British Studies* 22(1982).

[39] This is arguably the view taken in Collinson, *Religion of Protestants* and in the early work of Nicholas Tyacke, especially in his "Puritanism, Arminianism and counter-revolution"; for the application of such a view of the Jacobean status quo to the problem

and Mr. White we are confronted with a vision of an "Anglican" "monarchical church" whose ideological tone and institutional structures were conditioned by an urge to unite as many people as possible within the national church created by Henry VIII. On this view, Laudianism or whatever one wants to call the religious policies and temper of the Personal Rule, represented no more than an intrinsically conservative, indeed rather uncontroversial search for order, uniformity and obedience, a continuation of the policies of Elizabethan conformists like Whitgift and Bancroft. Indeed, for Dr. Sharpe Laudianism represented the natural ecclesiastical effects of a unitary Elizabethan world view, centered on notions of hierarchy and degree enshrined in both the microcosm of human nature and human society and the macrocosm of the entire created world. For both Sharpe and Bernard the values enshrined in these policies and the monarchical church which produced and conditioned them were naturally inimical to Calvinist protestantism. On their view, the only people likely to be alarmed by Laudianism were Puritans, a group marginalized by Bernard to a radical fringe teetering on the edge of separation or at least exile in the New World.[40]

There is a marked structural similarity between these two positions; they both share a vision of a consensual early Stuart church, the one distinctly protestant or reformed, the other calmingly "Anglican"; they both want to marginalize the notion of Puritanism, the one by collapsing it into the religion of protestants, the other by excluding it altogether from an "Anglican" mainstream. Moreover, both positions rely heavily on the view of themselves taken by particular contemporary ideological factions. For there can be no doubt that while the godly saw themselves as defenders of orthodoxy, order and obedience and construed the Laudians as innovating, cryptopopish agents of disorder, the Laudians, with no less certainty, construed the godly as Puritans, carriers of a heterodox and inherently destabilizing and schismatic ideology. Moreover, both groups could

---

of the origins of the civil war see J. S. Morrill, "The Attack on the Church of England in the Long Parliament" in D. Beales and G. Best, eds., *History, Society and the Churches* (Cambridge, 1985).

[40]G. Bernard, "The Church of England, c.1529-1642," *History* 75(1990); K. Sharpe, *Politics and Ideas in Early Stuart England* (London, 1989), chaps. 1 and 4; Sharpe and Bernard's views draw on those of Peter White now usefully collected in his *Predestination, Policy and Polemic* (Cambridge, 1992). For a view of Puritan radicalism rather less nuanced than that presented here and rather more in line with the opinions of White and Sharpe see A. Zakai, *Exile and Kingdom: History and Apocalypse in the Puritan Migration to America* (Cambridge, 1991). But also see the rather more satisfactory account of the same phenomenon in T. D. Bozeman, *To Live Ancient Lives* (Chapel Hill, N.C., 1988).

mobilize powerful arguments and evidence from the ambiguous and always heavily contested history of the English reformation to support their case. If we take the foundation documents and history of the English church as a text, that text was clearly ambiguous enough to be subjected to a number of mutually exclusive glosses or interpretations.[41] Now it is undoubtedly the case that we cannot hope to understand the period without imaginatively inhabiting the various rival readings produced by contemporaries of the position of the English church, the nature of order in a Christian society, and of the most urgent threats to that order. But nor can we hope to produce a satisfactorily total interpretation if we simply accept the view of one party to the resulting contemporary disputes. On the contrary, we have to accept that we are dealing with ideologically and polemically constructed views of order and disorder, orthodoxy and heresy, normality and deviance and above all that there was no such thing as a unitary Elizabethan or Anglican settlement but merely a number of competing readings of a series of inherently ambiguous, even unstable, legal, social, institutional and theological "texts." If we are to understand how those divergent readings were generated and the dialectical and dialogic relations between them we need to be able to use the word and concept of Puritanism. Without it we will miss a crucial category used by contemporaries to cut up and explain their world and more important still we will run the risk of marginalizing or obscuring a crucial strand in English religious opinion of the early seventeenth century.

[41] It is the ambiguity of those foundation documents and the contested and contestable nature of that history that renders the term Anglican so problematic as a category for analysis in this period, since it assumes the existence of a stable Anglican essence beneath the exegetical claims and counter claims, the polemical maneuvers and interpretations of contemporaries many of whom were making rival claims to define and embody the spirit of the English church. The lamentable consequences of these assumptions for the conduct of sensible historical research are best exemplified by Peter White's recent *Predestination, Policy and Polemic* with its curious attempt to distinguish definitively between theology and polemic (p. 11) and its assumption of a coherent entity called "English theology" inherently moderate, "a middle way," concentrating on "fundamentals" avoiding "extremes" but nevertheless "comprehensive and eirenic" (p. 202). This is "Anglican essentialism" with a vengeance and provides Mr. White with a license to construct and vindicate his own version of "Anglicanism" out of the materials provided to him by contemporaries and in the process to suppress many of the priorities and polemical commitments which alone make the positions adopted by various ideological fragments within the English church historically intelligible.

Not What But How—Thomas Minor and

the Ligatures of Puritanism

Stephen Foster

PURITANS FIGURE prominently in the history of both England and America in the seventeenth century, but any attempt to juxtapose the respective secondary literatures on the subject of Puritanism is liable to be a disconcerting business, even a depressing one. Take the matter of the "social basis" of the Puritan movement. Are certain social and economic circumstances in England and America more conducive than others to people becoming Puritans? Yes, say English and American historians with equal confidence, and then proceed to specify exactly opposite conditions. In general both groups assume a cataclysmic shift in English culture and society in the sixteenth and seventeenth centuries, baldly put, from a communal and traditional to an individualistic and modern regime, but English Puritans are numbered among the agents of the change, their American counterparts are presented as in full flight from it. The sort of undercontrolled, commercialized, and nascently industrial parishes plagued by overpopulation and growing inequalities that supposedly breed Puritans in England are the background to the allegedly desperate attempts to recreate the vanishing world of corporate custom and stable social relationships of the subsistence "peasant" villages of New England.[1] Put side by side, the two lines of argument suggest an easy triumph of historiographic mind over hapless historical matter.

Real Puritan villagers, when we know anything about them, do not

---

[1] For discussion and citations see Stephen Foster, *The Long Argument: English Puritanism and the Shaping of New England Culture, 1570–1700* (Chapel Hill, N.C., 1991), 15–16, 323–324, nn. 30–31.

seem to fit either model very well. Just at the moment the parish of Earls Colne in Essex seems to be the *locus classicus* of English Puritanism at ground level, at least judging from the number of studies in which the place is given a central part. It was certainly a cloth-working village in the right area and enjoying the right kind of field system (fully inclosed commons) and the right kind of progressive, commercial farming. But however ready a fraction of the villagers were to be Puritanized, in actual fact the Puritan characteristics of the parish seem to have been imposed from above when (and only when) the Harlakenden family came into possession of the lordships of the manor of Earls Colne and used their control over the local courts and the benefice to good effect. The Harlakendens, in turn, did use their lordships, and particularly entry fines, in an appropriately "rational" (that is, acquisitive) manner; their hapless tenants, however, continued a very unindividualistic, irrational habit of trying to keep their tiny holdings together and within their own lines of descent despite the difficulties Harlakenden rapaciousness put in their way. Just the sort of people to populate New England, it would seem, in helter-skelter flight from the breakup of the old order. But then why are there two Harlakendens, Roger and Mable, among the migrants, and why did their formidable elder brother Richard, lord of the manors of Earls Colne and future Parliamentary commander, also contemplate moving to Massachusetts?[2]

The discomfiture of the social historians can be of little value to their colleagues who have all along insisted that Puritanism "remains an obstinately religious phenomenon, and its common characteristics must be sought in its religious teachings."[3] Equally glaring anomalies plague the various English and American attempts to find any Puritan religious teachings that are both common and characteristic, in the sense that they both identify Puritans and set them off from the larger Protestant culture of which they were also a part. In the case of this enterprise, however, the two historiographies are not so

---

[2] Cf. Alan Macfarlane, *The Origins of English Individualism: The Family, Property, and Social Transition* (New York, 1979), 62–70; Robert von Friedeburg, "Reformation of Manners and the Social Composition of Offenders in an East Anglian Cloth Village: Earls Colne, Essex, 1531–1642," *Journal of British Studies* 29(1990): 347–385; Govind Sreenivasan, "The Land-Family Bond at Earls Colne (Essex), 1550–1650," *Past & Present* 131(1991): 3–37. For the evidence that Richard Harlakenden contemplated joining his brother and sister already in the Bay Colony see *The Records of the Town of Cambridge (Formerly Newtowne), Massachusetts, 1630–1703* (Cambridge, Mass., 1896–1901), 2: 26, 31.

[3] This is a classic statement from a classic work: A. G. Dickens, *The English Reformation* (New York, 1964), 319.

much mutually incompatible as internally inconsistent and yet so alarmingly parallel in their course as to raise the suspicion that changing interpretations are responses to some more powerful force than new data and new insights. Was there a distinctive Puritan segment or spectrum within English Protestantism between the Elizabethan Reformation and the eve of the Civil War? No, goes one revisionist school: the whole body of English reformers was so dominated by a dour, crabbed, and impossibly demanding predestinarian theology that Protestantism never really took hold at all in England except among a fraction of the governing class. Yes, there was a Puritan strain in English religion, counters another revisionist school, but it was an unpalatable Continental import and repeatedly failed to impose its lugubrious will on a compromise Anglican Reformation settlement more suited to the native character. And, no, there wasn't any such thing, according to a third form of revisionism, which posits a Calvinist consensus both broad and popular and itself at one with the Reformed Protestantism of the continent. Until the 1630s the Church of England was disrupted by nothing more than relatively short lived arguments, passionate for a time but lacking sufficient substance to make for lasting division. The admitted religious schisms of the Civil War, in turn, are accounted for either as a cloak for economic conflict (old-style Marxist) or as a phenomenon of very recent origin created by the Laudian apostasy backed by royal perversity (new-style revisionism).[4]

Comparing revisionist accounts of the English Reformation with equally revisionist attempts to explain the origins of the English Civil War is an entertaining exercise for an Americanist just so long as no thought is given to the various attempts to answer the same kinds of question about Puritan identity on this side of the Atlantic. The New World cacophony, in fact, bears a distressing resemblance to its Eng-

[4]The efforts to define a distinctive English Puritan tradition are reviewed and summarized in Richard L. Greaves, "The Puritan-Nonconformist Tradition in England, 1560–1700: Historiographical Reflections," *Albion* 17(1985): 449–486. The most recent attempt at the question, which has the virtue of conceiving of what will become Anglican Protestantism as also in the process of development over time, is Peter Lake, *Anglicans and Puritans?: Presbyterianism and English Conformist Thought from Whitgift to Hooker* (London, 1988). The controversy over the nature and efficacy of the English Reformation is reviewed in Patrick Collinson, *The Birthpangs of Protestant England: Religious and Cultural Change in the Sixteenth and Seventeenth Centuries* (London, 1988); Diarmaid MacCulloch, "The Myth of the English Reformation," *Journal of British Studies* 30(1991): 1–19. A very recent claim for a paganization of the English governing classes simultaneous with (and ultimately more successful than) the Reformation is C. H. George, "Parnassus Restored, Saints Confounded: The Secular Challenge to the Age of the Godly, 1560–1660," *Albion* 23(1991): 409–437.

lish counterpart. Various schools of revisionism in early American historiography do have one signal advantage: they are agreed upon what it is they want to revise, and that is the received wisdom of the 1930s through the 1950s. In that classic account a distinguishable English Puritan movement, frustrated by its failures at home, migrated in part to New England and there shaped the culture of that region in the seventeenth and early eighteenth centuries, so that after the Revolution New England was able to use its intellectual and organizational skills to put its stamp on the character of the newly formed nation. The assaults on this fixed position have taken a variety of forms, yet all of them anticipate or echo the strategies of their English equivalents.[5] For example, it may be admitted that there was an American Puritanism but also claimed that it was so dour, crabbed, and impossibly demanding that it did not last long or attract much more than an elite following and so made little lasting impact on American history. Alternatively, the distinctiveness of American Puritanism is admitted and it is even allowed a certain lease on life, but only with the proviso that it was a hothouse growth, able to survive only in hermetically sealed New England villages. When the modernity the Puritan migrants had fled to America to avoid finally caught up with them (the exact date of the lapsus is subject to negotiation among the proponents of this argument), then Puritanism expired and New England came to look like the rest of America. Or, in a more radical formulation, one can claim that what is taken to be Puritanism is just the characteristics of seventeenth-century English culture generally, and New England was different from the other colonies because they were deviant. As the rest of colonial America anglicized it caught up to and became more like New England because all the colonies were beginning to resemble their common English forebear ("modernizing") as the paradoxical event of political inde-

---

[5]The course of scholarship on American Puritanism since 1960 is plotted in detail in Michael McGiffert, "American Puritan Studies in the 1960s," *William and Mary Quarterly*, 3d ser., 27(1970): 36–67; David D. Hall, "On Common Ground: The Coherence of American Puritan Studies," ibid., 44(1987): 193–229. To my knowledge there is no single overview of the recurring war of the regions in early American historiography. However, the subject is treated *inter alia* but very usefully in two articles by Ian K. Steele whose titles do not fully convey the extent of their coverage: "The Empire and Provincial Elites: An Interpretation of Some Recent Writings on the English Atlantic, 1675–1740," *Journal of Imperial and Commonwealth History* 8(1979–1980): 2–32; "Empire of Migrants and Consumers: Some Current Atlantic Approaches to the History of Colonial Virginia," *Virginia Magazine of History and Biography* 99(1991): 489–512. The most sustained treatment of the respective contributions of the colonial regions to the creation of a common American culture is Jack P. Greene, *Pursuits of Happiness: The Social Development of Early Modern British Colonies and the Formation of American Culture* (Chapel Hill, N.C., 1988).

pendence drew near. (Lord North plays the role of Archbishop Laud in this one, and George III is given the quirks usually assigned to his collateral relation Charles I.) Diverse as these cases for the insignificance of American Puritanism are, they share a common concern for eliminating New England's peculiarity, earlier, later, or *ab initio*, in order that by 1776 the thirteen clocks may chime as one. But there is still another way to do it. It may actually be admitted that American Puritanism was a distinctive phenomenon and that it was of lasting importance within its region. The concession is made, however, in order to read New England out of American history, which is held to be dominated after 1776 by some combination of amorphous pluralism and racial tensions allegedly characteristic of the rest of the colonies at the time of independence. On this showing the union of 1789 was premature and the divided politics of the period 1794 to 1815 and again from 1828 onwards are so many temporarily successful attempts to contain New England traits (a defining passion for organization, discipline, regulation, and intellectuality) until economic change New Englandizes the North more than the South. Then the war comes. America, that is, also has its Civil War, to be explained at the moment by cultural dimorphism, although moral conflicts, the inexorable clash of economic forces, and adventitious short-range disruptions and clumsy, reckless politicians operating through inadequate institutions have had their day too. Most English revisionists probably had not read nor even in every instance have so much as heard of their American namesakes of forty years before when they began their assault on Gardiner, et al., but the earlier movement is so uncannily predictive of the later that it would do no harm to advise ambitious historians of Stuart England just entering the profession to study carefully the debates over the American Civil War in order to find a currently underutilized line of interpretation.

This review of the literature is not really intended to counsel either opportunism or despair. If Puritanism is liable to such diverse uses on both sides of the Atlantic, this is a point of interest in itself, a clue to its identity. We write about "Puritanism and" whatever so often— just think of all those titles and subtitles—that we might do well to ask if these recurring conjunctions do not point to something both essential to the nature of our subject and yet peculiarly liable to set off disagreements about it or render it vulnerable to appropriation for nonhistorical purposes. (Prove that indisputable Puritans behaved in an unseemly manner—as in "Puritanism and race" or "Puritanism and gender"—and you supposedly prove that this behavior was a component of Puritan*ism,* and, therefore, to the extent that it can be claimed that we continue under the influence of the past, has been passed down intact like original sin to the current generation.)

Now, there is no point in demanding of the past that it be logical. It has not been so. Accordingly, the study of the past needs to be endowed with a certain healthy illogicality, a willingness not to think too straightly about crooked and confused paths. But when we as historians do find a genuine past phenomenon, one recognized as such by contemporaries and necessary to our explanation of certain past events, that is entangled with so many other developments and yet repeatedly resists exclusive identification with any of them, surely we have a right to suspect that our thinking may be clouded by a Category Mistake. Most of us (if we are of the age of the present author or older) have probably first encountered the Category Mistake in our undergraduate reading of Gilbert Ryle's polemical attack on Cartesian notions of the mind/body problem. (What Ryle derisively termed "the ghost in the Machine.") It will be recalled that in Ryle's first exemplum a visitor from another country, or maybe another planet, is being shown a university, and after the usual tour of students, faculty, and buildings and grounds demands a little petulantly to be shown the university.[6] Puritanism, too, is often sought in the wrong place or at the wrong level of definition. It is no more a collection of things than Ryle's university but rather a purposive arrangement of them and even more a technique and a passion for purposive arranging. (It was still possible to think of universities in this way in Ryle's day.) The Puritan starting point was the axiom that "great and diligent teaching" would be necessary to redeem humanity "because men are made of a dull metall, and hard to conteine spirituall and heavenly things."[7] Posed negatively, the proposition contains a cautiously optimistic implication: if the limited yet real potentials of the culture of the day could all somehow or another be pressed into service, it might be possible to civilize and Christianize some meaningfully large fraction of the English people. The particular resources employed necessarily would vary from place to place and time to time, and in the course of our respective Category Mistakes we are in the habit of identifying some one or another passing combination as definitive according to our differing agendas. But it was only the insistence on combination that endured.

[6] Gilbert Ryle, *The Concept of Mind* (New York, 1950), 16.
[7] George Gifford, *A Brief Discourse of Certaine Points of the Religion, Which is among the Common Sort of Christians . . .* (London, 1581), f.84 (recte 83)r.

The argument can be made a little less abstract by detailed exposition in a particular instance. The subject chosen will not be familiar to most readers—no Nehemiah Wallington or Samuel Sewall he, to leave a hefty written corpus to perpetuate his memory. He is, in fact, an apparently unlikely choice, a layman of no great importance or intellectuality who spent most of his adult life in a small farming town in a colony that did not even have its own printing press. The argument will accordingly gather force from its application to a case not ready made to substantiate it. Additionally, the affairs of the aptly named Thomas Minor of Stonington, Connecticut, when examined closely have the advantage of turning the tables on the present author by exposing something *he* got wrong.

Minor came to New England from Chew Magna in Somerset early in the Migration, possibly in the *Lyons Whelpe* in 1629. Young, unattached, and single, lacking even an East Anglian affiliation, he is the sort of person one would have expected to find on the passenger list of a Chesapeake-bound ship instead, and in the current round of debate over the motives of the New England migrants his vital statistics alone are probably enough to consign him to the fishing rather than the praying camp.[8] As it turns out, however, his first definitive appearance in America is on November 2, 1632, as (at age twenty-four) a founding member of the church of Charlestown, proving once again the obvious, that little can be told about what goes on inside someone's head from a few scraps of demographic data. Minor married in 1634 and moved from Charlestown to Hingham about 1638, but in 1645 or possibly the next year he joined the younger John Winthrop in Connecticut to found the settlement later named New London, and then, finally, in 1653 (the year he began to keep a diary) he settled a few miles to the eastward in the area that became Stonington, where he remained until his death at an advanced age in 1690. A later generation of Minors endowed their progenitor with membership in an armigerous Somerset family (a claim subsequently withdrawn) and a line of descent leading to President Grant (a more credible proposition) and also published the diary he kept for thirty years.[9]

For all that time it was first Sergeant, then Lieutenant, never Mis-

---

[8] The assignment to the *Lyons Whelpe* comes from Charles Edward Banks, *The Planters of the Commonwealth* (Boston, 1930), 61; no source is given, however, and another account puts him in the Winthrop fleet of 1630, again without any evidence adduced. Minor's age, however, can be established: he was baptized on April 23, 1608. John A. Miner and Robert F. Miner, "The Curious Pedigree of Lt. Thomas Minor," *New England Historical and Genealogical Register* 137(1984): 182–184.

[9] Richard D. Pierce, ed., *Records of the First Church in Boston. 1630–1686*, Colonial Society of Massachusetts, *Publications*, 39 (Boston, 1961), 15n., 16n.; Clarence Almon Torrey,

ter Minor. He held every office in Stonington, concurrently or seria-
tim, yet never rose to anything higher except for infrequent stints as
an assistant to the magistrates on the New London County Court
and some important assignments during King Philip's War. The diary alone can lay claim to any share of our attention and even it contains little detailed description or much information of any sort about
the world outside Stonington. Although Minor made frequent trips
to other parts of Connecticut and sometimes ranged further afield,
he never describes what he did when away from home, only the bare
fact that he left and came back again. January of 1676, for example,
might have had an interesting story to tell if the concluding entry
had gone beyond "the Rest of this moneth I spent in the war."[10] The
descriptive entries concerning life in Stonington itself are a little fuller, but the bulk of them do little more than provide the skeletal details of their author's farming activities and domestic history. There
is nothing at any point in the diary concerning Minor's affective life
(though he presumably had one) except during a single cryptic episode that prompted him to keep two different sets of entries in 1662
and to lapse most unusually into verse:

> The 8th. of februarie 1661 [O.S.; i.e., 1662] I went To speake with a
> frend: but found I none: this is the secound time I tried a man: but I
> wile for beare the third if that I can: the first he witnessed with a Rattan
> the second he turned me of[f] with a slam: oh the 22 of July 1662 what
> bitter curses from him did I heare pray god to keep me in thy feare[11]

Circumstantial evidence suggests that Minor is referring to problems over local land titles occasioned by conflicting claims from
neighboring Rhode Island and the Bay, where the General Court had
cheerfully granted away chunks of Stonington land in the brief period when the town was under its jurisdiction.[12] In any event, Minor
was never again so personal or so poetical. A more typical monthly

---

New England Marriages Prior to 1700 (Baltimore, 1985), 511; *The History of the Town of Hingham, Massachusetts* (Cambridge, Mass., 1893), 3:71–72; Frances Manwaring Caulkins,
History of New London, Connecticut (New London, 1895), 44–45; Richard A. Wheeler, *History of the First Congregational Church. Stonington, Conn.. 1674–1874* (Norwich, Conn.,
1875), 294–295.

[10] Sidney H. Miner and George D. Stanton, Jr., eds., *The Diary of Thomas Minor,
Stonington, Connecticut, 1653 to 1684* (New London, 1899), hereafter *Minor Diary,* 133.

[11] Ibid., 189. The word "Rattan" here could refer either to a club of that material or, as
a variant of "rataplan," to a drum roil (possibly as a metaphor for noisy belligerence).

[12] Wheeler, *History of the First Congregational Church,* 36–37, 37n.; idem, "The First
Original Church in New London County," *Records and Papers of the New London County
Historical Society,* 1, pt. 3 (New London, 1891), 22–23. Although providing no further
details, *Minor Diary,* 190, indicates that its author's quarrel was with Thomas Stanton and
William Cheesborough. Whatever the experience, it gave Minor nightmares. (Ibid., 192).

entry (selected by opening the diary at random) in the year 1669 reads:

> The second moneth is Aprile and hath 30 dayes Thursday the ffirst manaseh and will begun at the ffarme Thursday The .8 we lined the house the .9. we Threshed the 10 bushells of Corne Thursday the 15 wee met at the meeting house and .13 or 14 gave in their nams to begin a Church and Thursday 22 my wife was at Tagwonck Joseph was heare & william more I had sowed my wheate saterday the 24 day I made an End of soweing in the plaine Thursday The 29. mr samuell mason Chosen leeftenant ffriday 30[13]

Even in this instance the mention of the formation of the Stonington church endows the entry with an unusual degree of importance. Such moments of heightened interest are vouchsafed only very rarely to anyone resolute enough to plow through this record of thirty years month by month. There is so little continuity between entries or reflection on their significance that one is almost tempted to conclude that Minor saw life in the mode currently being touted for a rock music channel on cable television, all ebb and flow. Yet there is an obvious organizing principle to the Minor diary, the same one found behind all diaries but in this case in markedly exaggerated form: the presence, indeed the ubiquity, of the author's sense of time. The declaration of the number of days in each month is a regular refrain punctuating the diary's episodic narrative on twelve occasions a year every year from the earliest entries. After ten years, in 1663, Minor also began the practice, continued faithfully thereafter, of opening the New Year on the appropriate Julian date with a calculation of the number of years that had elapsed since Genesis 1.1, evidently figured as March 25, 3949 B.C. Sixteen Sixty-Three, for example, is "from the Creation the yeare .5612."[14]

This engaging trait reserved for Minor a place in my opening paragraph for *The Long Argument,* in the course of which I suggested that his terminus a quo was taken in slightly revised or garbled form from *A Table from the Beginning of the World to this Day,* compiled by the Apostle of Norwich, John More, and published posthumously in 1592. There is by implication a nice epitome here of early New England: the farmer deacon living out his life in a cosmos filled up entirely by his acreage, his town, and his God, numbering the years as they pass according to some scheme of salvation history lined out

[13] *Minor Diary,* 89–90.
[14] Ibid., 5, 56.

by an Elizabethan prophet almost a century earlier. Unfortunately, whether treated with sensitivity and respect for the naive certainties of a lost era, or handled ironically for the humor inherent in Minor's ego- and anthropocentrism, this portrait of the man and his world, very much a still life, is in error in almost every particular.

Readers who are quicker on the uptake than I have been will have realized already that each New Year's Day entry in the diary is dutifully transcribed from the title page of that year's Harvard almanac. There were many more points of reference in Minor's world view than the single pair of Stonington and God, and all of them had been constructed in the course of the running engagement between laity and clergy that has been going on for generations before Minor set foot in Stonington. The almanac for 1663, compiled by Israel Chauncy, H.C. 1661, son of the president of Harvard and soon to be the minister of Stratford, Connecticut, finishes up with a brief but competent and lucid "Theory of Planetary Orbs." Later almanacs that Minor used expounded the Kepplerian discovery of elliptical orbits and explained that "the fixt Stars" seemed not to move because "their distances are so great: that their Inequality in motion is not at all to be perceived by us." Indeed, the distances involved were so great, they were beyond parallax measurement and "cannot be by any man determined."[15] Stonington was already, even in the mid-seventeenth century, a small dot on a small planet located somewhere in a universe of immeasurable vastness.

Lonely in some ultimate sense the inhabitants of the Connecticut town may well have been; isolated they most certainly were not. The very presence of the almanacs on a regular basis is a witness to just how far from autarky Stonington was. New London, less than ten miles away, possessed the best natural harbor in Connecticut, and contacts with Boston were relatively frequent. Minor or one of his sons went up to Boston, the entrepôt of British America, more years than not in the period covered by his diary, while Manasseh Minor, also a diarist, recorded a round trip in 1699 of only four days. When New London's minister wanted news of Bay Colony politics in 1683, he cautioned his correspondent, no less than Increase Mather, to

---

[15]John Langdon Sibley and Clifford Shipton, *Biographical Sketches of Graduates of Harvard University in Cambridge, Massachusetts* (Cambridge, Mass., and Boston, 1873–), 2:82–87; John Sherman (or Jeremiah Shepard), *An Almanack of Celestial Motions . . . for the Year of the Christian Æra 1674* (Cambridge, Mass., 1674), 15; John Foster, *An Almanack of Celestial Motions for the Year of the Christian Æra, 1675* (Cambridge, Mass., 1675), 15–16. Cf. Bernard Capp, *English Almanacs, 1500–1800: Astrology and the Popular Press* (Ithaca, N.Y., 1979), 191–194.

skip the gossip more than five days old—that was already available.[16] For Stonington and for its hinterland generally New London functioned as, in effect, an English market town, connected in turn to the provincial capital, in this instance Boston, which, like Hull or Newcastle or Norwich, was a point of contact with London and through the great city with the continent. Without these commercial ties spanning two continents Minor would have lacked even the paper on which to write his diary. Indeed, at some point in his life he would have lost the ability to read or write anything, for on December 19, 1676, Minor records, "I payd mr Hide six shillings six pence for Two paier of specttecles no cases."[17]

It is in this interconnectedness—not in some portrait after Henri Rousseau or Grant Wood—that the truest emblem of Minor's and New England's Puritanism can be found.[18] Puritans needed above all else an external arena rich in incidents and struggles that could serve as palpable metaphors for their internal pilgrimages. Or to put the proposition a little differently, since the English-speaking world of the period was not noted for its Arcadian conditions, people were drawn to Puritan forms of perception, if and when they were, because these endowed the confused din of events with salvific and teleological significance. In the development of the Puritan movement over time word and world were always assumed to be linked; the question in dispute, to which different answers were given in different periods, was how to turn the linkages to good use.

For the Elizabethan Presbyterians the most obvious means had been the mechanisms of ecclesiastical polity. Without the biblically prescribed church government, wrote John Udall, "the gospell can take no roote, nor have any free passage."[19] Doctrine alone, however correctly and forcefully expounded, required some kind of regular exposition by deeds to attain real meaning. In a church where con-

---

[16]Thomas's own trips are noted in *Minor Diary*, 20 (1656), 31 (1658), 39 (1660), 45 (1661), 52 (1662), 64 (1664), 75 (1666), 86 (1668), 90 (1669), 174 (1682). For Mannaseh's four-day round trip in 1699 see Frank Denison Miner, ed., *The Diary of Manasseh Minor, Stonington, Conn., 1696–1720* (n.p., 1915), 33–34. Simon Bradstreet's letter to Increase Mather is in *Mather Papers*, Massachusetts Historical Society, *Collections*, 4th ser., 8 (Boston, 1868), 477.

[17]Carl Bridenbaugh, *Cities in the Wilderness: The First Century of Urban Life in America* (New York, 1938), 32–34; Bernard Bailyn, *The New England Merchants in the Seventeenth Century* (Cambridge, Mass., 1955), 95–98; Alan Everitt, "The Marketing of Agricultural Produce," in Joan Thirsk, ed., *The Agrarian History of England and Wales*, 4 (Cambridge, 1967): 467–506; *Minor Diary*, 137.

[18]Cf. Collinson, *The Birthpangs of Protestant England*, chap. 2.

[19]John Udall, *A Demonstration of the Truth of that Discipline. Which Christ Hath Prescribed in his Word*, ed. Edwin Arber (1588; rpt. London, 1880), 4. Cf. Albert Peel, ed., *The Seconde Part of a Register* (Cambridge, 1915), 1:158; John Field and Thomas Wilcox, *An Ad-*

gregational discipline was lacking, "although there be never so sound & good preaching with Catechising, against sin and wickednes, yet the edge therof is so dulled, that it is fruitlesse and of little force"—words alone, without the referents to flesh out their significance.[20] This insistence on the necessity of polity to complement preaching earned the more militant Elizabethan Puritans the nickname "Disciplinarians." The distinguishing label of the American branch of the Puritan movement, "the New England Way," was intended to draw attention in the same way to a continuing insistence on the importance of church government, including especially discipline at the congregational level. Ecclesiology remained a perennial issue in the history of the Puritan movement, surfacing at intervals in both England and America with predictably divisive results on each and every occasion. Nevertheless, schemes of polity were only especially clear and vital instances of the broader imperative to harness a multitude of means to the same end, locating the message of the gospel in a temporal, experiential framework. Accordingly, the definition and implementation of polity could be placed on the backburner for one reason or another for long intervals while central Puritan goals were pursued by alternative routes. Thomas Minor did not have to worry about interference from the High Commission or Star Chamber, as John Udall did, yet, as we shall see, even in his happy, bishopless part of the world forms of ecclesiology were of secondary importance during long periods of his life. Near the beginning of his diary an entry describes his own reconciliation with the church of New London in 1654 after a quarrel with its minister, but apart from this one instance, in the course of thirty years a prominent member of, successively, the churches of New London and Stonington showed less recorded interest in the great cause of discipline than in a controversy over the branding of horses.[21] What does bulk large in the Minor diary are two other nexus for world and scripture: the sabbath and, from 1660 on, days of public humiliation or thanksgiving. Both were longstanding Puritan rites, but the uses to which they were put varied over the long course of the Puritan movement. Both also could be owned by English Protestants generally. Yet for Puritans they also possessed a special organizing function that was distinctive and potentially divisive.

Sabbatarianism, in fact, came to the Elizabethan Puritans late in

---

monition to the Parliament, in *Puritan Manifestoes: A Study of the Origin of the Puritan Revolt,* ed. W.H. Frere and C.E. Douglas (London, 1954), 16.

[20]Robert Cawdry, *A Treasurie or Storehouse of Similies,* 2d ed. (London, 1609), 220–221.

[21] *Minor Diary,* 12–13.

the day and did not initially command universal acceptance. Nor at any time before the Civil War did English Puritans have a monopoly on the proposition that the fourth commandment, as opposed to the Jewish ceremonial law, imposed a perpetually binding obligation unaltered by the coming of Christ. Divines of all stripes concurred on the point, and the repeated campaigns to secure Sunday legislation enjoyed support from a broad front of members of Parliament.[22] Yet, for all the apparent consensus, James I knew what he was doing (he generally did) when he referred to the restrictions on Sunday activity proposed in the Parliament of 1621 as "the Puritan Bill," implied that the ostentatiously nonpartisan chair of the committee in charge of the legislation "smelt a little of puritanism," and described the Book of Sports of four years earlier as an "edict against Puritanes"; he was throwing the potential opposition in the Commons off balance and creating a division in its ranks between those for whom the banning of certain activities on Sunday was desirable and those for whom the re-creation of a neo-Hebraic sabbath was the cornerstone of English achievements in practical divinity.[23] His son Charles I ran equally true to form when he signed sabbath legislation in 1625 and 1628 (James had always vetoed the bills) and then reissued the Book of Sports in 1633 as a shibboleth to identify and purge the very people he had tried to conciliate at the beginning of his reign and again at the opening of the fateful sessions on the eve of the Personal Rule. There were sabbatarians and sabbatarians, not to mention proponents of the continuing relevance of the fourth commandment who scrupled at the Judaizing and partisan implications of the term "sabbath." Laudian ruthlessness in the 1630s merely exposed the unpleasant truth that the general agreement on the fourth commandment had for long concealed very different ways of putting the consensus into practice. After their early hesitation, Puritan writers on the subject had closed ranks to promulgate a series of bans on ordinary activities on Sunday that none of the Parliamentary bills ever approached, with the partial exception of the act of 1628 (which

[22]Patrick Collinson, "The Beginnings of English Sabbatarianism," in *Godly People: Essays on English Protestantism and Puritanism* (London, 1983), 429–433; Kenneth L. Parker, *The English Sabbath: A Study of Doctrine and Discipline from the Reformation to the Civil War* (Cambridge, 1988); Joan R. Kent, "Attitudes of Members of the House of Commons to the Regulation of 'Personal Conduct' in Late Elizabethan and Early Stuart England," *Bulletin of the Institute for Historical Research* 46(1973): 41–71.

[23]Wallace Notestein et al., eds., *Commons Debates, 1621* (New Haven, 1935), 4:76, 6:362; Esther S. Cope, *The Life of a Public Man: Edward, 1st Baron Montagu of Broughton, 1562–1644*, American Philosophical Society, *Memoirs* 142(1981): 82.

had to be watered down before final passage).[24] They did so because the enormous hollow in time they sought to create was to be used to coordinate and reflect upon the whole previous week's spiritual strivings—"the market day of the soul" in the familiar metaphor—and at the same time to serve as an audible, visible, almost tactile validation of the claim that the English godly stood heir to biblical Israel.[25] Puritan clergy and laymen alike had come to endow sabbath activities with a centrality to their religious life that was idiosyncratic enough to make them easy targets in 1633, when the Book of Sports was reissued. The Book offended many and diverse sensibilities, but only Puritan ministers lost their pulpits rather than read it to their congregations, only a Puritan yeoman from Cambridgeshire could date the beginning of his conversion from the moment when his minister reluctantly read the Book, only a Kentish glover could tell the church of Cambridge in New England, "when the book of liberty [of sports] came forth and being afraid I should not stand in trials, hence I looked this way."[26] In the diary of Thomas Minor, who had looked the same way a few years earlier, "sabbath" is far and away the single most frequently recurring noun; he could not always be bothered to record what happened on the day but in thirty years he only occasionally failed to note its occurrence.

Public days, and especially days of humiliation, had a very similar history to the sabbath: a common ordinance of the Church of England was employed in a special way and as such aroused so much hostility that it became identified with one party only, "deemed as hatefull as conventicles the frute of the vestry elders there vestry doctryne and the disciplinarian faction."[27] Indeed, fast days were con-

---

[24]As it passed the Commons the sabbath bill of 1628 really would have put a substantial crimp in Sunday activities by providing "that no victualers nor alehouse keepers sell beer and victual," inhibiting long distance travel, not to mention tavern haunting. This provision, however, along with a prohibition on travel for judges of assize, was lost when the bill became a statute. cf. 3 Car. I c. 2 with Richard Johnson et. al., eds., *Commons Debates, 1628* (New Haven, 1977–1983), 2:228, 231.

[25]Charles E. Hambrick-Stowe, *The Practice of Piety: Puritan Devotional Disciplines in Seventeenth-Century New England* (Chapel Hill, N.C., 1982), 96–99; Foster, *The Long Argument*, 78–82, 95–97, 136–137.

[26]Margaret Spufford, *Contrasting Communities: English Villagers in the Sixteenth and Seventeenth Centuries* (Cambridge, 1974), 231–232; George Selement and Bruce C. Woolley, eds., *Thomas Shepard's "Confessions,"* Colonial Society of Massachusetts, *Publications,* 58 (Boston, 1981), 176–177. See also the comments of Thomas Shepard, *Theses Sabbiticæ: Or, The Doctrine of the Sabbath* (London, 1649), 48 (4th pag.); Richard Mather and William Tompson, *An Heart-Melting Exhortation Together with a Cordiall Consolation* (London, 1650), 24–25.

[27]Allyn B. Forbes et al., eds., *Winthrop Papers, 1498–1649* (Boston, 1929–), 3:306.

ceived of as essentially exaggerated sabbaths. The occasional nature of the activity, however, rendered it inherently more political from its inception. Even an uncontroversial subject could receive an argumentative gloss, as when Nicholas Bownd attributed severe weather and poor harvests to the failure to enforce the sabbath more strictly, or Thomas Hooker took the practice one step further and blamed the same phenomena on Charles I's marriage to the Catholic Henrietta Maria.[28] And if no fast should be called officially after some given provocation, the decision to hold one anyway without authorization was virtually a comment on government laxity or complicity in the provoking sin. Unabashed provocateurs, such as Henry Burton and Hugh Peter, used these occasions for blatantly political statements, as when Peter prayed for the conversion of Henrietta Maria or Burton held forth on *"that damnable Hierarchie."*[29] They were, however, merely bending to their own "pragmatical" purposes the motor forces of Puritan practical divinity in general. Thomas Hooker was no "cashiered courtier" like Burton, nor an ambitious apparatchik like Peter, but a soul doctor of such power and acumen that the thirteenth edition of his *The Poore Doubting Christian* was in print in 1700, fifty-four years after his death. Yet he was also "a great inquirer after News" who used a funeral sermon to compare the troubled state of the soul to the perils of the English state in 1626, menaced, he said, in both instances less by simple weakness or foreign enemies than by "our treacherous hearts at home."[30] Hooker arguably makes use of a strained analogy, but his sermon still does what all Puritan evangelism was meant to do: turn doctrinal abstraction into experiential knowledge. To do so meant, amongst other things, taking advantage of occasions to give believers multiple analogies for their private travails and to guide their individual journeys by placing them within the ongoing struggles of the church militant and the Elect Nation.

In the Connecticut that Thomas Hooker exchanged for wicked

[28]Nicholas Bownd, *The Doctrine of the Sabbath . . .* (London, 1595), 94, 224 (Margin); Cotton Mather, *Magnalia Christi Americana: Or, The Ecclesiastical History of New England,* ed. Thomas Robbins (Hartford, 1853), 1:345.

[29]Stephen Foster, *Notes from the Caroline Underground: Alexander Leighton, The Puritan Triumvirate, and the Laudian Reaction to Nonconformity,* Conference on British Studies, Studies in British History and Culture, 6 (Hamden, Conn., 1978), 17–18, 50.

[30]Oliver Heywood, *Oliver Heywood's Life of John Angier of Denton,* ed. Ernest Axon, Chetham Society, *Remains,* 97 (Manchester, Eng., 1937), 68–69; George H. Williams et al., eds., *Thomas Hooker: Writings in England and Holland, 1623–1633* (Cambridge, Mass., 1975), 47–48.

England he was hard put to find the traitorous heart and subtle un-derminers that had been so useful to his preaching before migration, nor was he or any other colonist again to experience the thrill of an unauthorized fast. Public days were called by all of the Puritan colo-nies in their early years on a rather infrequent basis when compared to the post-1660 period, and if the silences in the Minor diary are anything to go by, the occasional fasts and thanksgivings called by the colony of Connecticut in the 1650s (thirteen in all from 1653, when the diary begins, through 1659) were not the great events they subsequently became or that they had been on the eve of the Migra-tion. The events simply lacked their full resonance until parallel, in-terlocked crises after 1660 revived their original force.

Minor first begins to keep a sustained record of these occasions while on one of his trips to Boston, with the Massachusetts fast day of June 21, 1660, even if he follows the entry with notations of paying out two-shilling bounties on wolves on two successive Fridays. The Bay colony General Court was invariably more overtly political in its justification for fast days than its Connecticut counterpart. On this occasion the fast day proclamation instanced "the present sad and deplorable condition of our deer native countrie," speculated on what so uncertain a future might hold for England and New Eng-land, and concluded with an acknowledgment of the colony's decline "from those primitive affections, as well to the Lord, his blessed ordi-nances and government, as also one to another."[31] Stonington after-wards returned to the jurisdiction of Connecticut, but that brief ex-posure to the Bay's fasts had been enough. Minor had discovered public days and from then on his diary records the Connecticut equivalents pretty regularly.[32]

In a more muted way the Connecticut fasts and thanksgivings do track the three great public themes articulated in the Bay proclama-tions from the Restoration onwards: the menace of imperial power, the simultaneous domestic conflicts over policy and polity, and the

[31]*Minor Diary,* 40; Nathaniel B. Shurtleff, ed., *Records of the Governor and Company of the Massachusetts Bay in New England* (Boston, 1853–1854), 4, pt. 1:417–418.

[32]The next public day Minor records is the Massachusetts thanksgiving of July 10, 1661, but he follows this entry by one recording a Connecticut thanksgiving on October 23, 1661, and thereafter all subsequent entries deal with fasts or thanksgivings in the latter colony. (*Minor Diary,* 46, 47, 52.) This practice is the more interesting in that in 1661 and for at least part of 1662 Minor still considered himself under the Bay's jurisdiction. (Shurtleff, ed., *Records of the Governor and Company of the Massachusetts Bay,* 4, pt. 2: 53, 54.) Witnessing the 1660 fast in Boston, where it would have been conducted with pecu-liar solemnity and force, primed Minor to take note of the more humdrum versions held at home.

putative decline of the children of the founding generation in spirituality and morality. Minor takes notes of these occasions more often than not but remains true to form in never commenting on the reason behind the fast or thanksgiving or on much of anything else for that matter. The one thing that can be said for certain on the evidence of his diary is that Minor was obliged to keep England and English power in mind after one of the four royal commissioners sent to America in 1664 showed up in New London in 1666. Thereafter every March 25th the diary adds the regnal year of Charles II to the reckoning of time elapsed since the Creation.[33] It would be particularly intriguing to know what Minor thought of the claims for the declension of the New England population from its "primitive affections," as he was, after all, a Founder of a sort himself. An attempt to transfer membership to the church of Norwich from the church of New London in 1669 (when Stonington first began to organize a church of its own) suggests that he may have not been happy with at least some of the forms of extended church membership then in dispute, since Norwich was at the time a bastion of conservatism. Otherwise, the diary gives no indication that Minor came in conflict with either Simon Bradstreet or James Noyes, respectively the ministers of New London and Stonington and both champions of liberal admissions policies.[34] Whatever his particular views on each of the three organizing conflicts of the last third of the century, Minor was perforce caught up in the rhythm of public days as they became increasingly frequent and as the issues they addressed became ever more urgent. As a local magistrate he was obliged to read and enforce the proclamations for the public days and as a frequent deputy to the General Court he had a part, however secondary, in enacting many of them. If he took his Puritanism at all seriously, their agenda became his, wherever he stood on it.[35]

The change in Minor's calendar after 1660 is an indirect measure of a dramatic shift in American Puritanism. After decades of backing and filling the New England clergy had finally figured out how to reconstitute the connections between public and private conflicts that had stood their evangelical efforts in such good stead before the Migration. Essentially, they embellished the public days, and especially the fasts, which outnumbered thanksgivings by a ratio of

[33] *Minor Diary*, 76, 78.

[34] *Minor Diary*, 90; Robert G. Pope, *The Half-Way Covenant: Church Membership in Puritan New England* (Princeton, 1969), 119–120.

[35] cf. Hambrick-Stowe, *The Practice of Piety*, 100–103.

roughly five to one. In the jeremiad they created a sermonic form for the public days that spelled out in detail the links between individual laxity, general cultural inanition, and the blossoming political crises, domestic and imperial. In the covenant renewals that became adjuncts to the ritual of fast days they developed a ceremony that dramatized the same themes and supplied an inclusivist pledge of allegiance for the population at large without quite abandoning the proposition that churches consisted of visible saints. The Puritan redaction of predestinarian theology once again had an epic narrative in the travail of the apostatizing Israel of the Prophetic period.[36]

Perhaps the most interesting feature of these new arrangements is the secondary role played by the more formal ecclesiastical institutions: baptism, the Lord's Supper, even the favorite ceremony of the founding generation of New Englanders, the public recital of a conversion narrative before the entire congregation prior to a candidate's admission to church membership. To be sure, there was intense controversy over these three rites in both England and America, but the noise and smoke of these arguments is no real measure of the importance of the contested institutions in practice. In the ordinary course of events the Puritan laity tended to drift into a fragmented and rather freeform religious life, far more a matter of browsing and eclectic combination than the organized, congregation-bound routine the clergy held as normative. It would be the last decades of the seventeenth century before a well-organized and sustained ministerial campaign managed to assign the role relinquished by the conversion narratives to the covenant renewal and to achieve a limited if real success in creating something like a workable congregational polity centered on baptism, communion, and allegiance to the particular congregation where these rites were administered.

In estimating the eventual success of the American clergy, one has first to begin with the situation in the locales from which the laity migrated. In Minor's own case, formal institutions of any sort could not have been especially important to the Puritans of the clothing villages north of the Mendip Hills in Somerset, his part of England. Both of the incumbents of Chew Magna in his youth were conformists and pluralists, but nearby Brislington and Keynsham were frequent resorts for sermon gadding, while at Chelwood in 1635 there were "private conventicles in stables and out houses." To Chew Magna itself in 1640 (after Minor had already left) came none other

---

[36]Ibid., 246–56; Foster, *The Long Argument*, 213–230.

than William Erbury, who held all ecclesiastical ordinances a dead letter, to preach to large audiences. It was a potentially radical milieu, but one the Puritan clergy had generally been able to contain.[37] If some of these potentials were finally realized in England after 1640, the New England ministry at least was still mostly able to keep their flocks from the Seekers and Baptists. Yet even in America lay habits of mind originally formed in extraparochial activities yielded to the clerical sense of priorities only grudgingly.

To begin with, the matter of baptism: the dramatic circumstances of the relatively few New Englanders who overtly embraced the Baptist cause obscure the practice of a larger number of church members who scrupled baptism for their children and quietly left them unbaptized but who did not suffer persecution because they avoided schism or organized protest.[38] Next, the sacrament: for all the controversy over who might take the Lord's Supper, those whose entitlement was beyond dispute were often in no hurry to exercise their rights. What would Christ think, asked Cotton Mather, when "the people do Throng so fast of out doors before a sacrament."[39] Communion was generally offered infrequently in most churches and was unavailable entirely for years at a time in "widowed" churches lacking an ordained minister. New London, for example, carried on without giving a call to anyone from the departure of Richard Blinman in 1659 until the ordination of Simon Bradstreet in 1670. Neighboring Stonington, after the short-lived Zechariah Bridgen failed to survive long enough to receive a call, secured the preaching of the younger James Noyes in 1664 but did not organize a church and ordain Noyes for a further ten years. In 1669 Minor acknowledged this anomalous situation—he was a member of a church that he did not attend and attended a church that strictly speaking was not a church—when he sought dismission to Norwich from both the church of New London and the "inhabitants" of Stonington. In neither of these two places, however, would communion have been given at the time or chil-

---

[37] Margaret Stieg, *Laud's Laboratory: The Diocese of Bath and Wells in the Early Seventeenth Century* (Lewisburg, 1982), 288–293, 325, 329, 343; Collinson, "The Godly: Aspects of Popular Protestantism," in *Godly People*, 1–17; Collinson, "The English Conventicle," in *Voluntary Religion*, ed., W.J. Sheils and Diana Wood, *Studies in Church History* 23(1986): 228–234.

[38] Foster, *The Long Argument*, 178, 351 n.6; *Hutchinson Papers*, Prince Society, *Publications*, 3 (Albany, 1865), 133.

[39] Cotton Mather, *A Companion for Communicants* (Boston, 1690), 67.

dren baptized. The Minor diary is silent about these ordinances for a long stretch because there could have been nothing to record.[40]

More remarkable still, sizable numbers of New England's visible saints seemed to have regarded church membership itself as a kind of personal status or enfranchisement rather than a fellowship of those who lived and worshiped together. There is ample evidence of individuals who moved but failed to transfer to the church of their new home for periods of years if they bothered to seek dismission at all.[41] The lack of any record of Minor's dismission from Charlestown may just be a clerical error, but the case of his neighbor at Stonington, Captain James Pendleton, is unambiguous. Pendleton lived successively at Sudbury, Watertown, and, finally, Portsmouth, where in 1671 he became a founding member of the church before moving on to Stonington in 1673 or 1674. He baptized two children in the newly organized Stonington church but did not get around to joining it himself until 1680, and then almost immediately he moved again, this time across the border to Westerly, Rhode Island, without seeking a dismission from Stonington.[42] Pendleton was unusually peripatetic but otherwise by no means unique, either in Stonington or in late seventeenth-century Connecticut generally, where locally born townspeople were much more likely to belong to any given town's church than were residents who migrated there as adults. From his vantage point in Northampton, able to look south down the valley to Connecticut and east across unsettled territory to Massachusetts Bay, Solomon Stoddard grumped that "the father is in Covenant with one Church, the Mother with another, the Child was Baptized in a third and lives in a fourth."[43]

After 1660 the New England clergy began a progressively more strenuous campaign to integrate church ordinances in to the improvisatory spiritual life the laity had fashioned for themselves in both England and America. If any one thing distinguishes the state of the

[40]*Minor Diary*, 208–209. The only alternatives would have been either to invite a minister at a neighboring church to administer communion to the "widowed" one or to go to that church and receive the sacrament by communion of churches. The laity, in fact, were very skeptical about the former practice, although the clergy upheld it.

[41]Pope, *Half-Way Covenant*, 141–142; Foster, *The Long Argument*, 178–179, 352 n.8.

[42]Pope, *Half-Way Covenant*, 118–119; Everett Hull Pendleton, *Brian Pendleton and his Descendants, 1599–1910* (n.p., 1910), 30–38.

[43]Gerald F. Moran, "The Puritan Saint: Religious Experience, Church Membership, and Piety in Connecticut, 1636–1776" (Ph.D. diss., Rutgers Univ., 1973), 117–119; Solomon Stoddard, *The Doctrine of Instituted Churches Explained and Proved from the Word of God* (London, 1700), 8.

Puritan movement in America at the end of the seventeenth century from the way things had stood in England at the beginning, it is this upset in the original, rough-and-ready balance of power between clergy, magistracy, and ordinary laity. The clergy made particular and effective use of extended baptism and of covenant renewals as a way of widening church membership and of affirming the membership of those whose status for one reason or another was problematic. They also began to put a much greater emphasis on the evangelical and nourishing value of both of the sacraments for participant and witness alike. When James Noyes was finally ordained in Stonington in 1674, he made sure that the church covenant gave prominent attention to the subject, and from that year onwards the Minor diary first takes notice of baptisms. Communion had reentered Minor's consciousness a little earlier, in 1670, when after the ordination of Simon Bradstreet at New London, he made his first notation about receiving the Lord's Supper in thirteen years.[44] Thereafter, the diary indicates that Minor found baptisms and communions significant points of reference worthy of recording as they never had been between 1653 and 1657, the last previous period in which an ordained minister had been available to administer them.

The Minor diary leaves off a few years too soon to reveal anything, however delphically recorded, about the use of covenant renewals in Stonington. The town's church records, however, indicate when the ordinance finally took hold and why. Covenant renewals had been inaugurated in New England in 1677 at Norwich, the town just to the north of Stonington, but the practice was not adopted widely until the English attack on colonial autonomy turned it into a patriotic rite where all the inhabitants of a town, in full communion or otherwise, could declare a common avowal of their threatened New England Way. At Stonington Noyes followed the example of other New England churches and bided his time until he could use the crisis of the colonial charters in the 1680s to reorient and extend church membership, making one degree or another of affiliation with a town's church available to virtually any resident who could be coaxed or coerced into desiring it. On April 18, 1689, "children of the church" (individuals who had been baptized in right of their parents but had never been able to proceed to the sacrament) "owned" (affirmed) their parents' covenant and had their own children bap-

[44]Wheeler, *History of the First Congregational Church*, 43–44; E. Brooks Holifield, *The Covenant Sealed: The Development of Puritan Sacramental Theology in Old and New England, 1570–1720* (New Haven, 1974), chap. 7; *Minor Diary*, 23, 100, 125.

tized in a mass ceremony. Thereafter, this battle won, Noyes was able to use the same halfway membership to embrace the majority of Stonington's inhabitants not in full communion.[45]

April 18, 1689, was, not coincidentally, the day the Dominion of New England was overthrown at Boston. Stonington cannot have heard of that event the same day that it happened but they must have known it was in the offing. News of the landing of William of Orange at Torbay had reached New London and Boston simultaneously in mid-February, and by late March Boston was well aware that the invasion was a success. A copy of William's proclamation authorizing the resumption of government charters forfeited under James II was even in print in the Bay early in April, although it would be three weeks from the Massachusetts revolution before Connecticut followed suit and resurrected its pre-Dominion government.[46] In any event, what was known in Boston was known in New London within a few days and so available to the inhabitants of Stonington, who on April 18 were presumably aware that extraordinary changes in England were about to presage equally dramatic revolutions at home, even if the ultimate success of both ventures would remain uncertain for years.[47] Precisely this lack of any alternative polity whose legitimacy was not either denied or dubious finally broke lay resistance to a broad admissions policy for the only distinctively Puritan institution left, the church, whose moral character and legitimacy were not in doubt. "*For Commonwealths* r[ead]. Jurisdictions," declares the final addendum to the Harvard almanac for the year 1686 by way of an epitaph on New England's political autonomy.[48] The Glorious Revolution did not really revise this judgment, for if charters and assemblies were restored, secure and undisputed autonomy was never really regained in any colony. The Dominion, its sudden and dramatic demise, and then the long drawn-out threat after 1689 that the royal government would "resume" its rights in the colonies ac-

---

[45]Pope, *Half-Way Covenant,* 117–21; Foster, *The Long Argument,* 223–230.

[46]Ian K. Steele, *The English Atlantic, 1675–1740: An Exploration of Communication and Community* (New York, 1986), 103–107.

[47]It *is* possible in one instance to determine more exactly the time needed for news to travel from Boston to Stonington. Queen Anne died on Aug. 1, 1714. Boston received unofficial news of the event on Sept. 15 and the official word on Sept. 17. The news was in Bristol (halfway to Stonington) on the afternoon of the seventeenth and in Stonington itself on the nineteenth. *The Boston News-Letter,* Sept. 13–20, 1714; Miner, ed., *Diary of Manasseh Minor,* 119; M. Halsey Thomas, ed., *The Diary of Samuel Sewall, 1674–1729* (New York, 1973), 2:769, 769n.

[48]Samuel Danforth, *The New-England Almanack for the Year of our Lord, 1686* (Cambridge, Mass., 1686), 16.

complished in New England at last the design roughed out more than a century earlier in England—to use participation in church affairs to vivify and provide meaningful context for each pilgrim's progress.[49]

One can, however, overstate the ministry's triumph in purely ecclesiological matters. They had, after all, more than a century's worth of ingrained bad habits to overcome. Even in 1704 the annual convention of the Massachusetts clergy was complaining once again of "such as have submitted unto the *Government* of CHRIST in any of His Churches" (the circumlocution they were obliged to use to comprehend all of the varieties of membership that had been created over the previous fifty years) and had then dodged the obligation by moving without seeking to be placed under the watch of the churches of their new towns. In Connecticut as well as in Massachusetts the more unremittingly inclusionist forms of polity ("Stoddardeanism" or "Presbygationalism"), which made no provision for distinction in degrees of church membership, mostly turned out to be flops in practice.[50] These instances of failure are hardly surprising: in seeking to make the institutions of the church central bosses of Puritan spiritual life the New England clergy were not returning to an old order but attempting the unprecedented. Rather than toting up the evidence of the incompleteness of their achievement, we should be remarking with surprise that they had even partial success. In any case, the clergy made their advances along a very broad front.

Puritanism, it will be remembered, took in but was never reducible to questions of church order. The closest we can come to a definition that will comprehend its various dimensions over so long a time span and so diverse a set of locales is to see it as a search for continuous, multiple means to bridge the gap between the God who created the universe in 3942 B.C. (or whenever) and the believers who strove to comprehend the purposes, revealed and hidden, that were already complete at the Creation. These means necessarily were both civil and ecclesiastical; ideally, they should be as multiform and ubiquitous as experience itself. If, for example, the sacrament symbolized and enacted the union of believers in the body of Christ, so did the sexual union of man and wife—it alone could provide a physical and

[49]Foster, *The Long Argument*, 237–240.
[50]Williston Walker, *The Creeds and Platforms of Congregationalism*, pbk. ed. (Boston, 1960), 484; Moran, "The Puritan Saint," 91–93, 131–132, 156; Paul Lucas, "'An Appeal to the Learned': The Mind of Solomon Stoddard," *William & Mary Quarterly*, 3d ser., 30(1973): 278–283.

emotional analogue for understanding the otherwise incomprehensible mystery of communion. To return to Ryle-like assertions, the important point was not any given comment at any given time but the need for continuous commentary. This much had always been the case, whether the devices involved for coordinating word and world were consistorial discipline, private mediation, public fasts, conversion narratives, or covenant renewals. What had changed was the role of the clergy, who had become by the late seventeenth century the recognized interpreters and organizers of the process by which abstract doctrine became operative knowledge. Lay autonomy had not been eliminated but it had been restricted or at least outflanked by clerical permeationism. The clergy's ascendancy extended to their dominance of the profession of author at a time when printed materials were increasingly available, their control of secondary education as their numbers increased, and their uncontested role as the official moralists at every public occasion, be it elections, assize sessions, militia days, fasts, thanksgivings, funerals, or executions. There was a sermon for them all.[51]

The diary of Thomas Minor, who has been the intermittent hero of this essay because his literary remains hardly allow him to be much more, ceases at the end of 1684—perhaps imported spectacles could no longer keep pace with failing eyesight—some six years before the death of its author. But if one were to look at his part of the world just a few years later, when his place had been taken by his son, Deacon Manasseh Minor, it would be possible to identify another two events that brought to fruition the developments Thomas recorded obliquely and sometimes opaquely. In 1709 Connecticut obtained a printing press of its own, set up in New London at the home of the former minister of the town, now become governor of the colony. Noyes at Stonington had published nothing in a fifty-five year tenure. Eliphalet Adams, who succeeded to the New London pulpit the year the town obtained the press, finished his own career with fifteen titles, almost all occasional pieces, including the funeral sermon for Noyes (dutifully acquired by Mannaseh Minor).[52] And if there were more clergy able to print what they preached in the eighteenth century, spinning out their web ever more widely, there were more preachers too, because of the college at Saybrook. In 1704 that institution had graduated its first real class, three individuals, of whom

[51] Foster, *The Long Argument*, 268–279.
[52] Sibley and Shipton, *Biographical Sketches of Graduates of Harvard University*, 4:189–198; Miner, ed., *Diary of Manasseh Minor*, 150.

two became ministers. By 1710 there were a further twenty-eight graduates, twenty-two of them clergy. The progressive inspissation of the clerical presence in colonial society first observed through the Harvard almanacs had reached its initial climax in the founding of Yale. Not to put too fine a point on it, in the eighteenth century, rather than the seventeenth, the Puritan clergy would find their apotheosis and—because, as it happened, a Greek rather than a Christian dramatic structure prevailed—their nemesis.

Part Two: The Character of the Puritan

Puritan Self-fashioning

Margo Todd

14 June 1595. My negligence in not calling upon God before I went to
the chapel, and the little desire I had there to call on God, and my
drowsiness in God's service. My sins even through the whole day, being Sunday: (1) my negligence aforesaid, (2) my hearing of the sermon without that sense which I should have had, (2) [*sic*] in not praying God to bless it to me afterward, (3) in not talking of good things
at dinner being the posteriorums day, (4) in the immoderate use of
God's creatures, (5) in sleeping immediately after dinner, (6) in not
preparing me to sermon til it tolled, (7) in sluggish hearing of God's
word, and that for my great dinner, (8) in hearing another sermon
sluggishly, (9) in returning home and omitting our repetition of sermons, by reason that my countryman Eubank was with me, (11) [*sic*]
in not exhorting him to any good thing, (12) in not going to evening
prayers, (13) in supping liberally, never remembering our poor brethren, (14) in not taking order to give the poor women somewhat at 7
o'clock, (15) my dulness in stirring of my brother to Christian
meditations, (16) my want of affections in hearing the sermons
repeated, (17), my sluggishness in prayer, and thus sin I daily
against thee, O Lord.

UPON SUCH DIARY entries as this one of Samuel Ward's, historians have built an edifice called "Puritanism."[1] It is rigid, narrow, and

Research for this essay was supported by grants from the American Council of
Learned Societies, the National Endowment for the Humanities, and Vanderbilt University. The author is also grateful to the Master and Fellows of Sidney Sussex College,
Cambridge, who generously granted her Visiting Scholarship in 1988 and as always provided ready access to Samuel Ward's diary and other papers in the college.

This article was originally published in the *Journal of British Studies* 31 (July 1992):
236-264 and is published here with the permission of the University of Chicago Press. ©
1992 by The North American Conference on British Studies.
[1] The quote is from Sidney Sussex MS 45, fol. 18v-19. In this and all quotes from the
diary, spelling and punctuation have been modernized.

quaintly absurd in design. It is the sort of structure on which twentieth-century people can look down with complacency from the heights of their own intellectual towers. It makes us glad to have escaped the confining corridors of faith and piety by rendering them dark, small, and rather shabby.

Unfortunately it does so by unconscionably distorting the past. What it reflects is less the thinking of a man like Samuel Ward than the inadequate perspective of historians on subjects to whom they unabashedly condescend, and whom they are more willing to caricature than to try fully to understand. And it reveals a great deal about how historians use and misuse their sources when looking at subjects with that faint amusement that comes from the scholar's conviction of his own superiority to the actors of the past.[2]

This is not to say that the above quote is inaccurate or not genuine. It is one of numerous entries for 1595 in Samuel Ward's own hand in a diary made common knowledge to English historians by M. M. Knappen's edition of it, together with Richard Rogers's diary, as *Two Elizabethan Puritan Diaries*. Knappen served scholars well by making the diary known and easily accessible to students; however, the convenience of this edition may well have blinded us to its problems. Countless scholars since that 1933 publication have quoted it as typical of Ward or of Puritanism without either recourse to the original manuscript or consideration of the circumstances in which it was written. Yet a glance at the original diary, in a volume with sixty closely-written folios, reveals that Knappen's edition is limited to selections from the middle thirty folios, a section strikingly different from the other half of the volume.[3] Nowhere else in this manuscript

[2]The most recent example of an historian misusing Ward's diary in this way is H. R. Trevor-Roper's *Catholics, Anglicans and Puritans* (Chicago, 1989), in which the author repeatedly refers to Ward as "our old plum-guzzling friend" on the basis of Ward's journal confessions about overindulging in fruit. Needless to say, Puritans in general come off badly in Trevor-Roper's work. In all fairness to current scholarship, however, it must be said that not all historians treat Puritans so. The work of Peter Lake, Patrick Collinson, and others has provided us with a more balanced view. See, e.g., Lake's *Moderate Puritans and the Elizabethan Church* (Cambridge, 1982) and his *Anglicans and Puritans?* (London, 1988); Collinson's *Elizabethan Puritan Movement* (Berkeley, 1967) and his *Religion of Protestants* (Oxford, 1982); and Jacqueline Eales, *Puritans and Roundheads* (Cambridge, 1990). The stereotype does persist, though. See, for instance, Whitney R. D. Jones's treatment of William Turner's narrow "puritan moralizing" in his recent biography of Turner (New York, 1988).

[3]Interestingly, the two manuscript transcriptions of the diary that are kept with it in the muniments room of Sidney Sussex, one done in 1879 by one J. Rickards, a fellow of the college, the other commissioned by the master and fellows in 1913 and produced by Alfred Rogers, of the University Library, also omit the other half of the diary (fols. 1–15, 49–60, and the last five folios, written back to front).

or, for that matter, in any of Ward's voluminous extant papers, is there anything like this thirty folios of guilt.[4] It seems an anomaly— hardly the sort of thing on which we ought to base our concept of Elizabethan Puritanism. On the other hand, we do find similar self-scrutiny in other Puritan writings: Knappen's companion piece, the diary of Richard Rogers, is one of many examples.[5] And Ward's Puritanism, at least in the 1590s, is unquestioned, so anything he wrote then must be taken into account by scholars of Puritanism.[6] How, then, ought we to use the diary?

If we are to understand the Puritanism of this young Cambridge scholar late in the reign of Elizabeth, we ought to look much more carefully at his diary, in two ways. First, we must set it in its immediate literary context, examining the middle thirty folios of the notebook as they relate to the rest of the volume. Second, we must ask a new set of questions of the whole document. It is not enough to set forth one portion as a demonstration that Puritans were neurotically obsessive about the most trivial sins. We must ask some very fundamental questions of the whole text: Why was the document written? What was Ward's intention in recording his sins, among other things, in the notebook which he also carried to lectures? Why did he make his diary entries in the way he did—sometimes subjectively, at other times concerned with affairs outside himself; sometimes terse and unconcerned with style, at other times agonizing over his word choice; sometimes in the form of a prayer, at other times (frequently in the same sentence) referring to God in the third person? What is the significance of his style or disregard of it? Finally, why did he keep the volume long after he ceased to make regular entries in it? What did the exercise of diary-writing signify for him, both as he wrote and long after?

A careful look at Ward's text will reveal that what he was doing in

---

[4]Most of the papers have been collected at Sidney. The 60 or so notebooks, sermons, commonplace books, and miscellaneous fragments there have been classified in my "Samuel Ward Papers in Sidney Sussex College, Cambridge," *Transactions of the Cambridge Bibliographical Society* 8(1985): 582–592. Numerous letters are also found in the Bodleian Library's Tanner Manuscripts.

[5]The prescription of self-examination by Renaissance humanists as by zealous protestants in the sixteenth century made a self-conscious fashioning of one's identity, generally in the guise of conversion, a characteristic requirement of Puritans. See, among other prescriptive literature in this vein, Arthur Dent, *The Plaine Mans Path-way to Heaven* (London, 1601). On the tradition of self-examination in the sixteenth century, see Margo Todd, *Christian Humanism and the Puritan Social Order* (Cambridge, 1987), 30–31, 192–195, and esp. 194, n. 53.

[6]On Ward's Puritanism, see Margo Todd, "'An Act of Discretion': Evangelical Conformity and the Puritan Dons," *Albion* 18(1986): 581–599.

the 1590s was what most thinking people more or less consciously attempt at some point during their youth: He was defining himself, designing for himself an identity. Scholars of literature have suggested that this activity was in fact a distinctive feature of the Renaissance, when there appeared (or was perhaps re-born) in western thought a sense that the self *could* be deliberately fashioned. In the sixteenth century, according to Stephen Greenblatt, we find an "increased self-consciousness about the fashioning of identity as an artful process." The self, defined as a characteristic "mode of perceiving and behaving," a "distinctive personality," "a structure of bounded desires," could be intentionally shaped.[7] As a scholar of literature Greenblatt sees the creation of a literary character as a reflection of this self-fashioning. Following Clifford Geertz,[8] he argues against dividing literary symbolism from symbolic structure operative in society: humans themselves are cultural artifacts, and as such he treats sixteenth-century literary figures like More, Tyndale, Spenser, and Shakespeare. Applying Greenblatt's assumptions to the lesser literary production of Samuel Ward, one might "read" the Ward that emerges from the diary as a symbolic structure of Elizabethan Puritan culture. Certainly that Ward would be more representative of his culture than the literary giants and martyr heroes that figure in Greenblatt's study, and so perhaps of more interest to historians of protestantism broadly conceived. A careful reading of the whole notebook, then, will give us a more comprehensive and accurate picture of a particular, rather ordinary Cambridge Puritan and of the self-fashioning process in which he engaged, and as we follow that process, we will derive a self-definition of Puritanism.

Samuel Ward recorded entries in the little volume that was much later labeled his diary from 1592 to 1601, that is, from age twenty to age twenty-nine. Most of the dated entries in the middle, "confessional" section quoted above are dated from May 1595 to November 1599, when Ward was a graduate student at Christ's College, Cam-

---

[7] Stephen Greenblatt, *Renaissance Self-fashioning from More to Shakespeare* (Chicago, 1980), 1–2. See also Paul Delany, *British Autobiography in the Seventeenth Century* (London, 1969), chap. 2; T. Price Zimmermann, "Confession and Autobiography in the Early Renaissance," *Renaissance Studies in Honor of Hans Baron*, ed. A. Molho and J. Tedeschi (Dekalb, Ill., 1971), 119–140. Ultimately, Greenblatt denies any real individual autonomy in self-fashioning: see especially his epilogue.

[8] *The Interpretation of Cultures* (New York, 1973).

bridge.[9] He chose to record his sins in a volume which he had kept since his undergraduate days, and which he also used as a lecture notebook. He would put the little book aside two years later and not record anything further in it until the 1620s, when he took advantage of blank pages in it to jot down a few notes—on the pros and cons of a prospective marriage partner (61–61v); on "sins of the land" and the university (62v) and reasons for fasting after the accession of Charles I (63); and on a crisis of conscience related to a scandal in university administration (37).[10]

Aside from the 1620s entries, the notebook can be divided for reference into six sections: The fifteen folios written from the front and dated March 7, 1591/2 are lecture notes, mostly on a series of lectures by Laurence Chaderton on the tenth chapter of St. John's gospel. There are also notes on a lecture by a Mr. Harrison on Malachi 1 (13). The five folios written from the back are commentary on the first chapter of Genesis and Psalm 15. Since Ward generally attributes lecture notes to the speaker, these are probably his own notes on the biblical text.[11] The third section is the 21 folios of frequent, dated entries from 1595 to 1599 from which Knappen drew most of his edition (15v–36v). There are significant gaps in the dates here, although not in placement of entries on the pages—for example, the January 17, 1598, entry is followed immediately by the May 27, 1598, entry (35). While in some months entries are made almost daily, there is nothing written between November 6, 1595, and January 29, 1596 (23v), September 10, 1596, and July 31, 1597 (32v), or June 5, 1598, and November 10, 1599 (36). Ward apparently intended to be more regular than this: He recorded the advice of the ancients to "Remember to take account of the whole day at night, for it is hard to remember the next morning" (19), and on September 12, 1595, his first entry since July, he confessed "my great negligence for a great time of noting my sins" (22v). This suggests that the diary accurately reflects unintended discontinuity in Ward's process of self-examination. The last journal-style entry in this section is dated No-

[9]Ward (1572–1643) matriculated pensioner at Christ's in 1589, took his B.A. in 1593 and his M.A. in 1596, and in 1599 moved to Emmanuel as a fellow of the college. In 1599 he became a fellow of Sidney Sussex College, where he remained (as master from 1610) for the rest of his life. He was made B.D. in 1603 and D.D. in 1610. See the *DNB* entry for Ward; John and J.A. Venn, *Alumni Cantabrigienses* (Cambridge, 1922), pt. I, 4:334; and John Peile, *Biographical Register of Christ's College, 1505–1905* (Cambridge, 1910), 1:195.

[10]Given the frequency of references in this paper to Ward's diary, folio numbers in Sidney MS 45 are indicated in parentheses in the text rather than in notes.

[11]Continuing foliation from the front, this section comprises fols. 91v–95v.

vember 14, 1599. A few blank folios (38–42v) separate this from the fourth section, which consists mostly of undated lists of "benefits" for which Ward was thankful, although there are appended journal entries dated August 29 and 30 (46v–47) and a reference to September 6, 1601.[12] The fifth section is a six-folio commentary on the Lord's Prayer (49–55v). Finally, there is a section of commentary on prayer in general and assorted lists—of characteristics of the unconverted, personal items for thanksgiving, and daily duties. Appended to this section are two folios of fairly formal prayers apparently composed by Ward (56–59v).[13] There are almost thirty blank folios between this section and the one written from the back.

Taken altogether, Ward's notebook shows us several aspects of the self-fashioning process in which he was engaged during his twenties and reveals a great deal about the Puritan identity that emerged from it. It reveals, first of all, the importance of authorities and models, both contemporary and ancient, for the definition of character. Above all, the power of the biblical text is apparent here: The Scriptures served as Ward's guide; provided his patterns both for behavior and for modes of self-expression; and measured, chastised, and forgave the outcome. Second, reading the diary in context suggests that Ward fashioned himself primarily in communal, rather than individualistic terms, identifying himself with the community of the godly in perpetual readiness to combat the enemy, the forces of Antichrist, whether in Cambridge or abroad. Finally, from the notebook emerge the tensions that were built into the Puritan character: Ward identified with Christ, yet recognized his own sinfulness. He was both preacher and penitent. He both served and questioned authority. There is throughout the volume a dialectic between fundamentally opposed, yet paradoxically incorporated sides of Ward's *persona*. The text can thus be read as a dialogue, between individual and God, conscience and actor, reader and text, the self and himself.

The twenty-year-old Samuel Ward began his process of self-definition within the context of a university atmosphere charged with religious tension, as an undergraduate in a college known for its commitment to training godly protestant preachers for the reformation of church and community.[14] Christ's bordered a new college, Em-

---

[12]Knappen tentatively dates the lists 1596.

[13]Handwriting and some internal evidence suggest dating in the 1590s.

[14]H.C. Porter, *Reformation and Reaction in Tudor Cambridge* (Cambridge, 1958), 323–413; Collinson, *Elizabethan Puritan Movement*, chap. 3; Lake, *Moderate Puritans, passim*.

manuel, founded in 1584 by a Puritan zealot formerly of Christ's, explicitly to train a godly preaching ministry.[15] Both colleges would send members in 1596 to yet another new Puritan foundation, Sidney Sussex, the college of which Ward would later serve for thirty-three years as master. As a young man, then, Ward found himself in the midst of a community in which religious zeal was marked, and in which academic endeavor was channeled to religious ends. It was, as Ward remarked in doubtless inadvertent rhyme, "a most excellent place for knowledge and grace" (18). It was from this community that Ward derived the patterns for his self-fashioning.

When Ward arrived in Cambridge, he may not have differed markedly in behavior from most undergraduates. (Perhaps this was why his family sent him to a notoriously Puritan college.)[16] The diary gives us a glimpse of a merry young fellow who enjoyed a good joke (21, 21v, 33) and occasionally a bad one (23v), was given to "quipping" to the delight of his friends (18), who enjoyed the pleasures of the table (19v, 20, 21, 22v, 23, 27, 28, etc.), and who was not by nature very patient with long prayers (16). He tended to oversleep (20) and to nod off during sermons (19v, 21–21v, 34–34v, *et passim*), and to take more pleasure in bowling, tennis, and boating (22, 27, 34, 25v) than in worship (28, 34, etc.). He was quick-tempered and sharp-tongued (19) and tended to be rude toward servants (20, 22v, 27, 34). It is clear that he was a good student, but this fed his tendency toward pride, particularly in regard to his command of Greek, Hebrew, and philosophy (19, 19v, 21).

From the beginning of his diary-keeping period, however, Ward was clearly intent on transforming this frivolous, fun-loving, proud self into a more somber, disciplined, pious character. "My purpose this day," he recorded in May of 1598, is "taking a new course of life . . . more diligently to serve God" (35v). He desired a life of "true sobriety" (54), and here, at least, his success was undeniable: There is not the slightest vestige of humor in Ward's later writing. He prayed for "prudence . . . to order my life and conversation aright, . . . to demean myself with [adopt a demeanor of] sobriety and dis-

---

[15]Lake, *Moderate Puritans*, 8, has justly called Emmanuel "the paradigm of a puritan institution."

[16]Beyond Thomas Fuller's brief description in *The History of the Worthies of England*, ed. James Nichols (London, 1811), 1:333–334, there is almost no extant information about Ward's family background. We do not know whether his family was of the godly sort. We do know that he was not the only member of his family sent to Cambridge: the diary mentions a cousin, Thomas (33), and a brother, Henry (23, 58v); the latter matriculated Christ's College in 1593.

cretion, . . . gravity in my behavior, deliberation in my speeches, purity in my thoughts, and righteousness in my actions" (59v). His diary is to be both a repenting of the old and a pattern for the new "demeaning."

As he cast about for guides in this transformation and for models on which to structure his new self, two very visible and highly esteemed Cambridge Puritans must have sprung immediately to mind. The godly of Cambridge late in Elizabeth's reign were followers of learned and charismatic Puritan dons, notable among them Laurence Chaderton, the "pope of Cambridge Puritanism" and master of Emmanuel from its foundation, and William Perkins of Christ's, a former pupil of Chaderton's, preacher at St. Andrew's, and arguably "the first puritan theologian in the systematic sense."[17] Given the values of Ward's immediate community and the prominence and power of these two leaders, it was natural for him to look to them as both authorities and models for his own development.

Ward's personal veneration of Chaderton was immense. "Think how good a man Mr. Chaderton is who hath such a living affection to the poor, which is certain token of a sound Christian" (18), Ward remarked in 1595. So great was his devotion to his mentor that when he thought that the great man had been offended by one Mr. Hutchinson's failure to keep a dinner engagement with him, his anger overcame him (33). When the opportunity arose to follow Chaderton from Christ's to Emmanuel, Ward agonized over the possibility that he might not receive the fellowship there: "How pensive I was all the afternoon (January 17, 1598) considering my standing at Emmanuel College, . . . I was (I thank God) somewhat willing to prepare myself against the missing of it [the fellowship]," but it would be among "the greatest evils which may befall" (35).

It is significant that when Ward began keeping a diary, he did so in a notebook initially devoted to notes on Laurence Chaderton's lectures. The notes are detailed, and Ward carefully included in them "uses" or applications to his own life and the life of the true church. In his lecture and sermon notes, each exegetical passage is followed by "This teacheth . . ." or "The use is . . ." or "Here we learn. . . . ," and first person pronouns predominate in the ensuing sentences. "Remember always," he exhorted himself on June 13, 1595, "at the hearing of God's word to be applying the things delivered always to

---

[17]Collinson, *Elizabethan Puritan Movement*, 125, 431. On Chaderton in Elizabethan Cambridge, see Lake, chaps. 1 and 3.

thyself" (18v), and this he clearly did upon hearing Chaderton preach or lecture. Accordingly, Ward's diary ought to be read as part of an ongoing endeavor to follow Chaderton's directions, to imitate his godly life, and to reflect his understanding of the church. Ward's concern with sin and confession in the mid-1590s journal entries is the logical outworking of Chaderton's lecture in 1592 on the necessity of "affliction in mind for sin" (1v). His perception of the church in the 1590s (and indeed throughout his life) was conditioned by Chaderton's teaching that dissension and schism are inevitable "that the godly and the wicked might be separated," and his recourse in the midst of conflict was always to follow Chaderton's advice and "do as the noble men of Berea, who seeing these schisms, searched the Scriptures" (2). The diary proper is replete with laudatory references to "Mr. Chaderton's good sermons." Of course, Ward's transformation into a godly youth was not instantaneous, as is attested by his occasional "wandering thoughts at Mr. Chaderton's church" (29), or his "not calling to mind of Mr. Chaderton's sermon as I ought" (31, cf. 26v), but these were lapses from his usual practice, listed with sins of which he repented. References to Chaderton and indirect uses of his 1592 lectures and sermons are numerous enough to indicate that the master of Emmanuel provided a model of authoritative biblical exegesis and godly preaching for Ward's edification. "Christ frameth men by the word preached," Ward noted in his commentary on the Lord's Prayer (51); his own "framing" in the diary must be understood in the context of Chaderton's preaching.

Chaderton further provided for Ward a personal model of behavior and even of vocation. Like Chaderton, Ward would devote his life to academic pursuits—to scholarship both theological and exegetical and to the training of preachers—and to preaching itself. He admired Chaderton's "plain preaching," one of the subjects on which he heard him lecture in 1592 (4), and he styled his own biblical commentary (91–95v) and later his own sermons on Chaderton's simple models.[18] He would, moreover, follow in Chaderton's footsteps in taking a moderate stance on the reforms for which Puritans called: He had accepted the conclusion of Chaderton's lectures on John 10,

---

[18] Sidney Sussex MS Ward O.8 is a collection of Ward's sermons all structured much like Chaderton's lectures: The text is dissected and analyzed phrase by phrase, then interpreted in context, then applied to the lives of contemporary auditors in a section generally called "use." This three-part structure characterizes many Puritan sermons of the period and reflects the success with which university Puritans taught homiletics, by example as well as formally. Sidney Sussex MS Ward E also contains notes on sermons by Chaderton and by William Perkins (e.g., fol 11–11v from the back).

for instance, that Scripture "teacheth us wisely to keep even the institutions of men, for we must not always condemn the ordination of man, because it is of man"; only those "ceremonies which did tend nothing to God's glory he [Christ] called foolish" (3v).[19]

William Perkins and his sermons likewise directly molded Ward's behavior and attitudes. That Perkins was much admired by Ward is abundantly attested by his diary; as a matter of fact, Perkins's approval of the young Ward was a matter of troublesome pride for him (e.g., 16v, 30).[20] He thanked God that "I came to this college, and that in Mr. Perkins' time" (46v), and when Perkins left Christ's upon his marriage in 1595, Ward feared the ruin of the college (20v).[21] Perkins's sermons, however, were his most immediate influence on how Ward would choose to style himself. Occasionally Ward had to repent of his "negligence in not praying before I heard Mr. Perkins' sermon at afternoon" (35v) or his "little care to call to mind Mr. Perkins' sermon" (31, cf. 28, 34v), but more often, Perkins's admonitions were firmly embedded in his mind and shaped him profoundly as much in their mode of discourse as by their substance. The August 30, 1601, entry in the diary illustrates this: "Remember," Ward told himself, "how when thou heardest Mr. Perkins preach of the dignity of God's children, and of the manifold comforts issuing from thence, thou had good actions and affections in thy mind" (47). These good results helped to make the preacher *as preacher* a model for Ward as he considered his own vocation: The August 30 entry continues, "Oh bethink thyself of the great comfort that cometh to a man by God's service, how this will breed true contentment of mind."[22] Ward proceeds experimentally to place himself simultaneously in the roles of preacher and auditor, exhorting himself to evangelical humility and piety: "Above all things, learn humility, pity men when thou seest them run with full stream to sin, bewail their case, insult not over them."[23] As he instructs himself, the vocation of preacher, called "by

---

[19]This moderation and Ward's willingness to compromise on "ceremonial" issues are discussed in the context of Ward's correspondence with William Bedell in Todd, "Act of Discretion."

[20]Perkins even lent Ward money: f. 46.

[21]Ward began collecting Perkins's works as an undergraduate; they are recorded among his book loans in Sidney Sussex Ward MS A, fols. 1v, 5, 84. He later called Perkins's death a "blow given unto the gospel of Christ" (British Library MS Harl. 7038, f. 348).

[22]It was Perkins who urged Ward to study divinity rather than mathematics, and to identify the ministry as his vocation (46v), despite a speech impediment that Ward feared would hinder his effectiveness as a preacher. CUL MS Mm 2.23, fols. 161–162v.

[23]He similarly preached to himself as he took notes on Chaderton's lectures: Note the shift from third to first person pronouns in the midst of a list of "uses" in his notes on Chaderton's 1591 lecture, fol. 7v. Ward identified with both preacher and congregation.

all gentle means to reclaim" sinners, seems to seize his imagination. If he can follow Perkins's instructions and so avoid the mistakes of other preachers, he might take on Perkins's role himself: "Think how God taketh away many worthy men which might have done much good in the church, as Mr. Esty of late. And therefore much more may such as thou art be spared" (47). He addresses himself as one who has already internalized the Perkins model for preaching humbly, with regard for the "dignity of God's children."

Ward likewise reflected his adoption of Perkins's and Chaderton's hortatory and evangelical model in his behavior toward his fellow students. He emulated the preachers by exhorting his companions to upright behavior and proclaiming the gospel at every opportunity. His resolution to do so is clear from his occasional confessions of "no care of exhorting my brethren, nor boldness in the professing of God's name" (15v) or of "my cowardice in Christianity, in exhorting others to the same" (16v) or of "not reprehending of my brother when he swore" (27v; cf. 16, 17, 18, etc.).[24] Ward's table companions may well have been secretly relieved on March 21, 1596, at Ward's "little care to exhort them with whom I supped at supper" (25), as might "Thomas my cousin" on July 31, 1597, at Ward's "negligence in exhorting [him] to some good things, and that on the Sabbath day" (33), but whatever its effects on his friendships, the preachers' mode of discourse was becoming Ward's own.

Contemporary Puritans may have been the most readily accessible of Ward's models, but he had others, the most important of whom were embodied in the texts that were most important to him and to those educating him. Readers of the diary recognize in its very form the influence of one of these: Ward's self-examination and casting of his sins and "benefits" in the form of a prayer is clearly modeled (albeit not altogether successfully) on St. Augustine's *Confessions*.[25] The list of sins with which this paper begins is one of many examples of Ward's diary as invocation: "and thus sin I daily against thee, O Lord," he appended to his list. It reads as an afterthought, and this, too, is typical. Ward generally seems much more concerned with lists than with prayers. This is one of the factors that makes his diary a pale imitation of Augustine; the other is his rather frequent forgetful-

---

[24]The general confession that he constructed for himself likewise repents "giving no brotherly admonition, gentle exhortations, holy example of life" (58v).

[25]The importance of Augustine to Ward is apparent in the frequency of citations to him in both his published works and his later MSS. See especially his *Gratia Discriminans* (Cambridge, 1626); *Praelectiones de Peccato Originali* in *Opera Nonnulla*, ed. Seth Ward (London, 1658); *Dissertatio de Efficacia Baptismi* (London, 1649); and Sidney Sussex Ward MSS C, D, K, L.8, M.4, O.8.g, O.9, O.13, Q and S.

ness that he is addressing God, evidenced by the trouble he had keeping his pronouns straight: He confessed, for instance, "My rising without thinking on thy God" (16v). He was, nonetheless, *trying* to do what Augustine did, and for the same theological reasons. Both cast essentially subjective writing in a form which acknowledged their belief that the proper focus of human attention ought to be outside themselves, on God and his providential direction of creation. The importance of individual actions lay in their relationship to the divine order of election and damnation, just as the City of Man must be defined in terms of the City of God. The concerns of Ward's diary must be read in the context of his notes elsewhere in the volume on the Kingdom of God and its realization in human history. The kingdom of God will ultimately triumph, he notes, but "in regard of the coming of it into men's hearts it is wonderfully stopped [hindered] of the devil and our corruption" (51v). Accordingly, "our subjection to Satan, 7 Rom. *fine* [25], this is to be wailed of every man" (51v).[26] His diary does just that.

Another feature of Ward's diary that is reminiscent of Augustine is the image of the orchard as a place of temptation, and of fruit as a means for sin to take hold. There are dozens of references in the diary to overindulgence in cherries, plums, and pears, and one of Ward's overarching concerns in July of 1596 was his "grief for being excluded out of the [college] orchard" (27; cf. 26v-27v).[27] Readers of the *Confessions* (Book II) recall the incident when the sixteen-year-old Augustine stole pears from a neighboring orchard. It is an incident often taken lightly by modern readers, but Augustine used it as an illustration of the pervasiveness and power of original sin, even in the young, and as a statement of the significance of every human action, however trivial, in the larger scheme of things. No sin can fail to separate the sinner from God; therefore, no sin is too small to bewail. Ward's confessions of petty bickering with his fellows, overeating and drowsiness at sermon time ought to be read in this context: his penitence imitated the greatest of the church fathers, in his estimation—a worthy model for any would-be saint. He recognized with Augustine the larger significance of every sin. Ward, who loved fruit and knew the works of Augustine well, thus found the orchard an apt image for an important theological concept. For him, as for

---

[26]Romans 7.25: "So then, I of myself serve the law of God with my mind, but with my flesh I serve the law of sin." (RSV)

[27]Ward repents overeating plums (26, 26v, 27v, 28, 29, 29v, 30), cherries (25v), pears (28v, 34), and fruit generally (28v, 29v, 33, 34, 34v, 35).

his admired saint, to avoid the orchard was to "avoid even the occasion of sin" (26v); to avoid the orchard was a triumph of God over the Enemy.[28]

The pear incident in the *Confessions* has another theological implication: For Augustine, and later for Ward, the material world and spiritual forces were intertwined. A converted Manichee, Augustine had come to recognize that the material world was God's ("Fair were the pears we stole, because they were thy creation, thou fairest of all . . .").[29] The sins of the flesh reflected and were related to fundamental spiritual conflict, but in their relationship even the weaknesses of the flesh could serve as a divine communication. Ward's relating of the physical to the spiritual was more crude than Augustine's, but he did acknowledge the interrelationship of the two. He frequently drew a didactic parallel between a desire for food and a desire for Christ: He confessed, "I could not find such a thirst after Christ, as after temporal food" (23v), and on another day "my longing after damsens when I made my vow not to eat in the orchard: O, that I could so long after God's graces" (29). With gluttony topping his list of offenses, Ward seldom failed to connect sins of the flesh with their immediate spiritual as well as physical consequences. He often noted, for instance, that overeating made him inattentive at afternoon sermons: On November 12, 1599, he admonished himself, "Thou wast overtaken with eating too much, which made thee somewhat unfit to hear the sermon when thou shouldest either have fasted, or have eaten but little, for thou must learn to take hold upon such occasions" (36v; cf. 23, 26). And when his sin led to physical as well as spiritual detriment the connection between the two was underlined: He confessed in 1597 "my gluttony in eating too much, notwithstanding that I had often before fallen into the same sin; yea hereby I disabled myself to the worthy receiving of the sacrament so much as in me lay, and so greatly offended my God and injured mine own health" (35). His ill health, which he recognized was in part his fault, drew his mind away from God—"My mind was altogether of my body" (23v), when it ought to have aided him spiritually: "Seeing I do not profit by the Lord's afflictions upon me, what can I hope,

---

[28] The influence of Augustine's *Confessions,* and in particular his pear-stealing escapade, is visible in other Puritans, too: e.g., Richard Baxter confessed that he was in his youth "much addicted to the excessive gluttonous eating of apples and pears. . . . I have oft gone into other men's orchards and stolen their fruit, when I had enough at home." *The Autobiography of Richard Baxter,* ed. N.H. Keeble (London, 1931), 5.

[29] *Confessions of St. Augustine,* tr. Edward Pusey (New York, 1961), Bk. II, p. 32; the theft is recorded pp. 30–31.

but either that the afflictions should be multiplied, or else that I shall grow to hardness of heart?" (24).[30] Spiritual zeal, on the other hand, could overcome physical infirmities. He thought medicines more effective if commended to God's blessing and taken "in holy manner" (36), and his commentary on Psalm 69 implies that "the zeal of God's glory" might aid in overcoming his speech impediment (50v), a major roadblock to his preaching career. Clearly, flesh and spirit were intertwined in Ward's self-concept. We cannot dismiss his lists of sins of the flesh as a neurotic obsession with the trivial, for as Ward noted in his own commentary on Genesis, "seeing God took such care for our creation . . . , to destroy our bodies and souls, practicing iniquity daily" (93) is doubly offensive to the Creator.

However significant a model Augustine provided, there was another even more important, derived from Ward's most revered text and greatest authority, the Bible. Puritans naturally find their place in the long history of Christians' attempts at *imitatio Christi*. As Chaderton told Ward in a 1592 lecture, Christians must follow Christ in doctrine, life, and "crosses." Not only must they believe his teaching, "they will consider all Christ's life and frame their lives according to it, in that measure which is given them of grace" (6). "Even so must we do" (8v) is a recurrent refrain throughout Ward's notes on the gospels. Setting the diary in this context makes its purpose apparent: it is a record of how close Ward comes in daily living to obeying the mandate of his chief authority, the Bible, and his chief model, Christ. Perfection of life is required, and of this Ward falls short, but his determination to "frame" his life by Christ's necessitates the continued penitence and renewed effort evident in the journal entries.

Christ as preacher also provided a model for Ward, and one that would reassure him and his fellow Puritans in the midst of persecution. Just as Christ was condemned by pharisees for preaching plainly and truly (9v), "much more shall God's true ministers be in our age. For he that preacheth truly and plainly and keepeth good order is counted a madman and hath slanderous names, as names of Puritans and precisians. But happy are they who suffer for thus doing, for herein they suffer with Christ and shall be partakers of his glory" (2v). In fact, the "state of all Christians . . . [is] to be partakers of affliction" (15v), for one who would imitate Christ must do so "in

---

[30] On occasion he tried to make deals with God in the midst of his illness: "Remember thy promise how when thou art not well, how if God restore thee to health, thou wilt [be] careful to perform all Christian duties. Remember this." (fol. 17).

crosses and afflictions, in poverty, in being counted rebels, in being marked, . . . For it is impossible that any man renouncing the world, but must ever be in afflictions, crosses and calamities" (6). Since persecution for the truth is inevitable for one whose life is patterned on Christ's, suffering becomes its own comfort and a reinforcement of one's conviction of the truth: Christ's experience "teacheth us not to be discouraged, though they say they persecute us for our evil works, but to stand still in defense of our cause. . . . Christ showeth us what do make a martyr, even the cause for which he suffer" (8v).[31] Suffering for Puritans thus became a visible sign of their success in imitating Christ.

Proper behavior in the midst of persecution was also defined by Christ's pattern. Christ "answereth mildly this accusation of the Jews [blasphemy, in John 10], giving example to his ministers so to do, that they should mildly suffer false accusations" (8v). In some instances, it would be legitimate to flee persecution, since Christ provided an example of this, too (John 10.39–40): "The flight of Christ from his persecutors doth warrant us that we in like cases should fly, for seeing the head flyeth, the members also may fly, seeing the head and the members can never be separated" (14). One must not flee out of material self-interest, however, since Christ "fled not for the loss of his goods or any other thing, for we must as he doth, fly only for loss of life" (14). Finally, in standing one's ground, one must follow the pattern "of Christ in confuting his malicious enemies by the written word of God, . . . not with man's testimony" (9). The identification of the godly person with Christ is to be complete.

Ward's self-fashioning, then, did not occur in a vacuum. For Ward as for other Renaissance writers, the process was not really an autonomous one at all; Renaissance self-fashioning always involved submission to something outside the self.[32] Ward shaped his identity according to patterns set for him, by charismatic mentors in a Puritan college, and by the powerful figures that emerged from his authoritative texts. A word about the shaping force of the text itself may be in order before proceeding to examine other aspects of the self-fashioning process.

Ward's was a text-centered age for thinking people, and his Cambridge was specifically a Bible-centered community. The word of

---

[31] When Puritans were accused of causing schism, they were to recall that Christ's teaching divided the Jews of his own day, but "he was not the cause [of schism], because his doctrine was true" (fol. 2).

[32] Greenblatt, *Renaissance Self-fashioning*, 1, 9.

God in printed form was for protestants a higher authority than any man or institution, and Greenblatt is quite correct to note that "this investment of power in the book has . . . important consequences both for self-fashioning and for the way we read."[33] The Bible shaped both Ward's inner life and his understanding of the world, and it conditioned how he would understand his relationship to that world. "The Scripture serveth not only to confirm the truth and to teach, but also to rebuke error, not only in doctrine, but also in manners and men's persons" (9). He looked to Chaderton and Perkins primarily as expositors of the Scriptures, to Augustine as an embodiment of the message of the gospels, and to Christ as that message and as the identity by which all believers ought to style their own. What this styling meant, however, was not the mystical union with Christ that medieval visionaries had desired, nor the imaginative experiencing of such sixteenth-century Catholic spiritual exercises as Ignatius Loyola prescribed. It was more objective than either, in part because it was more text-centered than either. Its authority was the written word, and perhaps in consequence so was its result: A written record of sins in the context of biblical commentary comprises a distinctly Puritan approach to self-structuring. Ward's diary is an objective attempt to "apply God's word to myself" (29v); it is no accident that it is sandwiched between sermon notes and biblical exegesis in a single written volume. Whether the word was read or orally expounded in a sermon, Ward busied himself "in the sermon time in applying the word heard to mine own soul" (22), "to mine own heart and conscience" (21v), so the diary follows hard upon the sermon notes. Ward's prayers were patterned on that prescribed in Scripture, so in his written notebook they conclude the diary and immediately precede his commentary on Matthew 6, the Lord's Prayer.

In that commentary, Ward notes that "in every petition, we will search the meaning of the words and the wants which we must bewail, the graces which we may desire" (49), so that Christ's words might be incorporated into the meaning that Ward intends his own words to have. In this process of searching for the meaning of the words, Ward incorporates Christ's identity into his own. The petition, "Thy will be done" is for Ward a declaration of intent to assume the identity of Christ in faith, sanctification of life, and even "the suffering of Christ: 8 Rom[ans] 21 [since] every tittle in God's word signifieth these three things" (52v). Fashioning the self, then, was for

[33]Ibid., 76.

Puritans subsumed by the objective "labor to know God's word" (53); the self was to be formed by an outward focus on the word of the Other, "in hearing, reading, meditating and conferring of thy holy and heav[en]ly word" (58v).

Because Puritan self-fashioning was conditioned by scriptural authority and models, its result was an identification that was fundamentally communal rather than individualistic in nature. Biblical images like the "children of God" and the "kingdom of God," the history of Israel and of the early church, and the biblical conflict between these communal entities and the enemies of the gospel or the forces of Antichrist, were potent forces for identification with a community of the godly.

This is not to deny the individualistic elements in Puritan diary-keeping. After all, "God's kingdom must come in our hearts" to replace "the kingdom of darkness" there before the petition, "Thy kingdom come," may be fulfilled in the communal and the cosmic sense (51). Thus, Ward's explication of the Lord's Prayer also explains his concern with individual sinfulness and redemption, with "private" and subjective sins like "not feeling of that reverence which I ought" or "my ill dreams" (17v).[34] It does so, however, as a prelude to an extended discussion of the kingdom of God that dwells on the embodiment of that kingdom in the community of the godly in Cambridge, in England, and in the world (51v). Ward explains that prayer for the coming of God's kingdom must proceed quickly from petition "in regard of ourselves" to prayers "for universities and schools of learning, because even as a men having an orchard, for the upholding thereof he hath a seminary, and doth transplant out of his seminary good plants into the place of trees which are decayed, that they may be as trees of righteousness and the plants of the lord, as saith Ezechiel" (52). This being the case, the failure of an individual student, like Ward's "neglect in the duties of my special calling, in misspending of much precious time which should have been employed in pursuit of my studies" (58v) undermined the progress of the gospel which was to emanate from his community, and his individual failure became the failure of the godly.

Ward acknowledged among "God's benefits" that "he hath set thee in a college where thou sufferest not contempt for the true service of

---

[34]The dream entry is recorded in a different ink from entries around it, suggesting that Ward may have recorded it in the middle of the night—so great was his anxiety over sins of the heart.

God, but rather art well liked, whereas others are condemned and mocked for the service of God" (46). As part of that college, he had acquired an evangelical obligation which conditioned his understanding of himself in relation to others. Sins that might otherwise seem private or personal took on a larger significance in light of this obligation. Thus, in the midst of the self-scrutiny of his diary, Ward frequently noted the impact of his individual failings on establishing the kingdom of God in Cambridge. His "no care of exhorting my brethren, nor boldness in the professing of God's name, . . . [and] shame in serving God" (15v) undermined the evangelical mandate by which Puritans were to transform the world. He confessed his sin in absenting himself from prayers on June 10, 1595, because of the "scandal" caused to his roommates by the failure of his godly example (18; cf. 29); his "dullness at [sic] sleepiness at sermon" was sinful in part because it "no doubt was scandalous to some" (26v); and his "little affection in prayer before bed" was more than a private sin because it "might justly have given offence to them which prayed with me" (21v). His use of "scandal" clarifies the nature of the sin: Ward used the biblical term for an occasion of stumbling—a cause for weak believers to fall from the faith (Rom. 14.13). To cause scandal was an offense against the evangelical aims of the church. The one instance in the diary where Ward indicates doubt as to his election was an occasion when his anger with a colleague was so great that he "was scandalous to my other [colleagues] there standing" (24).[35] On the positive side, when he managed "to talk much upon the vanity of this life" at the death of Mr. Nowell (May 29, 1595), he was pleased so to edify his chamberfellows. Ward's sense of membership in a godly community and of the responsibility of that community to provide an example of piety to the world shaped his vision of himself and his obligations to the world.

He identified himself also with the godly ministry which was to transform the church in England by preaching. "Thy kingdom come" was in his commentary a prayer for "God's ministers, because they are the Lord's instruments to build his church. . . . For the devil is most busy to overthrow the ministry and preaching of the word. Zachar[iah], Proverbs: When prophesying faileth, then the people perish" (51v). When Ward identified his own vocation with that of Perkins and Chaderton, he placed himself in the midst of a commu-

---

[35] "Hereby I bewrayed my great corruption, whereby I might run to doubt whether ever I had any true taste of God's spirit" (fol. 24).

nity that had originated with the Old Testament prophets that he cited, holy men confronting a corrupt world; that continued with Christ and the apostles, pronouncing truth and suffering for it; and that was visible in his own day in the harassment of the godly. His prayer for God's kingdom to come thus logically extended from the individual heart to the university and the ministry, and finally to the church of England and all the world, for whom he prayed "that God would increase the number of godly kings and princes, for they are the nurse-fathers and nurse-mothers of God's church: 49 Isaiah" (51v-52; cf. 55). The list of those for whom he prayed "at home" likewise extended down from the king to his council and the magistracy, to the ministry and "our college," to "all the afflicted members of Christ" (58).[36] Ward saw himself as part of the beleaguered godly at all levels and throughout the Christian world. In praying, "Preserve thy whole church dispersed. Our realm enlarge round about us" (59v), he was praying for himself in the plural.

Ward devoted several pages of his notebook to constructing and revising a formal, general confession—one rather more demanding than that in the Book of Common Prayer, and here he can be seen struggling to make clear the dual nature of his identity, individual and communal, in the grammatical structure of the prayers. After one false start, addressing God as the "fountain of all my happiness, who only knowest all my wants . . . ," he omitted the first person singular pronouns and designed a more inclusive version: "O Lord God, the author of all true happiness, the fountain of all mercy . . ." (58v). In what follows, and in Ward's instructions to himself on praying, "we" and "I" alternate, as if the individual *per se* and the member of a community were vying for center: "We are to give thanks. . . ," "My prayer must not be performed carelessly. . ." (58–58v). That this was not a mere oversight is suggested by a list of God's mercies in which Ward wrote, "In giving me now and then to feel our wants," then crossed out "me" and substituted "us" (57). And in his comments on the Lord's Prayer, he remarked on the plural first person in "Give us our daily bread" thus, "Not me, because whatsoever riches that are given of God must not only be for a man's self. . ." (54v). Ward may have spent a great deal of time examining himself, but not to locate this introspection properly, in the midst of an overpowering concern with the Christian community, leads to a distorted notion of Puritans as individualists.

[36] He left blank the space under the heading "We are also to pray for, abroad:" (58).

The communal nature of the Puritan identity is perhaps even more clearly gleaned from Ward's identification with the godly over against the enemy—the foes of the gospel in Cambridge and within the Church of England, and the forces of popery in England and abroad. Scholars have observed that Renaissance self-fashioning is always achieved in relation to something perceived as hostile—an "alien," portrayed as a perversion of order, even as a demonic force.[37] For Protestants, the Catholic Church was the obvious "demonic other," but even less zealous protestants were useful as foils against which the godly could identify themselves. "The world" for Puritans was full of "incredulous and wicked men" who "harden their hearts as [the] Pharisees did" against the gospel (5). Ward complained about "many in our own time which will not come to the church to hear God's word, which remain still in their former ignorance" (15), and expressed gratitude that God "kept me from evil company" (46v). The godly must learn to recognize the wicked and "not favor nor keep company with a wicked man" (91v); accordingly, Ward goes to the trouble of listing characteristics of "the man that liveth here in this world not being in Christ" (57). That man is "in far worse estate than the vilest creature upon earth. He is under the power of darkness, having the devil for his prince and god" and so is in perpetual "danger of eternal death and damnation in hell fire" (57). He specifically mentions one such man "that was somewhat too bitter against good men" and so suffered in this world as well as the next, dying "in great pain, having (1) an empostume in his liver, (2) the dropsy, [3] the strangurion, [and] (4) the yellow jaundice"(47).[38]

Unfortunately, the wicked are not always so easily recognized: "Many bear a show of religion, . . . when indeed they are dissembling brethren" (92). With such as these, unfortunately, the Church of England is troubled. Much of Ward's identity as a Puritan derives from his efforts, following Chaderton's lead, to discern these subtle "aliens" and distinguish himself from them. It is significant that the lecture notes with which his notebook begins are on John 10—a passage of crucial importance to those who wished to distinguish true from false sheep (and pastors) in the Church of England. Chaderton's lecture on this passage is a not very subtle critique of the

[37]Greenblatt, *Renaissance Self-fashioning*, 9, 85, 88.

[38]By contrast, he exclaimed on June 5, 1598, "Remember the difference of the death of the godly and the wicked, how the godly dying leaveth a good report behind him, as D. Whitak[er]" (36). On Whitaker, the Puritan master of St. John's, see Lake, *Moderate Puritans*, chap. 6.

Church's laxity toward sheep "only in name and esteemed so," as opposed to "true sheep," who are "ruled by God's word" (1–5v). The fears that Ward expresses in the diary and elsewhere in the notebook, that "calamity" will befall Christ's College (21v) by the wrong sort getting fellowships, for instance, and his lists of "sins of this land" and "sins of the university" (62v) are fears that these false sheep will lead the church and her seminary astray. Ward's understanding of his own identity is closely tied to his fears for the true church—naturally enough, given the harassment of Puritans by "false sheep" close to home at Christ's in the 1590s. He accordingly records his anger at Bishop Bancroft's censure of his Puritan tutor (19), and he vaguely connects his own "backwardness in noting my sins" to the "great calamity . . . incident to our college, by reason of new elections of fellowships" (21v) in 1595. Ward's identification of himself with the godly was all the more necessary when the ungodly seemed to be seizing the day in the very nursery of the church. The diary is in part his attempt to draw the line clearly, "that the godly and the wicked might be separated" (2), lest the godly be contaminated by the wicked. Failure to make this separation has led to a false "security in the midst of God's judgments" (62v), one of the "sins of the land" for which the godly will surely suffer. Ward's clear view of the enemy within the fold thus underpinned his self-identification with the community of the godly. By separating themselves from the wicked, the godly are "hallowed to Christ," as the temple of Jerusalem and its priests were hallowed for God's service, "when they are severed from all the corruptions of the world to everlasting life" (49).

The truly demonic other were, of course, the papists. These "impediments of God's kingdom, as the devil, the pope, and his prelates" (51v) were foreshadowed in the Scriptures in the Jews who dissuaded people from hearing the words of Christ, "the very essential note of a false church, and an unchristian spirit. The same spirit is in the papists, who . . . dissuade all men from hearing us" (2v). Puritans reinforced their own identification with the Word preached by identifying Catholics as enemies of the Scriptures and as distorters of biblical truths. As Chaderton said in a sermon on Christ as the only mediator, "When the pope doth arrogate this power [to forgive sins] to himself, he thrusteth himself in the place of God" and so "speak[s] falsely, for God hath only given this power to Christ" (1v). On the central issue of salvation by faith, Ward in his own commentary found the papists perverting John 3, which proclaims that the "love of God is the efficient cause of our salvation, contrary to the papists, who say that *praevisu opera* are the cause of election" (12). That Catholics thus "derogate from the glory [of] God" (12) places zealous protestants like Ward squarely in the right camp. Ward has fashioned himself as part of God's ministry defending the Almighty in the battle against Antichrist.

Ward's notebook is an anti-Catholic document not only in the explicit denunciation of popery in its biblical commentaries, but also in the confessional form of the diary in the midst of the notebook. Ward's attempt at daily written confession of sin is itself a study in contrasts to Catholic seasonal shriving. For Protestants, the Christian life was to be under perpetual scrutiny. The hotter sort in particular denied the relegation of penitence to particular times and seasons.[39] The scrutiny, moreover, was self-scrutiny, without the mediation of a cleric. Just as the written text of Scripture served as Ward's authority, so the text of his diary "heard" his confession. The written word is here an image of the priesthood of all believers, and Ward's notebook is a palpable identification of himself as foe of the Roman Antichrist.

If Ward's self-fashioning involved drawing battle lines between himself and the enemy, there were lines to be drawn and battles fought within his own identity as well. Ward's notebook provides abundant evidence for the formation of fundamental tensions within the Puritan identity—tensions that must have produced considerable stress not only during Ward's youth, but throughout his life. These tensions originated in the paradoxes of Christianity itself, especially in the evangelical protestant form of Ward's Christianity; for that reason, their expression in the diary is expanded and illumined by the sermon notes and biblical commentary within which the diary finds it place.

We have seen that Ward's conclusion from Chaderton's sermons and from his own reading of the Scriptures was that he must identify primarily with Christ—in doctrine, life, and suffering. The problem with this mandate is obvious. Ward stated it in a scholastic "objection" to sinners praying, "Hallowed be thy name. . . . Ob[jection]: God's name is holy itself. How, therefore, can we sanctify it, being sinners?" His orthodox "Sol[ution]: God's name is sanctified when we acknowledge God's name is holy, and manifest it. . . ." (49) is

---

[39]This would be one of their many objections to Arminians later: cf. the exaltation of the church calendar in the work of Ward's later enemy John Cosin, *A Collection of Private Devotions,* ed. P.G. Stanwood (Oxford, 1967), first published 1627.

unsatisfactory, since his own susceptibility to sin leads even to "my inability to think a good thought" (20), let alone "to think on God" (23) or to manifest God's holiness by living in a godly manner. The diary as a record of how closely Ward managed to approximate the life of Christ is largely a record of failure, for the sinlessness of Christ and the endless recounting of sins in the diary stand in stark contrast. Ward affirmed that "For afflicted consciences, when they are troubled for their sin, if the devil object to us our unrighteousness, Christ is our righteousness and *sic in caeteris*" (11). Yet he was impelled by his own infidelity to identify himself no less with Antichrist than with Christ. His conclusion from Chaderton's explication of "Cursed is he who will not hear the word" is accordingly in the first person: "If we believed this we would hear it. But incredulity reigneth in us" (5). His pronouns here are a departure from the third person in previous and subsequent notes on this discussion of true and false sheep. Having denounced the latter roundly as "they," he must nonetheless stand back and identify himself with them. He recognizes in himself that "hardness of heart which keepeth him [the Pharisee] from seeing God's glory" and will later list among his "wants" in prayer the ability to "wonder at God's . . . glory" (50). "Even so are we naturally prone to overthwart, and to break God's commandments" (52v). His identity with Christ and the Enemy is thus simultaneous. Ironically, to identify the "other" is to identify *with* the "other," and Ward finds himself to be the man without Christ, whose characteristics he had listed to include "3. he is in danger of all the judgments of God . . . , 4. He is [in] danger of eternal death and damnation in hell fire" (57).

When Ward described that man in his notes, however, he did not stop at the threat of damnation. He continued, "5. God hath appointed every man a time of repentance which, if he misspend without repentance, he can never be saved. 6. Eternal life is prepared for all them who will fear him" (57). Ward's twenties were that appointed time of repentance. His objective was a complete transformation of his natural condition into the righteousness of Christ—a conversion in the largest sense of that word. The diary was to chronicle his turning around, or conversion, not, perhaps, as a narrative of the sort that New England Puritans tended to produce, but rather as an account book.[40] (Ward was of a less adventurous sort than the emigrants,

[40] A good example of the New England Puritan narrative is Thomas Shepard's autobiography, edited by Michael McGiffert as *God's Plot* (Amherst, Mass., 1972). See also Daniel Shea, *Spiritual Autobiography in Early America* (Princeton, 1968) and Patricia Caldwell, *The Puritan Conversion Narrative* (New York, 1983).

given more to lists than to dramatic stories.) As it turned out, however, the debit column was very full. Ward could not even manage to
make daily entries for more than a few weeks at a time. Finally,
he was forced to acknowledge his inability and build the resulting
tension into his theology.

The Protestant assertion of human helplessness before the power
of sin led one whose overriding aim was permanent conversion to an
abject reliance on what Protestants termed the grace of God for that
transformation. Ward thus identified God as his transformer: "It
pleased God at night to give me good meditations" (23v). He prayed
passively to be "brought to repentance, to . . . living to thee in new-
ness of life and that not only for a time, but so long as we live in this
world" (43; cf. 32v). Any failure in the process Ward saw as his own,
although even failure found a place in what he saw as God's design:
"It pleased God to detain the sense of my sins from me in my prayer,
howsoever I called often for the sight thereof, but I must attribute it
to mine own wants in prayer" (17). Ward would spend his life as
a theologian trying to reconcile the logical impasse here, trying to
reconcile, finally, himself as Christ-imitator with himself as helpless
sinner.

Reading the diary contextually reveals other tensions within the
Puritan self. Ward fashioned himself as both preacher and auditor,
exhorter and penitent, and the resultant tension stands out as much
in the form as in the content of his notebook. Part of the book is
essentially a confessor's manual, instructions to himself as a confessor hearing his own confession (58). Having adopted the preacher as
model, moreover, Ward wrote much of his diary in a didactic, even
hortatory mode. He upbraids himself for his sins and preaches at
himself, addressing himself in the second person as if he were among
the "brethren" in need of exhortation. "Remember God's mercy toward thee . . ." (16v); "Remember how thou couldst not meditate on
God . . ." (25v).[41]

The most consistent self-exhortation in the diary comes during a
crisis in his life as a tutor in Emmanuel—a crisis that caused Ward
to resume his diary-keeping after seventeen months' lapse. It seems
that during a time of lax supervision by Ward, one of his pupils acci-
dentally injured his leg, which apparently became infected and
caused his death. Ward assumed the role of preacher in entries for

[41] He outlines an order of confession of sins in particular categories, a requirement of
contrition, a description of prayer for pardon, and an order for amendment of life (58).

November 10, 11, 12, and 14, 1599, all of which exhort him to "re-member" the events as judgments of God: "Remember the great agony thou wast in for Luke's leg, thy grief thou hadst in part for that thou hadst been so negligent in looking to thy pupils, and therefore God had laid this heavy cross upon thee. . ." (36). Functioning as his own pastor, he instructed himself to repent his negligence and take greater care of his charges henceforth: "Remember how the 11 of Novemb[er] 1599, upon consideration of this great judgment upon thee (in Luke's leg) and upon consideration of thy negligence . . . , thou hadst a holy purpose to break off that sin, and to be careful in looking to all their [his pupils'] studies . . ." (36). Only when Luke died did Ward depart from his second person pronouns for a few sentences: "God make me thankful for his happy departure. . . . He confessed his sin before his death, prayed heartily, was very desirous to be informed in his duty towards God, desired that he might leave behind him a good example of his death unto others" (36v). At this point in the events, Ward was functioning as pastor to Luke, and his diary simply records his observations and prays for gratitude that Luke's end was joyful. But when he came to his conclusion, he re-verted to admonishing himself: "Remember that his death be an in-sinuation unto thee in the government and care to thy pupils. Look thou profit by God's chastisements. Look to thy pupil Robinson as thou art purposed" (36v).

The fact that Ward's identity included both preacher and penitent is one of the explanations for the very inconsistent use of pronouns in the notebook, even within sentences: "Remember *thy* cowardice in exhorting W.J. at Royston to prayer when *I* was with Mr. Bourne," (16v) he wrote on one occasion; on another he recorded "*thy* glut-tony at dinner, which distempered thy body; also *my* little care to pray. . ." (25v); and again, "*My* dullness to good talk all the ways *thou* came home" (30v).[42] Such examples of Ward simultaneously rebuking himself and confessing his sins reveal the dual identity he was adopting and the difficulties associated with it. He spoke for God in admonition, and for himself as sinner, carrying on an awkward dialogue within himself.

The other frequent example of mixed pronouns that bespeaks this tension within the Puritan self is in the use of the second person. On the model of St. Augustine, Ward used "thou" for God; on the model

---

[42]Examples of this sort can be found in his notes on Chaderton's sermons as well (e.g., the list at the top of 7v). Emphasis mine.

of Chaderton, he used "thou" for the hearer of an admonition—
himself as sinner. One might add the model of the Psalmist addressing his own soul as "thou." But again, Ward's conflicting uses of
"thou" in the same sentence suggest an uneasy melding of two models, penitent and preacher: "Remember God's mercy toward thee
[Ward] in giving thee [Ward] grace at the end of thy prayer, to pray
heartily unto thee [God] when as in the beginning thou [Ward] wast
blockish" (16v). Rather than writing this sort of thing off to care-
lessness or wretched grammar, readers of the diary ought to take it
as an index of the complexity and difficulty of Puritan self-definition.

One other tension that emerges from Ward's notebook relates to
the nature of authority and the capacity and responsibility of individual judgment. Ward both revered and challenged authority, and at
the same time he both exercised and denigrated individual judgment.
Protestant replacement of ecclesiastical authority with *scriptura sola*
was fraught with paradox. On the one hand, the Bible was the ultimate authority, and believers were responsible to read and interpret
the text to discern the truth there, as well as to render judgment
on the word preached or asserted by other authorities. Ward clearly
recognized this responsibility and its difficulty. In recording Chaderton's counsel to use the Scripture to discern "false sheep" within the
church, he cautioned, "We must learn that we must not judge rashly
of the word heard, nor condemn without premeditation, but must
[use] our judgment til we try it, and then seek the good of the person" (2v). One must exercise judgment even on the authorities of
church and state: "Let us . . . compare minister with minister, and
they which preach true doctrine and practice the same, let them be
preferred before those which preach and do not follow it in their life"
(15), and in regard to secular authorities, one must remember that
"Christ is over magistrates. [They] are annointed with men's hands,
and with material oil, Christ by God" (10). On the other hand, like
most Puritans in the 1590s, Ward was not politically or socially radical. At the same time that he judged particular preachers and even
bishops, the protestant ministry wielded great authority for him as
interpreters of Scripture in the preached word.

Given the pervasiveness of sin, moreover, individual judgment can
easily err. "Bethink thyself how many good matters are overthrown
by wrong judgment," Ward exclaimed in 1601. Replacing the false
authority of Catholic interpretation with individual reading of Scripture itself has threatened to undermine the true authority of the Bible
once again because of the individual's "sins of knowledge, especially
of presumption" (56). In Greenblatt's terms, in the process of self-

fashioning, the power to attack an alien," in this case popery, "is produced in excess and threatens the authority it sets out to defend."[43]
Ward accordingly asserts that "we must never in the matter of belief
consult with ourselves, for there is a great untowardness in man naturally to believe God's word" (5). But he has received from Chaderton and given himself conflicting advice. He *must* exercise his own
judgment, but he dare not. The resultant dilemma over where authority resides and how true judgment is to be rendered in light of
the depredations of sin created yet another fundamental area of tension in Ward's self-definition.

The problem of sin within even the redeemed self, and the tensions that this created, made Puritan self-fashioning a process at
once constructive and destructive. In the creation of the self, there
must necessarily be a loss of self. As Greenblatt puts it, "self-
fashioning occurs at the point of encounter between an authority and
an alien" and partakes of both, so that "any achieved identity always
contains within itself the signs of its own subversion." The "act of
self-fashioning is an act of self-cancellation," entailing "simultaneous
affirmation and effacement of personal identity."[44] This makes self-
fashioning simply another expression for what protestants called
"conversion." Certainly the language recording that personal transformation in Ward's notebook is a vocabulary of denial, loss, and
mortification: For the kingdom of God to "come in our hearts," to
be "framed to obedience to God's word," is to "give up ourselves to
be governed by God's holy spirit," to desire "thy will, not our own
wills" (51–51v, 52v). At the heart of his most formally styled prayer
is the plea, "Mortify and kill in me all unruly passions, bridle my
appetite with thy grace, and quench in me the fire of all unlawful
desires" (59v). His metaphors may be mixed, but the language of
self-denial is consistent. One of his most frequently confessed sins
was pride—in his academic excellence, in spiritual accomplishments, in being seen with admired men, all incidents of self-
exaltation rather than the self-destruction required to prepare for
the building of a new self.[45] Ambition, which he also confesses frequently,[46] is likewise a form of self-promotion rather than the required "giving up" of the self.

[43] Greenblatt, *Renaissance Self-fashioning*, 9.
[44] Ibid., 9, 57.
[45] He boasted of excellence, e.g., in geometry (22v, 23v), in Greek (19), and in philosophy (24v, 26, 29); of spiritual accomplishments (34v); of keeping exalted company (e.g.,
31v, 32v). For other expressions of penitence for pride, fols. 16v, 18v, 33, 56.
[46] e.g., 21v, 25, 30, 31v. Ward was in his own estimation overly concerned with securing
a fellowship at Emmanuel. The goal was surely an understandable and laudable ambition

It is not just his sinful behavior that Ward wants to mortify. He also identifies what modern readers tend to view as positive attributes and, because they are easily perverted to sinful ends, requires their abolition as well. Ward was devoted to the study of classical literature and apparently excelled in philosophy, but because this tended to feed his pride, he confessed as sin "my over great care of humane studies, when the Lord hath called me to the study of mortification" (22) and "my earnest meditation on philosophy, when I should have been occupied in thoughts tending to edification" (28). Edification, the construction of his godly self, required first demolition. It required that he renounce "confidence in myself" (34v) and indeed much that he had accomplished, since "a man cannot be saved, unless he condemn himself for his best works" (53v).

Ward saw the self-destructive elements of his conversion in terms of the ongoing conflict with the demonic other. That adjective describing the alien here is in fact his: His commentary on the Lord's Prayer traces the self-exaltation "settled in every man" to the Garden of Eden, where "the devil told Eve that she and Adam should be gods" (50). Likewise, to attribute one's promotion in this world to one's own achievements rather than to God's favor he labeled "satanic" (31v). And the first item in his list of "Blessings to be desired" is "to have grace to deny ourselves, for we differ little in will from the devil's will." At that "point of encounter between authority and alien" where Ward's self-fashioning occured, then, destruction of the alien entailed considerable destruction of the self.

What is constructed at the end of this complex and in many ways paradoxical process is a self-defined Puritan. By 1601, Ward had come to recognize himself as one of the community of the godly, defending the gospel in its orthodox protestant purity against the assaults of papists and "false sheep," carrying out the evangelical mandate, embodying the transformative power of the biblical text in his own life. His definition was sufficiently complete that he only had need to return to the volume in which he had accomplished it on three later occasions in his life. All three were times of crisis or occasions of redefinition. The first was in 1621 when he began to consider a major change in his life—marriage, which often entails some new understanding of the self in relation to others (61–61v). The second

---

for a Puritan, but for him the ambition itself, with its attendant sins of boasting and flattery of potential patrons (30, 21v), inhibited his spiritual development.

was a change in political regime, the accession of Charles I, that would prove to have a significant and negative impact on Ward and all Calvinists in the university. The "increasing popery, by the permission of the new queen" and "the prevailing of the enemy in Germany" (63) proved portents of troubles to come; Ward seems to have sensed that the godly were about to face the alien in new guise. The third occasion was more personal. In 1630, Ward acted against the dictates of his conscience in endorsing a man whom he knew to be corrupt.[47] How appropriate it was for him to return to the diary of his youth to record his violation of the self that he had there fashioned.

A glance at these events and at Ward's later life more broadly suggests that he was in his youth a successful self-fashioner. He managed to incorporate the tensions of his authorities into a workable amalgam—of Christ and sinner, of preacher and penitent, of individual and community. The identity that he framed in his twenties would continue to determine his actions and self-understanding in his maturity. Having defined himself in biblical terms, he would devote his life to that text—to its explication for students as an academic, to the exhortation of its precepts as a preacher, and to its availability to the laity as a translator of the Authorized Version of 1611. Having defined himself as a defender of protestant orthodoxy, he would devote his life to the defense of Calvinism—at the Synod of Dort in 1618–1619, and against Arminians in the university in the 1620s and '30s. Having defined himself with Chaderton as a moderate reformer in the 1590s, he would maintain that alignment in the face of increasing radicalism in the '40s, to his own hurt in 1643 when forces allied with his own former student, Oliver Cromwell, ordered his imprisonment for failure to support Parliament in the war.

It may seem more accurate to say that Ward was a functional product of his own culture, or at least that he fashioned himself in strict accord with the guidelines provided by his culture. It is certainly true that moments of apparently autonomous self-fashioning visible in Ward's diary as in other Renaissance texts, involved choices "among possibilities whose range was strictly delineated by the social and ideological systems in force."[48] But there

---

[47]Jerome Beale, Master of Pembroke, whom Ward had previously complained of for his "impetuousness and violence" (37). Ward apparently felt pressured by Vice-chancellor Butts to sign a testimonial that he later wished very much to repudiate in light of his dishonesty.

[48]Greenblatt, *Renaissance Self-fashioning*, 256.

were choices to be made. Ward need not have followed the moderate path of Chaderton and Perkins as closely as he did. He might well have taken the course chosen by the other Samuel Ward, also of Sidney and later preacher of Ipswich, or of that Samuel's brother Nathaniel, who became preacher at the new Ipswich in Massachusetts. All three Wards had sat under Chaderton's and Perkins's tutelage, and Nathaniel was in fact Ward's colleague at Emmanuel.[49] All adopted the Calvinist theology, reformist zeal and anti-popery of their models. But the brothers opted for a more radical form of that Puritan pattern than the moderate diarist. Samuel of Ipswich was suspended for "puritanical preaching," imprisoned for an anti-Spanish engraving in 1621, and forced to flee to Holland, returning only in 1638. Nathaniel was likewise suspended by Archbishop Laud for his Puritan views; he then made the long voyage to Massachusetts in 1634, not returning to England until 1646. If the stories of these men are cultural artifacts, they tell us of a Puritan culture in which the process of self-fashioning, however conditioned by the need for conversion and the requirement to define and combat the enemy, might produce various results. If the process was not autonomous, neither was the precise outcome predetermined by the culture.

The identity that emerged from our Samuel Ward's choices was, moreover, an historically active one. If the literary Ward of the diary is a symbolic structure of Elizabethan Puritan culture, it is no less true that the living, breathing Ward of Sidney Sussex College and the Synod of Dort and the Vice-chancellor's court of a beleaguered university in the 1640s acted out and helped to define for others the Puritanism of the seventeenth century. His moderate Puritanism in fact became that of at least one of the radicals' sons. While Nathaniel Ward's son John, who followed his father to Emmanuel in 1622, likewise followed him in his radical course to New England in 1639, the son of Samuel of Ipswich (named Nathaniel after his uncle), who followed *his* father to our Ward's Sidney in 1628, subsequently pur-

---

[49]Nathaniel was admitted sizar at Emmanuel 1596 (B.A. 1600, M.A. 1603). Samuel of Ipswich was admitted scholar at St. John's, also known for Puritanism, in 1594 (B.A. 1597, M.A. Sidney Sussex 1600, B.D. 1607). This Samuel was one of the original fellows of Sidney. A third brother, John Ward, was admitted sizar at Emmanuel in 1596 and appears to have followed the moderate Puritan course of Chaderton, Perkins and the diarist Samuel. John and J.A. Venn, *Alumni Cantabrigienses* (Cambridge, 1927), Part I, 4:332–334.

sued the college master's moderate course rather than his father's radical one.[50]

The fashioning of the Puritan self, then, was as complex a process as the Puritanism of England and New England was a complex phenomenon. To understand both the common characteristics of radical and moderate Puritans and their divergent paths, whether in old or New England, the next step must be to place side by side our careful readings of the diaries of moderates and radicals, and the narratives of the emigrés. For that purpose, this paper would have to be much longer, but the conference from which it has come was an important beginning.

---

[50]Venn, *Alumni Cantabrigienses,* 4:333. Nathaniel *fils* became rector of Hadleigh, Essex, in 1639, rector of Hawkwell in 1640, and prebendary of Lincoln in 1660. (His master, the diarist, was prebendary of Wells and canon of York.) Young Nathaniel's brother Samuel also came up to Sidney (1621); their brother Joseph came to Emmanuel in 1629. Nothing is known of either's subsequent career.

"A Suffering People":

Bunyan and the Language of Martyrdom

John R. Knott

A VISITOR TO John Bunyan in the County Gaol of Bedford, where he was imprisoned from 1660 to 1672, reported that his library consisted of two books, the Bible and the "Book of Martyrs."[1] Foxe's *Acts and Monuments* was one of a handful of books, including Luther's commentary on Galatians, that deeply influenced Bunyan. His frequent references to it, often citing the volume and page, sometimes quoting or paraphrasing, demonstrate a close familiarity with the text. Yet the influence is more pervasive than specific references reveal and can be found throughout his career. Through the *Acts and Monuments* Bunyan was exposed to the classic protestant view of church history as the struggle of true and false churches as well as to numerous models of resistance to persecution. It suggested ways of framing his experience and that of the persecuted church in his own time. Reading Foxe in the early years of his imprisonment, Bunyan could empathize with the Marian martyrs and see himself as one of their spiritual heirs. The *Acts and Monuments* offered him dramatic and persuasive affirmation of New Testament lessons about the centrality of suffering in Christian experience and, with the Bible, gave him ways of talking about it.

Early and late, Bunyan's writings show a fascination with the drama of martyrdom. The acts of martyrs presented the demands of

---

[1] John Brown, *John Bunyan: His Life, Times, and Work,* rev. ed., F.M. Harrison (London, 1928), 154. W.R. Owens, ed., *Grace Abounding* (London, 1987), 126n., attributes the comment to the anonymous author of *An Account of the Life and Death of Mr. John Bunyan,* published in 1700. A copy of the three-volume 1641 edition of the *Acts and Monuments* thought to be Bunyan's is in the Pierpont Morgan Library.

Christianity in their most extreme form and gave testimony of the power of faith that captured his imagination. In *Light for Them that Sit in Darkness* (1675) Bunyan writes: "How have the Martyrs despised death . . . having peace with God by Jesus Christ, scorning the most Cruel Torments that Hell and Men could devise and invent."[2] In *Come, and Welcome, to Jesus Christ* (1678) he links coming to Christ with forsaking the world and draws his illustrations from Foxe's accounts of early Christian martyrs as well as from the Bible (Abraham, Daniel, Stephen). He quotes the declarations with which Ignatius and Romanus embrace their torments and shows Eulalia expressing pleasure at Christ's victories, "as they was pulling her one Joynt from another," and Agnes telling her executioner that she will draw the sword into her breasts, "*that then I, being married to Christ my Spouse, may Surmount and escape all the darkness of this World.*"[3] Such *exempla* served Bunyan the preacher as startling instances of the love of Christ with which to challenge a congregation.

Bunyan was particularly drawn to the Marian period, which provided a closer analogue for the experience of those he addressed and compelling scenes of faith triumphant over persecution. A hundred years after Foxe wrote this period had receded into a legendary past. In *Of Antichrist and His Ruin,* published posthumously but probably written in the early 1680s, Bunyan represents it as a time when God was close, ready to comfort the persecuted and to rain burning coals upon the persecutors, as if punishing them with their own fires:

> In the Maryan days here at home, there was such sweet songs sung in the fire, and such providences, that coals of burning fire still dropped here and there upon the heads of those that hated God; that it might, and doubtless did make those that did wisely consider of God's doings, to think God was yet near, with, and for, a despised and afflicted people.[4]

Bunyan's "still" distances the Marian era from a diminished present, and his idealizing vision erases Foxe's grisly detail, the slow fires and the blackening limbs, to emphasize the sweetness of suffering for one's faith. In *A Holy Life* (1684), he looked back nostalgically to the early days of Puritanism and especially to the "*Marian* days" that preceded them as a time in which one could see "another life than is now among men, another kind of conversation than now is among

---

[2] Roger Sharrock, ed., *The Miscellaneous Works of John Bunyan* (Oxford, 1979), 3:98.
[3] Ibid., 383–384.
[4] George Offor, ed., *The Works of John Bunyan* (Glasgow and Edinburgh, 1859), 2:45.

professors."[5] In *Seasonable Counsel* (1684), another work of the same period of heightened enforcement of the laws restricting worship by Nonconformists, Bunyan seized upon striking examples of Marian martyrs defeating affliction by rejoicing, to show that God's support makes such victories possible. Hawkes and Bainham "could shout for joy, and clap their hands in the very flames for joy"; God can make "*Paul* sing in the stocks, and good *Rowland Taylor* dance, as he goeth to the burning stake."[6]

Seasonable Counsel offers Bunyan's most sustained exploration of the nature and purpose of the sufferings endured by Christians. Nonconformist worship had been restricted since the collapse of Puritan power and the restoration of Charles II in 1660, first under Elizabethan laws and then, beginning with the Act of Uniformity of 1662, under the series of new acts designed to enforce worship according to the Book of Common Prayer and to prohibit other forms of religious assembly that came to be known as the Clarendon Code.[7] The Conventicle Acts of 1664 and 1670 subjected to severe penalties those meeting for unauthorized worship in groups of more than four. The Five Mile Act made it illegal for an ejected minister to live within five miles of where he had formerly served as pastor. These and other penal laws were enforced more or less aggressively depending upon political circumstances and the efforts of Charles II and James II to secure greater toleration. There were periods of relief, notably after Charles's Declaration of Indulgence in 1672, but until 1688 Nonconformists lived with the likelihood of persecution for acting upon their religious beliefs. In the early 1680s increasing numbers were arrested for involvement in conventicles. They might have their property seized for failing to pay the large fines levied, be left in prison indefinitely, or be sentenced to banishment. In *Israel's Hope Encouraged*, published posthumously, Bunyan pictured exaggerated fears of such punishments as the work of Satan's subtlety: "He can make the loss of goods, in our imagination, ten times bigger than it is; he can make an informer a frightful creature, and a jail like hell itself; he can make banishment and death utterly intolerable."[8] Bunyan's object was to control such fears by helping his audience to understand the perse-

---

[5] Sharrock, ed., *Misc. Works*, vol. 9 ed. by Richard L. Greaves, 9:345.

[6] Sharrock, ed., *Misc. Works*, vol. 10 ed. by Owen C. Watkins (Oxford, 1988), 10:22, 81.

[7] See Gerald R. Cragg, *Puritanism in the Period of the Great Persecution: 1660–1688* (Cambridge, 1957), especially chap. 1. In his introduction to vol. 10 of *Misc. Works*, Owen Watkins describes persecution of Nonconformists and debate about toleration in the early 1680s as background to *Seasonable Counsel*.

[8] Offor, ed., *Works*, 1:531.

cution with which they had to reckon as an episode in the long history of suffering for truth and a part of God's plan. If one could see it in this fashion, it would more nearly be endurable.

In *Seasonable Counsel,* repeating a favorite argument of the Marian martyrs, Bunyan argues that "the people of God are a suffering people" and that their trials are sent by God to test and strengthen them.[9] Periods of persecution are to be welcomed, because "the best Christians are found in the worst of times" (36). His message is one of reassurance, that God will console and reward those who can detach themselves from worldly preoccupations and trust their souls to him.[10] Bunyan sought to portray the afflictions of his audience, typically loss of property and imprisonment, as part of the grander drama of persecution and martyrdom. Thus he makes the threats they face seem part of a continuum leading to martyrdom: "The ruin of an estate, the loss of liberty, a Gaol, a Gibbet, a Stake, a Dagger" (93). He reminds them of modern massacres of protestants in Ireland, Paris, and Piedmont "where the godly in the night, before they were well awake, had, some of them, their heart blood running on the ground" (25). His strategy was to establish a sense of the present as a time of crisis that demanded an absolute commitment to God. He cultivated in his audience a state of mind akin to that of the martyr, a readiness "to chuse to be gone, though through the flames, [rather] than to stay here and die in silken sheets" (20).

Bunyan, like Foxe and many others, used images of physical torment to insist upon the abuses of the flesh suffered by martyrs and demonstrate their capacity to endure them. Making these abuses concrete encouraged an imaginative identification with the experience of martyrdom and prepared the faithful to confront their own, lesser forms of suffering. In *Seasonable Counsel* Bunyan invokes Hebrews 11, adding torture to the familiar list of afflictions ("they were *Tortured,* had *cruel* mockings and *scourgings:* they were *stoned,* were *sawn asunder,* were *slain* with the *sword*" [22]), and claims that Christ enabled the "good men of old" to bear such suffering with patience and rejoicing. In another place he asks: "Is thy body to be disfigured, dismembred, starved, hanged, or burned for the faith and profession of the Gospel?" (82). Bunyan multiplies images of the abused body here to suggest the power of persecutors over the bodies of the persecuted and consequently the intensity of the suffering the Christian

---

[9] Sharrock, ed., *Misc. Works,* 10:95.

[10] His text is 1 Peter 4:19: "Wherefore let them that suffer according to the will of God commit the keeping of their souls to him in well doing, as unto a faithful Creator."

must be prepared to face. Yet Bunyan's continuing emphasis upon real or imagined torture, even dismemberment (in recurrent images of bodies *"sawn asunder"* or torn to pieces by wild beasts), enables him to insist upon God's power to restore and even transform the abused body. The contrasting image is that of the glorified body of the saint.

In the prison verses he published as *One Thing is Needful* (1665), Bunyan imagines martyrs in heaven with restored bodies:

> Those bodies which sometimes were torn,
> And bones that broken were,
> For God's Word, he doth now adorn
> With health and glory fair.[11]

The body must be resurrected, Bunyan argues in *The Resurrection of the Dead* (1665), a work of the same period in which he continues his quarrel with Quakers and Ranters, because "it is the body that feels the stocks, the whip, hunger and cold, the fire and rack, and a thousand calamities."[12] Such physical suffering, for which Bunyan showed a remarkable empathy, is transcended by the resurrected body he imagines raised by God "in all its features and members, inconceivably beautifull." The resurrected body will be free from infirmities ("There shall be no lame legs, nor Crump-shoulders, no blare-eyes, nor yet wrinkled faces") and incorruptible. This was his version of what it would mean for Christ to fashion our "vile" bodies "like unto his glorious body" (Phil. 3:21).[13]

Bunyan needed to convince his audiences of the larger significance of their sufferings, to show them that they were part of the same struggle of the godly against persecuting power as the faithful of Hebrews, Paul and Stephen, and the long line of Christian martyrs who imitated the apostles. In his *Prison Meditations* (1663) he assimilated his own experience to this perspective:

> Here [in prison] we can see how all men play
>   Their parts, as on a Stage,
> How good men suffer for God's way,
>   And bad men at them rage.[14]

He returned to the metaphor in *Seasonable Counsel:* "a man when he suffereth for Christ, is set upon an *Hill,* upon a *Stage,* as in a *Theatre,*

---

[11] Sharrock, ed., *Misc. Works,* vol. 6 ed. by Graham Midgley (Oxford, 1980), 6:86.
[12] Sharrock, ed., *Misc. Works,* vol. 3 ed. by Sears McGee (Oxford, 1987), 3:210.
[13] Ibid., 210.
[14] *Misc. Works,* 6:47.

to play a part for God in the World" (62). To play such a part one needed the kind of faith that would make it possible to embrace suffering and an understanding of the larger drama that gave it significance. It helped to have models, of the sort that Bunyan drew from the Bible and from Foxe's pages. Insofar as he generalizes the role, he describes it as that of the martyr, defined in *Seasonable Counsel* as one who not only suffers for the truth but suffers "after a right manner," that is, "in that holy, humble, meek manner as the Word of God requireth" (30).

In *Seasonable Counsel* Bunyan insists that God appoints who will suffer, and when and how they will suffer, and also controls the persecutors: "Gods bridle is upon them, Gods hook is in their nose: yea, and God has determined the bounds of their rage" (73). He uses familiar biblical metaphors of refining and pruning to justify persecution as a trial meant to purify and strengthen Christians,

> To refine them as Silver, and to purge them as gold: and to cause that they that bear *some* fruit, may bring forth *more*: we are afflicted, that we may *grow*.(73)

Suffering, then, is discipline imposed by God, and a means to spiritual growth.[15] One should accept its inevitability for the godly ("persecution always attends the word, that of the *Tongue,* or that of the *Sword*") and seek to understand its purpose.[16]

Bunyan speaks to the fears of the individual Christian (*"But I am in the Dark"* [18]) by urging him to trust his soul to God and by showing how God will comfort him and give him a "holy boldness" before his persecutors, like that of Peter before the Sanhedrin. Part of his strategy of reassurance in *Seasonable Counsel* was to portray what he calls God's "comforting, supporting, imboldning, and upholding presence" (23). Consciousness of this presence enables the faithful to bear suffering with patience, even with rejoicing, like Paul or such

[15] See Owen Watkins's discussion of Bunyan's view of persecution in *Seasonable Counsel. Misc. Works,* 10:xxi–xxvii. Richard Greaves has placed *Seasonable Counsel* in the context of widespread Nonconformist praise of suffering. See "Bunyan and the Ethic of Suffering," in Anne Laurence, W.R. Owens, and Stuart Sim, eds., *John Bunyan and His England, 1628–88* (London, 1990), 63–76. Bunyan would have encountered traditional arguments justifying suffering in a continuation of Foxe's *Acts and Monuments* printed with the 1641 edition. This begins with *A Treatise of Afflictions and Persecutions of the Faithfull,* which describes persecution as inevitable, to be borne patiently, profitable, and even pleasant. Bunyan would of course have regarded all such arguments as grounded in the New Testament, characterized by Barrie White as "a textbook for martyrs, the product of a martyr community." See "John Bunyan and the Context of Persecution, 1660–88," *John Bunyan and His England,* 51–62.

[16] *A Holy Life, Misc. Works,* 9:290.

Old Testament precursors as Daniel. Bunyan sought to shift his audience's attention from the afflictions they faced, from the facts of material loss and prison life, to the power of God to enable the Christian
to turn suffering into triumph:

> Is it not a thing amazing to see *one* inconsiderable man, in a Spirit of
> faith and patience, overcome all the threatnings, cruelties, afflictions,
> and sorrows that a whole World can lay upon him?(77)

His task was to convince the fearful Christian of the reality of this
power of God, as against the visible power of his persecutors, and to
"kindle in his soul so goodly a fire of love to, and zeal for God, that
all the waters of the World shall never be able to quench" (77).

In a posthumously published work, *Paul's Departure and Crown*,
Bunyan presented a case study of exemplary suffering. In the words
of his text (2 Tim. 4:6–8), Paul describes himself as ready to depart,
having "fought a good fight," and anticipating a "crown of righteousness." Bunyan shows Paul acting out his own teachings about suffering through his willingness to "embrace the cross for the Word's
sake,"[17] for example, by going to Jerusalem when his enemies are
sworn to kill him. His readiness, for Bunyan, depends upon a heart
"unclenched from the world" and an eye fixed upon the heavenly
glory that is the reward of the sufferer. If Paul offered a model for
individual suffering, he could also illustrate the role of the martyr in
the life of the church, exemplifying the suffering of the saints that
strengthens the church by confirming the gospel and recovering
truths that have been "lost in antichristian darkness." The trial of the
saints by persecution becomes the trial of the Word:

> What is this furnace of earth but the body of the saints of God, in which
> the Word is tried, as by fire in persecution. . . . While their flesh did fry
> in the flames, the Word of God was cleansed, and by such means puri-
> fied in these their earthen furnaces, and so delivered to us.[18]

Those who burned the Marian martyrs thought they were purifying
the body of the church. Bunyan's arresting metaphor, which gives a
new twist to biblical metaphors of refining, makes the actual bodies
of the martyrs the furnaces in which the Word itself is purged. The
implication is that such violent means are necessary to burn away the
dross of tradition and restore the Word to its original purity. In his

---

[17]Offor, ed., *Works*, 1:727.
[18]Ibid., 725. Bunyan is commenting on Ps. 12:6: "The words of the Lord are pure
words: as silver tried in a furnace of earth, purified seven times."

later works Bunyan focused increasingly on the collective suffering of the true church, seen as a means of waging war against the power of Antichrist.

In his early commentary on Revelation, *The Holy City* (1665), Bunyan portrayed the drama of "the Gospel-Church returning out of her long and Antichristian Captivity" and the glorious restoration of this church that he expected at the millennium, the thousand-year rule of the saints on earth.[19] Bunyan regarded the millennium as imminent but unlike some who produced commentaries on Revelation, he did not try to predict when it would arrive. Nor did he deal with the means by which it would begin, except by trying to lay the specter of political insurrection, reassuring the "Governours of this World" that it would not be by "outward force or compulsion" directed against them.[20] Bunyan was more interested in representing the perfection the millennium would bring and the long struggle of the church with Antichrist, understood in typical protestant fashion as Roman Catholic power, that preceded it. He drew upon the prophets as well as upon Revelation in representing the figure of the suffering church, "rent and torn among the briers and thorns of the Wilderness" (80) but to be adorned as a bride and recovered "to her Primitive Purity" (98). And he invoked familiar and powerful Old Testament images of God restoring the scattered remnant to the fold: "*He that scattered Jacob, will gather him, and keep him, as a Shepherd doth his Sheep*" (193).

Bunyan anticipated the emphasis on persecution of his later works, particularly those of the 1680s, in passages describing the destructiveness of persecutors and the trials of the godly. The "venemous Dragons, fierce Lions, and ravenous Wolves" of Jeremiah and Isaiah become persecutors "in their spirit of outrage against the Church and People of God" (169).[21] Bunyan celebrates Isaiah's prophecy that the grass will flourish, and flocks lie down, where dragons formerly made the land barren.[22] He would give Apollyon the wings and the roaring of a dragon, and the mouth of a lion, in Part I of *The Pilgrim's Progress;* in Part II , with Apollyon gone, the Valley of Humiliation has become "fat Ground" where sheep graze. As in later

---

[19] Sharrock, ed., *Misc. Works,* 3:79.

[20] Ibid. See Sears McGee's discussion of *The Holy City* in relation to protestant commentary on Revelation. Ibid., xxxii–xlv.

[21] Isa. 35:7–9; Jer. 51:34–39. Jeremiah compares Nebuchadnezzar with a dragon (Jer. 51:34).

[22] Bunyan uses the same imagery from Isaiah in *Of Antichrist and his Ruin.* See Offor, ed., *Works,* 2:63–64.

works, Bunyan associates persecution with trial, in *The Holy City* expressed through the image of refining fire. The "People of God," he says, "are thrown into the burning Fiery Furnace of Affliction and Temptation, and there they are tried, purged, and purified" (139). This becomes the "King of *Babylon's* Furnace," from which Jerusalem "*comes out a City of Gold.*" The extended passage in which Bunyan develops this image, drawing upon Job and Daniel as well as various prophetic books, becomes a soaring meditation on the value of trial.

If Bunyan found the images that he elaborates in *The Holy City* in the Bible, he derived his sense of church history largely from Foxe. Although he projects the millennium into a vague future, he conveys a strong sense of the progress already made in reforming the church, praising "our famous and holy Worthies,"

> that before us have risen up in their place, and shook off those Reliques of Antichrist that intrenched upon the Priestly Office of our Lord and Saviour, even worthy *Wickliff, Hus, Luther, Melancton, Calvin,* and the blessed Martyrs in Q. *Maries* dayes (134).

Bunyan saw their "Altar-work" in reforming worship as yielding to the "Temple-work" of gathering churches of believers in his own time, to be followed by the "City-work" of restoring the New Jerusalem.[23] He regarded the saints of his day as seeing beyond "what the holy and goodly Martyrs and Saints did in the days that were before us, *Hus, Bilny, Ridly, Hooper, Cranmer,* with their Brethren" (154). Like Foxe, Bunyan understood the work of reform as restoring the ideal of the primitive church, shaped for him by Foxe's accounts of the acts of the martyrs as well as by the New Testament. Unlike Milton and others in the thick of the battle against prelacy, he was not bothered by the fact that some of these were bishops. Bunyan's fullest representation of the idea of the suffering church can be found in several posthumously published commentaries of the 1680s, written after he had witnessed more than twenty years of persecution of Nonconformists. In *The House of the Forest of Lebanon* Bunyan treats Solomon's house, which he distinguishes from the temple, as a type of the church in the wilderness. His tireless allegorizing of detail from the description in 1 Kings 7 provides the framework for his commentary, but he draws upon Revelation and various Old Testament books to dramatize the afflictions of the church and the power of the truth to beat back the dragon and his angels. He portrays the church both

---

[23] See McGee, in Sharrock, *Misc. Works,* xxxviii-xxxix.

as the woman in the wilderness, weeping and in pain, and as a strong building able to outlast the assaults of Antichrist: "yet some of the pillars stood, they were not all burnt, nor cut down."[24] One of Bunyan's themes is the capacity of the church to endure, another the way God answers suffering with comfort. He construes the golden vessels of Solomon's house as two cups signifying the extremes of Christian experience. The woman drinks from "the cup of blood, of fury, of trembling, and of astonishment" but also from the sweet cup of consolation and salvation.[25] Bunyan quotes at great length from a letter printed by Foxe in which the Italian martyr Pomponius Algerius, burned in Rome in 1555, insists that the "cold winter" of prison is to him "a fresh spring-time in the Lord" and recounts a vision in which he sees the martyrs, horribly mutilated in ways he details, cured of their wounds and alive in heaven.[26] The letter gives exuberant expression to one of the favorite themes of Foxe's martyrs, the capacity to find spiritual joy in physical affliction ("O how delectable is this death to me!"). Bunyan describes Pomponius Algerius as "in the church in the wilderness" when he wrote the letter, drinking of both the bitter cup and the sweet.

In his unfinished commentary on Genesis, Bunyan traced the lineage of persecutors from Cain. With his descendants, Nimrod in particular, Cain represents the cruelty of tyrants and their rage against the church, stirred up by Satan. Bunyan stresses that God will hear the cries of the victims for vengeance: "O the cries of blood are strong cries, they are cries that reach to heaven."[27] The flood becomes for Bunyan "a type of those afflictions and persecutions that attend the church," the ark a type of the remnant gathered together by God and preserved from the "rage and fury of the deluge."[28] The subsiding of the flood, dried by wind that is a type of the "breath of the Lord's mouth" that slays the wicked, offers a dramatic demonstration of the power of God to deliver the righteous. Bunyan consistently emphasizes the survival of the church, through persecutions that will "kill and crucify" some. Seth replaces Abel, "a living saint . . . to maintain that truth which but now his brother bled for."[29]

It was in *Of Antichrist and His Ruin* that Bunyan offered his most

---

[24] Offor, *Works*, 3:519.

[25] Ibid., 529. Bunyan combines the "cup of consolation" of Jer. 16:7 and the "cup of salvation" of Ps. 116:13.

[26] Ibid., 530.

[27] *On The First Ten Chapters of Genesis.* Offor, ed., *Works*, 2:447.

[28] Ibid., 473, 468.

[29] Ibid., 475, 483, 454.

sustained commentary on the historical drama of persecution and deliverance. As in *The Holy City,* he mingled the apocalyptic visions of Scripture with detail from Foxe's account of the progress of the true church. Bunyan saw the "lying legends, and false miracles" of medieval saints' lives that Foxe sought to expose as kept alive "in the body of Antichrist, which is the church and synagogue of Satan." His case against Antichrist (whose works are seen as including "unscriptural councils," outrages committed upon the bodies of the saints to promote "blasphemous rites and ceremonies," and Constantine's introduction of riches into the church) depends heavily upon Foxe.[30] Bunyan celebrates the Marian martyrs and praises Henry VIII, Edward, and Elizabeth for their victories in the war against Antichrist.[31] Yet the dominant vein of the work is biblical and apocalyptic. Characteristically, Bunyan draws heavily upon the Old Testament, the experiences of David and those of the Israelites in Egypt, and, especially, in the Babylonian captivity. Daniel is a critical book for him. He invokes two symbols of persecution that recur in his work, "the burning fiery furnace, and the den of lions"; as they supported the "horrible" religion of the Babylonians, "so popish edicts are the support of the religion of Antichrist now."[32] Bunyan calls up the imagery of Revelation to represent Antichrist, and the whore of Babylon drunk on the blood of saints and martyrs, and that of Thessalonians (2 Thess. 2:7–8) to assure his readers that the Lord shall "consume him with the spirit of his mouth, and shall destroy him with the brightness of his coming."[33] Yet while Bunyan proclaims his confidence that Antichrist will be destroyed, and exults in Revelation's prophecies of the destruction of Babylon, he focuses upon the present suffering of the church, seen as in the last stages of the reign of Antichrist.

As he does elsewhere, Bunyan justifies suffering for truth as ordained by God. Antichrist came into the world, he argues, that the church "might be tried, and made white by suffering under his tyranny, and by bearing witness against his falsehoods." Saints overcome by suffering, "when they are imprisoned, banished, and killed for their faithful testimony."[34] Bunyan's principal strategy for dealing with suffering in this work, however, is to read the worsening afflic-

---

[30] Offor, ed., *Works,* 2:51, 76–78.
[31] Ibid., 45, 50.
[32] Ibid., 50.
[33] Ibid., 47.
[34] Ibid., 46, 65.

tions of the church in the early 1680s as signs of the coming ruin of Antichrist, improvising upon Revelation. Thus "when God's church is absolutely forlorn, and has no hiding place any longer in the world," Antichrist will begin to fall. When Babylon has become the "habitation of devils," a place of "implacable madness of spirit," then the desert will blossom.[35] Bunyan found the best example of the truth that deliverance follows the darkest time in the slaying and resurrection of the two witnesses of Revelation 11. He understands these witnesses "mystically," as referring to the "succession of good men" who form the continuing church, and their death as signifying the damage done the spirit of Christianity, so that there will for a time scarcely be found "a true visible church of Christ in the world."[36] Bunyan took hope from the biblical pattern of deliverance from apparent disaster; David triumphed over Saul soon after the destruction of his refuge of Ziklag. In *Of Antichrist and His Ruin* Bunyan imagined deliverance coming through the Spirit of God working in magistrates and especially in protestant kings. Like the kings of the Medes and Persians who broke the Babylonian yoke of the Israelites, they would destroy the power of Antichrist, which he identified with the penal laws under which the Nonconformists were persecuted.[37] Yet this remains a generalized hope, located in an indefinite future and divorced from any suggestion of political action by the oppressed. Bunyan consistently urges patient suffering and obedience to kings and magistrates. In *Of Antichrist and His Ruin* he distances himself from those who plotted against the government, among them some of his acquaintances:

> I do confess myself one of the old-fashion professors, that covet to "fear God, and honour the king." I also am for. . . . *praying* for them that *despitefully use me, and persecute me.*[38]

In the preface to this work he urges "quietness and patience" under affliction; Christians should not try to "work their deliverance" but leave this to the disposition of God.[39] In his later works Bunyan renders persecutors and their actions with a biblical harshness, but he

---

[35]Ibid., 60, 62–63. W.R. Owens discusses *Of Antichrist*, especially Bunyan's refusal to specify a time for the millennium and his loyalty to the crown, in "'Antichrist must be Pulled Down': Bunyan and the Millennium," *John Bunyan and His England*, 77–94.

[36]Ibid., 65–66.

[37]Ibid., 50, 72–74.

[38]Ibid., 74. Christopher Hill, looking for signs that Bunyan intended to urge political resistance, finds this statement ambiguous and sees other comments urging obedience as reflecting a fear of censorship. See *A Tinker and a Poor Man*, 328–330.

[39]Ibid., 44.

explicitly discourages resistance to civil authority, focusing instead on the necessity and value of suffering.[40] The frame of mind he cultivates in his audience is that of the martyr who patiently accepts what is done to him: "suffer with Abel, until your righteous blood be spilt."[41]

Bunyan's emphasis on passive suffering is striking, particularly in his later works. He could value bold speaking in defense of scriptural truth but interprets Scripture, in *Seasonable Counsel,* as requiring that one suffer in a "holy, humble, meek manner" (30). Even allowing for the influence of censorship, which may explain why a work such as *Of Antichrist and His Ruin* was not published in his lifetime, one must conclude that Bunyan's commitment to patient endurance of persecution was deeply rooted. Foxe, publishing his work in Elizabethan England with the approval of state and church, was much more inclined to praise boldness in the martyrs whose stories he told. Their aggressiveness in denouncing the false doctrine and corrupt practices of their examiners mattered at least as much to him as their capacity for patient suffering.

Bunyan's rendering of his own experience in *Grace Abounding* and *A Relation of the Imprisonment,* both prison works, shows him writing about persecution and suffering in ways that he had learned in part from Foxe. The preface to *Grace Abounding* takes the form of a pastoral letter that recalls the prison letters of the Marian martyrs. As Felicity Heal has observed, Bunyan begins with a Pauline salutation ("Children, grace be with you, Amen") and establishes his situation ("I being taken from you in presence") and his pastoral concern in language that echoes Paul's.[42] One might add that Bunyan also proceeds, Pauline fashion, from greeting to thanksgiving ("I thank God

[40] On Bunyan's political passivity in the period, see Owen Watkins, in Sharrock, ed., *Misc. Works,* 10:xix-xx; Richard Greaves, in Sharrock, ed., *Misc. Works,* 9:xxiii–xxiv. See also Greaves, "John Bunyan and the Fifth Monarchists," *Albion* 13(1981):83–95, and "The Spirit and the Sword: Bunyan and the Stuart State," Robert G. Collmer, ed., *Bunyan in Our Time* (Kent, Ohio, and London, 1989). In the latter Greaves discusses Bunyan's sense of the necessity of righteous suffering, as expressed in *Seasonable Counsel* and elsewhere, in the context of an exploration of his commitment to the principle of Christian obedience of rulers.

[41] *An Exposition of the First Ten Chapters of Genesis.* Offor, ed., *Works,* 2:451.

[42] Felicity Heal, "Grace Abounding to the Chief of Sinners: John Bunyan's Pauline Epistle," *Studies in English Literature* 21(1981): 147–160. See also Margaret Olofson Thickstun, "The Preface to Bunyan's *Grace Abounding* as Pauline Epistle," *Notes and Queries* 230(1985): 180–182. Roger Pooley suggests that Bunyan uses metaphor in the preface as "the code of the persecuted." See "*Grace Abounding* and the New Sense of Self," in *John Bunyan and His England,* 105–114. Roger Sharrock, ed., *Grace Abounding to the Chief of*

upon every remembrance of you") and offers his own version of a Pauline benediction: "God be merciful to you, and grant that you be not slothful to go in to possess the land." His preface is rich in the affective language characteristic of the Pauline epistle. Bunyan speaks as spiritual father to his "children," drawing those to whom he has ministered into a particularly intimate sense of community in the Word.

Bunyan's use of Paul's experience as an analogue for his own is a striking feature of *Grace Abounding* as a whole and one of the ways in which it recalls the writings of those, like Foxe's protomartyr John Rogers, who described their experience of the Marian persecution.[43] Yet one cannot help but be struck by how strongly Bunyan's imagination was gripped by the Old Testament. In the preface he invokes not only Paul but Samson and Moses and David, who recurs in the body of the work (with Job) as an example of the kind of spiritual wrestling in which Bunyan was engaged. The central figure of the preface is that of the "Journeyings" of the Israelites through the wilderness from Egypt to Canaan, the paradigm for the difficult spiritual journey to which Bunyan summons his readers ("The Milk and Honey is beyond this Wilderness" [4]).

Bunyan created his own version of the Pauline epistle in his preface, fashioning a "Scripture language" which he fuses with the concrete experience of his readers (*"Have you forgot the Close, the Milk-house. the Stable . . . where God did visit your Soul?"* [3]). He found in the frequent Old Testament references to lions a metaphor for the danger and persecution of his prison existence: *"I stick between the Teeth of the Lions in the Wilderness"* (1). Bunyan knew David's prayer ("Save me from all them that persecute me, and deliver me: Lest he tear my soul like a lion, rending it in pieces" [Ps. 7:1–2]) as well as the New Testament characterization of the devil as walking about "as a roaring lion" (1 Peter 5:8). The metaphor enabled him to suggest both inner and outer afflictions, both the assaults of fears and temptations and the oppression of those responsible for his imprisonment, and also, by a startling inversion, the good that could come of such afflictions. Bunyan represents himself as finding honey in the carcass

---

Sinners (Oxford, 1962), 1. All quotations from *Grace Abounding* and *A Relation of the Imprisonment* are taken from this edition.

[43] See Dayton Haskin, "Bunyan, Luther, and the Struggle with Belatedness in *Grace Abounding*," *University of Toronto Quarterly* 50(1981): 300–313, for a discussion of Bunyan's use of Pauline patterns, as mediated by Luther's commentary on Galatians, to represent his spiritual experience.

of the lion, like Samson, and sharing it with his readers.[44] He speaks in the preface as from "the Lions Dens," but he speaks with the assurance of someone who knows that God will deliver those, like Daniel, of sufficient faith. The lions remain, but they have lost their terrors for him, and he suggests that they can for his readers as well if they will only remember "*the very beginnings of Grace with their Souls.*"

In the narrative of *Grace Abounding* Bunyan takes his readers into a world in which the terrors of doubt and despair frequently appear overmastering. His spiritual anguish seems unbearably intense because he renders it in bodily terms, as excruciating physical torment. Bunyan represents himself "as tortured on a Rack for whole dayes together" (42) when he believes that he has yielded to the temptation to "sell Christ." Elsewhere he describes himself as "racked upon the wheel" (46) and "tore and rent in heavy case, for many days together" (45) by the thought that he has lost grace. Bunyan imagines himself suffering tortures of the sort he associated with martyrdom, but without the deeply grounded faith and the sense of divine support that would enable him to endure them. At one despairing moment he says: "If now I should have burned at a stake, I could not believe that Christ had love for me. Alas, I could neither hear him, nor see him, nor feel him" (26). The irony is that even the most extreme suffering he can imagine has no meaning without the assurance of grace. Christ should stand between his soul and "the flame of devouring fire" (55), Bunyan writes, but instead has turned "lyon and Destroyer" (56).[45]

Bunyan eventually overcomes his sense of alienation, of course, and in his newly strengthened faith can visualize himself in heaven by Christ, now understood as his "Righteousness and Life" (73). He imagines his deliverance from spiritual torment as a release from figurative bondage: "Now did my chains fall off my Legs indeed; I was loosed from my affliction and irons, my temptations also fled away" (72). Yet one of the chief consequences of this deliverance is an ability to accept the fact of his actual imprisonment. He was "cast into Prison," Bunyan says, "to confirm the Truth by way of Suffering, as I was before in testifying of it according to the Scriptures, in a way of Preaching" (86). Before, Bunyan felt helpless under debilitating

[44]The *Treatise of Afflictions* printed with the 1641 edition of the *Acts and Monuments* cites Samson's experience as showing how God extracts "sweets" from the "tartest troubles." See sig. B2.

[45]Bunyan cites Revelation 6, which describes the "wrath of the Lamb" but makes no reference to lions.

mental torment, a form of suffering that only seemed to confirm the horrors of damnation; in prison, he embraces suffering as part of God's design for him and a way of witnessing to the truth. New texts press upon him, urging prayer that he might be strengthened *"unto all patience and long-suffering with joyfulness"* (97),[46] and promising *"Blessed are ye . . . when men shall revile you, and persecute you"* (93).[47]

Bunyan's acceptance and apparent understanding of suffering offers the most telling evidence that he has found the assurance reflected in the preface. His fears that his sentence of banishment will be carried out are real enough for him to imagine himself miserably abandoned by Christ in exile ("at last it may be to die in a ditch like a poor forlorn and desolate sheep" [99]), but he controls them by recollecting the sufferings of the heroes of faith of Hebrews 11 and Paul's courage in going to Jerusalem knowing "that bonds and afflictions abide me" (99). Bunyan's imaginings in periods of despair are haunted by thoughts of death. When he tries at one point to hold onto a consoling thought, he feels himself "driven with force beyond it, like a man that is going to the place of execution, even by that place where he would fain creep in, and hide himself, but may not" (50). This imagined scene conveys a real sense of terror, like that other one in which Bunyan sees himself judged by the elders of the city of refuge while he stands trembling at the gate "with the avenger of blood at my heels" (66). Yet Bunyan's attitude toward death undergoes a remarkable transformation as he works through fears of execution so vivid that he imagines himself "on the Ladder, with the Rope about my neck" (100).

Bunyan's worst fear is that he will play his part on this stage badly, with tottering knees and a pale face, thus betraying his lack of the constant faith that sustained the martyrs with whom he instinctively identifies. The thought that his last words would offer a splendid opportunity for a sermon to a transfixed multitude offers some consolation, but the real transformation comes with his sudden resolve to "stand to" God's Word whether he experiences the comfort he craves or not. This takes the form of his famous declaration that if God "doth not come in":

> I will leap off the Ladder even blindfold into Eternitie, sink or swim, come heaven, come hell; Lord Jesus, if thou wilt catch me, do; if not, I will venture for thy Name (101).

[46] Col. 1:11.
[47] Matt. 5:11.

This leap, so strongly imagined that it seems real, turns Bunyan from fearful victim into decisive actor on God's stage, witnessing to his faith with a startling and irrevocable physical act.

Bunyan the narrator (and preacher) presents this "trial" as another episode in his spiritual education, offering his readers a "use" of his experience: "I am comforted everie time I think of it, and I hope I shall bless God for ever for the teaching I have had by it" (101). Yet the leap itself is the true climax of his narrative. Through it Bunyan acts out a martyr's death in his imagination, demonstrating the strength of his faith in the boldest, most public fashion conceivable to him. The way he imagines martyrdom here is strikingly different from anything he could have found in Foxe, who represents martyrs as able to hold still in the flames (or to raise their arms in gestures of faith) because they are assured of divine support and of the reward that awaits them. Bunyan created a new version of the drama of martyrdom with his blindfold leap into eternity, unsure of whether Christ would be there to catch him yet certain of his resolution to "venture all for God" (99). It is an electrifying moment, of a kind that seems wholly appropriate to an emotionally charged narrative in which Bunyan so often feels his spiritual condition in physical terms.

Bunyan shows that he could "play a part for God in the World" on another kind of stage in *A Relation of the Imprisonment,* a series of five letters to the Bedford congregation evidently written between 1660 and 1662 but not published until 1765.[48] He describes the events from his arrest for preaching in Lower Samsell in November of 1660 to his unsuccessful effort to appear at the Assizes in January of 1662 in terms that recall the accounts of examinations for heresy that he knew from Foxe.[49] Bunyan contended with civil rather than with religious authorities, over the right to preach rather than over such doctrinal issues as transubstantiation, but the confrontation he represented strongly resembles those recorded by Foxe's protestant

---

[48]See Roger Sharrock, "The Origins of *A Relation of the Imprisonment of Mr. John Bunyan,*" *Review of English Studies,* new ser., 10(1959): 250–256, and Sharrock, ed., *Grace Abounding,* xxii–xxvi. Sharrock discusses the circumstances surrounding the eventual publication of the work and speculates that it originated in letters from Bunyan to his congregation.

[49]The five letters deal with Bunyan's examination by the magistrate who sent him to prison to await trial, Francis Wingate; his trial at the Quarter Sessions, presided over by Justice Kelynge; his discourse in prison with the Clerk of the Peace, Paul Cobb; his wife's appearance before the Assizes in his behalf; his unsuccessful efforts to have himself brought before the next Assizes.

martyrs who reported their examinations for heresy. Like them, Bunyan reconstructed dialogue from memory and added framing commentary that characterized the struggle as one between God and the enemies of truth (the devil's "vassals"), unfolding according to God's will: "Let the rage and malice of man be never so great, they can do no more, nor go no farther than God permits them" (113). The outlines of the drama Bunyan presents are familiar from Foxe: a solitary hero of faith taking his stand upon the Word, examiners who become progressively more annoyed and hostile as their sensible arguments are rejected, an impasse resolved only by an act of judgment. Bunyan faced prison rather than the stake, with the threat of banishment if he did not submit, but he played his role as if he were choosing martyrdom. Like the protomartyr John Rogers, he continued to preach despite the danger of arrest, conscious that he was setting an important precedent at the beginning of a time of persecution. He shows himself dismissing the advice of a friend to cancel the meeting at which he is subsequently arrested, arguing that if he flees he might make others "afraid to stand," and declaring his willingness "to suffer upon so good an account" (106). Bunyan saw his imprisonment as a form of witnessing, praying that it might be "an awakening to the saints in the country" (113). When the Clerk of the Peace (Paul Cobb) comes to him in prison to urge him to submit after he has served the twelve weeks to which he was sentenced at the Quarter Sessions, Bunyan cites Paul and Christ and declares that rather than act against his conscience he is "willing to lie down, and to suffer what they shall do unto me"(125).

We see Bunyan consciously acting the role of martyr here, as earlier when he asserts that he will stand to the truth "to the last drop of my blood" (112). By embracing suffering, in his case indefinite imprisonment and the possibility of banishment, he dramatizes his faith and provides a compelling example for a congregation whose will to resist pressures to conform he hoped to strengthen. Another way of doing this was to establish a sense of divine presence, of the sort that one typically finds in accounts of Foxe's martyrs. Biblical texts come to him in the course of arguments ("God brought that word into my mind" [115]), suggesting that the Holy Spirit is tutoring him. When he returns to prison after his friends make an abortive attempt to gain his release, he asserts that "I did meet my God sweetly in the prison again, comforting and satisfying of me that it was his will and mind that I should be there" (113). After being sentenced at the Quarter Sessions, he finds his heart "sweetly refreshed" by his examination and claims that "his [Christ's] peace no man can take from us" (119). Such insistence upon the sweetness of experiences one would expect to be bitter, like the rejoicing in suffering that one finds so frequently in Foxe, spoke to the fears of those less strong in their resolve than Bunyan.

Bunyan gave the events surrounding his jailing the appearance of a classic confrontation between persecutors and potential martyr and at the same time recorded the kind of detail that grounds it in the social and political realities of the Bedfordshire of the early 1660s. His antagonists treat him as a "breaker of the peace" who must be ruled if public order is to be maintained, using the Elizabethan Conventicle Act of 1593 to silence him.[50] Their repeated insistence that he follow his calling of tinker comes across as a form of social intimidation. At the examination following his arrest both Justice Wingate and his friend Mr. Foster chide Bunyan for not following his calling, and Foster dismisses those he gathers for worship as "none but a company of poor simple ignorant people" (111). Bunyan is consistently put down when he claims to be called to preach as well as to practice his trade. When he tries to justify himself by appealing to Scripture at the Quarter Sessions (*"As every man hath received the gift, even so let him minister the same unto another"* [117]), Justice Kelynge treats the text as referring to Bunyan's "gift" of tinkering. Kelynge had previously dismissed Bunyan's talk of having the "presence of God among us" at the proscribed meetings as "canting." He is willing to argue Scripture with Bunyan to a point but becomes increasingly overbearing and abrupt, finally cutting off Bunyan's praise of his meetings by imposing sentence.

In reconstructing his series of encounters with authority Bunyan showed a dramatist's eye for telling exchanges. One cannot know exactly how much shaping he did, but it is clear that his reporting was selective. He describes Kelynge as asking where he had his authority, "with many other such like words" (117), and says of his dialogue with Paul Cobb in prison: "We had much other discourse, which I cannot well remember" (123). His secondhand account of his wife Elizabeth's appeal to judges Hales and Twisdon at the Midsummer

---

[50] Christopher Hill comments on the political context of Bunyan's arrest and trial. See *A Tinker and a Poor Man* (New York, 1989), 105–109. See also the introduction and notes to *A Relation* in W.R. Owens, ed., *John Bunyan: Grace Abounding to the Chief of Sinners* (London, 1987). Cragg, *Puritanism in the Period of the Great Persecution*, 44–45, sees the manner of Bunyan's examination as typical of the way dissenters were treated in the period.

Assizes of 1661, "*the which I took from her own Mouth*" (125), draws out the drama of the encounter. The sympathetic Hales receives her petition "very mildly" while the consistently hostile Twisdon, responding to a petition thrown into his coach, "snapt her up, and angrily told her that I was a convicted person, and could not be released, unless I would promise to speak no more, &c" (126). Bunyan represents his wife as coming to the chamber to make her plea "with a bashed face, and a trembling heart" (126), then shows her repeatedly challenging the court despite intimidating comments by Chester and Twisdon ("she thought he would have struck her") and rising to a moment of great dignity when she picks up on a comment that Bunyan is a tinker: "Yes, said she, and because he is a Tinker, and a poor man; therefore he is despised, and cannot have justice" (128).[51] Bunyan concludes the account on a note of pathos, with his wife weeping when she sees that no arguments will work.

Bunyan was writing for his congregation, making a record of his own and his wife's confrontations with "the adversaries of God's truth" for their edification. Like many of Foxe's martyrs, and others in the mid-seventeenth century who reconstructed their examinations or trials, he was preserving acts of witnessing by recording them for an intended godly audience ("The Lord make these profitable to all that shall read or hear them"). The Bunyan that we see in *A Relation of the Imprisonment* appears less aggressive in contending with authority than some of Foxe's heroes or than his contemporary George Fox, more patient than contentious under examination, but unwilling to compromise his determination to continue preaching. He praises Paul Cobb for his "civil and meek discoursing" (104) yet remains unmoved, recalling Foxe's account of Wicklif's counsel not to be dissuaded from preaching by threats of excommunication and insisting that he will be judged by the Scriptures, and by the "church of God" as expressed in Scripture. The self-portrait that Bunyan creates reveals a patient, composed defender of the Word, unshaken by the persuasion or the threats of those determined to put him back in his social place and ready to "lie down" and suffer what he imagines as a martyr's fate.

Recent commentary on *The Pilgrim's Progress* has had much to say about the subjectivity of the "way" Bunyan's pilgrims travel, the sense in which their faith or lack of faith determines whether they are in

---

[51] See Hill, 229.

the way or not and where they are along it. Or whether they can be said to progress at all.[52] My interest here is in Bunyan's perception of the way as one that necessarily entails suffering, as a way of the cross, and in the implications of this perception for the dramatic development of the work.[53] In *The Heavenly Footman* Bunyan elaborated on what was to become the central metaphor of *The Pilgrim's Progress* in expounding his text, "*So Run, that ye may Obtain*" (1 Cor. 9:24). In the course of trying to arouse the "slothful and careless people" he addresses in the epistle, he insists that "there is no Man that goeth to Heaven but he must go by the Cross."[54] The cross is the traveler's "*standing way-mark*," a sign of the "*tribulation*" and "*Persecution*" inevitably suffered by the godly.[55] In arguing the need for perseverance, Bunyan imagines an immensely long and wearying journey, "with Briers and Quagmires and other incumbrances,"[56] a projection of ordinary experiences of the road colored by Isaiah's description of the wilderness. Then he takes his readers into a different kind of imagined world, one of persecution met by heroic endurance:

> The Saints of old, they being *willing* and resolved for Heaven, what could stop them? Could *Fire* and *Faggot:*, *Sword* or *Halter,* stinking *Dungeon, Whips, Bears, Bulls, Lions, cruel Rackings, Stoning, Starving, Nakedness,* &c.[57]

Bunyan cites Hebrews 11, but the torments he evokes owe as much to Foxe as to the Bible. He presents a composite image of martyr-

---

[52] See, among others, U. Milo Kaufmann, *The Pilgrim's Progress and Traditions in Puritan Meditation* (New Haven, 1966), 106, 117, and *passim;* Stanley Fish, *Self-Consuming Artifacts* (Berkeley and Los Angeles, 1972), chap. 4; John R. Knott, *The Sword of the Spirit,* chap. 6; Vincent Newey, "Bunyan and the Confines of the Mind," and Philip Edwards, "The Journey in *The Pilgrim's Progress,*" both in Vincent Newey, ed., *The Pilgrim's Progress: Critical and Historical Views* (Liverpool and Totowa, N.J., 1980).

[53] The story of Christian's journey through the world's wilderness, with its attendant fears and afflictions, had a special resonance for readers in colonial America. In the verses with which he prefaced the second part of *The Pilgrim's Progress,* Bunyan boasted that the first part was received in New England with "loving countenance." David Smith's study of Bunyan's works in America reveals that *Grace Abounding* was reprinted more than *The Pilgrim's Progress* before the nineteenth century and that *The Holy War* was also popular; at least twenty different works by Bunyan were reprinted between 1681 and 1830. See Smith, "Publication of John Bunyan's Works in America," *Bulletin of the New York Public Library* 16(1962): 630–631. David Hall comments on the appetite for works evoking the fate of sinners such as Bunyan's *A Few Sighs from Hell,* published in Boston in 1708. See Hall, *Worlds of Wonder, Days of Judgment* (Cambridge, Mass., 1990), 56. Smith sees Puritan faith in the millennium as one reason for what he characterizes as an "Immediate and sustained colonial interest in Bunyan's works." *John Bunyan in America* (Bloomington, 1966), 4–5.

[54] Sharrock, ed., *Misc. Works,* 5:159.

[55] Ibid. Bunyan quotes from Acts 14:22 and 2 Tim. 3:12.

[56] Ibid., 161.

[57] Ibid., 164.

dom, here and in another passage in which he moves from the afflictions "run through" by Paul to win the "prize" to the horrific torments of the early Christian martyrs whose stories Foxe had found in Eusebius:

> It [the prize] made others endure to be *Stoned, Sawn asunder,* to have their eyes bored out with *Augers,* their Bodies broiled on *Gridirons,* their Tongues *cut* out of their mouths, boiled in *Cauldrons,* thrown to the *wild Beasts,* burned at the *Stakes,* whippt at *Posts,* and a thousand other fearful Torments.[58]

Bunyan's readers were in no danger of being thrown to wild beasts, or even of being burned at the stake, but by using the martyrologist's shock tactic of cataloguing grotesque abuses of the flesh he might hope to spur them to lesser acts of endurance. He complains that "There are but few when they come at the Cross, cry Welcome Cross, as some of the Martyrs did to the Stake they were Burn'd at."[59] If he could bring his readers to identify with the role of martyr, to the point of being prepared to embrace suffering, he might hope to persuade them to abandon the *"shifts and starting-holes"* ("I have Married a Wife, I have a Farm, I shall offend my Landlord")[60] by which they avoided his call to the demanding journey he described. His object was to help them find the "Will, and Courage" to undertake it.

Christian makes renunciations of the sort Bunyan urged in *The Heavenly Footman* when he heeds the warning to *"Fly from the wrath to come"* (10), but he only gradually understands what kinds of suffering his pilgrimage will involve. In *The Pilgrim's Progress* the way leads early to a natural hazard that metamorphoses into a psychological one, as the quagmire Bunyan imagined in *The Heavenly Footman* becomes the Slough of Despond, and moves by stages to the episode that epitomizes the kind of persecution Bunyan evoked in the earlier work, the martyrdom of Faithful in Vanity Fair. In describing heaven to Pliable at the outset of his journey Christian shows what seems a precocious awareness of the persecution experienced by the faithful. It is as though he has been reading Foxe on the early martyrs:

> There we shall see Men that by the World were cut in pieces, burnt in flames, eaten of Beasts, drownded in the Seas, for the love they bare to

---

[58]Ibid., 167. This catalogue of torments draws upon those that Pomponius Algerius describes in the letter that Bunyan quotes from Foxe. See Offor, ed., *Works,* 3:530.
[59]Ibid., 162.
[60]Ibid., 165.

the Lord of the place; all well, and cloathed with Immortality, as with a Garment.[61]

This is the kind of lurid imagining that Bunyan indulged in *The Heavenly Footman,* here associated with a particular state of mind appropriate to the pilgrim. The comment serves to place Christian in the long line of sufferers for truth, yet it also reveals how little he understands about the actual form his own trials will take. When Worldly Wiseman conjures up a vision of the ordeals of the way ("*Wearisomeness, Painfulness, Hunger, Perils, Nakedness, Sword, Lions, Dragons, Darkness; and in a word, death*" ([18]), Christian appears to shake off the threat ("methinks I care not what I meet with in the way, so be I can also meet with deliverance from my burden") but in fact yields quickly to the appeal of an easier way that will avoid the dangers. Evangelist has to step in to tell him that he must "abhor" Worldly Wiseman's "labouring to render the Cross odious to thee" (22). The episode teaches an important lesson early, that the way of the cross is the only true way. To take sensible advice about how to avoid danger and suffering is to set one's feet on the way to destruction.

The lions of Hill Difficulty suggest the kind of danger Bunyan associated with the way of the cross. Lions recur in his work as a symbol of the potential violence of persecution, and some of his most powerful images of the physical torments of martyrdom play on the fear of dismemberment by wild beasts. Mistrust's story of fleeing the lions triggers Christian's dread of being caught by them as they range for their prey in the night: "how should I escape being by them torn in pieces?" (45). He trembles with fear as he walks between the roaring lions, assured by the Porter of Palace Beautiful that they are chained. This straightforward "trial of faith" tests Christian's courage and his trust in divine protection.[62] His success in overcoming the danger takes him beyond the state of mind in which he was susceptible to Worldly Wiseman's cautions.

The episode is the first of a number that demonstrate the need for the pilgrim, like the martyr, to conquer the fear of death. Christian's continuing vulnerability to this fear, which takes the form of "a great darkness and horror" (157) when he enters the river at the end of his

[61] J.B. Wharey and Roger Sharrock, eds., *The Pilgrim's Progress,* 2nd ed. (Oxford, 1960), 14. Quotations from *The Pilgrim's Progress* are taken from this edition.

[62] Sharrock, *The Pilgrim's Progress,* 320n. and 321n., sees the lions as representing civil and ecclesiastical persecution; he takes the fact that they are chained as pointing to a time when enforcement of the penal laws against Nonconformists was relaxed. Whatever

journey, is one of the chief sources of the drama of Part I. As a Christian soldier primed for battle, he quickly masters fear in his fight with Apollyon, although he needs the help of the grace that enables him to recover his sword and deliver the decisive scriptural thrust. Christian thanks God for having delivered him "out of the mouth of the Lion" (60), in his case a persecuting tyrant turned into a monstrous embodiment of demonic power. He learns that he can resist Apollyon's "hellish" rage to destroy only by trusting in the promises of the Word. The texts that Christian cites were classic justifications of suffering and martyrdom as means to victory, particularly Romans 8:37 (*"Nay, in all these things we are more then Conquerors, through him that loved us"* [60]).[63]

A disorienting fear of death is the central danger of the Valley of the Shadow, which Bunyan represents as a "very solitary place" where hellish sights and sounds threaten Christian's psychological balance. The first image of the Valley we get comes from those who have turned back, telling Christian of hobgoblins and dragons and "a continual howling and yelling, as of a People under unutterable misery; who there sat bound in affliction and Irons" (62). Such suffering terrifies because it is without apparent meaning or limit, unlike suffering endured in imitation of Christ or Paul and in hope of a crown of glory. This evocation of suffering contributes to the sense of confusion and disorder that hangs over the place. The human voices, if that is what they are, blend into the phantasmagoric scene in which Christian soon finds himself, beset by "hideous noises," reaching flames, and an approaching company of fiends. He can dispel the terrors and keep to the way, Bunyan shows, only by praying and reciting Scripture that affirms God's power to bring light out of darkness. The actual return of light reveals, at the end of the Valley, the victims of the long history of persecution by Pope and Pagan: "blood, bones, ashes, and mangled bodies of men, even of Pilgrims that had gone this way formerly" (65). By introducing this image of martyrdom Bunyan links the persecutions of Roman empire and Roman church with the demonic forces of the Valley and at the same time suggests that they have lost their threat. Pagan is dead and

---

topical allusions Bunyan may have intended, the chains function as a dramatic device that makes Christian's trial possible and as a reminder of God's power to restrain evil.

[63] See the two preceding verses, Rom. 8:35–36: "Who shall separate us from the love of Christ? shall tribulation, or distress, or persecution, or famine, or nakedness, or peril, or the sword? As it is written, For thy sake we are killed all the day long; we are accounted as sheep for the slaughter."

Pope a grinning old man in a cave. What is missing here is any sense of the victory of individual martyrs and the regeneration of the church through their deaths. Bunyan supplies this in the episode of Faithful's martyrdom.

Evangelist's preparation of Christian and Faithful for their experience in Vanity Fair provides the strongest statement in *The Pilgrim's Progress* of the relationship between pilgrimage and suffering. Bunyan boldly raises the stakes with this episode. Christian and Faithful have come through trials, for which Evangelist praises them, but they have not "resisted unto blood" (86); they must now "run" for the incorruptible crown. Evangelist's warnings distill the Pauline message about the inevitability of suffering for the faithful, echoing Acts: "you must through many tribulations enter into the Kingdom of Heaven," "in every City, bonds and afflictions abide in you" (86).[64] His predictions that one or both of them must seal their testimony with blood echoes the formulation of John Rogers and other Marian martyrs. The promise he holds out is the one that sustained all Christian martyrs: "be you faithful unto death, and the King will give you a Crown of life" (Rev. 2:10).

Bunyan's Vanity Fair was shaped by his knowledge of legal proceedings, and no doubt by his experience of the commercial hubbub of the annual Stourbridge fair, but it has a universality that makes one feel that it could be one of Paul's cities of "bonds and afflictions."[65] The reception of Christian and Faithful suggests the world of primitive Christianity as well as that of contemporary Bedfordshire, with its hostility of the establishment to sectarians whose behavior appeared to challenge civil as well as religious order. They meet with mockery and reproaches (like Christ or Paul), a generalized examination at which their strangeness is the central issue, imprisonment, and beating. Bunyan shows them suffering abuse, including the indignity of being displayed in chains, with a Christlike "meekness and patience." Like Bunyan himself in *A Relation of the Imprisonment,* they seem prepared to "lie down" and suffer whatever is to be done to them.

The trial of Faithful loosely follows contemporary court practice and builds upon a tradition of personifying vices that Bunyan is likely to have known from Richard Bernard's *The Isle of Man.*[66] Bunyan de-

---

[64] Acts 14:22; 20:23 (Paul says "abide me").
[65] See Sharrock, *The Pilgrim's Progress,* 327n., for a description of the Stourbridge fair.
[66] Roger Sharrock, "The Trial of Vices in Puritan Fiction," *Baptist Quarterly* 14(1951):3–12, traces the morality tradition to which Bunyan's fictionalized trial scenes belong and compares his management of allegorical characters with Bernard's.

lighted in the possibilities for satire that allegorical naming afforded, here and in the trials of the Diabolonians and of the Doubters in *The Holy War*. Lord Hategood exemplifies both the injustice and the class bias of the court and would have reminded readers of such implacable enemies of Dissent as Judge Jeffreys. Pickthank, witnessing against Faithful for having "bespattered most of the Gentry of the Town" (95), could be one of the informers who harried Nonconformists. Yet if Bunyan used the trial scene to expose the persecution he knew firsthand, he avoided the kind of detail that would have limited it to a particular historical moment. Individual characters may be sharply realized, as Pickthank is, but the indictment is atypically general, charging the prisoners with causing "Commotions" in the town and winning others to "dangerous Opinions"; the judge commends the severity of Pharoah and Nebuchadnezzar and Darius, all regarded as notorious persecutors, in his charge to the jury; the only crime mentioned by the jury is heresy, and the penalty they demand is "the most cruel death that could be invented" (97).[67] The trappings of the court are those of Bunyan's day, but the attitudes could be those of persecutors in virtually any time. In defending himself against the accusations of the witnesses, Faithful displays "bold" speaking and a defiant stance of a sort that one could find in Foxe's heroes, or early Christian martyrs brought before Roman proconsuls, or the apostles themselves:

> And as to the King you talk of; since he is *Beelzebub*, the Enemy of our Lord, I defie him and all his Angels.(93)

Bunyan gives the episode a mythic character, making it embody central elements of a drama that originated with the primitive church and assimilating contemporary persecution of Nonconformists to this larger drama.

Bunyan's stylized treatment of Faithful's execution turns him into an idealized figure exemplifying the martyr's constant faith under torment in all ages of the church.[68] The cruelties that Bunyan shows

---

[67] C.E. Dugdale, "Bunyan's Court Scenes," *Studies in English* 5(1941): 64–78, sees Faithful's trial as skeletal by comparison with the trials of *The Holy War*, in which standard courtroom procedure is more fully represented, and takes it as pointing to Roman Catholic persecution of protestant martyrs rather than to current oppression of Dissenters.

[68] For a differing view of Faithful's trial and execution, see Brean S. Hammond, "The Pilgrim's Progress: Satire and Social Comment," in Newey, ed., *The Pilgrim's Progress*, 120–122. In this collection, see also Newey's "Bunyan and the Confines of the Mind," 29–30. Roger Pooley argues the influence of Foxe, and Hebrews 11, on Bunyan's rendering of the execution. See "Plain and Simple: Bunyan and Style," in N.H. Keeble, ed., *John Bunyan: Conventicle and Parnassus* (Oxford, 1988), 106–107. Sharrock, *The Pilgrim's Progress*, 328n., also notes the influence of Foxe. For a discussion of the influence of Acts

him suffering invite comparison with Christ and the apostles, including Stephen, and with the host of protestants who were burned:

> First they Scourged him, Then they Buffetted him, then they Lanced his flesh with Knives; after that they stoned him with Stones, then prickt him with their Swords, and last of all they burned him to Ashes at the Stake.(97)

By having the chariot carry Faithful immediately to heaven, Bunyan transforms the scene into an emblem of the martyr's victory and reward. Christian plays martyrologist, memorializing Faithful with his song and demonstrating his new understanding of the fundamental Christian paradox that one dies to live:

> Sing, Faithful, *sing; and let thy name survive; For though they kill'd thee, thou art yet alive.* (98)

The sudden appearance of Hopeful shows another way that Faithful lives and symbolically enacts the belief that the blood of martyrs is the seed of the church: "Thus one died to make Testimony to the Truth, and another rises out of his Ashes to be a Companion with *Christian.*"

Bunyan's narrative reaches a preliminary climax with the death of Faithful. Evangelist's warnings and exhortations point to this experience, which reveals the injustice and cruelty of persecution and the exemplary suffering of a protestant saint as nothing else in *The Pilgrim's Progress* does. Yet Bunyan was too interested in other kinds of trials, and in the longer journey that represented the continuing struggles of a more representative life, to let Christian take Faithful's shortcut to the New Jerusalem. The most significant of the remaining trials, Doubting Castle, shows another face of the persecution that the Christian could expect to encounter and effectively renders the psychology of despair.[69] The episode demonstrates that Christian remains vulnerable to doubt and can lose the way at any point, as critics have noted, but it also represents the prison experiences common to many Nonconformists and, with a few differences, to the Marian martyrs whose prison ordeals were reported by Foxe. The "dark Dungeon, nasty and stinking to the spirit of these two men" (114) and the treatment of Christian and Hopeful by the giant

---

and the example of Stephen on this episode, see Dayton Haskin, "Bunyan's Scriptural Acts," in Collmer, ed., *Bunyan in Our Time,* 83–85.

[69]John Stachniewski characterizes *The Pilgrim's Progress* as "exorcising persecutory fears" and sees Christian as impelled in his pilgrimage by a "terror of the inauthenticity of elect experience." See *The Persecutory Imagination* (Oxford, 1991), 207ff.

suggest the worst of these experiences. Prisoners often had to endure an overwhelming stench, the darkness of confinement in the dungeon of the prison, even beatings and periods of being deprived of food.[70] The "continual howling and yelling" of the Valley of the Shadow that Christian hears as that of a people who "sat bound in afflictions and Irons" (62) offers a nightmarish vision of such prison experience, reduced to an inarticulate howl of despair.

Bunyan may have gotten the idea for the giant and his castle from folktales or chap-book romances,[71] but he made him a caricature of the more tyrannical and abusive jailers in the prison experience of Nonconformists. His giant displays the rage and violence of the stock persecutor, not only beating the pilgrims but threatening to tear them in pieces. Hopeful encourages Christian by recalling the memory of his courage under persecution before: *"Remember how thou playedst the man at Vanity Fair, and wast neither afraid of the Chain nor Cage; nor yet of bloody Death"* (117). Doubting Castle calls for a similar exercise of courage and faith. Bunyan's powerful images of physical suffering suggest the force of the assault upon spiritual health Nonconformists could expect in prison and teach the lesson that faith is the only stay against despair.

Christian and Hopeful make their miraculous escape with the key of promise, as Christian is saved once more by the recollection of Scripture, when the reality for many Nonconformists was indefinite imprisonment, often ending in death from the fever or plague to which those in crowded, unsanitary prisons were especially susceptible. The experience of Doubting Castle and Vanity Fair, along with other ordeals, enabled Bunyan to evoke suffering of a variety of kinds, all of which contribute to the sense of the extreme difficulty of the pilgrim's journey through the world's wilderness. One important effect of this suffering is to intensify the joys of Beulah and the New Jerusalem. When Christian and Hopeful ask what they must do in the New Jerusalem, the Shining Ones respond that they must receive comfort for their toil and "joy for all your sorrow":[72]

---

[70] See Cragg, *Puritanism*, chap. 4, *passim.*

[71] See Harold Golder, "Bunyan's Giant Despair," *Journal of English and German Philology* 30(1931): passim; Sharrock, *John Bunyan*, 85; Nick Shrimpton, "Bunyan's Military Metaphor," Newey, ed., *The Pilgrim's Progress*, 205–224.

[72] See John 16:20 ("your sorrow shall be turned into joy") and Hebrews 12:11 ("chastening. . . . yieldeth the peaceable fruit of righteousness unto them which are exercised thereby").

You must reap what you have sown, even the fruit of all your Prayers and Tears, and sufferings for the King by the way (159).

The sufferings "by the way" form one of the major themes of *The Pilgrim's Progress*. By giving them meaning and making visible the rewards they would earn, Bunyan appealed strongly to the experiences and the yearnings of his immediate audience.

If the sufferings of Part II of *The Pilgrim's Progress* are less dramatic than those of Part I, they still lie at the heart of the journey. Christiana's angelic summoner tells her that *"The Bitter is before the sweet"* (180) and that she must endure "Troubles," as did Christian. She leaves the Interpreter's House resolved, as she and her family sing, *"To take my Cross up day by day,/ And serve the Lord with fear"* (209). Part II offers a different kind of education in suffering, focused on the collective experience of persecution. At one point Interpreter leads Christiana and her family into the slaughterhouse to watch a sheep patiently accepting death: "You must learn of the Sheep, to suffer: And to put up wrongs without murmurings and complaints" (202). The passage, which echoes Paul's characterization of Christians as "sheep for the slaughter" (Rom. 8:36), could be read as an unconscious revelation of Bunyan's attitude toward women; Christiana is taught to be a sheep, her husband to be a Christian soldier.[73] In *Seasonable Counsel* and elsewhere Bunyan makes it clear that all Christians should be prepared to suffer patiently, but the lesson is particularly appropriate to Part II, given Bunyan's emphasis on the life of the suffering church. Christiana herself, who recalls the woman in the wilderness of Revelation, bears much of the burden of this emphasis.

The trials faced by Christiana and her growing company of fellow pilgrims have less to do with the terrors and uncertainties of the individual Christian than those of Part I and more to do with the experience of the church in a threatening environment. In the Valley of the Shadow Christiana thinks of Christian in the same place, "all alone in the night" (242). Her comment is prompted by sensations of the sort he experienced and by similar, if less intense, fears, but Chris-

---

[73] For discussion of Bunyan's patriarchal sense of woman's subordinate role and its implications for Part II, see Margaret Olofson Thickstun, *Fictions of the Feminine* (Ithaca, 1988), and N.H. Keeble, "'Here is her Glory, even to be under Him': The Feminine in the Thought and Work of John Bunyan," in *John Bunyan and His England*, 131–147. I differ from both these critics in seeing Christiana as rising above whatever vulnerability and dependency she displays to embody a convincing dignity and heroism by the end of Part II.

tiana can share her experience with Mercy and be comforted by the
reassurance of Great-heart. The presence of Great-heart, offering
protection as well as guidance in the Valley of the Shadow and at
critical points in the journey, reflects Bunyan's growing interest in the
role of the Nonconformist pastor in nurturing a spiritual community,
one that he had come to play with great energy himself. Great-heart
comments more than once upon the folly of setting out on a pilgrimage without a guide. The pilgrims learn to recognize their dependence upon him and the importance of participating in the life of the
Christian community.[74]

The appearance of Giant Maul at the end of the Valley of the
Shadow, where Christian had encountered the ineffectual figure of
Pope, suggests the revival of fears of Rome after the Popish Plot, as
do the forays of the "devouring" monster from the woods outside
Vanity Fair, described in the language of Revelation.[75] Great-heart's
defeat of both typifies the role he plays as defender of the faithful and
illustrates the extraordinary power with which Bunyan invests that
role. The shift from Evangelist to Great-heart implies a new role for
the Nonconformist pastor as heroic protector of the flock. The giant
fights of Part II reflect the renewed persecution of Nonconformists
in the early 1680s and Bunyan's confidence in the ability of the true
church to withstand this with the help of strong spiritual guidance.
The lions of Hill Difficulty represent a greater threat of persecution
than in Part I because backed by Grim (Bloody-man).[76] His usurpa-
tion of "the Kings High-way," together with the comment that the
way had become grassy with disuse, suggests the effectiveness of penal laws that restricted Nonconformist worship. Yet Great-heart, as
idealized minister to the threatened flock, responds in the fashion of
a romance hero, killing the giant and clearing the way. The women
tremble as they pass but as in the Valley of the Shadow and other
places of peril appear to suffer less than Christian at comparable
stages of his journey.

Great-heart's ferocity, here and in similar encounters, suggests the
vigor of Bunyan's confidence that God will deliver the faithful from
the "power of Satan" and also the strong desire to see God's ven-

---

[74]See my "Bunyan and the Holy Community," *Studies in Philology* 80(1983): 200–225,
for an extended discussion of the role of the church in Part II of *The Pilgrim's Progress.* I
have adapted this article in portions of my discussion of Part II.

[75]See Hill, *A Tinker and A Poor Man*, 200, 217–218.

[76]Sharrock, *The Pilgrim's Progress,* 344n., takes Grim to represent "the evil power which
puts into effect the penal laws against Nonconformists" and cites the persecutions of
1681–1684 as explaining the fact that the way is "almost all grown over with Grass."

geance on persecutors that surfaces frequently in his work. Great-heart tells the cannibalistic Slay-good, who threatens the King's highway in the neighborhood of Vanity Fair, that he has come "To revenge the Blood of Pilgrims" (267) and does so by cutting off his head and displaying it as a "Terror" to those who might try to imitate him, as he subsequently displays the head of Giant Despair on a pole by the side of the highway. Such incidents constitute Bunyan's dramatic equivalent of Foxe's accounts of God's terrible judgments upon persecutors. They suggest a similar need to demonstrate that those who suffer for truth will be vindicated.

The giants of Part II have an analogue in the army of Bloodmen in *The Holy War,* published two years earlier in 1682. The Bloodmen, with their fury against the town of Mansoul, embody the history of persecution as well as contemporary attacks upon Nonconformists.[77] Their captains include Cain, Esau, and the Pope, whose *"Scutcheon* was the stake, the flame, and the *good man in it"* (229). In their ferocity the Bloodmen are like mastiffs ready to "fasten upon" anyone, "upon father, mother, brother, sister, Prince, or Governour, yea, upon the Prince of Princes" (230). They are captured and bound over for the *"great and general Assizes"* (234) of the Last Judgment, as if to suggest that their sins are too consequential to be dealt with at a local trial.

Diabolus himself takes on some of the attributes of a persecutor. He rules Mansoul tyrannically and after being displaced by Emmanuel battles to recover the town with "Hellish rage," unleashing Captain Cruel and Captain Torment, among others. Bunyan expresses the ravages of his army of Doubters in terms of physical abuse, showing them making "great havock," dashing children to pieces, and raping women. They so wound Conscience, "and his wounds so festered, that he could have no ease day and night, but lay as if continually upon a rack" (205). The captains of Emmanuel, having retreated into the castle at the center of Mansoul, play the role of the persecuted church in the "barren wilderness" that the town has come to resemble.

In the subsequent trial and punishment of the Doubters, after Diabolus has withdrawn once more from Mansoul, Bunyan reversed the

---

[77] See Hill, *A Tinker and a Poor Man,* 247. Sharrock and Forrest take the episode of the Bloodmen as referring to the persecution of Nonconformists after the Restoration and also to the forces of Antichrist in the last days. Roger Sharrock and James F. Forrest, eds., *The Holy War* (Oxford, 1980), xxxii, 275n. Quotations from *The Holy War* are taken from this edition.

injustice done Faithful in Vanity Fair by means of a similar if more elaborate kind of allegorical courtroom drama. The device of the trial of the enemies of faith, for which he could have found precedent in Bernard's *Isle of Man* and Richard Overton's *The Araignement of Mr. Persecution,* enabled him to take a symbolic revenge for the abuses of the legal system under which Nonconformists suffered. He provided a counterpoint to Faithful's martyrdom by showing the convicted Doubters, like the Diabolonians earlier, crucified for their offenses. One, Election-doubter, parodies Faithful's act by declaring that he will "die a martyr" for his "Religion" (240). One can explain the harshness of the punishments as reflecting Bunyan's conviction that one must suppress ruthlessly those worldly impulses that threaten faith, yet the scenes themselves convey a shockingly fierce sense of exultation in the defeat of satanic power.[78] Bunyan shows Lord Wilbewill relentlessly hunting down and punishing the followers of Diabolus. One is sentenced "to be first set in the Pillory, then to be whipt by all the children and servants in Mansoul, and then to be hanged till he was dead" (243); others are described as dying in prison. In such scenes Bunyan visited the fate of the persecuted upon the persecutors in an ironic reversal of roles, enacting the divine vengeance in which he needed to believe. Great-heart's decisive acts in Part II of *The Pilgrim's Progress* express a similar confidence that the persecuting power will be defeated, in this case through the leadership of the pastor acting as an instrument of God.

Christiana and her company can endure their trials and keep to the way because they learn to follow Great-heart and because they draw strength from each other and from the communities of Christians that they encounter in their journey. In Part II Bunyan evoked the ideal that stands behind all such holy communities, the primitive church, particularly in the experience of the pilgrims at the Inn of Gaius and in the house of Mr. Mnason at Vanity Fair. Gaius and Mnason exemplify the charity of the primitive church with their hospitality and encouragement. Honest greets the pilgrims with the "holy Kiss of Charity" (248) urged by Paul.[79] In their sojourns with both Gaius and Mnason the pilgrims become part of vital communities practicing a simple Christianity, nurtured by communal feasting and pious discourse. These communities play a role comparable to

---

[78]Dugdale, "Bunyan's Court Scenes," 73ff., defends the punishments as Bunyan's representations of "the struggles of an elect soul against religious errors and fleshly lusts" (p. 74).

[79]Rom. 16:16.

that of the scattered churches of Acts, as centers of faith in a predominantly hostile world. The pilgrims' dangerous journey through this world recalls the journeys of Paul in Acts, although they do not share his evangelical and pastoral mission.

Gaius draws Christiana and her children, through Christian, into the larger "Family" of those who "have stood all Tryals for the sake of the Truth" (260). Christian's "Relations," as celebrated by Gaius, include martyred apostles (Stephen, James, Peter and Paul) and early Christian martyrs (from Foxe's redaction of Eusebius):

> There was *Ignatius,* who was cast to the Lyons, *Romanus,* whose Flesh was cut by pieces from his Bones; and *Policarp,* that played the man in the Fire (260).

By naming these "men of great Virtue and Courage," and their torments, Gaius establishes a heroic ideal for Christian's sons and the other pilgrims to emulate.

The examples of Christian and Faithful provide a more immediate stimulus to the pilgrims and a link with the heroic past. In Part II both take on the character of protestant saints. Great-heart points out the signs of Christian's battle with Apollyon: Christian's blood on the stones, pieces of Apollyon's broken darts, the trampled ground. The inscription on the monument to Christian's victory records how he "*so bravely play'd the Man. / He made the* Fiend *to fly*" (240). As they leave Vanity Fair, the pilgrims linger at the place where Faithful was martyred:

> There therefore they made a stand, and thanked him that enabled him to bear his Cross so well, and the rather, because they now found that they had a benefit by such manly suffering as his was (279).

Bunyan does not create shrines, or relics, or invest these sites with the *potentia* associated with medieval saints, but he makes them quasi-sacred places that invite meditation upon two essential attributes of the pilgrim: the heroic resistance to evil illustrated by Christian, and Faithful's "manly suffering."

By recalling such acts, and those of more distant exemplars such as Stephen or Polycarp, the pilgrims can learn to see themselves as part of the "Family" of the faithful who constitute the true, universal church. In the less demanding environment of Part II, they are not called upon to demonstrate heroism on the scale of Christian's or Faithful's. Apollyon is gone, and there are no more burnings in Vanity Fair. Only Stand-fast, praised by Great-heart in words that echo

Evangelist's for having *"resisted unto Blood, striving against Sin"* (291), seems to belong to Christian's world. The best illustration of the kind of heroism appropriate to the pilgrims of Part II, and of the kind of community they become, can be found in the series of death scenes with which the work concludes. The deaths of Christiana, Stand-fast, and others of their generation are natural ones, acts of holy dying that seem a fit conclusion to lives that have become increasingly holy in the course of their pilgrimage. The manner of those who are summoned is disarmingly natural, particularly that of Christiana: "however the Weather is in my Journey, I shall have time enough when I come there to sit down and rest me, and dry me" (305). Yet the scenes themselves are highly stylized.[80] Those who cross the river receive a divine summons validated by a token (usually a verse from Ecclesiastes), make bequests, and speak last words to the attending community of friends. In fact, Bunyan's pilgrims imitate the pattern of courageous and holy dying established by Foxe's martyrs and take on some of their heroic qualities, with the key difference that these qualities have become attributes of Christians living out normal lives in a world perceived to be hostile.[81]

Foxe's martyrs usually receive a summons, give away possessions, offer parting advice in the form of letters, and speak a few last words at the stake. Some make arrangements for their families, as do Christiana and Stand-fast. Foxe shows most of them ready for their summons, some eager for it. They typically conquer the terrors of death by such actions as kissing the stake and continuing to pray aloud amid the flames. The calmness of Bunyan's pilgrims reflects this tradition. Stand-fast in particular suggests the martyrs' habit of reassuring the faithful as he speaks from the river of death: "This River has been a Terror to many. . . . But now methinks I stand easie" (310). Christiana's parting advice, including the admonition to Mr. Valiant-for-Truth to "be Faithful unto Death, and my King will give you a Crown of Life" (305), recalls the letters of the Marian martyrs. Her brief exhortations catch the characteristic tone of these letters: "Be ye watchful, and cast away Fear; be sober, and hope to the End" (306). Foxe reports George Marsh writing "a certain godly Friend" : "Only tarry ye the Lord's leisure; be strong; let your heart be of good

---

[80]See Sharrock, *John Bunyan*, 152–153. Sharrock notes the formulaic character of the scenes.

[81]Sir Charles Firth noticed Foxe's influence in the farewell speeches of the pilgrims, although he did not develop the point. See *Essays Historical and Literary* (Oxford, 1938), 138.

comfort; and wait ye still for the Lord" (7.67). The last words of Foxe's martyrs, usually in the form of a cry to God, offered a pattern that Bunyan imitated. Where Foxe reports Ridley as saying "Lord, Lord, receive my spirit" (7.550), Bunyan has Stand-fast exclaim *"Take me, for I come unto thee"* (311). Bunyan elsewhere quotes the early Christian martyr Julitta, from Foxe, as saying *"Fare-well life, Welcome Death."*[82] In Part II Mr. Despondency varies the formula: *"Farewell Night, welcome Day"* (308). Mr. Ready-to-Halt (*"Welcome Life"* [307]) echoes Foxe's Laurence Saunders.[83]

Foxe's stories of the Marian martyrs offered the most compelling evidence outside the Bible of individual acts of faith and courage and of the strength of a holy community in a period of persecution. His death scenes, with their realistic dialogue and abundant detail, provided Bunyan with a model of Christians, artisans as well as preachers and bishops, conquering death by submitting patiently to it. Bunyan offered only a glimpse of the pilgrims being welcomed to the New Jerusalem in Part II, choosing to concentrate on the fully human drama of their leave-takings. This was a kind of drama that Foxe had represented skillfully, although in his case it is intensified by the unnaturalness of the deaths and the pressure of a relentless authority. Bunyan's death scenes, by contrast, convey a remarkable sense of normality. One is struck by the dignity of the leave-takings and by the mingling of natural grief and rejoicing in the reactions of those left behind.

Christiana sets the tone for the concluding scenes with her quiet bravery and her composure. We see her courage earlier, when she meets Grim's challenge by declaring: *"Now I am Risen a Mother in Israel"* (219). She seems to be trying out a new identity at this point, without fully recognizing that she needs Great-heart to remove Grim from the way. In her final scene, she speaks out of a deeper faith and an assured sense of her role in the Christian community. Bunyan presents her summons as unavoidably sharp yet seemingly benign and providential in its working; her token is *"An Arrow with a Point sharpened with Love, let easily into her Heart, which by degrees wrought so effectually with her, that at the time appointed she must be gone"* (305). The bitter dissolves into the sweet. If Bunyan gives her an easier passage than he does Christian, who briefly experiences the "Terror" to which Stand-fast refers, he endows her with a commanding dignity

---

[82] In *Come, and Welcome, to Jesus Christ. Misc. Works,* 8:384.
[83] I owe this parallel to Roger Pooley, "Plain and Simple: Bunyan and Style," 107.

and authority. In meeting her final trial, Christiana displays a new kind of heroism, stimulated by the examples of Christian and other predecessors in the way but tempered by the needs of the community. She sets the example for the others, paying homage to the strong (Valiant-for-truth, Stand-fast, and Honest) and exhorting the weak (Ready-to-Halt, Dispondencie, Feeble-Mind). At the end, she usurps the pastoral role of Great-heart, who fades in importance at the close of Bunyan's narrative. The other significant role goes to Stand-fast, who shows how the fear of death can be conquered and in his farewell speech from the river voices the sense of triumph and anticipation of any pilgrim at the end of the journey. The two roles complement each other. Christiana leads the way and shows her solicitude for the spiritual health of the community she leaves behind; Bunyan associates her, through her children and their families, with the continuity of the church ("I heard one say, that they were yet alive, and so would be for the increase of the Church in that Place where they were for a time" [311]). Stand-fast, here and earlier a surrogate for Christian, makes the climactic exit and points to the joys of the New Jerusalem.[84]

The conclusions of both parts of *The Pilgrim's Progress* show the sufferings and uncertainties of the way replaced by the victorious and lasting joys of the New Jerusalem. We see the bitter yielding to the sweet in the lives of successful pilgrims. In Part II, especially, Bunyan found a convincing way of rendering the persecution and of anticipating the eventual triumph of the suffering church, a theme that engaged him in many of the works of the 1680s. One can find numerous signs of Foxe's continuing influence in this period, twenty years and more after Bunyan read the *Acts and Monuments* in prison, particularly in his conception of the history of the church and his sense of martyrdom as embodying the essence of the Christian experience. The conclusion of Part II, the most interesting evidence of this influence, illustrates how Bunyan could transmute Foxe's very human drama of martyrdom into his own powerful vision of the holy community in the presence of death.

[84]For a different reading of the ending see Thickstun, *Fictions of the Feminine,* 103–104.

Part Three: Communities of the Godly

Epistolary Counseling

in the Puritan Movement:

The Example of John Cotton

Sargent Bush, Jr.

IN RECENT YEARS we have come much more fully to understand that Puritans at various points in history, from the sixteenth century in England well into the eighteenth century in America, were part of a large, complex, and enduring "movement."[1] Despite striking differences among themselves at any given moment in history and, even more, over time, Puritans were bound together by a common thread of beliefs, interests, and values which were manifest not only in theological and ecclesiastical contexts, but in the social and politi-

My research on this portion of Cotton's correspondence has been aided by numerous people and institutions. I should like especially to thank Dennis Perry, Katherine Leake, Mark Hodin, and Jean Marie Lutes for their research assistance. I express my debt to George Goebel elsewhere in this paper. Grants in the form of a resident fellowship from the Massachusetts Historical Society, a summer stipend from the National Endowment for the Humanities, a Vilas Associates Grant from the University of Wisconsin, and support in various forms from the Graduate School of the University of Wisconsin have been invaluable aids to my work on the materials which form the basis of this paper. Since the present essay relies heavily on quotation from manuscript sources, I am particularly grateful to the following libraries for permission to quote from letters in their collections: The British Library, The Bodleian Library, the Massachusetts State Archives, the Massachusetts Historical Society, and the Boston Public Library.

[1]The work of Patrick Collinson has led the way in establishing this view of English Puritanism; see especially *The Elizabethan Puritan Movement* (London, 1967), where Collinson most comprehensively makes the case for a "puritan movement, as distinct from puritanism" (p. 11). Recently Stephen Foster has made the case for continuity of this movement from England to New England in *The Long Argument: English Puritanism and the Shaping of New England Culture, 1570–1700* (Chapel Hill, 1991).

cal dimensions of their lives as well. The movement had its effect on its members in the way they conducted their personal lives and in the way they thought about community, from local to national levels. Like other powerful movements, Puritanism depended on certain key leaders to voice its values and principles. While the sermon was the most common form of discourse through which Puritan ideology received and sustained its fundamental identity, more private channels of communication were also of central importance. Recognized leaders were called upon to counsel, in both speech and writing, those who were less informed, less confident, or simply less experienced in Puritan ways. The subjects of such consultations ranged from the broad principles of church polity or doctrine to very personal, specific questions from individuals facing particularly worrisome dilemmas in their own lives and careers. Such informal interchanges served as the glue that gave coherence to the movement. The career of John Cotton (1584–1652) provides a useful case in point.

Cotton's prominence in the Puritan movement, first in England and then in New England, is a well established fact. At Cambridge he was at first well known for his florid preaching and later equally famous for his Puritan plainness, which caused the conversion of John Preston. His movement toward Puritanism was clearly signaled by his move in 1603 from Trinity College to Emmanuel. He was in Cambridge for fifteen years, up until 1612 when he became the vicar of Boston's St. Botolph's Church in Lincolnshire. Despite recurrent pressure from both local opponents and the church authorities, Cotton managed to remain in that position for twenty-one years, finally resigning in 1633 when it was clear he would be called to account for his nonconformity by the High Commission Court. The same year, at age forty-eight, recently recovered from a long illness, widowed and remarried, Cotton embarked for New England, where he became the Teacher at the first church in the new Boston. He served that congregation only two years less than he had served in the first Boston, some nineteen years, until his death in 1652. His career was thus neatly divided in half, in a manner of speaking, by the Atlantic Ocean. In both places, he played a key role in defining, strengthening, and consolidating the notion of what it meant to be a nonconformist, an Independent, a Puritan.

From the beginning of Cotton's tenure at St. Botolph's, the congregation was sharply divided on the question of conformity to the prescribed forms of worship. When desecrations to the church building in the spring of 1621 signaled the severity of local divisions, the attention of the church authorities focused more intently on Boston.[2] These Boston disagreements were at a high point when the diocese of Lincoln received a new bishop in the person of King James's favorite, the Welshman John Williams. Over the next dozen years Williams's indulgence of Cotton's Puritan predilections became well known in English ecclesiastical circles. During those final twelve years of Cotton's Lincolnshire ministry he developed a widening reputation as an exemplary Puritan minister, one who knew how to keep his Puritan conscience clear while bending the tolerance of ecclesiastical authorities about as far as it could be bent. At the same time, Cotton increasingly put his learning, his judgment, and his experience at the disposal of others in the Puritan movement. With remarkable consistency his extant correspondence for the 1620s and 1630s indicates his growing importance as a pastoral counselor to clerical colleagues during his final decade in England. In fact, he provides a classic example of those who were central to "the growth in the sense of solidarity and autonomy among the godly" that characterized what Stephen Foster has called the middle period of the Puritan Movement.[3]

Although a few of Cotton's letters have achieved some notice, he is not generally remembered today as a letter-writer.[4] But this was not the case in his own time. His first biographer, Samuel Whiting, wrote that "he answered many letters that were sent far and near, wherein were handled many difficult cases of conscience, and many doubts by him cleared to the greatest satisfaction."[5] Whiting spoke from personal experience with Cotton as a correspondent, as we

---

[2] See Larzer Ziff, *The Career of John Cotton: Puritanism and the American Experience* (Princeton, 1962), 50–54. An aggressively Anglican critique of Cotton's Lincolnshire career appears in [Nicholas Hoppin], "The Rev. John Cotton, A.M.," *The Church Monthly* 4(1862): 161–167, 5(1863): 40–54. Jesper Rosenmeier's recent work on the period sheds further light on the way local politics contributed to the church dissension, as evidenced in an unpublished paper, "'Eaters and Non-Eaters': John Cotton in Boston, Lincolnshire, 1621–22," delivered at the Modern Language Association conference, Chicago, Illinois, December 1990.

[3] Foster, *The Long Argument*, 97.

[4] His letter to Samuel Skelton of Oct. 2, 1630, which deals with the central issue of Separatism, is probably the most frequently discussed; see David D. Hall, "John Cotton's Letter to Samuel Skelton," *William and Mary Quarterly*, ser. 3, 22(1965): 478–485, the only twentieth-century edition of the letter. Everett Emerson included five other Cotton letters in his valuable *Letters from New England: The Massachusetts Bay Colony, 1629–1638* (Amherst, 1976).

[5] Samuel Whiting, "Concerning the Life of the Famous Mr. Cotton, Teacher to the Church of Christ at Boston, in New England" in Alexander Young, *Chronicles of the First Planters of the Colony of Massachusetts Bay, from 1623 to 1636* (Boston, 1846), 425–426. Whit-

know from the survival of two of his letters to Cotton written while Whiting was the minister at Lynn in the Massachusetts Bay Colony. Cotton's departure from England, in fact, was lamented by numerous correspondents. Matthew Swallowe, for instance, writing "From [his] Study in *London, May* 20, 1641," cited Cotton's letter-writing as an important part of his value to his English colleagues over "the whole Land almost, as also divers forraine parts, the Divines whereof came to converse with him, others had intercourse with him by letter, have beene acquainted with, and doe retaine in memory his parts and graces."[6] Even after his emigration, correspondents quickly learned that separation by some 3000 miles need not prevent the continuation of exchanges with Cotton. Numerous transatlantic correspondences are still on record, both in actual surviving letters, and in preserved remarks about such exchanges. As Francis Bremer has demonstrated, a transatlantic Puritan "network" was present from the very beginnings of the Great Migration that continued into the next generation, though far fewer of the actual letters survive from the first generation than from the second. Cotton was a central crux of that network.[7]

By examining Cotton's exchanges with several Puritan contemporaries—especially younger ones—during the 1620s and early 1630s, up to the time of his withdrawal from the Lincolnshire scene, we can at least fragmentarily reclaim a dimension of Cotton's importance to the Puritan movement in his role as clerical counselor. In doing so, we can bring into focus the fundamental importance of letter-writing among the Puritans in the 1620s.

The evidence begins with Cotton's earliest known letter, a Latin

---

ing's account is limited almost entirely to the period of Cotton's English career. It was not published until the nineteenth century but the manuscript was a primary source for the earliest published biography, John Norton's *Abel Being Dead, Yet Speaketh; or, The Life & Death of that deservedly Famous Man of God, Mr John Cotton. . . .* (London, 1658). On the relationship between Whiting's and Norton's accounts see Edward Gallagher, "Introduction" to the facsimile edition of *Abel Being Dead* (Delmar, N.Y., 1978), xx–xxi.

[6]Epistle "To the Christian Reader" in John Cotton's *God's Mercie Mixed with His Justice* (London, 1641), sig. A2v.

[7]See Francis J. Bremer, "Increase Mather's Friends: The Trans-Atlantic Congregational Network of the Seventeenth Century," *Proceedings of the American Antiquarian Society* 94(1984): 59–96. Figure 1, p. 63, illustrates the network created by ongoing contact between Puritans on both sides of the Atlantic Ocean. Larzer Ziff has maintained that "the Puritan party throughout the kingdom" became increasingly aware of Cotton's activities in Boston: "From conservative Archbishop Usher to zealous young Roger Williams, they sought correspondence or interviews with him, and Cotton's name was the most respected in a lengthening list of clergymen who were destined to serve in crucial public positions," *The Career of John Cotton*, 45.

epistle to John Williams written on September 11, 1621.[8] The letter, which has never been published, offers Cotton's own highly charged defense of his disagreements with the local and national church. When the letter was composed, Williams, recently invested as Lord Keeper of the Great Seal, had also been selected to become the new bishop of Lincoln, but was not to be consecrated in that post until two months later. So Cotton's letter is an attempt to reach the new bishop with his own point of view on his conformity before Cotton's opponents could get to Williams. A sharp edge of bitterness about recent attacks upon him shows through Cotton's rather formal and deferential style. A translation of the central point follows:

> The church which flourishes among us English I support—as is only right—with pious zeal in my heart and the most scrupulous observance. The creed it believes, I believe; whom it worships, I worship; its laws— nearly all—I respect, none do I condemn. All authority, whether ecclesiastical, or civil . . . I humbly revere. All schisms, whether of Separatists or Anabaptists, I heartily detest, and wish that they were driven completely from the hearts of the faithful. . . . Only ceremonies remain—and by no means all of them. Because in my doubt I do not embrace them with a confident enough spirit, they in turn—as if I were an enemy to the church, a rebel against the authorities, a disrupter of the public peace, a troublesome revolutionary, a scourge of schism, in short as if I were a useless burden on the Church's land—they seek to drive me out of the vineyard of the Lord, to render me exiled from my own home, and even to tear me from the altars of the Lord and cast me into the hateful tomb of silence.[9]

This colorful self-portrait of a man who conforms to the dictates of Church authority in all but a very few (and by implication, minor) details is a carefully constructed picture of a hounded but faithful cleric who now humbly presents himself before Bishop Williams, his "Most Reverend Father, most Eminent Lord," hoping he "will not take it ill . . . if I, subjected to the rigors of ecclesiastical law, . . . knock at the door of your patience and clemency." Cotton's sense of the real danger of being "cast into the hateful tomb of silence," even

---

[8]The present essay draws on my ongoing work on an edition of Cotton's complete correspondence. See my "John Cotton's Correspondence: A Census," *Early American Literature* 24(1989): 91–111. "The letter mentioned here to Bishop Williams was incorrectly recorded in the published census as dating from 1631. The correct date is Sept. 11, 1621.

[9]MS: Bodleian Library MS. Add. D.23, f.246. I wish to thank the Bodleian Library for permission to quote from this manuscript. The English translation from the Latin of the text is by my University of Wisconsin colleague, George Goebel, classical language specialist on the *Dictionary of American Regional English,* to whom I am especially grateful. I also owe thanks for consultation on the Latin to both James Lowe and Kevin Van Anglen.

at this early stage, four years before the death of King James and the subsequent ascendancy of King Charles and his bishop of London, William Laud, is striking. He was already very much involved in the ongoing search for a workable balance between the kind of conscientious refusal to engage in certain of the ordinances of worship that had characterized normal practice at Emmanuel College and a literal carrying out of all the church's dicta on the subject. This is of special interest here because what he had so thoroughly experienced himself in the previous decade would become the basis for his advice to numerous younger Puritan ministers in the decade to come. He was in the process of gaining a reputation as a non-conformist survivor at a time when others were not faring so well. Eventually, Samuel Ward would admiringly observe that "Of all men in the world I envy Mr. Cotton, of Boston, the most; for he does nothing in way of conformity, and yet hath his liberty, and I do everything that way, and cannot enjoy mine."[10] Ward was simply reflecting a collective awareness of Cotton's special success in continuing his very popular ministry well into a period of widespread silencing of his fellow Puritans.

Cotton's next surviving letter, also written to Bishop Williams (but this time in English), is on the same topic. On January 31, 1625, Cotton answered an inquiry he had received from the bishop about reports of his "Inconformity." He points out that he already conforms in using the ring in the wedding ceremony and in standing to recite the creed. Other stipulations give him more trouble, namely wearing the surplice, making the sign of the cross in baptism, and kneeling to receive the sacrament of communion. He begs continued patience from the bishop, observing that he has recently, through study, conference, and "seeking vnto God," come to see the "Weakenesse of some of those groundes against kneelinge, which before seemed too stronge for me to dissolve." Having shown this willingness to learn his failings in his analysis of the question, he asks that he be allowed "yet further time, for better Consideration of such doubts, as yet remayne behinde," cagily noting that in the meantime, throngs of worshippers are flooding in to St. Botolph's so that, in fact, there is some question as to whether the congregation's failure to kneel to receive communion is a matter of conscience or simply a function of a sanctuary too crowded to permit room for kneeling.[11] However much Williams was hearing complaints from the more strictly con-

---

[10]Whiting, "Concerning the Life of the Famous Mr. Cotton," 427.
[11]British Library Additional MS 6394, f.29. I am grateful to the British Library for permission to quote from this manuscript. This letter has been published several times;

formist church members in Boston, it was clear that people were voting with their feet in flocking to Cotton's services from the surrounding countryside.

The success of this and probably other such appeals to Bishop Williams permitted Cotton another seven years' continuance at Boston. During those years his importance to the strength of the Puritans' resistance of ecclesiastical coercion in the matter of the ceremonies was repeatedly certified in the kind of requests for advice and counsel that he received. Single letters or exchanges with nineteen different individuals have survived for the years from 1626 through 1632. Exchanges with eleven of these individuals demonstrate the extent to which Cotton had become known as one whose wise counsel was available for the asking. In a time long before clerical counselors were a distinct service group to the profession, such availability of a proven, respected veteran of the disagreements with ecclesiastical authority was welcome news to many. Several of these individuals were younger ministers facing the question at the outset of their careers or at moments of crisis or danger. The present context does not allow full examination of all of these cases, but the exchanges with six of these men—Ralph Levett, Edward Reyner, Charles Chauncy, Timothy Van Vleteren, Jeremiah Burroughes, and Nathaniel Ward— will serve as illustrative examples. We can be sure there were many more such exchanges than we now know about. These few have survived by chance and they demonstrate Cotton's central importance as an experienced veteran in the conformity wars.

Ralph Levett, a Yorkshire native, had completed his B.A. at Christ's College, Cambridge, in 1621/2, and received his M.A. in 1624, the year of his ordination. The opening sentence of his letter to Cotton, written March 3, 1625/6, seems to indicate that Levett was one of the many recent students from Cambridge who spent some post-graduate time in Cotton's Boston household, preparing for formal entry into the ministry.[12] Cotton has often been prominently mentioned among those influential Puritan ministers who created "seminaries" in their households where a polishing of clerical

---

see Pishey Thompson, *The History and Antiquities of Boston . . . in the County of Lincoln* (Boston, Lincs., 1856), 418–420; *New England Historical and Genealogical Register* 28(1874): 137–139; Massachusetts Historical Society, *Proceedings* 42(1908–1909): 204–207.

[12]He begins, "first, i give you thanks for your kindnes to me at my being with you both first & last," and he ends the letter by sending "my best to Mistriss Cotton" and to others in Boston. MS: Massachusetts State Archives, vol. 240, Hutchinson Papers, vol. I, f. 1. Published in Massachusetts Historical Society, *Collections*, ser. 2, 10:182.

skills and knowledge could be accomplished, often with more than one such apprentice in residence at the same time. Patrick Collinson, for instance, noting a 1580 conference of Puritan ministers which resolved that each minister ought to entertain a student of divinity, training him for the ministry, mentions as a later example of the practice that "John Angier was brought up under John Cotton." John Morgan has discussed the practice as it existed in the early seventeenth century, listing Anthony Tuckney, Thomas Hill, and Samuel Winter as some of Cotton's resident protégés.[13] There were many more. Indeed, after John Preston became the master of Emmanuel College in 1622, he recommended so many of his graduates to Cotton that Cotton became known as "*Dr. Preston's seasoning vessel.*"[14]

Levett's case is interesting because at the time of his letter to Cotton he was serving as a private chaplain to the Wray family at Ashby-cum-Fenby in Lincolnshire. In such a position, he was protected from the direct oversight of the larger church and was more or less free to practice his Puritanism, subject only to the will of his employers. But he found the situation posed problems of conscience to a young Puritan cleric all the same, and he writes to Cotton seeking advice on some very particular practical issues that have arisen. He wonders whether—and how—to pray for "my good lady," his patroness, when she is present in the congregation. More tied to his Puritan inclinations is his doubt about entertainments, especially those he witnessed at Christmas-time, where there was "cardinge" (card-playing) and "mixt dancinge." Valentines Day had also taken him unawares, as he was approached by the household's "2. young Ladyes" to draw a name out of a hat; "every one drawes a Valentin (so they terme it)."[15] His Puritan principles were clearly being challenged as he considered what was an appropriate response for him as a minister of God on the one hand and an employee of the family on the other. So he resorts to his mentor for advice.

Cotton's answers are direct and detailed, providing just the sort of assistance and, in most cases, support for Levett's inclinations that

[13]Patrick Collinson, *The Religion of Protestants: The Church in English Society 1559–1625* (Oxford, 1982), 119. See John Morgan, *Godly Learning: Puritan Attitudes towards Reason, Learning, and Education, 1560–1640* (Cambridge, Eng., 1986), 293–300. On John Cotton's practice, see also Ziff, *The Career of John Cotton*, 43–44.

[14]Cotton Mather, *Magnalia Christi Americana* (Hartford, 1820), 1:238.

[15]R[alph] Levett to John Cotton, March 3, 1625/6. MS: Massachusetts State Archives Vol. 240, Hutchinson Papers, Vol. I, f.1. Published: Massachusetts Historical Society *Collections,* ser. 2, 10:182. I am grateful to the Massachusetts State Archives for permission to publish from this and other manuscripts, as identified in subsequent references.

the younger man had sought. He tells Levett how to pray in public so as not to invite the charge of flattering his patroness, opposes carding and drawing names for Valentines on the ground that they are lotteries, but finds no fault with dancing, opposing only "lascivious dauncinge to wanton dittyes & in amorous gestures & wanton dalliances especially after great feasts." [16] Interesting as these answers are, they are of less importance here than the very fact that the exchange occurred. Levett clearly feels justified in troubling Cotton with these questions because of his experience of Cotton's "former love" in his household in Boston. In his first ministerial post, Levett is somewhat uncertain in attempting to establish a ministerial presence that will make the right statement of principles while also meeting the needs of the family in whose service he ministers. Nothing in Cotton's answer could have given Levett any reason to think he had presumed too much in asking these questions. Cotton is available as a resource to help this young minister get his clerical feet firmly under him.

The situation for Edward Reyner thirteen months later was similar in one respect: he too was conscious of being a neophyte in the matter of applying Puritan principles to his performance of his new duties. Reyner was an exact contemporary of Levett, having been educated at St. John's, Cambridge, with a B.A. in 1620/1 and M.A. in 1624/5. After schoolmaster jobs in Lincolnshire towns, he became a lecturer at Welton, just five miles north of Lincoln, then in 1626 lecturer at Benedicts in Lincoln. On February 17, 1626/7, about six weeks before his letter to Cotton, he was made lecturer at Peters at the Arches, Lincoln.[17] The surviving letter to Cotton is written from Lincoln and dated simply April 5, omitting the year. The context suggests that it was probably very soon after he arrived in Lincoln in early 1627.

The letter implies an ongoing acquaintance with Cotton and ends by saying, "My wife and I remember our loue to you and yours," suggesting that this single letter is part of a much larger context of friendship and, doubtless, counsel by the older minister.[18] Unfortunately, Cotton's reply has not survived. Reyner's letter was written,

---

[16] John Cotton to Ralph Levett, undated. MS: Massachusetts State Archives, vol. 240, Hutchinson Papers, vol. I, f.2; Published: Massachusetts Historical Society, *Collections,* ser. 2, 10:183–184.

[17] A. G. Matthews, *Calamy Revised* (Oxford, 1934), 408; Edmund Calamy, *Nonconformist's Memorial,* ed. Samuel Palmer (London, 1802), 2:421–427.

[18] Edward Reyner to John Cotton, April 5, [1627]. MS: Massachusetts State Archives, vol. 240, Hutchinson Papers, vol. I, f.84.

however, in order to carry out the requests of two other ministers, both of whom had asked Reyner to put a case of conscience before Cotton so that they in turn could advise troubled parishioners. This seems to presume that Reyner already had Cotton's ear, just as it also suggests that by now Cotton was being appealed to from "far and near." The first request, Reyner says, came from "Mr. Langley of Treswell," Nottinghamshire, the adjacent county to the west. Langley was much older than Reyner, having received his B.A. at Christ's College, Cambridge, in 1603, placing him very close in age to Cotton himself, though his approach to Cotton through Reyner suggests no immediate acquaintance between them. Langley's question is unknown to us, since it was detailed in an enclosure which Reyner sent along with his cover letter. The other case was put to Reyner by "Good Mr. Wales (whom you know)," who "is much perplexed as you may understand by Mr. Petchels Letter [another enclosure] and hath longed after your resolution of his doubts to help him out of the briers." The inquirer is Elkanah Wales, who was Perpetual Curate at Pudsey, Yorkshire, from 1616 to 1662,[19] but good Mr. Wales's question also remains unknown to us. Reyner then says, "Troubling you thus with the doubts of others, I am not willing to trouble you further with my owne," though he proceeds to do so anyway, saying, "I haue beene put upon it in my self lately to study the point, whether a man may be safely ignorant of the lawfulnes or Unlawfulnes of church-Ceremonyes in the word." He concludes that he "must search the Scripture for a Ground of doing or refusing them." Having expressed this much, of course, he has implied an invitation to Cotton to help him answer the question. Thus, in one brief letter, Reyner presents Cotton with three prickly questions from three different ministers. As was said of Thomas Hooker's role during this same period among the local ministers and students around Chelmsford, Essex, he was their "library."

Only three weeks before Reyner's letter arrived, Cotton had gotten a lengthy missive from a man just seven years his junior, Charles Chauncy, announcing, "I am now (by God's good hand) vickar of Ware, and desire your best direction how I may, with most profit

---

[19] Reyner probably had been acquainted with Wales's preaching for some time since he grew up near Leeds and "greatly frequented sermons in his childhood . . . at Leeds, Pudsey, Halifax, and other places," Benjamin Brook, *Lives of the Puritans* (London, 1813), II, 421–422; Ronald Marchant, *The Puritans and the Church Courts in the Diocese of York, 1560–1642* (London, 1960), 289.

and edification of my charge, proceed in the Lord's work."[20] Such a sweeping request for assistance from a thirty-five-year-old vicar can only be explained by the fact that Chauncy had until then been protected from the real struggles of the parish ministry by his appointment as fellow of Trinity College, Cambridge, where he acquired a reputation as an outstanding scholar of both classical and oriental languages. He was briefly vicar of St. Michael's in Cambridge before taking the post at Ware in his home county of Hertfordshire. The inexperienced but brilliant minister, it seems, thought first of asking advice from John Cotton, whom he may well have known in Cambridge fifteen years earlier. This is another form of evidence of Cotton's growing reputation as a ministerial consultant and counselor.

Chauncy complains of the "dissolute town" and of the previous lack of adequate instruction from which the people in this "barren wilderness" suffer. He is particularly concerned about the challenge his principles will meet "in regard to the government and discipline of our church." He expects he will face troubles because of his opposition to certain aspects of the Thirty-Nine Articles, "which we are bound to read publicly and to yield our assent unto." He says "the article concerning the ordination of bishops and ministers doth somewhat trouble me, as also the ceremonies which we are bound unto, which though I forbear myself, yet I know not how to avoid but that my curate must use if I will stand here." He then renews his request to Cotton: "I pray afford your wisest advice herein."

Coming from this particular man, the letter is especially poignant, now that we know his subsequent history. He was cited by the Court of High Commission three years later, on April 30, 1630, for a variety of misdeeds, most of them typically Puritan:

> the omission of Athanasius's Creed, the Lesson from the Old Testament, the Litany, the surplice, the Cross in Baptism, and the exhortation in Matrimony, 'With my body I thee worship,' with various speeches in the pulpit and elsewhere, in praise of the Puritans, in disparagement of the authority of the church and state, in expectation whereof he asserted that some families were preparing to go to New England.[21]

---

[20]Thomas Hutchinson, *The History of the Colony and Province of Massachusetts-Bay,* ed. Lawrence Shaw Mayo (Cambridge, Mass., 1936), 1:223. No manuscript is known to exist.

[21]*Calendar of State Papers, Domestic Series, Charles I, 1629–31* (London, 1860), 4:233.

After protesting his innocence briefly, he submitted to Bishop Laud's direct accusation within six weeks. This bought him some time, at least, and he remained at Ware for three more years, until October of 1633, when he became vicar at Marston St. Lawrence in Northamptonshire. Two years later he was again in trouble with the High Commission, being charged with contempt of the church and of his ecclesiastical jurisdiction (the bishopric of London) for outspokenly opposing the building of a kneeling rail around the communion table at his former church at Ware. He was sentenced, fined, and imprisoned, and finally knelt before the court to read a statement of abject submission to the prescribed forms of church worship, including kneeling to receive communion. Thus, he was made an example by Laud, who may in the end have regretted it because the instance was later cited in Laud's own eventual trial in the next decade as evidence for his oppression of the clergy.[22] Still, succumbing to this ecclesiastical pressure was in Chauncy's own mind in later years a shameful failing which even his service in the role as president of Harvard College from 1654 to 1671 could not serve to obliterate from his consciousness. In his last will and testament he compulsively rehearsed his "so many sinful compliances with and conformity unto vile human inventions and will-worship and hell-bred superstition, and patcheries sticht into the service of the Lord, (which the English *Mass* book, I mean, the *Book of Common Prayer,* and the *ordination of Priests,* &c. are fully fraught withal)."[23]

Chauncy was well aware in 1627 of the danger that lay before him in serving in the public ministry at just the time of the unleashing of the wrath of William Laud against the vile Puritans. His earnest plea to Cotton for advice was not idle. But Chauncy proved much less successful than his advisor in keeping clear of ecclesiastical justice. We do not have Cotton's reply to Chauncy, but he doubtless offered his best advice on this and other occasions. Chauncy invited him to stop at Ware "in transitu" as he traveled south, as it was exactly on the way from Boston to London. On his part, Chauncy promised to make personal contact with Cotton "once a year."

While all three of the men mentioned thus far were Cambridge-educated English Puritans, Cotton's "seminary" in the 1620s often included refugees from abroad, especially Germany and Holland,

---

[22] See William Prynne, *Canterburies Doome* (London, 1646), 361–362.

[23] Mather, *Magnalia,* 1:421. Mather italicizes the quotation, using roman type for emphasis. I have normalized the style by reversing the use of roman and italic type.

who had fled the Wars of the Palatinate. Other surviving letters include examples of Cotton's exchanges with four of these individuals. The first is a letter from John Nicolaus Rulice (or Reuliss) a German minister from Heidelberg who had fled the Catholic persecutions in the early 1620s, apparently going first to Cambridge and then at some point to Boston before moving on to Kent and finally to Holland. His letter, written on November 29, 1628, as he prepares to embark for Holland, is mainly about his political maneuvering to obtain a lectureship in Kent. He goes into detail on this not so much because he thinks Cotton can help him, apparently, as to report his hopes to a mentor whose interest and encouragement he assumes. He ends by asking for advice on how to conduct himself in his ministry once he is safely established in Holland. Other Cotton correspondents associated with continental Puritanism include Hugh Goodyear, an English minister Cotton probably knew from Cambridge days who had been at the English church in Leiden since 1616, and John Dinley, a Lincolnshire graduate of Christ's College, Cambridge, who was secretary to King James's daughter, Elizabeth, the Queen of Bohemia, in her forced exile in the Netherlands. Finally, there was Timothy Van Vleteren, a Dutch minister who had not been a member of Cotton's household seminary, but who knew—and mentions—others who had. One thing that characterizes all of these letters is that the writer, whether it is Cotton or his correspondent, mentions other churchmen who are mutual acquaintances and share a common interest in the Puritan movement. Their mutual reliance, even interdependence, is one of the most striking cumulative messages we can glean from these letters.

Both sides of Cotton's exchange with Timothy Van Vleteren have been preserved. Van Vleteren was from a Dutch family, though both his father and he were born in England—he at Sandwich, Kent, just across the channel from Holland. When he wrote to Cotton on October 26, 1629, he was the minister of the Dutch Church in London (Austin Friars), though before that he had ministered at Souteland, near Middelberg in southwest Holland. In fact, in his letter he refers to two other men who were associated with the same region in the Netherlands and who were known to Cotton. His letter is written on the occasion of his forwarding a package of "papers" to Cotton from Maximilian Teelinck, whom Van Vleteren had known when Teelinck was minister at Vlissingen (or Fleissing) in 1627–28 and Van Vleteren was at Souteland, just a few miles away. The other mutual friend is

Isaac Bishop, Van Vleteren's successor at Souteland, "who hath vsed your table and ro[o]fe."[24] Van Vleteren comments that "both these frindes have often spok of their ædification conversing with your reverence, and communicated their writings from you vnto me namely Catechisme, on the Canticles, of predestination, sence witch time [I] have desired to be acquainted with such a servant of Christ." His lack of acquaintance with Cotton does not prevent his putting a question to him: "it hath troubled me much in the matter of an oath, meditating on the 3 commandment whet[h]er a subiect is bound in Consience, when higher powers can affirme nothing against him, but surmise or suspect of his faithfulness to swear vpon interrgatories, or propositiones of their one framing against him." Cotton's reply notes his pleasure at hearing of both Teelinck and Bishop: "I waite for an opportunity to write unto them both, as men whom I much esteeme and affect, me[an]while let me intreate you when you write into those parts Commend my deare affection to them and tell them they are both written in my heart though I can seldome get liberty to write to them, and many other good friends as I gladly would." The comment that keeping up with his correspondence had become a burden helps fill out our picture of the increasing role he was playing in just this way as advisor to his colleagues on points of discipline and interpretation of fundamental rules of Christian (and ministerial) behavior. His household seminary's alumni obviously held an important place in his memory and he faithfully retained a recollection of their merits. Some became prominent in the Puritan movement, while others did not, but all knew Cotton as valued confidant and advisor.

The process of training such men and releasing them into the field to do their work was continuing. The 1630 letter to Goodyear at Leiden identifies the bearer of Cotton's letter as "Petrus Griebius, a German, who lived sometime here with vs, & whom God hath now graciously fitted for publique service in his Church."[25] Even as this "good yong man" leaves Cotton's household, another arrives, recommended by Goodyear. Cotton's seminary accommodations apparently had no vacancy at the time, but he found a way to welcome the unnamed newcomer from the continent anyway, as he explains:

[24]Timothy Van Vleteren to John Cotton, Oct. 26, 1629. MS: Massachusetts State Archives, Vol. 240, Hutchinson Papers, Vol. I, f. 16.

[25]John Cotton to Hugh Goodyear, April 12, 1630. Published in facsimile and transcription in D. Plooij, *The Pilgrim Fathers from a Dutch Point of View* (New York, 1932), 86–87. The MS at the Gemeente Archief, Leyden (Weeskamer 1355), has been lost since at least 1982.

"The yong man, whom you recommend hither, is receyved to Table in my house, & (for want of roome with me) to lodging, in a neere neighbours." Always remembering that the surviving fragments from Cotton's large correspondence must be just a small portion of the total, the recurrence of references to the young men whom Cotton nurtured at this critical early stage of their careers suggests the project must have occupied a considerable part of his energies.

With the arrival of the 1630s, Cotton's career was reaching a critical stage at just the time of the founding of the Massachusetts Bay Colony. His attentions were certainly drawn that way, as we know from his journeying all the way to Southampton to preach the farewell sermon to the Winthrop party and from a letter of October 3, 1630, to the Massachusetts Bay Company's Herbert Pelham in London to arrange for sending a quantity of meal to Cotton's Boston friend, William Coddington, already in New England. We also have Cotton's famous pre-emigration letter to Samuel Skelton at Salem (October 2, 1630) as well as less well known ones to Coddington, who early became a magistrate in New England, as he had been at old Boston. While Cotton was remaining aware of the colonial experience, however, he was also more conscious that political pressures were tightening, for him and for others.

Just a month after his letter to Skelton, he received one from Jeremiah Burroughes, who was then a parish minister at Bury St. Edmunds, Suffolk. He was not a particular friend, as Burroughes indicates in starting his letter: "Though my acquaintance with you be small, yett the necessitie of the cause in which I shall desire your helpe, putts me on to repaire to you."[26] This "cause" proves to be a major career decision. Burroughes had been having a falling out with local community leaders and he felt he was being eased out of his salary and his welcome in the community. He had received an offer from "a gentlewoman, whom yett I never sawe, & I thinke she neuer sawe me, wherein she offered me a liuinge." Even though he senses he is no longer valued by many in Bury, he is reluctant to take the

---

[26]Jeremiah Burroughes to [John Cotton], Nov. 1, [1630]. MS: John Davis Papers (012.3), Massachusetts Historical Society. I wish to thank the Massachusetts Historical Society for permission to quote from this manuscript. A transcript of this letter appears in Kenneth W. Shipps, "Lay Patronage of East Anglian Puritan Clerics in Pre-Revolutionary England" (Ph.D. diss., Yale University, 1971), 404–405. Burroughes dated the letter from Bury simply "Novemb: 1." Shipps suggests the year was 1631, but it should be 1630 since we know that Burroughes "was instituted to the Rectory of Tivetshall in Norfolk, April 21st, 1631," John Browne, *History of Congregationalism and Memorials of the Churches in Norfolk and Suffolk* (London, 1877), 115.

new offer. Bury St. Edmunds "is a greate place & so perhapps some
hope of more good then in a country village to which I am called."
He wants to stay, but fears he must go, so he appeals to Cotton to
"helpe vs in our streights, & lett your answere be as full as it may
conveniently," adding that "you and my tutor Hooker I esspecially
rely on for Counsel vnder god."

Cotton's answer is brief. He explains, as he had in the much longer
letter to Skelton a month earlier, that he is weakened from having
lately suffered greatly from ague. He does say, though, that one ought
not "to pitch vpon a place, or remooue without the joynt approba-
cion of your brethren mett together, to consider aduisedly of your
case." But he promises to write again soon and try to answer the
question then "according to my weaknesse." We know that Burroughes did indeed become installed at Tivetshall, Norfolk, on April
21, 1631, just under six months after this appeal for Cotton's advice.
Whether in the meantime Cotton had found it possible to say more
to him on the subject we do not know. Even though the move seemed
a setback to Burroughes's ambitions at the time, it did not forever
condemn him to anonymity, as he seems to have feared. He ultimately became well known in Puritan circles as one of the five Independents at the Westminster Assembly.

Another committed Puritan minister who would later achieve another kind of prominence with his pen wrote to Cotton on December
13, 1631. Nathaniel Ward was at a crucial point in his life when he
wrote a strongly felt but brief note from his home at "Stondon
Mercy" [i.e., Stondon Massey], Essex. He addresses Cotton as his
"Reverend and dear friend," telling him bluntly in the first sentence
that the ultimately dreaded hand of the authorities had just been laid
on his shoulder: "I was yesterday convented before the bishop, I
mean to his court, and am adjourned to the next term."[27] The bishop
is Laud, who in the same year had already been responsible for
Thomas Hooker's fleeing the country to Holland and indeed for a
great deal of talk of emigration throughout East Anglia. Ward's letter
is a valuable document for the way the spare prose emits a strong
sense of emotional agony as he confronts the implications of the
hardening of the lines of confrontation between bishops and Puritan
preachers. The letter contains only eight sentences after an initial
"Salutum in Christo nostro," and just enough metaphoric enforcement to dramatize the very real fear and isolation in his trouble that

[27]Nathaniel Ward to John Cotton, Dec. 13, 1631. Hutchinson, *History,* 1:104.

Ward feels. Yet he is writing to Cotton as a friend, one who has proven his friendship and support of Ward in the past and who is being brought up to date on the fate of one of his dear clerical brethren. The letter summarizes much that has been implied in others discussed here regarding Cotton's centrality to a large circle of ministers who were attempting to practice "purity in the ordinances" in their various locations throughout southeast England. The letter implies an expectation of personal suffering, whether that should take the form of imprisonment or, in Cotton's own terms of a decade earlier, the hateful tomb of silence. Because it carries so thoroughly this sense of crisis and personal pain over the condition of the faithful in England, it is worth quoting in detail:

> I see such giants turn their backs,[28] that I dare not trust my own weak heart. I expect measure hard enough, and must furnish apace with proportionable armour. I lack a friend to help buckle it on. I know none but Christ himself, in all our coast, fit to help me, and my acquaintance with him is hardly enough to hope for that assistance my weak spirit will want and the assaults of tentation call for. I pray therefore, forget me not, and believe for me also if there be such a piece of neighbourhood among Christians. And so blessing God with my whole heart, for my knowledge of you and immerited interest in you, and thanking you entirely for that faithful love I have found from you in many expressions of the best nature, I commit you to the unchangeable love of God our Father in his son Jesus Christ, in whom I hope to rest for ever.[29]

Unlike all of the other letters noticed above, this is no questioning appeal for help on various difficult points or on achieving identity as a Puritan minister. This is, rather, a statement of heroic resolution. Ward knows who he is and how his previous actions in his ministry have clearly identified him as an opponent of much that Bishop Laud stood for. He knows he will be punished; all that is uncertain is the severity of the sentence, though he is well aware that it will be harsh. He feels, like any person having to face the music individually, very

---

[28] One of the "giants" Ward has in mind is surely Thomas Hooker, who had left for Holland earlier in 1631. Ward was one of the forty-nine signers of a petition to Bishop Laud urging "the continuance of [Hooker's] libertye and pains" at Chelmsford, calling him "orthodox, . . . honest, and . . . peaceable," all to no avail, however, as another petition from the conforming clergy of the region urged their bishop to require conformity to preserve "the credite . . . of our ministerie," T. W. Davids, *Annals of Evangelical Nonconformity in the County of Essex* (London, 1863), 158–161. See also George H. Williams, "The Life of Thomas Hooker in England and Holland, 1586–1633" in *Thomas Hooker: Writings in England and Holland, 1626–1633*, ed. George H. Williams, et al., Harvard Theological Studies, no. 28 (Cambridge, Mass., 1975), 19–20.

[29] Hutchinson, *History*, 1:104.

much alone. He seems in effect to be saying good-bye to his past life and to those, like Cotton, who had helped him in it. That Cotton *had* been an important resource for him is clear from the final sentence. Other letters and personal contacts between the two had clearly preceded this one, and Ward thankfully acknowledges that friendship, even as he prepares to face enforced removal from the active ministry in England.[30]

In less than a year after receiving Ward's letter, Cotton was himself on the run. He had recently lost his wife after a childless marriage of nearly two decades and after a few months he had married Sarah Story, a Boston widow. On October 3, 1632, he wrote a letter to his bride of five months from a hiding place already apparently well removed from Boston. Cotton does not disclose his whereabouts but assures her he is "fitly & welcomely accommodated." He regrets that his "Sweet Hearte" cannot yet join him, but acknowledges his fugitive status in saying, "if you should now traveyle this way, I feare you will be watched, & dogged at the heeles. But I hope, shortly God will make way for thy safe comming,"[31] which did indeed happen within no more than six weeks. It is interesting that even during this undercover period in London, "Addresses . . . were made unto him privately by divers persons of worth and piety, who received from him satisfaction unto their Consciences in cases of greatest concernment."[32] John Norton quotes John Davenport's account of his meeting with Cotton in London at this time, a meeting which is said to have brought both Davenport and Thomas Goodwin over to the Puritan position on non-conformity.[33] Cotton departed for New England on about July 10, 1633.

The story goes on, of course, as Cotton continues his role as advisor and counselor to all comers even during his errand into the wil-

---

[30]The upshot for Ward was as expected. In 1632 he was suspended, excommunicated, and deprived of his benefice. He emigrated to New England in 1634. John J. Teunissen, "Nathaniel Ward (c. 1578–1652)," *American Writers before 1800: A Biographical and Critical Dictionary*, ed. James Levernier and Douglas R. Wilmes (Westport, Ct., 1983), 1517. For the only book-length treatment of Ward's life, see Jean Béranger, *Nathaniel Ward* (Bordeaux, 1969).

[31]John Cotton to Sarah Cotton, Oct. 3, 1632; MS: Boston Public Library, MS Am. 1502, V. 1, no. 1. This letter has been published in *Chronicles of the First Planters of the Colony of Massachusetts Bay, from 1623 to 1636* (Boston, 1846), 432–433 and in Massachusetts Historical Society, *Collections*, ser. 4, 8:543–544. I quote from the manuscript by courtesy of the Trustees of the Boston Public Library, where Dr. Laura Monti, Dr. Giuseppe Bisaccia, and Roberta Zonghi have been both gracious and immensely helpful on my several visits to the Department of Rare Books and Manuscripts.

[32]John Norton, *Abel Being Dead, Yet Liveth* (London, 1658), 21.

[33]Norton, *Abel Being Dead*, 32–33; see also Ziff, *The Career of John Cotton*, 68.

derness. Although he continued to answer letters from clerical colleagues in England, his emigration permanently altered his relationship to the Puritan movement. But of course his and many others' flights from Laudian repressions signaled the change of the movement itself. If he was no longer in as convenient a position to be the spiritual and professional counselor to young Puritans, his reputation survived his departure so that in the next two decades—especially in the 1640s—he was one of the spokesmen for New England's version of church polity to whom the English brethren repeatedly had written recourse.

Still, while in the later years of his New England period his counsel more often took the shape of books of controversy, his clerical counseling skills were discovered anew, now by his fellow emigrants. He had a continuous correspondence with Peter Bulkeley, the minister at Concord, from the time of Bulkeley's settlement there in 1635 until at least 1650. Although they were in disagreement on some of the basic issues of the Antinomian Controversy in 1636–1638, Bulkeley was given to asking Cotton for help in resolving doctrinal dilemmas as well as practical congregational challenges. Similarly, we know that in 1639 the ministers at Plymouth, John Rayner and William Brewster, wrote to him to seek his professional advice on church matters. Others in New England, including Samuel Whiting, sought personal spiritual comfort, seeing Cotton as a minister to ministers. At the same time, those in England who had valued Cotton's counsel earlier continued occasionally to resort to him. One John Elmestone, a schoolmaster in Kent, sought his advice in 1640 and as late as a few weeks before Cotton died in 1652. And he continued to express a loving concern for his former neighbors and friends in Lincolnshire. Indeed, a prefatory Epistle to a late publication, *Of the Holinesse of Church-Members* (London, 1650), is truly a personal letter from Cotton to civic and church leaders "together with the whole Congregation and Church at Boston" in Lincolnshire. The book which this letter introduces is, in fact, written as a response to letters from Boston and elsewhere in England, on the subject of church membership and what it entails for the believer.[34]

The 1620s in England, as any number of historians have explained, was a critical decade for the shaping of Puritan dissent, a decade in which a generation of ministers was forced to negotiate the

---

[34]Cotton says, "I have for the satisfaction of your selves, and of sundry others, who have written to me about the same, penned this ensuing Treatise," *Of the Holinesse of Church-Members* (London, 1650), sig A2v.

narrow path in their own local circumstances between principled non-conformity and the limits of tolerance by ecclesiastical authority. John Cotton, through his household seminary and through his correspondences with many who trusted his counsel, was a key figure in the training of that generation in England. The fragments of correspondence, surviving here like the shards of a Greek vase, tell a story that is only partially present, but that is strongly and clearly enough suggested by the surviving evidence so that we can safely infer the rest of the picture. But whether his correspondents, like Cotton, emigrated to establish new conditions for their spiritual lives or whether they remained behind to experience the further troubles and triumphs of English Puritanism in the dramatic decades ahead, they knew that Cotton's loving advice filled a strongly felt need. Wise and sympathetic counsel from a fellow-sufferer and fellow-believer surely strengthened the bonds that held the Puritan movement together well beyond the limits of the life of any one person. The surviving fragments of Cotton's correspondence provide clear evidence of the importance of these personal, informal exchanges to the inner strength of the Puritan movement before, during, and after the period of the Great Migration.

Sects and the Evolution

of Puritanism

Patrick Collinson

THE INVITATION was to offer a paper on the theme of "Puritans and the Evolution of Sects." This embodies a conventional teleology and one which is built into the standard historiography of "Puritan" dissent and nonconformity. We begin with an ostensibly monolithic and almost unchallenged Catholic Church. We end with—shall we say?—California, a licensed and potentially limitless plurality of religious entities, both cults and sects. From this promised land there is, or so far has been, no return. Sir Nicholas Bacon (the father of Francis) expressed an Elizabethan fear that a certain train of undesirable events would determine that religion "which of his own nature should be uniform, would against his nature have proved milliform, yea, in continuance nulliform."[1] It was polemically conventional to proceed from the uniform through the milliform to the nulliform. The opposite course of events had not occurred to Bacon and is still less likely to coincide with our modern expectations. It is now impossible to believe that Christendom can lie in the future, except perhaps eschatologically. Progressive fissiparation, whether or not concluding in the "nulliformity" projected by Bacon, is seen as virtually a law of Protestantism, somewhat resembling the biological law of evolution from simple to more complex forms: Bossuet subsumed in Darwin.

So far as the religious history of the English in the second half of the sixteenth century and the seventeenth is concerned, we move by a series of primary, secondary, and tertiary processes from Pro-

---

[1] *The Remains of Edmund Grindal,* ed. W. Nicholson, Parker Society (Cambridge, 1843), 471.

testantism through Puritanism to Separatism/Sectarianism. The strength of this version of the *longue durée* of Post-Reformation religious history is that it is not only more or less true to what in fact happened but that it provides historical justification for all of the main religious interests concerned, as we find them institutionalized in the principal churches of the English-speaking world. Both Roman Catholics and those Anglicans who adhere to an essentially catholic ecclesiology within the Church of England can exclaim, in effect, "We told you so." Sectarian anarchy is the inevitable outcome of the exercise of wilful and private religious judgment. As Hilaire Belloc once wrote: "The moral is, it is indeed,/ You must not monkey with the Creed." Meanwhile, what used in England to be called "free churchmen" have turned vices into virtues. From their side of the fence, they have agreed with high Anglicans that the principles of the Reformation have necessarily tended towards a radically decentralized and individualistic religious experience. So at least have reported Congregationalists, Baptists, and, *a fortiore*, Quakers. Presbyterians might have had a different tale to tell if they had not been gobbled up by, on the one hand, the rational dissent of Unitarianism, the brain-child of the eighteenth century, and on the other by Scottish and Scoto-Hibernian Presbyterianism, the legacy of nineteenth-century migration within the British Isles, a species not so much of nonconformity as of religious tribalism. What follows can be read as a kind of apology or lament for the lost tribe of the English Presbyterians.

Meanwhile, in another part of the forest, investigations of religion as a social "factor," whether more or less Marxist or Weberian in their understanding of what that factor is and of how it operates, have added reinforcement to these ecclesiological and church-historical perspectives. Christopher Hill tells us that by some historically necessary process, compulsory communities in early modern England were giving way to voluntary communities, as parishes broke up into conventicles and house churches. These were the ecclesiological analogues and facilitators of proto-industrial units of production and capital accumulation.[2]

For the purpose of this paper it is necessary to note only in passing the suggestion of Richard Niebuhr and his disciples among religious sociologists that these centrifugal tendencies tend by a generational

---

[2]Christopher Hill, *Society and Puritanism in Pre-Revolutionary England* (London, 1966); especially the chapters called "The Spiritualization of the Household" and "Individuals and Communities."

process to which most if not all sects are prone to give way to renewed centripetal forces which turn them into those denominations whose instinct it is to secure a new kind of *modus vivendi* with society and its majority values, a society which, in the case of the United States especially, became simultaneously pluralistic and consensual.[3] Nor is it necessary to become embroiled in the "ecumenical" aspirations of many twentieth-century churchmen in the radical protestant tradition towards so-called "Unitive Protestantism," motives arising in the perception of some critics of ecumenism from the pathological degeneration and even disintegration of once confident religious traditions, including the tradition of independency: for example, British Congregationalists swallowed up in something called the United Reformed Church.[4] The experience and fortunes of religious bodies in liberal, competitive, and pluralistic conditions lie beyond the chronological scope of this paper and were no concern of a conference devoted to the seventeenth century.

What this paper will suggest is that the conventional teleology of "Puritans and the Evolution of Sects" tends to obscure, in the second half of the sixteenth century and the first half of the seventeenth, strong currents running in the opposite direction, from a relatively incoherent and disorganized sectarianism towards that version of "unitive Protestantism" which English Puritanism in the rhetoric of its own apologetics aspired to be. An East Anglian minister published a book in the early years of the seventeenth century which claimed to contain the sum of that unitive divinity (in a thousand pages!), demonstrating "in how many truths, that is in particulars above number, we do agree, teaching the same things from one and the same word, by one and the same Spirit, with a sweet consent, in comparison of those few things wherein the jugementes of some doe differ."[5] It is not necessary to believe that this witness was telling the whole truth and nothing but the truth. But it is helpful to acknowledge that "sweet consent" was a positive value for ministers in the Puritan tradition, which they not only sought but claimed, for understandable polemical reasons, actually to enjoy. It is also necessary to attach due importance to the insistence of the Puritan mainstream

---

[3]H. Richard Niebuhr, *The Social Sources of Denominationalism* (New York, 1929).

[4]John T. McNeill, *Unitive Protestantism: The Ecumenical Spirit and its Persistent Expression* (London, 1964, but deriving from lectures delivered in Chicago in 1928); Ian Henderson, *Power Without Glory: A Study in Ecumenical Politics* (London, 1967). This book was provocatively dedicated "to the good Christians in every denomination who do not care greatly whether there is one Church or not."

[5]Robert Allen, *The doctrine of the gospel* (London, 1606), Sigs. *4–5.

on the involuntary constraints imposed on private judgment by true belief. Richard Bernard of Worksop in Nottinghamshire and Batcombe in Somerset denounced among other errors of his time willworship, defined as "a voluntary worshipping of God in and by such meanes as man inventeth." This led to schism, "which is an uncharitable division, and an unlawfull separation from the true church of Christ, . . . forsaking the fellowship of the Saints wilfully in a factiousness of spirit, making unlawfull assemblies within and among themselves." "We depart from this iniquity."[6]

According to conventional perspectives, the first (if by no means the last) time that English-speaking religious history ran into the sectarian sand was in the mid-seventeenth century: the consequence of migration, revolution, and civil war. In fact, the mid-seventeenth-century experience was not unprecedented. An earlier chapter is half forgotten, or consigned to somewhat marginal literatures on something called the Freewill Men of mid-Tudor England and on an Elizabethan phenomenon called the Family of Love. These movements are understood to have borne the same relation to "orthodox" English Protestantism as continental Anabaptism to the "magisterial" Reformation: conventional teleology again. Where the still older sectarian tradition of Lollardy fits in, whether it was indeed sectarian, or a tradition, and what it may have contributed to the Reformation on the one hand and to mid-sixteenth-century sectarianism on the other, are questions which continue to confuse historical discourse but need not detain us. Here we may only note that the protestant version of history created by the sixteenth-century martyrologist John Foxe proposed an alternative teleology of Lollard sects as the progenitors of a national Protestant Church, a scenario with which some nineteenth-century Anglicans felt by no means comfortable.

What does concern us is that the Reformation and pre-Reformation chapters of sectarian history were separated from the revolutionary sects of the mid-seventeenth century by a hundred years in which sectarianism was evidently not rampant and which we may call the Puritan century. This major feature of the religious-historical landscape is obscured in the special pleading to establish the continuity of radical, centrifugal dissent to be found, for example, in Christopher Hill's essay "From Lollards to Levellers," an argument which assimilates Puritanism itself to that continuum, at

---

[6]Richard Bernard, *The good mans grace or his stay in all distresse* (London, 1621), Sigs. C3v–4v.

least to the extent of making it a Trojan horse with a belly-full of sects.[7] It is possible that what happened between the Lollards and the Levellers was the religious equivalent of one of those rivers in limestone country which run for half their course underground; and that part of that underground was the Puritan consciousness itself. The first is uncertain, the second contestable. What is more certain is the consolidation in the later sixteenth and early seventeenth centuries of centripetal Puritanism, "radical" in a rather different sense, which assimilated and domesticated the sectarian tendency by a process which some would want to describe as the reception of Calvinism, others as routinization, but those pursuing the studies represented in this conference as "the rise of Puritanism."

It is possible, if the unpredictability and arbitrariness of the historical process is accepted, to understand Puritanism as comprising a series of developments opposite to those which we tend to take for granted. The rise of Puritanism, if sustained and stabilized, could have meant not the triumph of pluralistic and eventually tolerant religious individualism, which William Haller thought was a historical paradox on the grand scale,[8] but the success of the opposite, unitive and intolerant. It would take a large book, or an anatomy of many books already written, to establish how and why the unitive and intolerant scenario proved implausible and impermanent. The most that a short paper can hope to establish, or at least to assert, is that Puritanism in its original intentions believed itself to be headed in a direction quite contrary to that implied in the phrase "Puritanism and the Evolution of Sects." The argument of what follows is fivefold:

(1) As a religious movement and as a godly community, Puritanism grew by subjecting scattered and disorganized elements to a process of church formation, albeit the formation of a church within the Church. The means of formation were educational, which is to say catechizing, preaching, and sermon repetition, on which few disabling restrictions were placed by the larger church authorities, except temporally and locally; and collective disciplines which on the contrary were significantly restricted. It is possible to argue that the

---

[7]Christopher Hill, "From Lollards to Levellers," in *The Collected Essays of Christopher Hill*, vol. 2: *Religion and Politics in 17th Century England* (Brighton, 1986), 89–116. See Dr. Hill's more recent uncertainty ("From Lollards to Levellers" having first appeared in 1978) whether there indeed was "a continuity underground from Lollards via Anabaptism and Familism to the sectarians of the 1640s" (*Three British Revolutions, 1641, 1688, 1776*, ed. J.G.A. Pocock [Princeton, 1980], 114).

[8]William Haller, *The Rise of Puritanism* (New York, 1938), *Liberty and Reformation in the Puritan Revolution* (New York, 1955).

combination of unrestricted preaching and restricted discipline produced the unintended and unwanted result of sectarianism.

Let us assume, as most historians of the Reformation do, that English Protestantism succeeded and even in some sense grew out of the antecedent Lollard tradition. Lollards were relatively incoherent and disorganized, or at least localized, according to a recent analysis.[9] It is not clear that they stood over against the late medieval Church as a counter-church. Their principles, or at least their strategies, were not separatist but allowed a posture of outward conformity and subterfuge and a measure of integration in the wider society. The first generation of Protestants differed from the last generation of Lollards not only in their solifidian theology, a matter noticed by all historians, but in their conviction that they constituted the true Church, and that this conviction must be articulated in separation from the false, popish Church. This idea was shared by one of the earliest of the protestant bishops, William Barlow, when he defined "the trewe church of God" as "where so ever ii or iii simple personnes as ii coblers or wevers were in company and elected in the name of God" and with the simple Cornish woman who told her own bishop that the true Church was "not your popish Church" "but where two or three are gathered together in the name of God." A Kentish weaver said the same, and of course all three were merely elaborating Matthew chapter eighteen verse twenty. "Come out from among them and separate yourselves," wrote the Essex curate William Tyms to "all Gods faithfull servants."[10] That was 2 Corinthians chapter six verse seventeen. One result of this new and uncompromising separatism was the unprecedented holocaust of Mary's reign. But if the immediate consequences of the new protestant ecclesiology were separatist, its longer-term implications were anti-separatist. There could be no separation from the true Church which had separated itself against the false. Gathered sect and universal church are, as Troeltsch perceived, congruous.

The enterprise of protestant church-building involved a secondary process of separation from surviving elements of pre-protestant dissent, insofar as these elements were not assimilated into "orthodox"

---

[9]Richard G. Davies, "Lollardy and Locality," *Transactions of the Royal Historical Society,* ser. 6, 1(1991): 191–212. But Professor Ann Hudson, as an authority on Wycliffite texts who is impressed with their endurance in the Lollard tradition, takes a rather different view in *The Premature Reformation: Wycliffite Texts and Lollard History* (Oxford, 1988).

[10]"Sermon of the Bishop of St. Davids 12 November 1536," British Library, Cotton MS Cleopatra E.V, fol. 415; *The Acts and Monuments of John Foxe,* ed. S.R. Cattley, viii (London, 1839), 499, 330, 118.

Protestantism. It is conventional to regard tendencies such as the so-called "Free Will Men" of the 1540s and 50s as breakaway sects. "Anabaptist" was a term used somewhat promiscuously in the England of Edward VI. But in the perception of these heretics themselves, it was the Protestants with their unfamiliar, academic theology and "clerkly" fluency who were the splitters and sheep-stealers. The leading freewiller (and in all probability old Lollard) Henry Hart (we know a man of the same name with a Lollard past in Kent) was given to saying that "all errors were brought in by learned men"; while the Somerset radical John Champneys claimed to speak for "the electe unlearned people" in a book "grossly compyled without any clearkly eloquence."[11] The evidence for the penetration of radical dissent by orthodox Protestantism is necessarily elusive, but some of it will be found in the prison debates and martyr letters of the Marian persecution, and especially in the writings of the Coventry weaver John Careless, not himself a learned man but content to submit to learned evidence. Careless advised a fellow prisoner what he should say to his judges: "I am a poor man without learning; but am commanded of God to follow the counsel of his constant preachers." "This kind of answer, my dear heart, it shall be best for you to make."[12]

It remains an open question what happened to the English "Anabaptists" after the accession of Elizabeth. The early 1560s saw a continuing polemic "to enarm and fence the true Church of God againste the pestiferous sect of the free will men of our time," but this was not sustained and perhaps there was no need to keep it going. English "Arminianism," when it took shape in the early seventeenth century, had no sense of any indebtedness to an earlier anti-predestinarian tradition, and of course the social and intellectual circumstances were very different.[13] There are three possibilities. The old heretics, or at least any effective leadership of the kind that Henry Hart seems to have exercised, may have been wiped out in the Mar-

---

[11] Henry Hart, *A godly newe short treatyse instructyng every parson. howe they should trade theyr lyves* (London, 1548); John Champneys, *The harvest is at hand. wherein the tares shall be bound, and cast into the fyre and brent* (London, 1548). On the freewillers and other mid-Tudor radicals, see J. W. Martin, *Religious Radicals in Tudor England* (London and Romcoverte, 1989), which corrects the terminologically anachronistic I.B. Horst, *Radical Brethren: Anabaptism and the English Reformation to 1558* (Nieuwkoop, 1972).

[12] *Acts and Monuments of John Foxe*, 8:187–188.

[13] The mid-Tudor freewillers are not mentioned at all in Peter White, *Predestination, Policy and Polemic: Conflict and Consensus in the English Church from the Reformation to the Civil War* (Cambridge, 1992).

ian persecution, in which case the Marian authorities did orthodox Protestantism an unintended good turn. Or they survived as a radical religious underground, to resurface in due course under new names, Christopher Hill's subterranean river. In the meantime, the Elizabethan Family of Love looks like a kind of residual category, the fag end of the old Lollard traditions: safe houses, covert ways, a "*secretum vocabulum*" and a cunning mixture of internal and external integration.[14] But the exceptionality of the Familists and (apparently) their very small numbers and spotty distribution point to the third possibility: that radical dissent was domesticated and re-educated within Elizabethan Protestantism and indeed Puritanism, which should be seen as a force making for integration rather than sectarian disintegration: the Careless model.

We should think of this as an ongoing process, a kind of acted-out version of John Coolidge's "Pauline Renaissance in England": practical edification. The interface separating the learned preaching ministry and the unlearned, unpreaching but informed and even opinionated body of "professors" is an area all but inaccessible to the historian of Puritanism, but the one which he most needs to understand. We catch stray glimpses of it in certain exchanges between the unseparated Puritan ministry in Elizabethan East Anglia and the Brownist movement, and especially in Robert Harrison's "treatise of the church and the kingdome of Christ," written in about 1580 against the rector of Booton in Norfolk, Edward Fenton. Some might suppose, wrote Harrison, that Fenton was the spiritual father of the godly in his neighborhood, "manie in whome some good towardnes did appeare." But in truth the children were more forward than their father and could be said to have begotten themselves "by fruitfull edifying of gratious speach and godly conference, of whome you chalenge to yourself. the honor of parentage."[15] Harrison's attack on Fenton (and Harrison was himself a minister, or at least a Cam-

---

[14] Alastair Hamilton, *The Family of Love* (Cambridge, 1981); J. W. Martin, "Elizabethan Familists and English Separatists" and other relevant essays in *Religious Radicals;* and, most recently and authoritatively, Christopher Marsh, "The Family of Love in English Society, 1550–1630" (Cambridge Ph.D. thesis, 1992).

[15] *The Writings of Robert Harrison and Robert Browne,* ed. A. Peel and L.H. Carlson, *Elizabethan Nonconformist Texts,* no. 2 (London, 1953), 26–69, and especially 52–53. Further light is shed on the background to Harrison's "Treatise" in the exchanges between Harrison and a fellow-Separatist Thomas Wolsey with Edward Fenton by Dr. Michael Moody in an unpublished paper which he kindly allowed me to read: "Thomas Wolsey, A Forgotten Founding Father of English Separatism and a 'Judaiser.'" See also Dr. Moody's article "Trials and Travels of a Nonconformist Layman: The Spiritual Odyssey of Stephen Offwood 1564–ca.1635," *Church History* 51(1982): 157–171.

bridge graduate and a schoolmaster) could have had no motive if Fenton and others like him were not successfully restraining the majority of the godly professors of the Norfolk parishes from the drastic step of Brownist schism. There were of course currents, probably less strong, running in the opposite direction. Thomas Wolsey, the third and most obscure member of the original Brownist troika, spent thirty years in jail as an incorrigible Separatist, advanced beyond Separatism to judaizing extremes and, according to later testimony given by Stephen Offwood, "perverted many zealous professors, of which I knewe twentie." The twenty allegedly included none other than Henry Barrow, who would carry the torch forward into the next generation of Separatism.[16]

(2) My second point is the logical counterpart of the first and may be more briefly stated. If Thomas Wolsey perverted as many as twenty zealous professors to schismatic Separatism, the bishops, and especially bishops like Edmund Freke of Norwich (whose episcopate coincided with the Brownist episode) or John Aylmer of London, and above all Archbishop John Whitgift of Canterbury, perverted many more. Insofar as these authorities within the greater Church frustrated the enterprise of lesser church formation, which is how we may characterize the enterprise of Puritanism and the counter-enterprise of "Anglicanism," they encouraged rather than discouraged sectarian tendencies which the Puritans deplored. Admittedly most of the evidence to this effect reaches us from the protesting pens of the Puritans themselves[17] (they would say that, wouldn't they?), but if biased it is also plausible. Godly professors whose faith was simple and robust and who were not versed in the theory of *adiaphora* would be offended by the sight of their minister in a surplice, perhaps even physically repelled into illegal conventicles. A minister who was silenced for nonconformity might join them in their conventicles and could do little to prevent his people wandering off to find

---

[16]My source is Michael Moody's use of Stephen Offwood, *An advertisement to John Delecluse and Henry May the Elder* (Amsterdam?, 1633?).

[17]See, for example, John Field's complaint to Anthony Gilby that the bishops' persecution had driven some into sectarian extremes, "as full of errors as opinions." (Field to Gilby, Aug. 4, 1572, Cambridge University Library, MS. Mm.1.43. pp. 443–4.) Cf. the Cambridgeshire ministers who told the Privy Council in 1584 that if they were deprived, their flocks would be corrupted by the local Familists: and the authors of a "generall supplication" made to Parliament in 1586 who protested that the "faithful ministers" were so far from schism that they "chieflie more than anie of those which laie this blame upon them have laboured with manie, and by Gods blessing prevailed with a number, to the keeping in the unitie of (the Church) such as otherwise would have departed from it." (*The Seconde Parte of a Register,* ed. A. Peel [Cambridge, 1915], 1:229–30, 2:81.)

sustenance elsewhere. Consequently it became a paradoxical commonplace in the seventeenth century to say that the bishops were the greatest sect-makers.

(3) It will be helpful to spend rather longer on the third point, which concerns the sustained polemical and practical resistance offered by mainstream Puritanism to what the Westminster divine Edward Staunton called "England's incurable wound," Brownist Separatism. This resistance can be considered under three sub-headings, since it was mounted in published apologetics and polemics, in face-to-face confrontations and conferences with Separatists or those threatening to separate, and in the encouragement of covenanted religious meetings best described as semi-separatist and designed to satisfy the appetite for the intensity of godly fellowship and to make the invisible visible, short of actual schism from the wider, more diffuse parochial and national christian community. Anti-separatism, as a broad plank in the Puritan platform, could be considered under a fourth sub-heading which would take due account of the heavy emphasis placed in the Puritan biographical tradition on the relentless opposition offered by the old Puritan divines to the Separatists in the days before and leading into the Civil War. The biographical collections of Samuel Clarke have been formative of three centuries of Puritan and nonconformist historiography (and not least for William Haller), but they were originally intended for a Restoration readership. There were obvious polemical advantages post-1662 in drawing attention to the antiseparatist convictions of the "old English Puritans" before 1640.[18] So this evidence may appear somewhat suspect.

However, there is no reason to suspect Clarke and the preachers of the funeral sermons who provided him with his raw material of inventing a spurious tradition and pedigree. The titles of a large number of books published between the 1580s and the 1620s are no inventions: Stephen Bredwell's *Rasing of the foundations of Brownisme* (1588), Richard Alison's *A plaine confutation of a treatise of Brownisme* (1590), the early Henry Jacob (*A defence of the churches and ministery of Englande* [1599]), two books by Richard Bernard (*Christian advertisements and counsels of peace: also disswasions from Brownisme* [1609], *Plaine evidences: the Church of England is apostolicall* [1610]), William Bradshaw's *The unreasonablenesse of the separation* (1614), John Darrell's *Treatise of the Church written against those of the Separation, com-*

---

[18]Patrick Collinson, "'A Magazine of Religious Patterns': An Erasmian Topic Transposed in English Protestantism," in *Godly People: Essays in English Protestantism and Puritanism* (London, 1983), 499–525.

monly called Brownists (1617). It is significant that, with the exception of John Paget's *An arrow against the separation of the Brownists* (1618) (and Paget lived and ministered in frontier territory, in Amsterdam), these attacks were made not from the presbyterian right (as it were) of the Puritan movement but by writers, including some of Perry Miller's so-called non-separating congregationalists, who were themselves, or had been, close to Separatism. Stephen Brachlow demonstrates that this was a very fine, if critically important, dividing line.[19]

One of the most uncompromising denunciations of separation came from the pen of a certain Randall Bate, an extremist in all respects but this, who died in prison as "a glorious Martyr of Iesus Christ." In what were posthumously described as his "daily meditations," Bate asked whether it were fitting to be buried in churchyards? ("Answer: It seems no.") and "whether it be not needfull to pull downe churches built for the honour of Idolls," that is, the parish churches, consecrated as they were to saints? ("Answer: It seems it is."). Yet Bate, while professing to love them as persons, rebuked the Separatists for a blind zeal which was self-willed, even Satanic. "Men must not separate till the Lord separate for gods people must follow the Lord, not goe before him." "This kind of separation obscures the good providence of god towards the land, which gives some liberty in his service, but with some paines, cost and other crosses, which usually accompany the pure worship of god. This is no small sin, to bereave the Lord of so great mercy in spirituall blessings, as he hath shewed towards our land."[20] In Bate's perception, and it was a perception widely shared, what he called "totall separation" (and it would be accurate to call Bate a semi-separatist) was a separation not from evil but from the great deal of good which was still to be found in the parish assemblies, to separate indeed from the true children of God. Like Henoch Clapham, of whom more presently, Bate regarded this as an error of the right hand, which is to say the pardonable error of excessive zeal. But it was none the less an error, indeed a sin, which Clapham had diagnosed as the sin against the Holy Ghost.

A telling part of the anti-Separatist polemic was to insist that op-

---

[19] Stephen Brachlow, *The Communion of Saints: Radical Puritan and Separatist Ecclesiology 1570–1625* (Oxford, 1988). Among other antiseparatist works now lost, note the Gloucestershire minister John Sprint's *Considerations* and *Arguments* (both 1607), which were answered in Henry Ainsworth's *Counterpoyson* (Amsterdam, 1608), and a third book by Bernard, also answered by Ainsworth, *The separatists schisme.*

[20] *Certain observations of that reverend, religious and faithfull servant of God, and glorious martyr of Iesus Christ, M. Randal Bate* (Amsterdam, c.1625). See Stephen Foster, *Notes from the Caroline Underground: Alexander Leighton, the Puritan Triumvirate and the Laudian Reaction to Nonconformity* (Hamden, Conn., 1978), 23, 89.

ponents of Separatism separated not from the Church but from notorious sins within the Church, sins which ranged from intolerable
but discardable ceremonies to the moral contagion incurred in the
course of unnecessary "company keeping," so-called "good fellowship" which was nothing of the kind. "Though a corporall separation
cannot be had, yet in spirit thou must separate thyself." This was said
to be the harder, more painful way. "We suffer for separating within
the Church."[21]

In October 1605, one Margaret Browne of Slaughterford in Wiltshire found herself part of a group of weavers and their wives who
were presented to the archdeacon for Brownism (not inappropriate
in her case!) and "going from the Church of England." When
Browne appeared in court, she alleged that she was now "better per-
swaded and doth and will acknowledge her error."[22] It is not unlikely
that the pressure applied by the ecclesiastical tribunal itself, the danger in which Goodwife Browne stood, persuaded her to abandon her
Brownism. But we must not discount the effects of a number of set-
piece encounters between Separatists and Nonseparatists, some of
them perhaps casual and opportunistic, others involving elaborate
arrangements, in pulling back from the brink some of those for
whose benefit they were staged. As it happens a conference of this
kind had been held in Slaughterford a year before Browne and her
accomplices appeared in court, and was connected with the well-
publicized defection from Separatism of the minister Thomas White,
as well as the conversion of a more obscure participant who having
once thought the religion of the Separatists to be "trew and right"
subsequently discovered it to be "false and erronious."[23]

Looking back from New England in the 1640s, John Allin and
Thomas Shepard recalled the tense atmosphere prevailing in some
of these encounters: "Yea, how many serious consultations with one
another, and with the faithfull ministers, and other eminent servants
of Christ have been taken about this worke is not unknowne to
some."[24] Some of these occasions were thoroughly ventilated in the

[21]John Sprint, as quoted by Ainsworth in *Counterpoyson*, Sig. A.

[22]Wiltshire Record Office, MS. D 3/4/2. I owe this reference to Dr. Michael Moody.

[23]Wiltshire Record Office, MS. QS/GR/E 1604, fol. 148v, MS. D 3/4/3 1607 (calen-
dared in *HMC Report. Various Collections* i. 76). I owe these references to Dr. Moody and
Dr. Martin Ingram. See M.E. Reeves, "Protestant Nonconformity," in *The Victoria
County History of Wiltshire*, 3:95–101. Light is shed on conferences in Wiltshire in Thomas
White's *A discoverie of Brownisme* (London, 1605) and in Francis Johnson's *An inquirie and
answer of Thomas White his discoverie of Brownisme* (Amsterdam, 1606).

[24]J. Allin and T. Shepherd, *A defence of the answer* (London, 1648), 6. See also their *A
defence of the nine positions* (London, 1645).

controversial literature of Dissent, such as the meetings in the East Midlands which involved John Robinson, John Smyth, and Richard Bernard, John Cotton recalling how Robinson "resorted . . . to many judicious divines in *England* for the clearing of his scruples, which inclined him to separation."[25] Other episodes are known only from the records of the ecclesiastical courts (and doubtless most are not known at all). Such was a two- or three-day conference hastily convened in a vicarage in the village of Ash near Sandwich in East Kent, when two notorious separatists from twenty-five miles away in the Weald were heard to be passing through.[26] "The assertions of John Silliman of Aldwinkle in the county of Northampton delyvered to be examyned and answered"[27] were evidently connected with a similar occasion. These gatherings, essentially for the resolution of vexed and wounded consciences, were in a tradition which was well-established long before the reign of James I. It cost the troubled conscience long cross-country journeys, such as those undertaken by the many who came to Richard Greenham at Dry Drayton outside Cambridge with their problems. Soon Greenham moved to London, which may have made it easier for some. So it had been in Mary's reign when the husbandman Henry Orinel from Willingham in Cambridgeshire tramped to Colchester to confer with the future Familist missionary Christoph Vittels, was disturbed by what he heard, and promptly set off towards Oxford seeking further resolution from the protestant bishops in prison.[28] Orinel's problem was not utterly different from that confronting radical Jacobean Puritans: what to do about the legal demands of the established Church. There has been a persistent tendency to underestimate the capacity of such people to make up their own minds on difficult religious problems, suitably assisted, or, where this has not been underestimated, to assume a radical conclusion to every such quest. (But apparently Orinel did later succumb to Familism.)

Another strategy of Puritan ministers concerned to find a prophylactic for the bacillus of separation was the semi-separated, semi-

---

[25] John Cotton, *The way of the congregational churches cleared* (London, 1648), 7. See also John Robinson, *A Justification of separation* (Amsterdam, 1610), in *Works of John Robinson*, ed. R. Ashton (London, 1851), 2:8; and Richard Bernard's account of conferences with John Smyth in *Christian advertisements* (London, 1608), 30–37.

[26] Kent Archives Office, Cathedral Archives and Library Canterbury, MS. Z.4.4, fols. 67v-9r.

[27] Bodleian Library, Ashmolean MS. 826, fols. 223r-6v. I owe this reference to Dr. Michael Moody. John Silliman is named as a convicted Separatist in Public Record Office, S.P. 38/6, s.v. 25 May 1599.

[28] Samuel Clarke, *Lives of Thirty-Two English Divines* (London, 1677), 15; John Rylands University Library Manchester, Rylands English MS. 524; William Wilkinson, *A confuta-*

gathered group, the church within the church realized in private meetings of the godly minority. Such house meetings were so commonplace as to make it unlikely that they were always related to a perceived separatist threat. Often they may have been unselfconscious, naive. But it is hard to tell. When the Essex preacher and diarist Richard Rogers brought together the super-saints of his parish, "well-nigh twenty persons," to subscribe a special covenant among themselves, we do not know whether there was a separatist problem in Wethersfield to which this was a response.[29] Yet when Richard Bernard established a voluntary covenant among a hundred of his Worksop flock ("which covanant long since you have dissolved"), it was allowed by the Separatists Ainsworth and Robinson that he had done this "only in policy, to keep your people from Mr Smyth."[30] And John Cotton admitted to the same motivation when he wrote of the covenant which he had initiated among "some scores of godly persons in Boston Lincolnshire," claiming that while this was "defective," yet it was "more than the old Non-conformity."[31]

(4) The fourth of my related points is that the debate between Separatism and Antiseparatism was conducted at the greatest intensity within the intelligences and consciences of individuals living very close to Stephen Brachlow's critically drawn, thin frontier. One Puritan has left it on record how "this twenty years and more" he had "sought out the truth through a world of controversies." After reading the Scriptures, presumably the most relevant texts, "not so little as fifty or threescore times," he could still find no justification for separation.[32] (But why then did he keep on searching?) The teleology of Puritanism to Sects encourages us to look for a progressive radicalization in such tortured souls. But, as in this case, progress was often regress. So it was, after all, with the founding father of Separat-

tion of certain articles delivered unto the Familie of Love (London, 1579), preface. Further information on Orinel will be found in Margaret Spufford, *Contrasting Communities: English Villagers in the Sixteenth and Seventeenth Centuries* (Cambridge, 1974), 245–248, and in Christopher Marsh, "The Family of Love."

[29] Richard Rogers, *Seven treatises containing such directions as is gathered out of the holie scriptures* (London, 1603), fols. 477–95. The Wethersfield covenant was publicized in further editions of the *Seven treatises* in 1604, 1605, 1607, 1610, 1616, 1627 and 1630, suggesting that historians should also take account of what in crime reports is called "the copycat factor." See Collinson, *Godly People*, 545.

[30] Henry Ainsworth, *A brief answer to Mr Bernards book intituled the separatists schisme* (part of his *Counterpoyson*), pp. 155–6; *Works of Robinson*, 2:101. See also *The Works of John Smith*, ed. W.T. Whitney (Cambridge, 1915), 2:334.

[31] Cotton, *The way of the congregational churches cleared*, pt. I, p. 20.

[32] Michael E. Moody, "Puritan Versus Separatist: A New Letter," *Journal of the United Reformed Church History Society* 2(1981): 243–245.

ism who gave it its name, Robert Browne: although historians more or less loyal to his memory have sought to dismiss the significance of his betrayals, making them a mere personal aberration, the actions of a man with diminished responsibility.[33] But Browne's case was not unique, not even all that singular. Witness Thomas White's thoroughly embittered *Discoverie of Brownisme* (1605), containing the memorable discovery: "I thought . . . that they had been all saints, but I have found them all devils."[34] Witness too the picaresque account of his adventures in Morocco and elsewhere recorded by the relapsed Brownist Peter Fairlambe, *The recantation of a Brownist, or a reformed Puritan* (1606).

The Separatist who, like Fairlambe, finished up in the arms of the bishops was perhaps the ultimate and arch-separatist, since he had separated against Separatism itself. One of these stormy petrels was Henoch Clapham, a failed poet turned preacher and biblical paraphraser who reached Separatism and the ancient congregation of Amsterdam by a checkered course, "sometimes haled by this faction, sometimes pulled by that faction." But presently Clapham had persuaded himself that Puritans, Separatists, and Anabaptists were all "flat Donatists." He claims to have been converted to this view, like some precursor of John Henry Newman, by patristic study, presumably St. Augustine. But we may suspect that, like Thomas White of Wiltshire, what got up his nose was the petty tyranny of Francis Johnson's Amsterdam "parlour." He recorded the caustic comment that "tell the church" meant, in separatist circles, "tell Tom Tyncker, tell Dick Cullier, tell Jone the Oyster Wench." Soon Clapham discovered that the faith professed in the Church of England was so far true that to separate from it was equivalent to the sin against the Holy Ghost. This was awkward, since by now Clapham was ministering to a tiny splinter group of half a dozen who with him had broken away from Johnson's congregation. He asked his pathetic flock why they should turn aside "as if there were no prophet but my selfe?" And yet something had happened between Clapham and those half dozen which it was hard to repudiate utterly. "You and I have gone a warfare at our own charges." There was, after all, no other destination for this prodigal than the established Church, which presently gave him a living in Kent. There he wrote two remarkable books, *Errour on the right hand* and *Errour on the left hand*, a series of recognizable portraits

---

[33] See Peel and Carlson's remarks in *Writings of Robert Harrison and Robert Browne*, 4–5, glossing items in their bibliography, 545–556.

[34] White, *Discoverie of Brownisme*, 25.

of the turbulent spirits of the age, taken from the safe and central ground of "Mediocritie."[35] Even as a reformed Anglican, Clapham's Anglicanism was not the same substance as the Anglicanism of the elder brother who had never left his father's house. Yet when it came to the crunch, Clapham and we cannot tell how many others found that the official Church with its patronage, the objective reassurance of its sacraments, its stability, had more to offer than Amsterdam.[36]

So it was that others drew back from the verge, like the Nottinghamshire minister Richard Bernard who confessed that he had been "tossed by the present tempest" and, according to John Smyth, "did acknowledge this truth wee now professe divers tymes and was upon the point of Separation with some of his people with him." Instead, Bernard was persuaded by the great and the good of the Jacobean Church to take on a new pastoral role of immense usefulness and great personal profit at Batcombe in Somerset.[37] Others strove to have it both ways. Henry Jacob wrote in 1611: "for my part I never was nor am separate from all publike communion with the congregations of England."[38] Much depended upon what was meant by "all." Such personal life histories made the religious history of early Stuart England. There are no such things as religious and social "forces": only individuals, trying to be both consistent and safe in a set of inconsistent and unsafe circumstances.

(5) The fifth and final point concerns "conventicles." Private religious meetings of the kind: formalized by Cotton in Boston and Bernard in Worksop and countless more informal meetings were called conventicles when they attracted the unfriendly attention of the authorities. Conventicle is a spectral term embracing at one extreme subversive, criminal conspiracies having nothing to do with religion,

---

[35]This passage draws freely upon the following works of Clapham: *A briefe of the Bible drawne first into English poesy* (Edinburgh, 1596), *Bibliotheca theologica* (Amsterdam, 1597), *The syn against the Holy Ghost* (Amsterdam, 1598), *The discription of a true visible christian* (Amsterdam?, 1599), *Antidoton: Or a soveraigne remedie against schisme and heresie* (London, 1600), *A manuell of the Bibles doctrine* (London, 1606), *Errour on the right hand* (London, 1608), *Errour on the left hand* (London, 1608).

[36]For an account of what may have motivated rank-and-file Separatists in retreating from their schism to the established churches of England or the Netherlands, among them the desire to secure regular baptism for their children, see A.C. Carter, *The English Reformed Church in Amsterdam in the Seventeenth Century* (Amsterdam, 1964), pt. I, chap. 4, and A. C. Carter, "John Robinson and the Dutch Reformed Church," in *Studies in Church History*, no. 3, ed. G.J. Cuming (Leiden, 1966), 232–241.

[37]John Smyth, *Paralleles, censures, observations* (Middelburg, 1609), in *Works*, 2:331 seq.; Richard Bernard, *Plaine evidences* (London, 1610); Kenneth Fincham, *Prelate as Pastor: The Episcopate of James I* (Oxford, 1990), 193–194, 300–301.

[38]Henry Jacob, *A declaration and plainer opening of certain points* (Middelburg, 1612), 5–6.

and at the other innocent religious gatherings without any subversive, criminal intent. Somewhere in the middle of this spectrum we find the religious conventicle which had, or was supposed to have, a subversive intent. That intent was to conduct religious proceedings contrary to the Act of Uniformity and, subsequently, to the Conventicle Acts. In the words of the Canons of 1604 they were secret meetings tending "to the impeaching or depraving of the doctrine of the Church of England or of the Book of Common Prayer." Bishop Bancroft's 1601 visitation of the diocese of London asked: "Whether any within your parish do resort into barns, fields, woods, private houses, or to any extraordinary expositions of Scripture, or conferences together: or that be drawers or persuaders of others to any such schismatical conventicles?"[39]

In a published article on "The English Conventicle"[40]—I have made the following observations. Many, and for all that we know to the contrary most, frequenters of so-called "conventicles," as practiced within the early seventeenth-century Puritan mainstream, denied, or would have denied, that their meetings were conventicles in any criminal sense, which is as much as to say that they were not considered by those who frequented them to be separatist in intent. The standard "conventicle" appears to have been held primarily for the purpose of sermon repetition, which consisted of confirmation in the ears and memories of the hearers of doctrine originally delivered in public sermons. A secondary activity may have been prayer. The Act of Uniformity of 1559 made illegal any form or act of public prayer conducted outside the liturgical forms and rubrics of the Prayer Book. It failed to define what was public prayer and presumably had no intention to inhibit private prayer. Puritans denied that their meetings for private prayer were public. In their perception, private religious duties were compatible with the public duties which the law required. In the words of the lawyer Roger Quatermayne: "I did alwayes thinke that publick duties did not make voyd private, but that both might stand with a Christian." An earlier writer distinguished between "godly societies and assemblies of the righteous" and the "ordinary assemblies and meetings together at the house of prayer."

Much of course depended upon the public-private distinction,

[39] *Elizabethan Episcopal Administration: An Essay in Sociology and Politics,* ed. W.P.M. Kennedy, iii. *Alcuin Club Collections,* no. 27 (Oxford, 1925), 350.
[40] Patrick Collinson, "The English Conventicle," in *Voluntary Religion, Studies in Church History,* no. 23. ed. W.J. Sheils and D. Wood (Oxford, 1986), 111–208.

upon who was making it and who was entitled to make it. The unrestricted, unlicensed voluntarism of private religious meetings might well have been thought incompatible with the kind of church-state that seventeenth-century England, as a civil society, aspired to be. Nevertheless the law, which was uninformative (before the eighteenth century) on the general subject of lawful and unlawful assembly, failed to define as unambiguously illegal the kind of private religious meeting often called a conventicle; although the 1664 Conventicle Act would later somewhat clarify the situation in terms of a certain number attending "over and above those of the same household," a principle which served to turn an ostensibly legitimate private activity into an actually illegal public activity. My article further argued that however honest and limited their intentions, however far they may have been from claiming the status of separated and gathered churches for their conventicles, some conventiclers did tend, especially in particular historical circumstances, to grow into the gathered churches which, existentially and in some sense, they already were. The long-lived religious society known as Broadmead Baptist Church Bristol, which grew from conventicle to gathered church in the course of the 1640s, is a case in point. But it was a protracted growth, the details of which were dependent at every point on arbitrary and unusual circumstances, nothing less than a revolution. The origins of many such churches, Congregational or Baptist, were more circumstantial than wholly intentional or predictable. Undue attention has been devoted to those conventicles which did so develop, to what we may call the Broadmead model, especially and for understandable reasons in histories written within and for these denominational traditions. The conventicle which never did become a gathered congregation, which I believe was the more typical conventicle, was necessarily ephemeral, leaving behind no formal record and attracting no historians.

This argument can be set in a model representation of the character and structures of English Christianity in the early seventeenth century, as accomodating and reconciling elements of compulsion and voluntarism, inclusion and exclusion, public obligations and private imperatives. Spontaneous expressions of these imperatives were integrated within the more permanent and legally prescribed structures of the Church with varying degrees of majority-minority friction and tension. As Peter Lake has shown,[41] two very different eccle-

---

[41] Peter Lake, "Presbyterianism, the Idea of a National Church and the Argument from Divine Right," in *Protestantism and the National Church in Sixteenth-Century England,* ed. P. Lake and M. Dowling (London, 1987), 193–224.

siologies coexisted uneasily in post-Reformation England. In principle they may appear incompatible. But in practice they were not and there were good and pragmatic reasons why the conflict was not tidily resolved, either before 1640 or after 1660–1662. This coexistence of church-type and sect-type Christianity (to use the Troeltschian categories) was of the very essence of Elizabethan and Jacobean Puritanism but it was a longer-lasting and more universal phenomenon than Puritanism. There was something of this hybrid situation, not necessarily fraught with friction, in the interwoven history of parishes (which Christopher Hill calls "compulsory communities") and voluntary religious fraternities, before the Reformation. And there was more of it in the history of successive versions of radical religious dissent, from the late fourteenth to the late seventeenth centuries. Recent studies have shown, especially the studies of rural dissent undertaken by Dr. Margaret Spufford and her pupils, that these "sects," Lollards, Familists, Baptists, and Quakers, were not really sects at all in the full-blooded Troeltschian sense. In many unsuspected respects they were integrated in the wider local community, in which their leading male members, often men of some substance, assumed the public and semi-public functions appropriate to their economic and social standing.[42]

Dr. Christopher Marsh has shown that the secret of the success of the Family of Love in certain villages of south Cambridgeshire, a success which seems to have consisted not only of surviving as a religious minority group in an ostensibly intolerant majority society but of conspicuous material prosperity, was a shrewd and advantageous strategy of both internal and external integration. The business they did with each other, the spiritual and material benefit cultivated by introversion and endogamy, by no means excluded "normal" relationships with other villagers and parishioners, the taking on of functions and responsibilities proper to their status. Among the Familists, this strategy seems to have been finely tuned to ensure not sectarian growth, for that may never have been their ambition, but the perpet-

---

[42]D.J. Plumb, "John Foxe and the Later Lollards of the Thames Valley" (Cambridge Ph.D. thesis, 1987), and his "The Social and Economic Spread of Rural Lollardy: A Reappraisal," in *Voluntary Religion,* 111–129; Marsh, "Family of Love"; William Stevenson, "The Economic and Social Status of Protestant Sectarians in Huntingdonshire, Cambridgeshire and Bedfordshire (1650–1725)," (Cambridge Ph.D. thesis, 1990). See also some of the contributions to *Religious Dissent in East Anglia,* ed. E.S. Leedham-Green, Cambridge Antiquarian Society (Cambridge, 1991). A forthcoming collection of essays, edited by Margaret Spufford, and mostly the work of her erstwhile pupils, is likely to revolutionize along these lines our understanding of sixteenth- and seventeenth-century rural dissent.

uation of a small religious elite which eventually, and unlike the Quakers, failed to transmit itself into the third and fourth generations and beyond. Among the Puritans, other strategies, in some ways more exclusive and socially rejectionist than those of the Family of Love, were destined to ensure that a religious minority could ensure the advantages and take on the responsibilities, and the power, of a moral majority. In the event, that strategy too failed, at least in Old England, and we are inclined to add, "of course." But who is to say that that would have been the outcome if seventeenth-century history had taken another course?

Puritanism and the Evolution of Sects; Sects and the Evolution of Puritanism; Separatism, Antiseparatism and Semi-Separatism; Integration and Disintegration. All these tendencies had some parts of the historical process going for them. But none was invested with inevitability or irreversibility.

Roots and Branches:

From Principled Nonconformity

to the Emergence of Religious Parties

Carol G. Schneider

OVER THE PAST two decades, scholarship on the pre-civil war period in England has disclosed the extent to which the church policies advanced by Charles I and Archbishop Laud were perceived by contemporaries as both radical and increasingly subversive of the Protestant Reformation in England. This scholarship has turned on its head several generations of earlier studies which viewed Puritanism—perceived as a way of thinking and behaving in the church—as itself a potentially revolutionary solvent that helped prepare its adherents to challenge regnant authorities in both church and state. In the newer analyses of dissent in the pre-revolutionary church it is Laud's Arminians who have emerged as the revolutionary agents, prodding into reaction both Puritan clergy and laymen who, under James I, had essentially made their peace with the institutional arrangements of the English church. While those who protested Laudian policies were labeled "Puritans," most of the protesters were in fact resisting a set of innovations that seemed to challenge both the theology and the established ritual practices of the English church.[1]

This way of viewing developments in the Laudian church helps answer the question how a church reform momentum was galvanized in the 1630s and especially at the outset of the Long Parliament. It is

[1] Nicholas Tyacke, *Anti-Calvinists: The Rise of English Arminianism c. 1590–1640* (2nd ed., Oxford, 1990).

especially useful in helping explain how so many moderates turned into dissenters. But describing Laudian bishops and policies as radical and "Puritans" as reactive tends to obscure the constructive aspects of the Puritan reform agenda—the issues that those seeking change (rather than an end to change) considered to be at stake as they began, in 1640 and after, to press for reform of the church. This interpretation of religious politics, in short, helps us to understand Puritan protests but tends to obscure the substance of Puritan commitments.

Analysis of clerical tracts from the late 1630s and early 1640s shows that one effect of Laudian policies was to inspire a renewed activism among godly divines who had long since accommodated to the imperfect reformation of the English church and who would probably have remained compliant were it not for the Laudian "innovations." Some of these godly divines, by their own confession, had not thought much about church order and governance until Laud challenged them to take up the subject. Other divines prodded by Laudian policies into a heightened disaffection had in fact believed throughout their ministries that "God had left a rule in his word for discipline" that was not followed in England. At the same time, however, most of those who held the latter view also believed that the scripturally established discipline pertained "not to the being, but well-being of a Church." Therefore, as one summary of their views explains, they "unchurched not those where it was otherwayes. Perfection in Churches . . . [they] thought a thing to be hoped for rather than expected. . . ."[2]

The "disorders" introduced by Laudian edicts forced both groups of divines to think again. Those who believed that Scripture provided standards for governance and discipline that were important but not absolutely essential were forced by what they saw as dangerously escalating corruptions to revisit questions of order, government, and discipline they had previously considered it both prudent and licit to set aside. Those who had previously considered issues of governance and discipline both elective and of secondary importance turned with new interest and attentiveness to those who had long held that Scripture set forth non-episcopal forms of governance and discipline.

[2]This topic is explored in detail in Carol Geary Schneider, "Godly Order in a Church Half-Reformed: The Disciplinarian Legacy, 1570–1641" (Ph.D. diss., Harvard University, 1986), 166–201 and passim. The quotations are from John Geree, "The Character of an Old English Puritane, Or Non-Conformist," ed. Maurice Hussey, *The Church Quarterly Review* 148(1949): 67–71 (Reprint of 1646 text.).

This escalation of interest in issues of church order and discipline did not mean that a latent tradition of thinking about church order was simply revived and more broadly disseminated. What ensued was rather a period of ferment and analysis in which godly divines reworked older themes into new configurations of thought and commitment.

In this essay, I explore some of the central issues at stake in discussions of church order and discipline as they can be discerned from debates among leading Puritan clerics in the 1630s and especially after 1637. In doing so, I hope to illuminate the terms of debate about church order as Puritan ministers reformulated them in the late 1630s and to describe the nexus of concerns that seemed most important to dissenting divines when they addressed church order and church authority. The essay explores in particular the church views of those who had been resolute but non-separating dissenters from episcopal order in the seventeenth-century English church. But it places their views in a larger, rapidly evolving context of controversies and emergent commitments.

The essay centers on the controversial tracts of John Ball of Whitmore, in Staffordshire. Ball, who died in 1640, was a nonconforming lecturer, theologian, and controversialist who, at the outset of his ministry, took ordination in Ireland rather than England in order to avoid subscription. Resolute in nonconformity throughout his career, he was deprived, imprisoned, released, and later confined again. His political travails notwithstanding, however, he spent much of his career working to define that middle ground that kept Puritan disaffection with the Church of England from crossing over into complete separation. In so doing, he wrote extensively about the beliefs and ideological commitments of divines who, like Ball himself, looked back to Cartwright and his colleagues *both* in their critique of the English church *and* in their insistence that, for all its flaws, the Church of England remained a true church from which the godly must not withdraw.[3]

Ball's work is significant for an understanding of Puritan clerical perception and aspiration in the Laudian period, not because he was a particularly original or creative theorist but precisely because he was not. A learned and methodical scholar, he viewed himself as

---

[3]There is a "Life" of Ball in Samuel Clark, *A general Martyrologie* (London, 1651), 442–451. Ball is also noticed in the *Dictionary of National Biography*. For a more extensive discussion of his work, see Schneider, "Godly Order," 202–246, 304–335, and 361–380.

working in a tradition of precept and practice, and he set out to establish systematically the principal tenets of that tradition.

Equally important, Ball did not work alone. Active, according to contemporary sources, in a broad network of clerical fasts, religious exercises, and "conferences," he wrote the three controversial pieces that present his views on church order at the behest of other nonconforming divines, several of whom can be identified. At least one of his controversial works explicitly received "persuall and joynt approbation" from his colleagues; a subsequent controversial polemic was written after he was "importuned to take further paines in that Contraversye [with New England churches]. . . ." When his works were published posthumously in the 1640s, they carried endorsements both from divines who were leaders in the Presbyterian efforts of that period and from lesser-known colleagues, who had been close to Ball in his ministry.[4]

What we have in Ball's controversial tracts, then, is an informative window into the closed rooms in which dissenting clerics discussed their views on the church as the Apostles had modeled it, on the Church of England as it then stood and on particular radical Puritan church reform initiatives which Ball wrote to critique.

The three controversial tracts discussed below were composed in the 1630s but published in the 1640s, after Ball's death. Two of the tracts, which circulated in manuscript in the 1630s, were composed before there was any significant hope that the Laudian regime in the Church of England would be challenged. Written in this period of apparent impasse, Ball's pages presuppose a continuation of the corruptions which he deplored and thus illuminate a vein of Puritan thinking which was simultaneously dissenting and yet resigned to stalemate. At the same time, since Ball wrote in part about the newly established churches in New England, his works make it clear just what kinds of reforms he—and the colleagues who charged him to write for them—welcomed and which reforms they felt called to repudiate.

Categorizing Ball with one or another of the available clerical la-

---

[4] Simeon Ashe and William Rathband, "Epistle to the Reader," published with *A Letter of Many Ministers in Old England Requesting the judgment of their Reverend Brethren in New England concerning Nine Positions. Written Anno Dom. 1637* (London, 1643). The Epistle further explains that this tract, which contains an exchange between Ball and New England divines, was made public at the request of the London Puritan ministers; Langley et al., *Preface to John Ball, An Answer to Two Treatises of Mr. John Can* (London, 1642). In this preface, Ball's colleagues provide both information on and justification for Ball's involvement in Nonconformist disputes.

bels proves difficult. After his death, on the basis of his writings in the 1630s, he would be termed "the Presbyterians' Champion." Yet if he was remembered as a proponent of Presbyterian views, he was also considered a mediator. In 1645, several leading Presbyterian divines, including Edmund Calamy, mourned in their preface to the posthumous edition of Ball's *Treatise of the Covenant of Grace* that, had Ball only lived, he would have been the man to find a way to resolve the controversies then raging between Presbyterians and Congregational Independents over the form of church government. On the other hand, as we will see below, Ball shared so many premises in common with Congregational Independents' views on church government that a 1640s pamphleteer writing in Delft became confused and termed Ball one of the Independents' own "tribe."[5]

The conflicting categories assigned to Ball in the 1640s underline a point made by many scholars: that it is more confusing than informative to attempt to delineate "presbyterian" and "congregational" clerical ideologies through most of the early Stuart period. Such positions do emerge in the late 1630s, however, and as we will see below, Ball's writings help us understand the circumstances of their assertion.

For understanding Ball's work and significance, however, it is more useful to adopt the nomenclature that Ball used to categorize himself. He called himself a "Nonconformist" and when he wrote his controversial manuscripts, he did so as an exponent and interpreter of a by then well-elaborated tradition of Nonconformist ideology in the Church of England.[6]

Ascribing the term "Nonconformist" to a tradition of thought about church order may seem problematic. Conventionally, scholars use the term nonconformity to cover Puritan behaviors rather than ideas: the refusal to use disputed church ceremonies, to wear vest-

[5] Clarke, *General Martyrologie*, 449; Reynolds et al., Preface to John Ball, *A Treatise or the Covenant of Grace* (London, 1645). The other signers of this laudatory preface were Thomas Hill, Daniel Cawdrey, and Anthony Burgess. Interestingly, these Westminster Assembly divines who thought Ball would have been of assistance in mediating their disputes represented all shades of Westminster 1640s Presbyterianism. Daniel Cawdry was a longstanding Nonconformist who vigorously opposed Independency; Calamy both supported a Presbyterian national system and fostered reconciliation with Congregational Independents; Hill preached two sermons in the summer and fall of 1644 that seemed to endorse a measure of toleration for Congregational Independent churches within a broadly defined Presbyterian church. The characterization of Ball as an Independent is from [Alexander Forbes], *An Anatomy of Independency. Or, a Briefe Commentary . . . upon the Apollogetical Narration* (London, 1644), 39.

[6] See especially *An Answer to Mr. Can,* where Ball's entire argument is couched as a representation of what Nonconformists "hold."

ments, to subscribe in conformity with the Canons of 1604 and the like. Even as restricted to such practices (or non-practices) "Nonconformist" is, like most of the rubrics associated with religious and secular Puritanism, a notoriously slippery category. Puritans differed among themselves on the significance of the disliked requirements that comprised "conformity," some seeing them as absolutely unlawful, some as merely inconvenient and some as wholly insignificant. Moreover, since nonconforming behaviors were not necessarily prosecuted, it is not always possible to discern whether particular Puritans were conformists or not. It is also very clear from contemporary testimonies that many of the clerics most active on behalf of godly piety prior to 1640 were conformists; as Richard Baxter observed, most of those who served in the Westminster Assembly fell into this category. It is also clear that there were extremely close ties of family and friendship between conforming and nonconforming divines.[7]

In the 1650s, Nathaniel Fiennes described the relations between conforming and nonconforming divines as he had perceived them:

> heretofore the Devil . . . had two other distinguishing names, Conformist, and Nonconformist, when Surplice and other Ceremonies were injoyned by the Prelates, wherein all men had not attained to the same measure of light, but were of different judgments, so that their difference . . . could be discerned . . . very easily, . . . yet it might be truly said of many reverend and godly men amongt them . . . both Ministers and Christian brethren, that notwithstanding such a difference, they prayed together, fasted together . . . and took so little notice of these differences of opinion . . . as that notwithstanding they were of one heart and one soul. . . . This I know myself to be a truth . . . having lived long with them, and . . . known their conversations.[8]

As Fiennes's text makes clear, the differences between divines on these issues were both real and significant but did not constitute a set of boundaries that divided groups of Puritan clerics from one another.

All these difficulties notwithstanding, it is still useful to accept as a framework for analysis Ball's own orienting assumption that there was a well-established tradition of Nonconformist writing and thinking about church order and church discipline. Clearly, many non-

---

[7] See Schneider, "Godly Order," 148 and 166–179, for a picture of the evolving relationships between conforming and nonconforming divines.

[8] [Nathaniel Fiennes], *Vindiciae Veritatis, Or an Answer to a Discourse intituled, Truth it's Manifest* (London, 1654). The authorship of this tract is discussed by Valerie Pearl, "The 'Royal Independents' in the English Civil War," *Transactions of the Royal Historical Society,* ser. 5, 18(1968): 93.

conformist divines may not have subscribed to this tradition. But the category is useful because it is in tracts written by Nonconformists, and as far as I have been able to tell, only in tracts written by Nonconformists, that we can find non-separating Puritans continuing to discuss in any detail, through the early Stuart period, their views on the nature of the church, church order, governance and discipline.

This is not to say that only Nonconformists held the views described in these tracts. (Indeed, as the Fiennes encomium quoted above implies, conforming divines had ample opportunity in their godly gatherings to encounter—and perhaps accept—the ecclesiological hermeneutics of their dissenting colleagues.) But it is extremely difficult to extract more than a few hints on issues of order, discipline, and governance from most Puritan writings prior to 1640. Nor did the lifting of censorship bring to press writings by conforming Puritans that show they had been writing on church order, discipline, and governance all along.

Leading Nonconformist divines, by contrast, felt called throughout the early Stuart period to assert and clarify their views on church order and church corruption. Their works therefore offer a comparatively rich vein of information about dissident thought concerning the church as it persisted, admittedly devoid of all political thrust, from the hey-day of the classical movement down to the new era which dawned for Puritans in 1640. Collectively, Nonconformists produced a substantial tract literature in which they enumerated their views, not simply on the relatively specific subjects of ceremonies and worship, but on the more encompassing issues of church order, government, discipline and the election of ministers as well.

This literature, which I have analyzed elsewhere,[9] reveals that many prominent Nonconformists persisted in and elaborated the disciplinarian tradition advanced by Cartwright and his fellows in the 1580s. They elaborated this tradition, not to press for reform, which they had largely ceased to expect, but rather to hold the line against those *misinterpretations* of their views that tended to result in separatism. For example, the Separatist leader John Canne wrote, in the early 1630s, to show that separation was the necessary consequence of what he termed the Nonconformists' own "principles." In that document, he said that almost all of those who moved to separatism had first been persuaded by the Nonconformists' own teachings.[10]

[9]Schneider, "Godly Order," 115–334.
[10]John Canne, *A Neccesitie of Separation from the Church of England, Proved by the Nonconformists Principles. Specially opposed unto Dr. Ames, his Fresh Suit against humane ceremonies, in*

Ball's first controversial tract was written to rebut John Canne's clever, if intellectually unscrupulous, attempt to demonstrate *A Necessity of Separation . . . Proved by the Nonconformists' Principles,* printed at Amsterdam, in 1634. Ball set out with some urgency to show that the Separatist had fundamentally misrepresented what the Nonconformists taught. He thus worked within Canne's promise that there was a discernible tradition of Nonconformist thinking on the church. What he contested was Canne's interpretation of that tradition, as well as his conclusion that the "Nonconformists' principles" left no alternative but separation.

To refute Canne, Ball set forth methodically what he termed the Nonconformists' views in order to show both what they actually believed concerning scriptural teachings on church order and discipline *and* that the Church of England, for all its flaws, met scriptural standards as Nonconformists understood them. Ball's self-consciousness about writing to correctly represent the views of a dissenting group within the Church of England is one of the reasons his writings warrant attention.

Ball's response to Canne remained in manuscript form until 1642, when it was printed posthumously as *An Answer to Two Treatises of Mr. John Can.* Ball's next discussion of church issues appeared in his commentary on New England's reply to "Nine Questions" which Ball and twelve other Nonconformists sent to New England divines in 1636. Ball's commentary, which secured the "joynt approval" of other nonconforming divines was printed together with the original "Nine Questions" and New England's reply, in 1643 as *A Letter of Many Ministers in Old England . . . Together With [the] . . . Answer thereunto. . . . and the Reply . . . unto the Said Answer.* The tract, which offered a fraternal but critical perspective on New England practices and judgment, was printed again in 1644 with the title *A Tryall of the New-Church Way in New-England and in Old.*

Ball's third and last statement on ecclesiastical matters appeared in a much fuller treatise on New England which he wrote to satisfy "both . . . Ministers and others from divers parts of this Kingdome"; this, his last work, was published in 1640, shortly before his death, under the title *A Friendly Triall of the Grounds tending to Separation.*

Each of these tracts reflects Ball's role as a Nonconformist spokesman. But the second tract, *A Letter of Many Ministers/Tryall of the*

---

the point of Separation only. Also Dr. Laiton, Mr. Dayrel, and Mr. Bradshaw, are here answered, wherein they have written against us, ed. Charles Stovel, Hanserd Knollys Society (London, 1849 [orig. ed., 1634]).

New-Church way, holds special interest for historians because we can identify several of the Nonconformist colleagues on whose behalf Ball wrote. This in turn helps us situate all three of Ball's controversial tracts in particular—and eventually influential—clerical networks.

The "Nine Questions" sent by letter to New England divines is still extant; it was signed by Ball and twelve other divines.[11] Prominent among them was the Puritan patriarch, John Dod, then living under the protection of Sir Richard Knightley at Fawsley, Northamptonshire. Dod was a figure whose dissident lineage stretched back to the Puritan organizing that preceded the Hampton Court discussions; he was closely associated with Thomas Cartwright and had served, together with Arthur Hildersam (who died in 1632) as co-executor of Cartwright's will and guardian of his papers. Dod, like Ball himself, was also close to John Cotton, one of the recipients of the "Nine Questions," and both held Cotton in the highest respect and affection.[12] Dod is reported to have helped Cotton overcome his original scruples about fleeing from persecution through the emigration to New England.[13] Two more signatories were closely linked to Dod: one was his son Timothy and another, Robert Cleaver, was co-author with Dod of a larger number of pastoral tracts.

A fifth signer was Julius Herring, a Nonconformist whose ministry at Shrewsbury had been repeatedly interrupted by suspensions and who had long been an intimate of both Ball and the deceased Hildersam. Herring would shortly leave England to take John Paget's congregation in Amsterdam and his parting from Ball at that time was

---

[11]John Ball, John Dod and others to John Cotton, Boston Public Library, Cotton Papers, Pt. 2, no. 9. The date, summer, 1637, is penciled in the MSS, but John Allin and Thomas Shepard give the date of 1636 in their tract *A Defence of the Answer made unto the Nine Questions* (London, 1648), 32. (Their preface is dated 1645). The original set of exchanges between Ball's group and New England was published by Simeon Ashe and William Rathband as *A Letter of Many Ministers in Old England Requesting the iudgment of their Reverend Brethren in New England concerning Nine Positions. Written Anno Dom. 1637: Together with their Answer thereunto returned. Anno 1639. And the Reply Made unto the Said Answer. . . Anno 1640* (London, 1643). References to this document in the text below are taken from a 1644 edition, published with the title *A Tryall of the New-Church Way In New England and in Old.*

[12]*D.N.B.*; Cotton Mather, *Magnalia Christi Americana,* ed. Thomas Robbins et al. (Hartford, Conn., 1853–1855), 1:263. Ball's friendship with Cotton is mentioned in Langley et al., Preface to Ball, *An Answer to Mr. Can.*

[13]William Haller, *The Rise of Puritanism* (New York, 1957 [orig. pub. 1938]), 61–62; Mather, *Magnalia,* Pt. I, 263. Allin and Shepard reported, however, in *Defence of the Answer,* 3–4, that many Nonconformists had urged the dissenting ministers to hold their peace and not preach against the corruptions that had made them want to leave England.

so affecting that the episode found its way into Herring's 1651 biography.[14]

A sixth signer, Simeon Ashe, had been launched on what would eventually be a distinguished career by both Arthur Hildersam and Thomas Hooker, the latter by that time in New England. In the 1640s, Ashe would emerge as a highly respected Presbyterian leader, part of the inner circle of London ministers, and a member of the Westminster Assembly. Ashe was also personally close to John Ball and following Ball's death in 1640 served as co-editor of Ball's posthumous publications. During his London years, Ashe became a close friend of Edmund Calamy, who was a leader among London Presbyterian divines after 1640.[15] Ashe, as Calamy's friend and Ball's co-editor, presumably solicited (and influenced?) the laudatory preface to Ball's *Treatise of Grace* in which Calamy and other Presbyterians hailed Ball as a lost authority on church governance who could have served as a mediator over the mid-1640s debates between Presbyterians and Congregational Independents.

Thomas Langley, of Middlewich, Cheshire, was another close colleague of Ball's; he reportedly accompanied Ball on a journey to London at the time of the Short Parliament to see what relief might be obtained for persecuted ministers, and he was one of the co-editors of Ball's *An Answer to Mr. Can*.[16] Two other signers of the "Nine Questions," William Bourne and Thomas Paget, were also well-known Nonconformists; both were reported to have been involved with other clerics in a "kind of consultative *classis*" in Lancashire.[17] Another reported participant in this same Lancashire "classis," William Rathband, did not sign the letter but later joined with Simeon Ashe in publishing Ball's controversial tracts. Rathband, like Ashe, would eventually sit in the Westminster Assembly.

William Huitt eventually emigrated to New England, taking a church at Windsor, Connecticut.[18] I have not discovered anything about the final three signers, Ralph Shearrard, John Armstone, and

[14] Clarke, *A General Martyrologie*, 469.

[15] Ibid., 385; Samuel Palmer, ed., *The Nonconformists memorial. . . . Originally written by Edmund Calamy, Abridged, corrected, and methodized*, 2nd ed., 3 vols. (London, 1802–1803), 1:94–95. However, *Calamy Revised*, ed. A.G. Matthews (Oxford, 1934), does not place Ashe in Staffordshire until 1627, when he became vicar of Rugelcy, and thus geographically close to Ball, Hildersam, and Herring. He had been ordained in 1619.

[16] Clarke, *A General Martyrologie*, 449–450.

[17] R. C. Richardson, *Puritanism in North-west England* (Manchester, 1972), 24–25, 60; Robert Halley, *Lancashire: Its Puritanism and Nonconformity*, 2 vols. (Manchester, 1869), 1:238–242.

[18] David D. Hall, *The Faithful Shepherd: A History of the New England Ministry in the Seventeenth Century* (Chapel Hill, N. C., 1972), 98.

Nathan Cottons. However, since Ball's rejoinder to New England purports to speak explicitly for Nonconformists, we can safely assume that these three, like the rest, were known refusers of surplice and ceremonies. This overview of Ball's connections helps situate his own self-representation in the tracts discussed below: he wrote as a Nonconformist; he wrote to assert the Nonconformists' view of specific issues; and when he wrote, he did so as the acknowledged colleague and appointed spokesman for a larger and well-connected group.

As we have seen, several of the colleagues who authorized Ball's critique of New England either were participants in earlier disciplinarian reform efforts, became emigrants to reformed churches in the Netherlands, and/or were close to the divines shaping new churches in New England. One eventually went to New England himself. Their biographies thus confirm what Ball's texts also show: that the ideological commitments of this group entailed belief in a reformed church order that stood over and against the established patterns of the Church of England.

This does not mean, it must be stressed, that the Nonconformists whom Ball represented felt inexorably compelled to work to establish this church order in England. Since Cartwright's day, Nonconformists had acknowledged that it was the magistrate's responsibility to reform the church and that, as long as the Church of England remained valid to its ministry of Word and Sacraments, they must resign themselves to its flaws. Even as Nonconformists refused participation in corrupt ceremonies, therefore, they did not view what was *missing,* namely clerical governance and disciplinary structures, as sufficient grounds either for separating or for challenging monarchical authority to determine the forms of government in the English church. While they certainly worked behind the scenes to turn "lesser magistrates" into patrons of godliness, they accepted rather than challenged the magistrate's right to authorize the forms and structures of church governance.

Thus Ball's texts (like earlier Nonconformist writings against Separatists), asserted views on church order and governance, not as a pattern for reform in England, but as a standard against which to test the writings and actions of reformers whose situation—whether in the Netherlands or in New England—made church reformation a licit option.[19]

What then, do Ball's writings show about Nonconformists' views,

---

[19] See Schneider, "Godly Order," 247–335 for a much fuller discussion of this point.

in the late 1630s, on church order and church discipline? The first and most striking aspect of all three tracts by "the Presbyterians' Champion" is that they share much common ground with what are usually taken to be congregational views on church order and governance. Like New England divines, Ball drew heavily on the writings of William Ames, the exiled Nonconformist theologian who retained close ties while in the Netherlands with Nonconformists in England. New England divines readily cited William Ames as one of their own authorities on scriptural precepts for church order[20] and Ball's tracts both cite and reflect the same source.

Ball agreed, for example, with Ames as well as with New England divines that a society of faithful people joined under lawful pastors, teachers and elders was a "true and compleat constituted Church of Jesus Christ," fully empowered to exercise government.[21] Like Cartwright before him, Ball was content that such a church should administer its own discipline, including excommunication, and might ordain its own ministers, providing only that it have a sufficient number of elders to preside. Ball followed William Ames in identifying a church united for worship as a church at least implicitly in covenant with God. He also gave a qualified approval to the practice of explicit and open church covenants, for which he believed there were scriptural precedents.[22]

Ball's discussion of church discipline located power and authority over church discipline in the properly constituted congregation. The *power* and *authority* of binding discipline, Ball wrote, had been delivered by Christ "to the whole church, that is, to every particular church collectively, because it perteineth to them to deny Christian communion to such wicked persons as adde contumacy to their disobedience, and to remit the punishment again upon repentance. . . ."[23]

Ball used this formulation, which had been earlier elaborated by William Ames, to argue—against the Separatists—that authority over discipline was an inseparable property of the church, so that even a church inhibited for one reason or another from *exercising* that authority could not be said to be altogether without order. Church

---

[20] Hall, *Faithful Shepherd*, 46–47, provides a useful discussion of Ames's relationship both to New England and to the English disciplinarian tradition extending back to Cartwright.

[21] Ball, *An Answer to Mr. Can*, Pt. 2, 35. See Schneider, "Godly Order," 308–313, for a more extensive analysis of Ball's intellectual debt to Ames.

[22] Ball, *Tryall of the New-Church Way*, 23–24, 49.

[23] Ball, *A Friendly Trial*, 265; *An Answer to Mr. Can*, Pt. 1, 135.

power, Ball explained to Canne, citing Ames's *Cases of Conscience,* "*de jure & quoddactum primum,* cannot be separated from the true Church, because immediately and necessarily it floweth from the essence it selfe, for it is contained in that covenant, whereby the faithfull are gathered into a Church." Or, as some of Cartwright's disciplinarian colleagues had written, as early as 1592, "Though none of our Assemblies did use this power [of discipline], it followeth not from thence, that we have it not. . . ."[24] Church discipline thus completed rather than constituted a true church. Where it was obvious that a society included persons who profaned the holy things of God, Ball acknowledged, it was a defect in that society if it did not exercise the censures to cleanse itself. But this was not a defect which nullified the legitimacy of the society's essential being. Citing Old Testament examples, Ball argued that God's covenants with the Hebrew people, many of whom were visibly disobedient and faithless, made it clear that the covenant bonds which made manifest a particular faithful church might outwardly encompass persons who in truth were not saints at all.[25]

In making the congregation his frame of reference, Ball was following a well-established tradition of argument, which has roots in Cartwright's own writings but which was much more fully elaborated by Nonconformists after the failure of the Hampton Court Conference. This exegetical tradition was highly instrumental for Nonconformists; negatively, it had allowed them to argue that Scripture showed no model for diocesan bishops, since all the first churches were parochial; constructively, it had enabled them to point to faithful congregations where the word was rightly preached, rather than to corrupt episcopacy, in their contention that the Church of England, in "essentials," remained a valid church. Ball faithfully elaborated the principle tenets of this tradition, following not only Ames but Paul Baynes, William Bradshaw, Robert Parker and other earlier exponents of the argument that all the first churches were congregational.

Ball's "congregational" conception of the church was firmly wedded, however, to a "presbyterial" understanding of the exercise and

---

[24] Ibid.; *The Church of England is a true Church of Christ. Published as a Most Grave Confutation of the Errors of the . . . Brownists or Separatists,* ed. W. Rathband (London, 1644). *The Church of England . . . a true Church* was probably written in the 1590s and had circulated in manuscript in Nonconformist circles until Rathband, one of Ball's editors, finally published it. See Schneider, "Godly Order," 253–263, for a fuller discussion of this very interesting tract, a committee effort to explain the bases for Nonconformist fidelity to a deeply flawed English Church.

[25] Ball, *An Answer to Mr. Can,* Pt. 2, 53–56.

administration of church authority. Even though particular churches were given the power of "binding and loosing," the exercise of that authority had been assigned to "that assembly of officers or governours in every church which the Apostle calleth a *presbytery*." To exercise church power, a church *must* have such a presbytery.

> If a societie enjoy but one Pastour or Teacher for the time, the power of government doth not belong unto him. For Christ hath not committed this power unto one but unto many. . . . But the power of guiding or governing is given to the Colledge Ecclesiasticall, or company of Governours, and must not be executed by any others.[26]

The "Colledge Ecclesiasticall" should also assume the leading role in church elections and ordinations. Again, Ball thought these functions should be exercised in the context of the particular church, and he, echoing a long line of reformed opinion, noted the right of the church to consent to its pastors and elders. But the presbytery should assume the primary responsibility. Ball judged, in fact, that Apostolic practice left the presbytery considerable latitude as to the degree of involvement a congregation might use in choosing leaders, "for sometimes men were propounded unto the Church to be chosen, and sometimes the choice was wholly left unto them. And was this not for our direction, that more libertie may be given where the danger [of an ill-informed selection] is lesse. . . ."[27]

Ball's language allows the inference that he thought elections and ordinations might be conducted entirely within the confines of an individual church so long as it was properly constituted. Thus he argued that the advice of other churches should be sought in instances where the people were "few, simple, apt to be deceived"; similarly, he wrote that ordination "belongeth . . . to the Presbyterie . . . and may and ought to be performed by the Presbyters of neighboring Congregations, if . . . [a church] has none of their owne, or not a competent number."[28]

In his descriptions of church order and governance, Ball revealed great commonality with the fundamental assumptions that guided the organization of New England's churches. What then prompted his critique, shortly after he finished writing against John Canne, of the "New-Church Way" in New England? As David Hall has amply documented, Ball and his fellows penned their nine questions to John Cotton at a time when lay fervor was at a peak in the New

[26]Ball, *A Friendly Triall*, 265; *An Answer to Mr. Can*, pt. 2, 36.
[27]Ibid., Pt. 1, 36.
[28]Ibid., Pt. 1, 24–25.

England colony. New England congregations were becoming actively engaged in the practice of discipline; they themselves initiated censures and were actively debating the merits of excommunication. The laity were participating in prophesying and had begun to question the minister after sermons. Moreover, the New Englanders had added to these other departures a wholly innovative practice, a test for church membership in which the whole congregation examined candidates to determine the extent of their spiritual probity.[29]

In the view of Ball and his colleagues, this renaissance of godly participation posed grave danger for the structures of church order and for church unity. Ball's tracts against New England explored both issues. The participatory practices being developed in New England seemed to Ball to jettison the carefully wrought sixteenth-century balance—well developed in presbyterian thought and codified in the *Directory of Discipline* —between ministers who functioned as the mouth of God and congregations who were supposed to acknowledge godly authority with their willing consent. Ball, Dod, and their fellows wanted to be told whether it was true that New England now considered the "power of Excommunication . . . [and government] so in the body of the Church that what the major part doth allow, that must be done, though the Pastors and Governors, and part of the assembly be of another minde, and peradventure upon more substantiall reasons." The Nonconformists were further concerned that New England churches were in many instances too tiny for the responsibilities being assigned to them; three, four, seven, or twenty persons was too small a group, Ball insisted, to claim the prerogatives and/or to establish the institutional structures of the original Apostolic churches.[30]

As the Nonconformists saw it, these newborn congregational presbyteries abroad were no sooner instituted than their Apostolic power and authority were being threatened by the disorderly introduction of democracy. Ball's group spied worse prospects ahead since "if the power of the keys be given first and immediately to the community of the faithfull, what reason can be alledged why in defect of Officers the Church might not rule, governe, feed, bind, loose, preach and administer the Sacraments. . . ."[31]

Ball's colleagues were not the only ones to object to these discon-

[29] Hall, *Faithful Shepherd*, 78–92.

[30] *A Directory of Church-Government* (London, 1645); "The Nine Positions," in Ball, *Try-all of the New-Church Way*, n. p. [the positions are the printed questions]; *A Friendly Tri-all*, 259.

[31] Ball, *Tryall of the New-Church Way*, 75.

certing developments. Another Puritan writer acidly reminded New England that *"Ministers have power over the people by the word of God, Heb. 13.17.1 Thes.5.12.1 Tim 5.17 and not be mens engaging themselves by Covenant."* A group of ministers in Lancashire wanted to know whether New England held it "lawfull and convenient that a company of private and illitterate persons (into a Church body combined)" should collectively conduct elections and depositions of "Ministers of the word." They also sought to know just how small a group—"seaven, or nine, or twenty, or fourty"—was supposed to be thought sufficient to have "all power, and exercise of Church Government." Even more explicitly, they wanted to be advised, "What act of Government. . . . may the Presbiters doe, more than any other member may doe, or without the particular consent of the rest, wee crave to have these particular Acts mentioned. . . ."[32]

The democratic tendency which Ball and other Puritans found so distressing in the New England churches was significant not only as an error in itself, but also for its larger implications. Undue enlargement of congregational prerogatives was, after all, an error Nonconformists had encountered before. In his writings against New England, Ball distinguished two theories on the relations between the faithful and the power of the keys. The first, for which he noted Dudley Fenner, Robert Parker, and John Davenport as examples, distinguished between "the power it self wch they given to the Church, and the execution and exercise of it, which they confined to the Presbytery." Despite his evident anxiety to curtail any claims that real power had been given to church members, Ball did not criticize this exegesis. Instead he moved directly to a second school of thought which gave "the power of the keyes with the exercise thereof to the whole body of the Church, or if in the dispensation they attribute anything to the Officers, it is but as servants of the Church." And here, said Ball, coming to the point:

> lyeth the stone at which they of the Seperation stumble, and which we conceive to be your judgement and practise, wherein we required your

---

[32] *Apologie of the said Elders [of the severall Churches] in New-England for Church-Covenant, sent over in Answer to Master Bernard in the yeare 1639* (London, 1643), 24. This tract was printed with Richard Mather, *Church-Government and Church-Covenant Discussed, In an Answer of the Elders of the severall Churches in New-England To two and thirty Questions, sent over to them by divers Ministers in England* (London, 1643) and with a third tract, John Davenport's *An Answer of the Elders of the Severall Churches in New England unto 9 Positions.* The Lancashire Questions come from Mather, *Church-Government and Church-Covenant*, 4–5. Mather, it should be noted, replied that New England considered consociation of Churches into classes and synods to be "lawfull and in some cases necessary." Ibid., 64.

plaine answer, with your reasons, but have received no satisfactions. You referre us to Mr. *Parkers* reasons to prove the power of the keyes to belong to the whole Church, who are of farre different judgement from Mr. *Parker* to the point it selfe. And if your judgement and practise be according to that of the Separation (which we feare) you dissent from him, and we cannot but dissent from you. . . .[33]

Had the New Englanders really stumbled into Separation? Perry Miller and numerous scholars after him have documented the painstaking casuistry colonial divines used to argue that they had not. Moreover, New England biography made much of the fact that their divines had left England only after seeking the approval of just such grave and reverend elders as now were writing to query their orthodoxy. Yet the truth was that New England divines had entered into a project of radical purification—or separation from corruption—far beyond anything possible in England. They had established the discipline, thrown out the liturgy, called and ordained previously ordained ministers in collective parochial elections, and zealously restricted the membership of their flocks to the certifiably godly. Perhaps inevitably, their tolerance lessened for the half-way measures, the mix of good and barely tolerable, which they had left behind. And no doubt equally inevitably, the zeal with which they stripped themselves of corruption grated painfully on their brethren who remained saddled, not only with English corruption, but with the increasingly difficult task of rationalizing continued tolerance of that corruption to those church members who saw New England as a source of moral and practical inspiration.

Ball's colleagues listened carefully to the commentary which accompanied purification in Massachusetts. New England, as anticipated, had established a reformed order of worship. But did they now regard it as *unlawful* to participate in a service where a set liturgy was read?[34] Presumably they were not reassured when Richard Mather answered inquiries on this point with the comment that "in England, we should willingly joine in some parts of Gods true Worship, and namely in hearing the word. . . ." English Nonconformists had long devoted their ministries to persuading scrupulous Puritans of the legitimacy of worshipping and receiving the sacraments in parish assemblies, Prayer Book, and ceremonies notwithstanding. Yet here was Richard Mather proclaiming the semi-Separatist doctrines

---

[33] Ball, *Tryall of the New-Church Way,* 71.
[34] "The Nine Positions," Questions 1 and 2; Ibid., n.p.

that Nonconformists had long opposed. Moreover, Dod's and Ball's good friend John Cotton evidently agreed with him.[35]

There was similar room for unpleasant reverberations over New England's procedures governing admission to the sacraments. English disciplinarians had long deplored the pell mell admission of all and sundry to the Lord's Supper, urging the necessity of restraining the ignorant as well as the sinful. Ball himself was reported "exemplarily careful to preserve Gods ordinances from pollution . . . and . . . was wont to tell his Auditors, that their . . . thrusting daggers into their Ministers bodies, would not be more grievous, than their unworthy communicating at the Lords table."[36]

Up to a point, Ball and his colleagues welcomed New England's zeal, exhorting the colonists to keep the ordinances pure. But the limits of their enthusiasm were breached when John Cotton wrote to friends in the fall of 1635 that, if he were in England, he would no longer be willing to communicate with them in the sacraments, even if the ceremonies were removed. It was too dangerous, Cotton now thought, to risk fellowship with the unregenerate; communion with them in the sacraments might be a fellowship with sin. Reminded that his stance echoed the semi-separatist "errors" of John Robinson twenty years earlier, Cotton was not deterred. If Robinson had turned away from the common liturgy, sacraments, and discipline in England, wrote Cotton, "yet since . . . it hath appeared, there was no just ground of coming on to them."[37]

Thus, in the face of a half-century of insistent Nonconformist teaching that the godly were not tainted when they received the Lords Supper in a "mixt" assembly, one of the Nonconformists' most esteemed colleagues had turned around and conceded this central point against them. Ball and his colleagues put their response succinctly in the "Nine Questions" they sent to New England:

> You know how oft it hath been objected that Non-conformists in practice are Separatists in heart but that they goe crosse to their own positions, or smother the truth for sinister ends. They of the Separation boast that they stand upon the Non-conformists grounds. . . . But both these are much countenanced by your sudden change if you be changed as it is reported. How shall your brethren be able to stand up in the

---

[35] Mather, *Church-Government and Church-Covenant Discussed*, 27.

[36] Clarke, *A General Martyrologie*, 448.

[37] John Cotton, *The Way of the Congregational Churches Cleared* (London, 1648) in Larzer Ziff, ed., *John Cotton on the Churches of New England* (Cambridge, Mass., 1968), 183.

defence of their innocencie, . . . when your example and opinion shall be cast in their dish?[38]

Both the content and the tone of the Ball-Dod commentary on New England confirm that the English correspondents had initially viewed themselves as colleagues and supporters of the New England enterprise. The New England churches had been expected to establish forms of governance and discipline consonant with the Nonconformists' exegesis of Apostolic precept. Their innovations came as a painful surprise.

What Ball and his colleagues viewed as New England's deviations from the expected church model did not merely disturb the English observers. It also helped generate deep fissures among Nonconformists. These fissures would eventually lead to the emergence of "congregational" and "presbyterian" parties among dissident Puritans.

In the letter to New England which conveyed their initial queries, Ball and his associates pointed out that New England's innovations had precipitated alarming divisions in the ranks of the godly still in England.[39] The letter mentioned no names, leaving an impression of anonymous zealots, disruptively following in the footsteps of more than one generation of Separatists before them. But as Thomas Edwards's 1644 *Antapologia* describes in some detail, those lured into a state of schism by New England's example included two future leaders among the English Congregational Independents, Thomas Goodwin and Philip Nye. Moreover, as we can tell from contemporary sources, John Ball was actively engaged in a resulting effort to dissuade one or both of these notables from their apostasy.

By the time Edwards penned *Antapologia* in 1644, Goodwin and Nye, joined by three other Westminster Assembly Congregational Independents, had already published their famous 1643 *Apologeticall Narration* which explained how each of them, once awakened to the sinfulness of the corruptions in the Church of England, had found it impossible to reconcile conscience and continued acquiescence in this corruption. This rejection of their former conformity they described as rejection of the "dark part" of the Church of England. Only in their subsequent exile in the Netherlands had they embarked upon a search for the "light part," that is, for the affirmative scriptural injunctions touching church government and church discipline. At that point, they said, guided by a study of scripture, the example

---

[38] "The Nine Positions," in Ball, *Tryall of the New-Church Way,* n.p.
[39] Ibid.

of Reformed churches, the writings of "the good old Non-conformists," and the New England models, the five divines had arrived at the congregational views on church order they defended in the Westminster Assembly.[40]

According to the Presbyterian Edwards's 1644 account, parts of this story were simply untrue. As Edwards recounted, or more accurately insinuated, the tale, Goodwin and Nye at least had "fallen" upon their "new" church way before they ever left England, following closely the example of the Massachusetts churches and in particular the precepts of John Cotton.[41] Robert Baillie's 1645 account of the same conversion fills out Edwards's account of Cotton's influence. According to Baillie, who, as a Scottish commissioner working closely with London Presbyterian ministers had access to the same sources as Edwards, John Cotton was instrumental in dissuading Goodwin from compliance with disputed ceremonies through their mutual participation in the conference where Cotton and other divines debated this issue. Then, "Master Goodwin, . . . with very little ado, was brought by his Letters from New England to follow [Cotton's views on church order]," boasting "beyond . . . moderation" of the "New Light" gained from this source.[42] According to Edwards's account, Goodwin, Nye, and others who departed with them for Holland made a pact to pursue the New England pattern in their exile.

Edwards was unspecific about the substance and the details of this reported pact, and offered no evidence at all to suggest that Nye and Goodwin had been public proponents, prior to their departure, of the full and complete jurisdiction vested in congregations which they defended in the *Apologeticall Narration*. But reading Edwards carefully, we see that the basis for his contention that the Dissenting Brethren became converts to the "new way" was his knowledge that both Goodwin and Nye, sometime in the late 1630s, had withdrawn from communion with English churches. They had taken this step,

[40] Thomas Goodwin, Philip Nye, Sidrach Simpson, Jer: Burroughes, William Bridge, *An Apologeticall Narration* (London, 1643), printed in facsimile with commentary, ed., Robert Paul (Philadelphia, 1962), 2–5, 9–10.

[41] Thomas Edwards, *Antapologia: Or, a full Answer to the Apologeticall Narration of Mr. Goodwin, etc.* (London, 1644), 18–23, 31–35. Edwards's account of this is anything but plain, since he names no one specifically. However, he gives enough information about each of the five brethren who wrote the *Apologeticall Narration* that, by process of elimination, we can see that he is talking about Goodwin and Nye when he speaks of some of the brethren as having remained public in England even after they discovered their New Church Way.

[42] Robert Baillie, *A Dissuasive from the Errours of our Time* (London, 1645), 56.

according to Edwards, because they were convinced by John Cotton's letters that it was not lawful to receive the Lord's Supper in congregations which mixed saints with the "civil and prophane" and further that it was unlawful to be present at worship which used a fixed liturgy.[43] Nye and Goodwin had withdrawn from parochial communion over the very issues which the Ball conference cited in its letter to New England:

> And letters from New England have so taken with divers in many parts of this Kingdome, that they have left our Assemblies because of a stinted Liturgie, and excommunicated themselves from the Lords Supper, because such as are unfit are not debarred from it. And being turned aside themselves, they labour to ensnare others . . . .[44]

Goodwin and Nye did not, it is important to stress, simply separate, denying the legitimacy of the Church of England. Rather, they argued that, even though it was a true church, its corruptions were such that the saints must form purer congregations within it. Or, to put it differently, they progressed rapidly from conformity to a semi-Separatist posture that effectively left the half-way house of principled Nonconformity well behind.

At the time of their defection, Goodwin and Nye were linked to the inner circles of both clerical and secular Puritanism by their editorial work on the sermons of those two foremost Puritan preachers, John Preston and Richard Sibbes. They would continue to be highly regarded in the 1640s, even by their opponents, for their learning and piety. This break with the carefully qualified insistence of nonconforming Puritans that the Church of England was a church in which the saints could lawfully communicate—while resisting specific ceremonial corruptions—was an important challenge to the Nonconformists' principles. When Dod, Ball, and their fellow Nonconformists wrote in 1636 to express their concern that New England was tipping the precarious balance of Nonconformity toward an outright separation, their concern was more than a matter of maintaining a shared ideology. The separation issue had cut through the inner ranks of the godly and it was men of acknowledged stature who were withdrawing themselves from communion with English churches and who were perceived to be laboring "to ensnare others. . . ."

When Nye and Goodwin reached their new judgment about par-

[43]Edwards, *Antapologia*, 18–19, 31–32.
[44]"The Nine Positions," in Ball, *Tryall of the New-Church Way*, n. p.

ticipation in English churches, both Ball and Dod were directly engaged in "conferences" that sought to change their minds. Edwards's *Antapologia* provides one version of this tale. According to Edwards, one of the Dissenting Brethren "did . . . both by preaching and another ways vent . . . against . . . Communicating in our assemblies, so that the Countrey thereabouts was much disturbed, and that painfull preacher Mr. Wheateley . . . much grieved by the falling off and withdrawing of some."[45]

Immediately thereafter, Edwards continues, "at the request of some great persons of worth, Mr. Ball . . . had . . . a conference and dispute with him at Mr. Knigthtlyes."[46] Offering a much later account of the same dispute, Richard Baxter included both Goodwin and Nye at the conference at Richard Knightley's.[47] Richard Knightley, the Northamptonshire Puritan who hosted this conference, was a long-standing patron and protector of John Dod. (He was also a friend of John Pym, who lived in Knightley's Fawsley home during the late 1630s.) So this conference which sought to reason with defectors from the Nonconformist middle ground between full conformity and *de facto* separation certainly included at least some of the divines who had attempted to bring home to New England the dangers inherent in their new opinions. It is quite likely that Ball's draft arguments against New England error were used in this conference as well.

In this breach between the New England divines and their English Nonconformist colleagues, we can see the emergence of positions, if not parties, that foreshadow the ministerial debates in the 1640s between proponents of a presbyterian reform and proponents of congregational independency. Even as we note this emergent divide,

[45]Edwards, *Antapologia*, 22.

[46]Ibid.

[47]Richard Baxter, *Reliquiæ Baxterianæ: Or, Mr. Richard Baxters Narrative of the most Memorable Passages of His Life and times*, ed. Matthew Sylvester (London, 1696), III, 19. According to Baxter, after Goodwin and Nye together had fallen away from "hearing or joyning in Common Prayer and Sacraments with the Parishes. . . . my Lord Sav and Mr. Pim and some others had got them to a dispute with Mr. John Ball, . . . who, as some saith, utterly baffled them." I suggest that the person who debated with Ball was Nye, rather than Goodwin, because Nye exhibited more concern over the sinfulness of using the liturgy than did Goodwin. See, for example, *Antapologia*, 99 and 240. According to Edwards, Goodwin specifically approved the London ministers' decision to continue use of the "best and least offensive" parts of the Common Prayer Book liturgy in order to avoid unnecessary religious divisions. So Goodwin seems not to have found the "stinted liturgy" utterly unlawful.

however, it is important to specify as precisely as possible, what was and was not at stake in these late 1630s discussions.

As the above discussion implies, the debate between the Ball group and New England did not center on what would be the most hotly debated issues in the Westminster Assembly: the juridical authority of classical and synodal assemblies over particular churches. As we have seen, Ball and his colleagues shared the New England premise that a properly organized congregation was, in the scriptural sense, a fully constituted church. They put no questions to New England about presbyterial organization beyond the congregational level; they did not ask anything about synods. New England in the 1630s established voluntary conferences to resolve questions and disputes among churches. The Ball group either knew what New England was doing in this sphere and approved it, or did not think it sufficiently important to query.

The Ball group's lack of interest in New England's supracongregational church government should not be taken to represent the views of all reform-inclined divines then scrutinizing news of the developments in New England. In 1637, a group of Lancashire ministers sent another set of questions to New England, thirty-two in number, all decidedly hostile in tone. The Lancashire group's thirty-two questions did include two queries about classes and synods. Classes, this group implied, using terms compatible both with William Ames's writings on church government and with the voluntaristic practices of English Puritanism, ought to provide individual churches with "counsell and consent" in significant matters. This Lancashire group placed greater weight on synods, as they implied in a question that demonstrated their preference for order over truth in any conflict between the two:

> Or give you any power to Synods and Councells to determine and order things that cannot otherwise be ended, so . . . that their determination shall bind . . . particular Churches . . . to due obedience, in case they decree nothing but according to Truth and right, and to peaceable suffering, in case they should doe otherwise? Or what other course you have, or intend to have for that end. . . . ?[48]

But even for this clearly critical set of observers, New England's supracongregational church organization and hierarchy were not the

---

[48]Mather, *Church-Government and Church-Covenant*, 4–5. Mather, it should be noted, replied that New England considered consociation of Churches into classes and synods to be "lawfull and in some cases necessary." Ibid., 64.

main sources of consternation. Like Ball and his colleagues, the Lancashire divines were mainly concerned with New England's views on church membership, with the closely related question of church covenants, and with the degree of power and authority being conceded to members of the congregation over their ministers.

When the first fissures emerged in the ranks of those who traced their views on church order and discipline back to the sixteenth century presbyterian reformers, it was these issues, centered on the constitution and spiritual order of the individual church, but holding far-reaching implications for church unity and for ministerial authority within the church, that were perceived to be at stake. On the other hand, it is also clear that there was an integral connection between these hotly disputed issues and what would later emerge as congregational and presbyterian positions on the structure and exercise of church government and authority. These connections also were foreshadowed in the Ball—Dod critique of New England churches.

For those who admired New England, there was a close and necessary connection between the determination to form "purer" churches and the insistence that the power of juridical authority must be retained in congregations and not delegated or diffused to "higher" institutions. Thomas Goodwin pointed to the connection in his late 1630s tract on the Book of Revelation. In that text, Goodwin did not address questions of polity and church organization. What concerned Goodwin in his study of Revelation was discipline rather than ecclesiology. The object of discipline, as he saw it, was the exclusion of the civil and the profane from the "inner temple" or individual church. As Goodwin interpreted Revelation, it showed that the faithful were called to put "a difference between men and men." This was by no means an impractical task; the whole thrust of Puritan ministry in England, Goodwin argued, "hath . . . run in this channel thus to distinguish men, and to separate the precious from the vile."[49] The reformation would be perfected when the winnowing and purifying of each of God's churches had been accomplished.

This was not a polemic against classes and synods, but rather a grounding of a new understanding of the work of church discipline in prophetic texts. Its immediate practical application was the kind of church practices which Goodwin and other radical ministers were

---

[49] *The Works of Thomas Goodwin, D.D.,* ed. John C. Miller, 12 vols. (Edinburgh, 1861–66), 3:147, cf. 3:128. See also Thomas Goodwin and Philip Nye, preface to John Cotton, *The Keys of the Kingdom of Heaven* (London, 1644) in Ziff, ed., *John Cotton on the Churches,* 85.

watching in New England: examining the faith of would-be communicants, acknowledging the purposes of church membership in a covenant taken upon entrance into the church, establishing an active and participatory congregational discipline that would involve those worthy of church membership—the saints—as well as their ministers and elders.

At the same time, this understanding of prophetic imperatives compelled its adherents to place fresh insistence upon the congregation as the locus of church authority. We can see something of the flavor of this imperative in yet another 1630s tract, this one a letter written "a yeer or two before the Long Parliament" and published in the 1640s as *The Saints Apologie*. *The Saints Apologie* was written by a Puritan who acknowledged the English churches to be true churches but nonetheless felt obliged to obey God by leaving a "mixt" congregation and joining a "purer" communion. It thus shows us the temper of those who agreed with Goodwin and Nye and who therefore most concerned the Nonconformists: godly folk who insisted that, even though the Church of England was a true church, obedience required a radical dissent from all contact with its corruptions of practice, membership, and governance.

The author of *The Saints Apologie* placed major emphasis both on the congregation's power of the keys and on each congregation's positive obligation to use that power to "separate the vile from the precious."

> This I conceive to be the present state of most of the Churches in this Kingdome, which although they be true Churches . . . yet being too ignorant wherein that consisteth, and what power and priviledge they have and ought to exercise by it; they suffer . . . a mixed multitude . . . among them to their own hardening, to the Churches leavening. . . .[50]

Church members contracted guilt, the author went on to say, by their failure to use the keys to exclude the ungodly. "There lyeth a duty upon every member of a visible Church, which hee is obliged to performe, or else he will partake of the guilt of other mens sins. To do anything less than what duty obligeth . . . is to live in sin against conscience: and that is, against Christianity. . . ."[51]

The Saints Apologie allows us to enter into the dynamics of the Congregational Independent world view *prior* to the point where leaders of that movement began their debate over the polity to be established

---

[50] *The Saints Apologie, Or, A Vindication of the Churches* (London, 1644), 3–4.
[51] Ibid., 9.

for a reformed Church of England. In this tract, the authority—or lack thereof—of church classes and synods is not yet at issue. But it is very clear why the saints must insist on congregational authority over discipline and excommunication: only by exercising that authority to control the composition of the church can they obey their stringent understanding of conscience and spiritual obligation. Hitherto, this kind of doctrine had characterized Separatists, now it was newly combined with the Nonconformists' insistence that English churches were true churches *and* with the New England assertion that churches could be both valid and yet intolerable to those of scrupulous conscience.

In his response to the challenge posed by the radical New England emphasis on winnowing and restructuring purer congregations, Ball, as the spokesman for fellow Nonconformists, reasserted the centrality of clerical authority as the divinely appointed instrument of true order within the church. In part, his arguments were staples of Nonconformist ideology. In apologia stretching back to William Perkins, Puritan dissenters had long insisted that the fundamental source of order and authority in the church was the Word of God, effectively preached by godly ministers. Ball argued this point once again when he contended that the "chiefe and principall meanes Christ useth . . . [for discipline] is the preaching of his Word, whereby he saveth his people, and conquereth his enemies."[52]

Similarly, as we have seen above, when he reasserted the guiding authority of the congregational presbytery over a more participatory decision-making process in the church, Ball was saying no more than the reformed tradition, both in England and abroad, had said before him. His arguments systematically reasserted earlier claims that the Scriptural injunction "Tell the Church" in disciplinary cases must mean in practice, "Tell the presbytery" which was authorized to act for the church.[53]

For the most part, then, we can see Ball as the exponent of a stable and, at least in his rendition, highly codified interpretative tradition, which he used to confront the deviations of misguided revisionists. There is, however, one argument in Ball's final tract against New England which itself seems to mark a departure from earlier Nonconformist traditions of ecclesiological argument, at least as these made their way into (eventually) public record. This departure is

---

[52] Ball, *An Answer to Mr. Can*, Pt. 2, 43–44.
[53] Schneider, "Godly Order," 366–368.

surprising and, because it connects Ball's ecclesiology to issues that move to center stage in the 1640s, potentially significant.

This unexpected argument is Ball's observation, offered in passing rather than as a major assertion, that Scripture provides more than one model for church organization and structure. Scripture, he suggested in his second tract against New England, showed that some of the Apostolic churches were clearly single congregations in their internal structure and covenant. But others, and in particular, the Church of Jerusalem, had probably subdivided once their numbers grew large, thus establishing a number of congregations which nonetheless remained united in one society and under one government.[54] This is unexpected because, as we have seen, all three of Ball's tracts on church order, authority and discipline take the individual "church society" as the primary unit of reference. Moreover, Ball shows no interest in the kinds of reformed church organization to be found in Scotland or the Netherlands, and says virtually nothing about supra-congregational structures of church authority, whether classes, synods, or church councils. It is also surprising because it undercuts the by then standard Nonconformist practice of equating the Apostolic churches with "particular congregations" in order to challenge the exegetical bases for diocesan episcopacy. If all the early churches were congregations, then the only bishops empowered to rule in the early churches were congregational pastors (and elders). It was not, in fact, at all easy to establish the congregational case since the Church of Jerusalem was known to have numbered at least five thousand (Acts 4:4) and was therefore overlarge for a worshipping assembly. But for more than thirty years, Nonconformists had generally argued that the first churches were parochial, and therefore not diocesan. Ball himself, in his second tract on New England, paraphrased Paul Baynes's much earlier "proofs" that Jerusalem had been a single church.[55]

He used these "proofs," however, to argue that it was inappropriate for a very small congregation to assume to itself all the prerogatives of church government:

> For that was not a division of the society [the Church of Jerusalem] into societies distinct, but an assignment of some particular officer to the oversight of one part of . . . the society, for the more fit . . . government

[54] Ball, *Tryall of the New-Church Way*, 25–27.
[55] Compare Ball, *A Friendly Triall*, 261–262 with Paul Baynes, *The Diocesans Tryall* (Amsterdam, 1621), 16.

of the whole. . . . And out of doubt this form or kind of a visible . . .
church is much nearer to the patterns and precedents set by the apostles
. . . then that two or three or few believers, uniting themselves in covenant, should be reputed the onely visible and ministeriall church, independent, from whom the officers should, as their servants, derive their
authority.[56]

This suggestion that Jerusalem had evolved into a "church" composed of multiple congregations is a minor rather than a major point
in Ball's argument. It was used not to counter congregational ecclesiology, but to check its potential excesses. Nonetheless, the assertion
is arresting, because it seems to suggest either division or an unexpected flexibility—or both—in the Nonconformist understanding of
the word of God on church government. The claim that there are
two Apostolic models for church order is potentially a recipe for diversity; it could be used, in principle, to endorse *both* congregational
churches, each with its church presbytery and governance *and* the
presbyterian model as it had evolved in Scotland, in which individual
kirks were united under one supracongregational or "classical" presbytery. While Ball's whole frame of reference on the church is markedly different from the "composite" church models that the Scots
would describe for the English the 1640s, Ball's observation on the
Jerusalem Church (crucially important for Scottish ecclesiology),
shows that he saw Scottish ecclesiology as one among various licit
options.[57]

If Ball's observation that there are two—different—scriptural
models for church order were merely idiosyncratic, it would not warrant attention. But in fact, as both later Puritan tracts and the Westminster Assembly debates reveal, there were other Presbyterian divines who took this same position. In the Westminster Assembly
debates on authority in the Apostolic churches, for example, Stephen
Marshall argued what turned out to be the minority view that the
Apostolic church at Ephesus had been but a single congregation.
This exegesis was critically important to the Congregational Independents' efforts to win approval or their own church order in the
Westminster Assembly debates.[58] The same claim is also found in *An
Answer to an Humble Remonstrance,* which Marshall, Edmund Ca-

[56]Ball, *A Friendly Triall,* 301–302.

[57]Schneider, "Godly Order," 469–471.

[58]George Gillespie, *Notes of Debates and Proceedings of the Assembly of Divines and Other
Commissioners at Westminster,* February 1644 to January 1645, ed. David Meek (Edinburgh, 1848), 50–52; Schneider, "Godly Order," 15–16.

lamy, and three other Presbyterians published against episcopacy in 1641.[59] On the other hand, Marshall also held, against the vehement objections of Goodwin, Nye, and their colleagues, that the founding church at Jerusalem had not been a single self-governing congregation. Rather, Marshall argued, the Jerusalem church had grown to include numerous congregations, which worshipped separately, but which remained a "church" because they were united under and collectively governed by a single presbytery. Echoes of this perspective can also be found in *An Answer to An Humble Remonstrance.*[60]

In 1649, the provincial assembly of Presbyterian ministers in London issued *A Vindication of the Presbyteriall-Government, and Ministry* which asserted the same position. According to this tract, which seems to have been largely the work of Edmund Calamy, "Scripture . . . tells us of a Church, consisting of no more than can conveniently meet in one place . . . and of a Church consisting of divers Congregations."[61] Other period publications make the same point.

Ball's assertion of disparate Scriptural models for church order, like so much else in his writings, thus reflected and reported on what seems to have been a largely underground tradition of discussion and interpretation. His tract tells us that, notwithstanding the dominance of the "congregation as Scriptural church" equation in earlier Nonconformist (published) argument, in the late 1630s, Nonconformists were evidently persuaded that there was more than one Apostolic model for church order. Thus their own practice of conceiving godly congregations as covenanted "churches" held Scriptural warrant; but so too would the alternative conception advanced in Scotland, where several congregations under one presbytery were held to constitute a fully ordered "church."

This, I believe, is the authentic "presbyterian" temper, asserting itself against the threat of divisions and disorders both in New England and nearer home. For what Ball's use of the two-model argument shows is the overriding priority assigned to the concept of a fully empowered "presbytery" in the Nonconformists' conception of a rightly ordered church. Church structures may vary with circumstances, as Ball's comments on small congregations make clear. There is more than one covering church pattern in Scripture and as

[59] Smectymnuus, *An Answer to An Humble Remonstrance* (London, 1641), 58. See an even longer discussion of the same point in Smectymnuus, *A Vindication of the Answer to the Humble Remonstrance* (London, 1641), 151.

[60] Smectymnuus, *An Answer to an Humble Remonstrance*, 80–81.

[61] *A Vindication of the Presbyterial Government* (London, 1649), 6.

Ball indicates in another place, where Scripture shows variation, it allows a "liberty." [62]

What may not vary, in Ball's representation of Scriptural warrants, is presbytery itself, which holds constant as a precept for governance across different ways of structuring a "church." For Ball, the heart of church authority was the "ecclesiastical college," ministers and elders gathered together to exercise governance and authority as the first congregations had known them. Optimally, there should be a presbytery in every congregation. Alternatively, where a particular church was too tiny to mount a full complement of pastors and elders, one presbytery might serve more than one congregation without violation of the Apostolic precedents. What mattered in all circumstances was that presbyteries—and not the membership of congregations—ought to exercise the power of the keys. This vigorous defense of presbyterial authority in church governance and discipline is surely what led contemporaries to remember Ball as "the Presbyterians' Champion," his substantial indebtedness to "congregational" intellectual sources notwithstanding.

What is puzzling about this entire picture is how we make the transition from Nonconformist views as Ball both codified and reflected them to the national church Presbyterian platforms of the 1640s. If we accept the arguments of this paper, those most actively engaged in explicating a reformed view of church governance in 1630s England were working within a framework more readily identified with congregationalism than with the Westminster Assembly. While their chief spokesman clearly espoused the authority of the presbytery over and against the insurgence of activist congregations, Ball's writing yields few hints of any interest in a plan for a national presbyterian system.

A full discussion of this issue falls outside the boundaries of this paper. Two points can be made, however. The first is that, as Baxter reported, many of those who came to be called Presbyterians had earlier been conformists. The clerical Presbyterianism of the 1640s drew on disparate traditions; only one of these was the interpretive tradition of the "good old Nonconformists." The second point is that the Nonconformists clearly formed a coalition in the 1640s with these more moderate colleagues, at least some of whom were much less persuaded than Ball and his Nonconformist colleagues that

---

[62] Ball, *An Answer to Mr. Can,* Pt. 1, 36.

Scripture had established non-episcopal patterns for church governance. (Cornelius Burges, for example, one of the central "Presbyterian" spokesmen, supported a moderate episcopacy at several critical junctures.)[63] Ball's friends and intellectual heirs did not form a separate ideological grouping in the 1640s; rather they are found contributing support to Presbyterian enterprises in and out of the Westminster Assembly and aggressively writing against the fatal errors of the Congregational Independents. Some of them were proponents of compromise with the Congregational Independents, but they did not form a separate group to advance the cause of accommodation.

To sustain a coalition with ministers representing a range of views, the Nonconformists had to be pragmatists. They had to adapt their reading of early church structures to the needs of a national church. Such pragmatism was not necessarily a problem for those who accepted the argument that there was more than one church model in Scripture: since, as we have noted above, diverse Scriptural examples implied a "libertie."

There is an interesting tract published in 1641 which offers clues to the kinds of conceptual translations Nonconformists evidently made between their ecclesiology and opportunity when the work of the Long Parliament seemed to open new doors of possibility and promise. The title of this suggestive tract is *The Beauty of Godly Government in a Church Reformed.* Although the author remained anonymous, it is clear from the tract's topic, language, and detailed plan for church governance that it was written by one or more ministers. Its gracious references to the success of church governance in "our neighbor Kingdome" Scotland further suggest that the proposal came from the circle of divines then actively conferring with the Scottish commissioners on ways to advance presbyterian reform in England. As we observed in the description of Ball's Nonconformist connections, several of his colleagues had ties to this group.

Whoever wrote *Godly Government,* its internal structure shows us how divines who thought as Ball did about Scriptural patterns for order and governance applied their principles to a plan for reformed church government in England. The tract's author, like Ball, Ames,

---

[63] *The Letters and Journals of Robert Baillie, 1637–1662,* ed. David Laing, 3 vols. (Edinburgh, 1841), 1:3–2. Cornelius Burgess, *An Humble Examination of a Printed Abstract of the Answers to Nine Reasons of the House of Commons, against the Votes of Bishops in Parliament* (1641), 67; British Museum Additional MSS 18,778, fol. 44, cited in Valerie Pearl, "Oliver St. John and the 'Middle Group' in the Long Parliament, August 1643–May 1644," *English Historical Review* 320(1966): 496. Thomason identified Burgess as the author of *An Humble Examination.*

and Nonconformist theorists generally, equates the first Scriptural churches with individual parish churches. This in fact is the tract's opening observation: "according to the order in holy Writ; the first Churches being Parochial: speciall care must be had, that parishes have in them the ordinances of Christ." A few pages later, *Godly Government* makes essentially the same point again, this time in a passage immediately following expressions of praise for Scottish forms of church governance: "[I]n the Apostles dayes were first founded parochial Churches, and in them the Elders and Deacons ordained, and all Christs ordinances exercised in them; and therefore to be admitted of us."[64]

With Scriptural warrant for parochial governance thus established, *Godly Government* spells out a pattern for parish government by pastors and elders, to be "chosen with the peoples consent, and admitted . . . in the face of the whole Congregation." Some of the "Laietie," said the author, thought that this would make "every Minister a pope in his parish." But this was an error, for the elders would be joined with each minister in government, "so as without them hee can doe nothing."[65] The benefits of establishing such "parochial government" were both spiritual and practical:

> Hereby will religious persons, religious meetings and pious exercises be had in esteeme, and the vertuous regarded; who will be watchfull one over another, being knit together in an holy communion, much with us wanting. Hereby will the vicious, the prophane and scandalous be suppressed. . . . [66]

Nonetheless, while a plan for parish government and discipline is the most fully developed and rhetorically enthusiastic discussion in *Godly Government,* the tract locates this authority in a national presbyterian system. Parish government is subordinated to a classical presbytery; classical presbyteries are to send delegates to county synods which will meet twice a year; these synods in turn are subordinate to a general assembly which will meet, as Parliament was henceforth expected to convene, every third year.[67]

Interestingly, the only parts of this edifice justified by references to Scriptural warrant are the authority of pastor and elders and the Apostolic models for parochial government. Classical presbyteries

---

[64] *The Beauty of Godly Government in a Church Reformed* (London, 1641), 1, 7.
[65] Ibid., 1–4, 7–8. The tract is mis-paged; there are no pages 2 and 3.
[66] Ibid., 5–6.
[67] Ibid., 7–11. See also the explicit endorsement of subordination on p. 12.

and synods are simply described. While the goods to come of them are favorably compared with the evils of episcopacy, the author of *Godly Government* makes no effort to ground classical presbyteries and synods in Scriptural texts. The church at Jerusalem, which would figure so prominently in the Westminster Assembly and 1640s Scottish justifications of classical presbyteries, is not mentioned.

The plan presented in this text can be seen as a middle ground between the views of Ball and his colleagues, who made congregational church authority their primary frame of reference—except when a church was too tiny to envision an adequate presbytery—and the dominant group in the Westminster Assembly, who would argue that the Scriptural model for government by presbyteries was that of Jerusalem: councils of pastors and elders exercising authoritative governance over multiple separate churches.

Godly Government's author stressed the Scriptural warrants for a full presbytery in every parish. Nevertheless, a national system of church assemblies was evidently also wanted. The text offers insight into the appeal of such a system in its final observation about the benefits of classical presbyteries: "By this wee see how the parochial government is upheld, and yet kept within bounds. . . . "[68]

Thomas Edwards provides a complementary picture of the way Nonconformists viewed synodal government structures as they moved from the apologetic principles reflected and codified in Ball's pages to the realm of practical reform. Writing in 1641 (against Independency) on the case for authoritative church synods as a structure for church government, Edwards argued:

> now where there is no Law forbidding, there is no transgression. for sinne is a transgression of the Law. . . . But here [i.e., in establishing synods] is no Law broke, this never being spoken against [in Scripture] . . . .but found agreeable to the Law and light of Nature concerning societies, to general rules in the word of edification, order, peace, purenesse, lovelinesse, etc. to examples also and practices in Scripture; and what though there be not an expresse precept of a common in *terminis* for it yet not being against Scriptures but so agreeable to it . . . no sober godly Ministers or Christian should refuse Communion with a Church . . . and foment a schisme for that. . . . [69]

The arguments here are consonant with the proposals of *Godly Government*. Synodal governance structures are not thought to be an

---

[68]Ibid., 8.

[69]Thomas Edwards, *Reasons against the Independent Government of Particular Congregations* (London, 1641), 16–17.

apostolic institution, but they are very clearly wanted: indeed, they are closely linked to the "law and light of nature concerning societies." There being no rule against them, and much in practical terms to be said for them, they can be incorporated in a national plan for government. Scriptural institutions and pragmatism thus combine in a plan for a church order that will both introduce a spiritual discipline and establish a national system to protect the integrity of that spiritual discipline.

When the Long Parliament opened new opportunities for Puritan ministers to seek a more fully reformed church, several of Ball's colleagues assumed positions of leadership in what would soon be described as Presbyterian circles. When they did so, they brought with them long-established commitments to the importance of establishing congregational government and discipline in order to advance godliness. But they also brought other commitments: to church unity, to the integrity of the parish structure against separatist impulses, and above all, to the spiritual and institutional authority of ministers when gathered in collective assemblies or presbyteries. We may infer from this review of Ball's controversial tracts that they had also developed a lively concern about the tendency of religious enthusiasm to foster dangerous innovations when congregations retained too much autonomy. Scriptural warrants for parochial government notwithstanding, Ball's colleagues and intellectual heirs perceived a practical need to embed godly government in a comprehensive national system. The scrupulous among them could learn from Ball himself that Scriptural church models provided the requisite "libertie" to legitimate this objective.

The Meanings

of Religious Polemic

Ann Hughes

ON MAY 4, 1651 an eminent Puritan, Thomas Hill, master of Trinity College, Cambridge, preached at Paul's Cross, London. It was quickly reported to John Goodwin, the radical minister of St. Stephen's, Coleman Street, that "in your sermon . . . before the Lord Mayor and Aldermen of this city, with many others, you [Hill] were pleased to vent yourself with much unseemliness of passion (which gave great offence to the sober and most considerate part of your auditory) against certain opinions." Specifically, Hill had denounced "Pelagian and Arminian" opinions which he associated with Goodwin's *Redemption Redeemed.* Such an attack on a prestitigious occasion, could not pass unchallenged; within a week Goodwin had produced a twelve-page open letter to Hill with the immodest title, *Moses Made Angry.*[1] In the lively, controversial religious atmosphere of the 1640s and 1650s in "old" England the spoken, the written, and the printed word were inevitably intertwined: a book prompted a sermon which in turn elicited a pamphlet response, and indeed, Goodwin's letter demanded a further response from Hill. If Hill had been wrongly reported, and would disown the attack on Goodwin, then Goodwin for his part declared his willingness to apologize.

Thomas Edwards's notorious heresiography, *Gangræna,* provides extended examples of the complex connections between published texts and oral confrontations. In the preface to his third part, published in December 1646, Edwards described reactions to his earlier

---

[1] John Goodwin, *Moses made Angry, or a Letter Written and Sent to Dr Hill, Master of Trinity Colleg in Cambridg* (1651); the "letter" is dated May 9, 1651 (p. 12).

volumes recounting the "errors, heresies, blasphemies" of the sectaries. He had been challenged in person, "some who having been
mentioned in letters written up to friends, and printed by me, have
come to my house, denying peremptorily those things spoken of
them in the letters, desiring to know who writ them, that they might
have reparations." With typical tactlessness, Edwards told them and
then wrote to his informants for further damning information. Other
victims "used devices and found out inventions to possess people
that relations in my book are false, when most true." It was easiest to
do this when different sectaries shared the same name, "Thus one
Webb, an officer in the army did, telling the people in the west where
he found *Gangraena* that the story of Webb was of him, I am that
Webb in *Gangraena* and 'tis all false, I never preached such things.
This a godly minister in the west of England told me he heard one
Webb an officer in the army speak thus to the people to possess them
against *Gangraena*." But this was disingenuous; as the army officer
Webb knew quite well Edwards's target was "another Webb, a
younger man here in London."[2]

Hitherto, discussions of *Gangræna* have been about the accuracy
of its content: some scholars, like Christopher Hill or Ian Gentles,
have used it as direct evidence for the nature and spread of radical
opinions while others (Colin Davis or Mark Kishlansky, for example)
claim that Edwards's obvious bias makes his work useless for such
purposes. They suggest that Edwards is constructing an exaggerated
picture of the sectarian threat in order to bolster support for a rigid
Presbyterian system.[3] More interesting insights, however, may be obtained by thinking about the making of *Gangræna* and about reactions to it as a text. *Gangræna* was a compilation of letters written
to Edwards, narratives of his personal experiences, and alarmed extracts from books he had read. It thus combines the intense and intimate emotions aroused by face-to-face encounters in London with a
more abstract sense of an "imaginary" community defined as those
who had read the same books or agonized over the same issues. This
last community of course included New England: through books,
hearsay, and rumor Samuel Gorton had come to Edwards's atten-

[2] Thomas Edwards, *The third part of Gangræna or A new and higher Discovery of the Errors,
Heresies, Blasphemies and Insolent Proceedings of the Sectaries* (December, 1646), sig A3–A4.

[3] Christopher Hill, *The World Turned Upside Down* (first published 1972; 1975 paperback
is quoted), 175–176, 187–189; Ian Gentles, *The New Model Army in England, Ireland and
Scotland 1645 -1653* (Oxford, 1992), 89, 101, 140–1; Mark Kishlansky, *The Rise of the New
Model Army* (Cambridge, 1979), ix; J.C. Davis, "Fear, Myth and Furore: Reappraising
the 'Ranters,'" *Past and Present* 129(1990): 79–103, especially p. 88.

tion.[4] "There is one Gorton, who was a great sectary in New England, holding many desperate opinions there; a copy of which, given by Mr Williams of New England (that writ the book cal'd *The bloudy Tenet*) unto a Reverend Minister now at London, I have seen and perused. . . . how Gorton escaped [from trial and imprisonment at Boston] . . . I know not; only this I am assured of from divers hands, that Gorton is here in London, and hath been for the space of some months; and I am told also, that he vents his opinions, and exercises in some of the meetings of the sectaries, as that he hath exercised lately at Lam's church, and is very great at one sister Stag's, exercising there too sometimes."

My concern in this essay is with the forms and meanings as well as the content of confrontations between "orthodox" Puritans and more radical figures. The focus is particularly on public formal or semi-formal debates or disputations over religion in old England during the interregnum and their writing up for publication. I am trying to avoid a stress on content alone by looking also at the broader forms and meaning of disputations both as events and as published texts. In a very preliminary and rather indiscriminate fashion, I am exploring how the insights developed by cultural historians and literary theorists influenced by post-structuralism or new historicism can enlarge our understanding of the Puritan religious literature of the 1640s and 1650s. A crucial argument is that language is constitutive of meaning, it does not merely reflect it. Forms of communication have an impact on the values and ideas available to people in societies, although in turn forms are used, adapted, appropriated by different groups in particular, specific ways. Louis Montrose has characterized new literary approaches as asserting, "'The Historicity of Texts and Textuality of History'. . . . the dynamic, unstable and reciprocal relationship between the discursive and material domains."[5] Although the "textuality of history" is asserted in a general fashion, particular studies of the historical context and significance of works that are an accepted part of a literary tradition are more common than examinations of more mundane historical sources as if they were literary texts. I wish, in other words, to exam-

---

[4]Edwards, *Gangræna* II, pp 174–5.

[5]Louis Montrose, "Renaissance Literary Studies and the Subject of History," *English Literary Renaissance* 16(1986), especially p. 8; for some other guides to these various influences see, out of a many possible references: Patrick Joyce, "History and Post-Modernism I," *Past and Present* 133(1991): 204–208; Lynn Hunt, ed., *The New Cultural History* (Berkeley, 1989); Richard Wilson and Richard Dutton, eds., *New Historicism and Renaissance Drama* (London, 1992).

ine the pamphlets as print culture, not just to ransack them for opinions on infant baptism or the nature of the visible church.[6]

The more immediate historiographical context for analysis of disputations is what seems to me to be the unsatisfactory treatment in much existing work of the attitudes and fortunes of the orthodox Puritan ministry in interregnum old England. Here orthodox, or mainstream, means those ministers who had supported Parliament in the civil war as a means of completing, at last, the reformation of the English church. They wanted a reformed national church, Calvinist in doctrine, with an effective, well-maintained, preaching ministry and a structure which could enforce a rigorous moral and religious discipline. Many preferred a Presbyterian church government, although doctrinaire views on this were rare and at times, at least, most "congregationalists" or "Independents" were part of this mainstream. Thus most English "Presbyterians" would regard the ministers of the "New England Way" as brethren, if erring brethren. Ultimately, of course, the aims of the orthodox parliamentarian clergy were frustrated: no satisfactory replacement for the episcopal prewar church could be established and pre-civil war Puritanism fragmented after 1640. But it is inadequate to characterize the experiences of the orthodox Puritans as marked simply by failure and division.[7]

There are currently two very different stresses in work on the religious divisions of the '40s and '50s although there are some interesting convergences in views of the orthodox clergy; the two versions are in turn connected to very different views of the Reformation itself. One strand can again be seen as represented in a most stimulating fashion in Hill's *World Turned Upside Down*. Here the radical, emancipatory potential of the Reformation (and its Lollard roots) is stressed: the priesthood of all believers, the importance of the bible in the vernacular and so on. This radical reformation culminated in the mechanic preachers and separatists of the interregnum while orthodox Puritans like Thomas Edwards are portrayed as increasingly conservative, embattled, and alarmed at the results of their fiery

---

[6]The major exceptions for early modern England are on popular literature: Margaret Spufford, *Small Books and Pleasant Histories: Popular fiction and its readership in seventeenth century England* (London, 1981); Tessa Watt, *Cheap Print and Popular Piety 1550–1640* (Cambridge, 1991).

[7]For further discussion of the experiences of the "orthodox" godly in interregnum old England, see my "The Frustrations of the Godly" in John Morrill, ed., *Revolution and Restoration* (London, 1993); the gloomy judgment is from Blair Worden, "Toleration and the Cromwellian Protectorate" *Studies in Church History* 21, ed. W. Sheils (Oxford, 1984).

preaching. In this account, furthermore, radical Protestantism is also seen as popular—in two senses: it is seen as appealing to large numbers of people, and as attractive mainly to men and women from below the ranks of propertied and educated elites. A very different approach is adopted by John Morrill who argues that religious radicals were seen as a bizarre and decidedly unpopular minority.[8] Morrill's account stresses the elitist and reformatory rather than emancipatory aspects of zealous Protestantism. For Morrill, Protestantism was an over-demanding, book-based religion, an inadequate substitute for the comforting rituals of the still vital pre-Reformation church. The orthodox clergy are not here the embattled conservatives described by Hill, but elitist failures, whose reforming efforts were sabotaged by an easy-going, accessible "Anglicanism" based on communal parochial ritual and straightforward morality as the paths to salvation. It is this Anglican "silent majority" which represents popular religion for Morrill: most people, he alleges, rejected the demanding, divisive Calvinist divinity of the orthodox "Presbyterian" clergy which harped on sin and irrevocable damnation, and had impossibly high standards for admission to the sacraments, excluding many judged as ignorant and profane.

Both Hill and Morrill agree however, that mainstream Interregnum Puritanism was elitist and unpopular—an aspect of educated, elite culture that despised and was rejected by the bulk of the population. In examining interregnum disputations both as oral debates and as printed pamphlets, I wish to question this view of Puritanism as unpopular, and, more generally, to explore the validity of cleavages between elite and popular culture, oral and literate forms. Disputations have an obvious value for exploring some general connections between religious literature and religious "experience" as well as for discussions about the accessibility and styles of Puritan religious writings. They may thus help us to see more broadly the meanings generated by other kinds of religious polemic like *Gangræna* in the ways suggested earlier.

In New England disputations seem to have been less common, but the complex interrelationships between different forms of religious controversy demonstrated in *Gangræna* are found clearly in the Antinomian controversy in the Boston church in 1636–1637—oral preaching and debate, manuscript correspondence and circulated

[8]Hill, *World Turned Upside Down*, 59–60 (amongst other examples); John Morrill, "The Church in England 1642–1649," in Morrill, ed., *Reactions to the English Civil War* (London, 1982).

arguments, published recapitulations and resumes. David Hall has recently argued that "people in New England perceived speech and writing as continuous and interchangeable"; his work on popular religious belief has served as inspiration as much as comparison for my discussions of old England. Hall has done much to elucidate the meanings of literacy in early New England and the ambiguous purposes and impact of religious literature; he has also stressed the accessibility and popularity of zealous Puritanism, the impossibility of distinguishing in any clear-cut way between the religion of the clergy and that of the people. There are of course sharp contrasts to be made between old and new England: the founders of New England were "more Protestant than most," and largely literate. "No town in New England had a maypole; no group celebrated Christmas or St Valentine's Day, or staged a pre-Lenten carnival!" Normal practices in New England were promoted by a minority in old England, but it was a significant minority whose character may be better grasped through Hall's approach.[9]

Interregnum disputations are a particularly striking reminder that the pamphlet sources we use to study theological ideas and religious debates were not themselves the product of remote, detached, academic research. They involved vital questions about the true church, salvation, and the relationship between God and humanity; furthermore, pamphlet controversies often had their origins in direct physical confrontations and debates between adherents of different religious positions, occasions that combined public challenges to opinions with intimate threats to status and position. These direct encounters took many forms, both casual and elaborate. In *Gangræna* Edwards reported numerous examples of heckling of parish ministers by radicals, often soldiers who then took over the pulpits and preached themselves, as well as arguments in the streets such as the debate over the nature of the Trinity between a "great sectary" and a "person of quality and a godly man" that occurred "near the House of Commons' door." During the Antinomian controversy Thomas Weld reported that "after our sermons were ended at our public lectures, you might have seen half a dozen pistols discharged at the face of the preacher . . . not once and away, but from day to day after our sermons."[10]

[9]David D. Hall, ed., *The Antinomian Controversy, 1636–1638: A Documentary History* (Middletown, 1968); Hall, *Worlds of Wonder, Days of Judgment: Popular Religious Belief in Early New England* (New York, 1989), 42, 22–30, 4–11.

[10]*Gangræna*, I, pp 106–8, 182; II, p 149; Hall, ed., *Antinomian Controversy*, 209–210.

Disputations were more extended and more formal than such ad-hoc encounters; they occurred in a variety of ways as these examples from old England will indicate. Sometimes, an orthodox minister was challenged by a radical sectary, as Ralph Josselin was by the general baptist, Samuel Oates, on a preaching tour in Essex. Josselin recorded in his diary, on June 29, 1646: "This day I held against Oates the Anabaptist morning and afternoon; argument that they had no ministry and that particular Christians out of office had no power to send ministers out to preach; he confessed it, and held only to do what he did as a disciple. I showed it was contrary to Scripture. Our discourse was without passion." Sometimes, however, it was the more orthodox minister who took the initiative. In September 1653 the baptist clergyman John Tombes preached at Abergavenny in Monmouthshire that "infant baptism was a nullity, a mockery," so offending local schoolmasters and ministers that they arranged a disputation for the following day. Francis Fullwood, a young Devonshire minister, gatecrashed a Quaker meeting in October 1656 and engaged in public debate with a Quaker missionary, Thomas Salthouse, on the validity of the public ministry and the Quaker notion of the inner light. Fullwood, like most ministers engaged in such debates, found it necessary to justify his actions, going to some pains to excuse his rashness in an account of the dispute published "out of a single and sincere desire that error may be shamed and the truth cleared." "It seemeth strange to some, that Mr Fullwood would venture to go into the Quakers' meeting; but his encouragement thereunto was, that that friend who desired him to go, hoped that much good might be done thereby; . . . It seemeth yet more strange, that Mr Fullwood would go himself, without giving any notice thereof to any of his friends who might have been helpful, at least, as witnesses to him, But . . . the warning was so short . . . Besides he had no thoughts of making a set dispute of it, 'till provoked by the Quaker's railing discourse. And had he not gone, some would have been ready enough to have said, he durst not."[11]

Frequently, public debate was a last resort when private measures failed to heal divisions in a community. Faced with the scandal of a president of Harvard College who no longer believed in infant bap-

---

[11] *The Diary of Ralph Josselin 1616–1683,* ed. Alan Macfarlane. British Academy Records of Social and Economic History, new ser., 3(1976):63; *A Publick Dispute betwixt John Tombs, B.D. respondent, John Cragge and H. Vaughan, M.A., opponents, touching Infant-baptism 5 September 1653* (London, 1654), dedication by J.W. (not paginated); *A True relation of a Dispute Between Francis Fullwood . . . and one Thomas Salthouse* (1656) sig B2.

tism, the leading clergy of New England, "laboured with extreme agony either to rescue the good man from his own mistake, or to restrain him from imposing them upon the hope of the flock." A more public debate, amongst the clergy, was arranged when private conference failed. The obscure, as well as the famous, resisted private persuasion. In the mid '50s, a young man in the congregation of the minister Adam Martindale in Cheshire was barred from the sacrament because his wife had been pregnant when they married, and as a consequence (Martindale felt) turned Quaker. When Martindale and a leading parishioner visited him to talk him out of his errors, they found him, "as yet raw in that way" and "offered him to dispute the case at his own house before a few select friends with the ablest he could procure; but nothing would serve their turn but a public disputation on Knutsford Heath, which we undertook, Mr Thomas Partington coming in to our assistance. They had got to their champion the famous Richard Hubberthorne, well-known by his printed pamphlets, and (to speak truth,) the most rational calm-spirited man of his judgement that I was ever publicly engaged against . . . Yet for all his dexterity we clearly proved against him the following points, by plain scriptures, vindicated from all his sophistical evasions, false glosses, and subterfuges." The points Martindale "proved" included the need to test the evidence of the spirit by the scriptures; the importance of a "sent ministry" rather than the light within in leading people to salvation; and the impossibility of becoming free from sin in this life. In his memoirs Martindale recorded that "This was the most calm, methodical and useful dispute with that sort of people at which I was ever present," one of several such encounters with separatists and Quakers in the 1640s and 1650s.[12]

These confrontations were modeled on the formal debates or disputations which were an important part of the education of the minority of English males who attended grammar schools or universities. Academic disputations were the means by which knowledge and skills were tested; degrees were awarded after a public demonstration of the scholars' abilities in a disputation rather than by the written examinations dominant in modern education. The most prestigious academic occasions were the Act at Oxford and the Commencements at both Cambridges when noted disputants and aspirants for

---

[12] Samuel Eliot Morison, *Harvard College in the Seventeenth Century*, 2 vols. (Cambridge, Mass., 1936), 1:305–308; the quotation is from Cotton Mather, *Magnalia Christi Americana*, in turn quoting Jonathon Mitchell's diary. *The Life of Adam Martindale By Himself* (Chetham Society vol. 4, 1845), 114–115.

higher degrees performed before eminent audiences. In old England before 1640 monarchs and courtiers might attend: John Preston caught the attention of James I at a specially arranged debate in 1615, while copies of Cambridge, Massachusetts, commencement theses were eagerly sought by up-to-date young men in the later seventeenth century. An academic disputation was formal, precise, and dignified. A respondent, given a question in advance, prepared and put forward arguments to support it; one or more opponents stated contrary positions, and attacked the respondents' reasoning; a moderator summed up the points on both sides, elucidated obscure or neglected aspects of the debate, and made a decision. Most disputations on matters of logic or grammar concerned formal matters where the answer itself was not important, the point was to demonstrate skill in debate: Preston's dispute before the king was with Matthew Wren over whether dogs could reason.[13] University disputations thus had a large element of ritual or game; and indeed were attended by the mockery and play of satirical commencement theses or bogus debates in both old and new England. The young Milton denounced university orations and disputations as trivial intellectual games, a diversion from a serious quest for truth.[14]

The educated consensus was that disputations provided an essential training but even in an academic context theological disputations, undertaken only by those attempting higher degrees, were more problematic for theology was about the fundamental truths of religion which ought to be uncontrovertible. Most of the time then the answer to a theological disputation was regarded as obvious, and again the disputant was tested on his capacity to muster the best arguments for a generally accepted truth. At the worst, during times of religious crisis, where truths were contested, disputations could be a means of demonstrating in a dynamic way the errors of opponents or of practicing arguments that would be effective against them. Hence aspirant ministers seeking ordination by the Manchester Presbyterian classis during the Interregnum had to show skill in

[13] Craig R. Thompson, *Universities in Tudor England*. Folger Booklets on Tudor and Stuart Civilization, Folger Library (Washington, 1959); M.H. Curtis, *Oxford and Cambridge in Transition, 1558–1642* (Oxford, 1959), 88–116; Rosemary O'Day, *Education and Society, 1500–1800* (London, 1982), 52, 112, 118; Morison, *Harvard College*, 1:67–69, 143–145, 156–157, 160–163. William Haller, *The Rise of Puritanism* (first published, New York, 1938; 1957 paperback quoted), 71, 298 for Preston; John Cotton, junior, to Cotton Mather, March 1678, in *The Mather Papers* (Massachusetts Historical Society, *Collections*, ser. 4, vol. 8), 248.

[14] Morison, *Harvard College*, 1:123–124; Haller, *Rise of Puritanism*, 300–301.

disputation before the classis. An attempt to maintain the formality of disputation in difficult times can be seen in Edward Johnson's account of the debates on antinomian "errors" at the Cambridge synod of 1637: "A catalogue of the several errors scattered about the country was there produced, to the number of 80 and liberty given to any man to dispute pro or con, and *none to be charged to be of that opinion he disputed for unless he should declare himself to be so.*"[15]

It was not possible for religious disputation to remain routine during the religious changes and conflicts of the sixteenth and seventeenth centuries. Traumatic ruptures occurred in old England during the 1550s and again during the rise of Arminianism, when previously outlawed opinions became uncontrovertible answers. Radical heretics and separatists had mounted occasional challenges to the orthodox from the time of the Lollards, while in the late 1630s desperately important semi-private debates on the issue of separatism were held amongst English Puritans themselves. In the 1640s and 1650s traumas multiplied for the orthodox as they faced numerous attacks from sectarian opponents who were not only arguing for unacceptable positions but were also refusing to follow the rules of dignified university debate.[16]

In New England disputations outside Harvard were rarer and retained their academic nature, confined usually to the clergy; the major exceptions were the two occasions in when the orthodox engaged in public debate with the baptists in the 1660s. An intimate and elaborate means of containing deviant or radical opinion through church discipline supported by civil power prevented the emergence of the licensed religious speculation of interregnum old England. There, orthodox Puritans did not have unequivocal backing from secular authority: they had more need to defend their beliefs in public while radicals had more opportunities for challenging ministers. More characteristic of New England debates were those held to resolve crises within orthodoxy, during the Antinomian controversy and the move to the "half-way covenant"; tightly organized, they involved

---

[15] *The Minutes of the Manchester Classis* (3 volumes, one pagination, Chetham Society, new series, vols 20, 22, 24, 1890–91), 298–299 for an example; Edward Johnson, *The Wonder Working Providence of Sion's Saviour in New England* (first published London, 1654; 1952, New York edition quoted), 171, emphasis mine.

[16] For the frequency of disputations in the Interregnum see Ann Hughes, "The Pulpit Guarded: Confrontations between Orthodox and Radicals in Revolutionary England," in Anne Laurence, W.R. Owens, and Stuart Sim, eds., *John Bunyan and his England, 1628–1688* (London, 1990) esp. 35–36; for earlier sectarian challenges and the debates of the late 1630s see the chapters by Patrick Collinson and Carol Geary Schneider in this volume.

displays of learning by the clergy, despite Thomas Weld's self-effacing account of the synod of 1637: "The other fortnight we spent in a plain syllogistical dispute (*ad vulgus* as much as might be). . . . In the forenoons we framed our arguments, and in the afternoons produced them in public, and next day the adversary gave in their answers, and produced also their arguments on the same questions; then we answered them, and replied also upon them the next day." The issues were real and important, but the forms were observed. More patterned and formalized still was the "dialogue" recorded by William Bradford in 1648. This conference between "some young men born in New England, and sundry ancient men that came out of Holland and old England" was intended to reassure the younger generation that the attacks on the "New England way" by Presbyterians like Robert Baillie were not justified.[17]

In old England the distance between participants in disputations varied enormously: the extremes can be illustrated by two very different debates on the validity of infant baptism. In January 1650 Richard Baxter of Kidderminster defended baptism against John Tombes of Bewdley; although Tombes had radical views on this one issue, he agreed with Baxter on most matters of theology and church government and indeed had a much more "establishment" academic background. These men were neighbors in more than a geographical sense. In November 1658, in contrast, two "several public disputations" before thousands of people took place in St. Clement Danes Church, London, where the participants could hardly have been more different: the Laudian Peter Gunning, a bishop after the Restoration, challenged Henry Denne, the general Baptist who wrote sympathetically of the Quakers.[18]

Episcopalian or Anglican participants in disputations can be found in the '40s and '50s: Clement Barksdale of Gloucestershire, with Gunning, and Henry Vaughan, one of Tombes's opponents in Abergavenny, are significant examples, while Francis Fullwood was one of those Interregnum conformists who became a pillar of the restored Church of England. But the most common "moderate" or "conser-

---

[17]Hall, *Worlds of Wonder*, 62–65; Weld, preface to John Winthrop, *A Short Story of the Rise, reign and ruine of the Antinomians, Familists and Libertines* in Hall, ed., *Antinomian Controversy*, 213; for the debates at the 1662 synod on the "half-way covenant" see Michael G. Hall, *The Last American Puritan: The Life of Increase Mather* (Middletown, 1988), 58–59. Bradford's dialogue is in Alexander Young, *Chronicles of the Pilgrim Fathers of the Colony of Plymouth from 1602–1625* (2nd edition, Boston, 1844).

[18]Richard Baxter, *Plain Scripture Proof of Infants Church-membership and Baptism* (1650); *A Contention for Truth in Two Several Publique Disputations* (1658).

vative" participants were the orthodox Puritan parish clergy. Such godly ministers had enthusiastically challenged Laudians in the early 1640s, only to find their own positions publicly assailed by radical sectaries. Debates thus took place on the nature of the true visible church as a national, comprehensive mixed company or a gathering of saints; and on the claims of an ordained, educated ministry, maintained through tithes, versus the right of gifted lay people to preach; on the validity of the parochial structure or the practice of infant baptism. The characteristic opponents of the orthodox godly in the 1640s and early 1650s were rigid separatists who were often also Baptists. The rise of the Quakers from the mid 1650s brought a shift in the nature of disputations as different aspects of Puritan orthodoxy were challenged. The importance of the scriptures; the historical nature of Christ as distinguished from his spiritual significance; Calvinist doctrines of sin and predestination versus ideas of perfectibility and the inner light, were all characteristic of debates involving Quakers. Although many orthodox parish ministers like Baxter or Fullwood debated the Quakers, in print or in person, Quaker ideas also outraged many who had themselves previously been radical opponents of orthodox "Presbyterians." The west country baptist Thomas Collier and the Cheshire Independent Samuel Eaton are amongst several examples of men who played a "radical" role in debates with parish clergy in the 1640s and early 1650s but later defended "orthodox" positions against the Quakers.[19]

This is important and useful information, but it is at least as revealing to examine disputations as events in their own right, as dramas or spectacles. Why did people participate in them, what meanings did they have for audience and participants? Of course, we usually know about oral disputations because they were written up and published; in several cases we are lucky enough to have rival versions from both sides of a debate. Here, disputations provide an excellent example of the insights that can be gained when we show sensitivity to historical sources as texts. We cannot present an "accurate" or "truthful" picture of what occurred in debates, what we have are the different strategies that witnesses or participants used for presenting *their* versions of religious truth to wider audiences. These reveal contrasting attitudes to the written and the spoken word, and to the links between religion and learning, and enable us to consider the popularity and accessibility of varying styles of religious writing.

[19] Clement Barksdale, *The disputation at Winchcombe* (Oxford, 1653); *A Publick Dispute;* Hughes, "The Pulpit Guarded," 33, 36.

Orthodox, educated ministers had more to lose by taking part in disputations than mechanic preachers and so their justifications for participation are especially interesting. In an important general account of disputations, the Presbyterian John Ley advised his fellow ministers to debate only where the rules were agreed in advance, the opponent was worthy, and the occasion could be dignified and edifying. The accounts of Martindale and Fullwood already quoted are ambivalent about their participation in public debate. Disputations could be "tumultary," as the Abergavenny debate was described, and were sometimes forbidden by secular authority for fear of disorder as was a famous projected debate in London between the eminent Presbyterian Edmund Calamy and the baptist leaders Kiffin and Knollys in 1645.[20]

More personally, orthodox ministers expressed contradictory fears: firstly that they were degrading themselves and their calling by agreeing to debate with the unlearned. In an earlier dispute involving Fullwood, with the baptist Thomas Collier at Wiveliscombe in Somerset in 1651, the orthodox account admitted, "Some men may possibly dislike the action itself, and question the prudence and discretion of the ministers, who could so much undervalue themselves as to contest with such ignorant wranglers." A Warwickshire minister wrote of his meeting with a general baptist, "I need not tell you how many dissuasions I had from entering the lists with an illiterate adversary. . . ." The orthodox feared sectaries' views would be given more legitimacy by an agreement to debate: "you enquire whether it may be fit to dispute, and confer with them, seeing their doctrine eats as a canker, for which cause the Empress would not suffer her son Theodosius to discourse with the heretic Eunomius."[21]

But there was a second, contradictory fear that native wit, experience of argument obtained through popular drama and story-telling, or through participation in legal processes, or indeed through catechizing exercises and the sort of private religious discussion groups that got Anne Hutchinson into trouble in New England, might enable the unlearned to make a good showing in disputations. Impu-

---

[20]John Ley, *A Discourse of Disputations Chiefly concerning matters of religion* (1656), 57–58, 69–72; Edwards, *Gangræna*, I, p.94.

[21]Francis Fullwood, *The Churches and Ministry of England, True Churches and true Ministry, Cleared and Proved in a Sermon . . . and a narrative (subjoyned) showing the substance of the dispute after the Sermon* (1652), Preface to the Reader by Charles Darby; *A Publick Disputation Sundry days at Killingworth in Warwickshire, betwixt John Bryan, Doctor in Divinity (Minister at Coventry) and John Onley, Pastor of a Church at Lawford* (1654); *A Publick Dispute*, dedication.

dent disruption by uneducated men who did not know, or refused to follow, the rules of debate might lead to educated ministers actually losing a disputation, and being heard to lose it in public before a credulous people. Ley, for example, warned that oratorical skills were not confined to the educated and the orthodox, and people might be won over by surface eloquence not valid arguments. Hence some preferred private conference as a means of dealing with doubts and opposition. Hence too the stress in orthodox accounts of public disputation on the superficial, showy, popular appeal of their opponents; and the paradoxical attempt to portray themselves, maintained, educated clergymen, in a defensive and apologetic manner as the most vulnerable participants. The Wiveliscombe disputation was presented as a contest between "three or four young despised ministers, and the whole strength of the adversary." This of course made the success of the orthodox all the more creditable for the young Fullwood was caught unprepared and was tired from the sermon he had preached, yet still managed to confute his crafty adversary. The orthodox account gives a dramatic picture of this hard-won victory: Collier and his allies "would ever and anon appeal to the people, especially when their arguing was plausible and specious, or if there had been some verbal falterings in any of the defendants. For they well know, that a stentorian voice and plausible speech, do much more prevail upon ignorant souls, than the strongest reason or the most forcible argument." Yet, they claimed that Collier was "put to silence more than once" and often, "so non-plussed, breaking all the laws of disputation, he would begin again, running back to his argument" so that his followers had to fill up his "vacancy" with "clamours." Sometimes, the attempts of the educated and orthodox to present themselves as the underdogs in disputations bordered on the absurd. The Cambridge academic Thomas Smith published his version of his dispute with the Quakers George Fox and George Whitehead as "Three eminent Quakers against one scholar of Cambridge." This provoked a well-judged satirical reply by Henry Denne addressed to "my learned friend, Mr Thomas Smith, Bachelor in Divinity, Reader of the Rhetoric Lecture in Christ College in Cambridge, Keeper of the University Library." The Quakers were, wrote Denne, "wholly unversed in learning" and for Smith to encounter them "was to incur disgrace . . . to fill the world with a victory so ignoble, what is it but to glory in his own shame?" Indeed Smith's learning had not brought him victory, and he was urged by Denne to return to the study of "his Arabic and other manuscripts."[22]

But orthodox Puritan ministers frequently participated in debates. Of course, where radical sectaries had issued a "challenge" (significantly the terminology of the tournament is often used), it was difficult to refuse without accusations of cowardice as Fullwood pointed out in justification of the debate with Salthouse. When the Baptists challenged the parish clergy at their regular Wiveliscombe exercise, "swift notice was given to all or the most part of the sectaries of the west. In the mean time many threatening and insulting speeches were given out by that party; as that no Presbyterian minister durst show his head there, with much to that purpose. Nor was anything more rife in every man's mouth, than the future dispute at Wiveliscombe." (This is not of course consistent with the claim that the young ministers were taken completely by surprise). Quakers could be even more "insulting": when Richard Baxter's assistant was attacked during a sermon, "because he avoided public disputing with them at that season, as not taking it for a profitable spending of the Lords day, they call him the hireling that flieth."[23]

The orthodox were by no means always to be found in a defensive position. Baxter himself clearly preferred oral debate to written polemic: claiming that he only published his *Quaker's Catechism,* dealing with the Quakers "in their own questioning way" because they "abhor syllogisms and disputings" and would not agree to public oral debate. Many orthodox ministers, as we have seen, initiated debates themselves. They were aware of their positive duty to defend the truth and confute error, and prepared to compete with radicals for popular support. If we find this surprising it may be that we should re-assess our view of the orthodox, Puritan clergy of the Interregnum simply as the conservative and defensive opponents of the sectaries. At Wiveliscombe the orthodox argued that conflict could be productive because it led to the defeat of error: "How many sparks of truth have been beaten out by the collision even of flints? That God who commanded light to shine out of darkness, doth often produce the best effects out of the worst causes." The conformist opponents of Tombes in Abergavenny argued eloquently against their own exam-

---

[22]Ley, *Discourse of Disputations,* 3–4; Fullwood, *The Churches and Ministry of England,* sig. C1r–v, C3v–C4r; T. S[mith], *The Quaker Disarmed* (1659); Henry Denne, *The Quaker No Papist* (1659) sig A2–3, 10 (in fact p. 18).

[23]Fullwood, *The Churches and Ministry of England,* sig. C2r; Richard Baxter, *The Quaker's Catechism* (1656), 'To the Reader,' sig A2r.

ple of Theodosius: "the sword of the spirit, which is the word of God, is the only weapon to wound the hairy scalp of false teachers; with this, Christ confounded the Sadducees; St Peter, Simon Magus . . . There are none that speak against seasonable disputes, but either those that understand them not, or with spiritual pride storm against those that are gifted with that faculty above them . . . when false teachers have infused poison, may we not apply an antidote? When they have sowed darnel and cockle, may not we weed them out? This is to set Towns and Cities on fire, and to deny buckets to quench them, to suffer invasions, and to permit none to rally together an army to resist them."[24]

Orthodox ministers' conception of their own responsibilities thus led them to debate their social and educational inferiors, but there were limits to this condescension. The Puritan clergy were not prepared to give women's opinions any legitimation by agreeing to refute them in public debate. "I wonder you should trouble yourself to discourse with that woman! She hath so much learning it makes her mad," exclaimed one witness of a later argument between a cleric and a woman over tithes. The relationships of male clergy with godly women focused rather on the private giving of advice or settling of doubts and difficulties, where the male cleric's superior role was clear-cut. John Ley's general account of disputations made it plain that women were not to dispute publicly. He condemned "heretical viragoes . . . women who have so much forgotten the frailty and modesty of their sex as to make challenges to learned men for disputation in matters of religion." The prominent role of Anne Hutchinson in the Antinomian controversy in New England heightened fears of its subversive impact. John Winthrop condemned "the impudent boldness of a proud dame, that Athaliah-like makes havoc of all that stand in the way of her ambitious spirit," and it should be noted that the orthodox never faced Mrs. Hutchinson in formal public debate as they did the ministers John Cotton and John Wheelwright. Mrs. Hutchinson had her say, but in the clearly subordinate role of the accused in trials conducted by the Boston church and the Massachusetts civil court.[25]

[24]Baxter, *Quakers Catechism,* sig A2v; Fullwood, *The Churches and Ministry of England,* sig. B4v; *A Publick Dispute,* dedication.

[25]Phyllis Mack, "The Prophet and Her Audience: Gender and Knowledge in the World Turned Upside Down," in Geoffrey Eley and William Hunt, eds., *Reviving the English Revolution* (London, 1988), 139; Ley, *Discourse of Disputations,* 16–17; Hall, ed., *Antinomian Controversy,* 275, chap. 9 etc.; Hughes, "Pulpit Guarded," 41–42.

The debates reveal how "orthodox" and "radical" men were appropriating some common asumptions and arguments, albeit with different emphases. They shared a belief that the truth would emerge inevitably through honest debate although they differed over what that truth was, and over who to blame when disputations were not fruitful. All were working within a tradition based on the authority of scripture although again there were differences over how exactly to interpret the "word," especially with the Quakers. All disputants therefore insisted that they took part in debate to vindicate the truth only, and not for any personal desire for glory. At Wiveliscombe, the clergy "aimed more at the maintenance of truth than at the praise of a victory and yet they aimed at victory also, but not to credit themselves, but the truth." The Baptist Thomas Collier in another dispute described himself as "the least of all the Saints" but insisted "let me be abused so truth be exalted"; and Quaker disputants, like Edward Burrough and James Nayler, often wrote that they strove not for mastery for themselves but only for "the lord and his truth." A similar rhetoric was used by Thomas Weld to justify his role in the trial of Anne Hutchinson, "myself asking why she did cast such aspersions upon the ministry of the country though we were poor sinful men and for ourselves we cared not but for the precious doctrine we held forth we could not but grieve to hear that so blasphemed."[26]

All disputants, orthodox and radical, predictably claimed to have silenced and confused their opponents, although they gave different reasons for this achievement. The orthodox usually silence the radicals through their learning; the radicals are "sorry disputants," lacking educated oral skills and ignorant or scornful of the rules of disputation. This was the case even when a radical figure was in fact more highly educated than his orthodox opponent: learning floundered in defending a poor case. Thus Richard Baxter was shocked at John Tombes's inability to keep to the rules of logic: when he was stuck he "breaks over the hedge, and turns all the dispute into a discourse and goes up and down at pleasure." At Abergavenny, Tombes was again accused of resorting to "his unwonted course of impertinent exposition," while Cragg, his opponent, argued that learning could not contradict the truth: "if he should but study the question so many

---

[26]Francis Fullwood, *The Churches and Ministry of England,* sig. C4v; *The Heads and Substance of a Discourse, First private and afterwards publike, held in Axbridge..March 1650* (1651), epistle to the Council of State; James Nayler, *Deceit brought to Daylight* (1656); Edward Burrough, *Truth (the Strongest of All) Witnessed Forth* (1657), 3–4; Hall, ed., *Antinomian Controversy,* 321.

hours as Mr Tombes hath done days, so many days as he hath done weeks, so many weeks as he months, or so many months as he years, the truth was so evident on his side, he would not fail (maugre all opposition to make it clear."[27]

For the orthodox educated skills were on the side of truth; they were the means by which truth was demonstrated, error confuted, and weak souls reclaimed. For most radicals, however, learning was frivolous and deceptive; it was opposed to, or contrasted with the truth. In New England, Quakers and Baptists held to this position and in Devon, old England, Thomas Salthouse contrasted "sound doctrine" with "cunning, devised fables and excellence of speech." For the academic Thomas Smith, logic was an essential attribute of rational humanity: "I pray ask any man in the world that knows what logic is, whether it doth not put a difference between a man and a beast?"; but George Fox put a very different view in his account of a debate with baptists: "the Baptists began with their logic and syllogisms, but I was moved in the Lord's power to thresh their chaffy, light minds, and showed the people that after that manner of light discoursing they might make white black and black white, and because a cock had two legs and they had two legs therefore they were cocks, and so turn anything into lightness, which was not the manner of Christ nor his Apostles' teachings and speakings."[28]

It would be a mistake to distinguish too sharply between "radical" and "learned" traditions. "Unlearned" sectaries could draw on sophisticated critiques of vain academicism constructed by the learned themselves: they were not simply reacting spontaneously to the arrogance of university educated ministers. Puritan attitudes towards learning were ambiguous and could be exploited in different ways: learning could pander to human vanity while faith came through the heart as well as through the understanding. True religion should be accessible to all; hence, as Hall has noted, Thomas Weld's description of the highly technical 1637 debates as a "plain syllogistical dispute." The traumas of the 1640s and 1650s provoked some qualification of earlier positions and a more determined defense of the value of learning just as in New England the Antinomian controversy led

---

[27]Baxter, *Plain Scripture Proof of Infant Baptism* sig. d1v; *A Publicke Dispute*, 43, 15.

[28]Hall, *Worlds of Wonder*, 62–66; Thomas Salthouse, *The Hidden Things of Esau Brought to Light* (1657), 9; Smith, *The Quaker Disarmed*, quoted in Paul Hammond, "Thomas Smith: a Beleaguered Humanist of the Interregnum," *Bulletin of the Institute of Historical Research* 56(1983): 194; Fox, quoted in C.W. Horle, "Quakers and Baptists, 1647–1660," *Baptist Quarterly* 26(1976): 344–362.

to a tightening up. As is well known, after 1637 strict limits were put on the previously accepted practices of questioning ministers after sermons and holding private meetings of the laity. A question might be asked for information, but "questions of reference . . . whereby the doctrines delivered were reproved . . . was utterly condemned." Meetings where sixty or more women met to expound the scriptures under Anne Hutchinson were "agreed to be disorderly and without rule."[29]

Nonetheless in old England a common Christian and biblical heritage qualifying the power of learning blurred the differences between disputants. The conventions of debate could also inhibit the full expression of hostility and abuse, especially by the educated ministers (although John Tombes does not seem to have been inhibited). Josselin and Martindale had civil comments for their opponents while the Wiveliscombe debate apparently ended as happily as any encounter at the Act: "They answered no more; and indeed it was now late; we did mutually congratulate the happy meeting and discourse of the day. Collier: I bless God that we have met with so moderate a man as you Master Fullwood. Fullwood: Truly, I did not expect to find a man so sober and rational among you, as you have been Master Collier."[30]

In their printed form, disputations demonstrate authors' sharp consciousness of the power of the press, and they vividly reveal the paradoxical nature of much religious literature, as recently emphasized in a New England context by David Hall. On the one hand, religious authors present their words as obvious and fundamental truths directly and immediately conveyed to men and women by God. On the other hand, writers have to stress the importance of getting *their* version circulated in a definitive form to a wider audience, and use, often *self-consciously,* a variety of *deliberate* strategies for presenting supposedly self-evident truth. John Tombes attacked his opponents' version of the Abergavenny dispute when he presented his own in a preface, "The reason of this writing is rendered": "there came to my hands a pamphlet wherein the intitler speaks like a vain braggadochio, as if the book had ripped up the Anabaptists and like a Prelate had silenced them." "I do account it a shameful practice," he continued, "which these men, and another before [presumably Richard Baxter] have used towards me, that after I have

---

[29]Hughes, "Pulpit Guarded," 44; Hall, *Worlds of Wonder,* 65; Hall, ed., *Antinomian Controversy,* 210n.; *Winthrop's Journal,* ed. James Kendall Hosmer (New York, 1908), 234.
[30]Fullwood, *The Churches and Ministry of England,* 71.

been drawn to a verbal extemporary dispute, and that no common notary agreed on, yet by answers are published by them without ever allowing me the sight of them, that I might either own them or amend them, afore the printing and publishing them." The printing of Francis Fullwood's debates with Collier and Salthouse was justified in similar fashion. John Ley regretted the naivety of his friend and neighbor, Dr. John Bryan of Coventry who had allowed his unlettered baptist opponent John Onley to organize the printing of their debate. The result, according to Ley, appeared as a debate between a John Bryan and a Dr. John Onley; the learned Doctor was made to appear he had "suffered a failing in his faculties."[31]

All accounts of disputations, and in particular rival accounts of the same debate, attack the truthfulness of opponents' versions while justifying their own truth-telling strategies. The Quaker Edward Burrough commented on his opponent's version of a debate at Drayton, Middlesex: he "hath given a relation of four times as much as he did speak at that meeting; and have related as though he spoke that which he never uttered, . . . and have not related so much by many times, as was spoken by me, . . . as many may witness. . . ." Philip Taverner, the author of this version, admitted he had "improved" on the oral debate. In his preface to the reader, he explained: "Thou hast here as orderly a relation of a confused discourse as the disorder in it would admit; the multitude of words which this day's work was filled up with, I do not undertake to set down; they were legions and far exceeding the largest memory, but the sum and substance of what was spoken on both sides is truly related; and here and there some few words inserted, for a further proof, and clearing of things spoken to."

The ways in which an appearance of truth-telling was combined with the presentation of a partisan argument could be very complex. Henry Denne's version of his debate with Gunning incorporated a narrative and direct speech account of the disputation itself within a second dialogue between a supposed witness and man who had merely heard about the contest. This made it possible to provide a critical commentary on Gunning's performance while posing as an "impartial relation."[32]

---

[31] John Tombes, *A Plea for Anti-Pædobaptists* (London, 1654), 1, 3; Francis Fullwood, *The Churches and Ministry of England*, sig D1; *A True relation of a Dispute Between Francis Fullwood*, sig. B2r; Ley, *Discourse of Disputations*, 77–78.

[32] E. Burrough, *Something of Truth Made Manifest (In Relation to a Dispute at Drayton)* (1658), 2; Philip Taverner, *The Quakers Rounds; A Contention for Truth in Two Several Publique Disputations* (1658), sig A2r, preface to the Reader.

Public disputations obviously illustrate the shifting, context-bound nature of concepts such as radical or orthodox in the religious debates of interregnum old England. The Baptist Thomas Collier who disputed with the orthodox parish clergyman Francis Fullwood at Wiveliscombe on the nature of the true church, the ministry and baptism, can be found five years later defending "orthodox" notions against the Quaker Thomas Salthouse as Fullwood himself was doing. Samuel Eaton, John Tombes and John Bunyan have similarly two-edged careers as controversialists. Both Eaton and Collier are amongst those who figure prominently in two notable collections of "errors": Thomas Edwards in *Gangræna* castigated them as grand sectaries, and proponents of "toleration" while George Fox in his *The Great Mistery of the Great Whore Unfolded* (1659) attacked them as lying, anti-Christian persecutors of the truth.[33]

But it is not simply that we need to have a subtler understanding of those who are usually seen as the religious radicals of the Interregnum. Crucially, the willingness of orthodox Puritan ministers to defend their notions of religious truth in public and to compete with radicals for popular support, should lead to a reassessment of the stance of such men. Hall's dynamic picture of mainstream Puritanism in New England can be applied in old England also. The godly were neither embattled conservatives nor elitist failures—or at least not only this. Contemporaries often commented on the time and energy "Presbyterians" spent on appealing to the people. The Quaker James Nayler sardonically described Presbyterian populism in his account of a dispute with several parish ministers at Chesterfield: "And now let every honest heart judge, by what spirit these men are guided, which for their own wicked ends make challenges and gather together many hundreds of people of their own sect, yea in their high places, and this they count no disturbance to state's government. But if the despised ones of the world do but meet to wait upon God in that ordinance in which they find him appearing to them, either in house or field (who are not thought worthy to meet in their towns but stoned and haled out) and this they persuade their magistrates is not fit to be suffered but inform and petition against it, under pretence of plotting against the present power."[34]

As Hall has stressed, we need to recover a sense of the radical and popular potential of mainstream Puritanism. The godly ministers of the '40s and '50s were the heirs to an activist and populist Protestant

---

[33]Hughes, "Pulpit Guarded," 33, 50.
[34]James Nayler, *A Dispute between James Nayler and the Parish teachers of Chesterfield* (1655), 16.

tradition of the sixteenth century, which stressed a plain and accessible preaching style and fought for the scriptures to be made available
to all. The Presbyterian Thomas Cartwright, writing in the late sixteenth century, provides a clear justification for the interregnum orthodox disputants: "For the scriptures declareth that women and
children and that from their infancy, that noble and ignoble, rich and
poor, wise and foolish exercise themselves in the holy scriptures . . .
the points of religion which the church taught were not only known
of doctors and masters but of taylors, smiths, weavers, and other
artificers . . . not of citizens alone but of country-folk, ditchers,
delvers, neat-herds, and gardeners disputing even of the holy
trinity."[35]

Orthodox ministers were thus prepared to take part in, and even
instigate the dynamic, open-ended, popular spectacles of public disputations. Religious debates attracted large audiences—at Chesterfield or at Clement Danes, London, where thousands were said to
be present at the debates between Gunning and Denne; their popularity itself suggests that a sullen and conservative response to orthodox Protestant reform or to radical speculation was neither as inevitable or as widespread as some work now suggests. The atmosphere
of debate is summed up in the common use of the language of the
tournament with challenges issued and champions coming to the
arena with their followers. Hubberthorne was the Quaker champion
against Martindale, Tombes, "so experienced a champion" against
Cragg. Richard Farnworth described a 1655 contest between the
Quakers and two Worcestershire ministers as "the great battle fought
(with the sword of the mouth only) at Underwood Hill." Contestants
faced each other like warriors in combat. At Clement Danes, Denne
"stood up in the pulpit, and entreating the multitude to be silent,
and to behave themselves civilly, and orderly and craving attention
he spake. . . ." Gunning faced him from an opposite gallery. Even in
the restrained atmosphere of the 1637 synod in New England, one
commentator wrote of "the valiant soldiers of Christ" at war for
truth.[36]

The drama of disputations is further revealed in examples of audience participation. At Wiveliscombe Thomas Collier denied that the

---

[35]Cartwright quoted in Hall, *Worlds of Wonder*, 22; see also Peter Lake, *Anglicans and
Presbyterians? Presbyterianism and English Conformist Thought* (1988), 79–80.
[36]Norman Penny, "The First Publishers of Truth," *Journal of the Friends Historical Society* (1907), 279n.; *A Publick Dispute*, 15; *A Contention for Truth in Two Several Publique Disputations*, 4; Johnson, *Wonder-Working Providence*, 174–175.

Reformation under Elizabeth had created a true church because the people had been compelled to agree by fear of the power of the magistrate. This was too much for "Mr Thomas Gorges, a very worthy, godly, and learned Gentleman, and Justice of Peace in the County," who interjected, "the renouncing of Popery, and embracing the Protestant Religion, was a voluntary act of the whole Land, in their Representative the Parliament, that sat in the first year of Queen Elizabeth's Reign." Fullwood rammed the point home. "Mr. Collier hearken to the Gentleman, he is a States-man, and knows what belongs to History better then you or I." The irascible Tombes, as portrayed by his opponents, did not take kindly to heckling: "C[ragg]: 'I see you have learned to vilify that argument you cannot answer. . . .' He hath answered nothing at all (says one under the pulpit) but shifts and denies all. T[ombes]: 'Thou art an impudent, brazen-faced fellow whosoever thou art, I have answered all, confuted all my adversaries' books.'"[37]

If we move from disputations as events to examining them as texts we get a similarly complex picture of the relationships between radical and orthodox Puritanism, and between religious literature and popular "culture." The forms of written disputations are complex, but it is by no means clear that "radical" accounts are more accessible than "orthodox." We are dealing with different ways of telling the truth and also with different forms of narrative, of telling a story. Orthodox versions often seem more straightforward, more frequently written in dialogue form as if they were scripts of plays. The craft or "style" is to appear to be simply presenting an obvious truth. Radicals usually write in indirect speech and are more obviously presenting a story; their narratives indeed are usually tidier and more coherent. There are exceptions to these patterns, and more work needs to be done on their significance, but nonetheless they suggest the difficulties in assigning particular genres in a simple way to "educated" or to "popular" culture. Printed disputations support the stress in recent work on cultural history on the interpenetration of elite and popular culture, and of oral and printed modes; and demonstrate the capacity of different groups to select or appropriate similar forms for contrasting purposes. "The 'popular' cannot be found ready made in a set of texts that merely require to be identified."[38] Popular protestant writers before the civil war frequently used dia-

[37] Francis Fullwood, *The Churches and Ministry of England*, 58; *A Publick Dispute*, 67–68.
[38] Roger Chartier, "Culture as appropriation: Popular Cultural Uses in Early Modern France," in Steven L. Kaplan, ed., *Understanding Popular Culture* (Berlin, 1984), 233.

logue "to give their writings immediacy and punch," as Christopher Hill has noted, but the dialogue form has also been an elite genre for conveying truth since Plato. Popular radical literature of the 1640s such as the early pamphlets of Richard Overton, or Leveller trial scenes mixed dialogue, narrative, and extracts from official records; but the impeccably orthodox Presbyterian Thomas Hall also used mock trials in his attacks on lay preaching or adult baptism. Both orthodox and radical accounts of disputations can be linked to accessible popular genres, the radicals' are perhaps nearer to the oral forms of popular story-telling, full of drama and repetition. Educated, orthodox ministers attempted to suggest exact verisimilitude, through dialogue or through self-deprecatory, hesitant descriptions. The Presbyterian minister Immanuel Bourne's account of the Chesterfield debate with James Nayler, is full of remarks like "or to that effect," "if my memory serves," and the like, asides which manage to foreground the authority of the writer, despite their self-effacing form. Nayler's version is a heightened, mystical dramatic story beginning "Being moved of the Lord to go to Chesterfield about the 20th day of the 10th month. . . ."[39]

Disputations reveal in a most suggestive way the complex and often contradictory relations between the spoken and the written word in religious discourse. Some literary theorists and anthropologists have argued for sharp distinctions between written and oral modes of communication. Walter Ong writes that, "oral communication unites people in groups" while writing and print isolate. Discussing religion specifically, Jack Goody suggests that the "written word belongs to the priest, the learned man . . . the oral is the sphere of the prophet, of ecstatic religion . . . the conflict between priest and prophet, between church and sect, is the counterpart of the fixed text and the fluid utterance." In studies of popular culture in early modern Europe the oral means the popular; the written implies educated, elite culture. The socially specific spread of literacy in early modern England, and some evidence from interregnum disputations, and pamphlet polemic could support such contrasts, but other aspects of this material could be marshalled behind an entirely contradictory

[39] Christopher Hill, *A Turbulent, Seditious and Factious People: John Bunyan and his Church* (Oxford, 1988), 134; Hughes, "Pulpit Guarded," 46; compare Immanuel Bourne, *A Defence of the Scriptures* (1656) with James Nayler, *A Dispute between James Nayler and the Parish teachers of Chesterfield* (1655). The Chesterfield disputation is discussed in Rosemary O'Day, "Immanuel Bourne: A Defence of the Ministerial Order," *Journal of Ecclesiastical History,* 27(1976): 101–114.

argument. For post-structuralists influenced by Derrida, it is the spoken which has authority over the written in western philosphical traditions. A text or message is most authentic when it is spoken by an authoritative individual voice; writing is more slippery: its meanings can be transformed by others as it passes out of the control of the writer. Writing, claims Christopher Norris, "occupies a promiscuous public realm where authority is sacrificed to the vagaries and whims of textual 'dissemination.' Writing in short, is a threat to the deeply traditional view that associates truth with self-presence and the 'natural' language wherein it finds expression."[40] The existence of disputation as an academic form; the preferences of some ministers, such as Baxter, for oral over written debate; the anxieties that opponents' printed works would distort authentic speech—all these would suggest the priority given to speech. Yet a third view, on "the equivalence of speech and writing," is represented by David Hall's discussion of the Bible as the living word of God as well as a written text, meant to be heard as well as read. Those who lacked fluent literacy in the sense of reading print easily might nonetheless develop a competency in understanding and quoting the word of God through oral means—engaging in and witnessing debate as well through catechizing, private discussions, or hearing sermons. In Chartier's terms, "between literacy and illiteracy there exists a wide range of reading abilities . . . between private, individual reading and passive listening to spoken words there exists a wide range of attitudes toward print culture." The late sixteenth and early seventeenth centuries were a period of sharply increasing technical competence in reading while the 1640s and 1650s saw, of course, a rapid expansion in the amount of printed material available.[41]

For now, we need to stress the importance of specific context in any evaluation of the significance of oral, written, or printed cultural forms. For both old and new England, two further paradoxical comments may be made: the first is that distinctions between oral and literate forms are much more blurred than much of the general literature suggests; the second is to note the sheer importance of written and printed material in both old and new England compared with more "traditional" societies. One has only to note the importance of

[40]Walter J. Ong, *Orality and Literacy: The Technologizing of the Word* (London, 1982), 69; Jack Goody, *The Interface Between the Written and the Oral* (Cambridge, 1987), 161; Christopher Norris, *Deconstruction: Theory and Practice* (London, 1982), quoted in Toril Moi, *Sexual/Textual Politics: Feminist Literary Theory* (London, 1985), 107.

[41]Hall, *Worlds of Wonder*, 25, 38–42; Chartier, "Culture as appropriation," 236.

the printing press to the Quakers who otherwise would fall on the prophetic, ecstatic side of Goody's dichotomy quoted above: the Quakers attempted to encode their fluid utterances in texts. In many controversies oral, manuscript, and printed forms are interwoven. Published works often prompted oral debates: two west-country clerics accused Thomas Collier of blasphemy after reading one of his pamphlets, and Collier in turn challenged them to repeat their accusations in a public debate. Pamphlets were used as evidence in disputations, as in the encounter between Nayler and the orthodox ministers of Chesterfield. The language of printed works often reveals an overlapping or even confused view of the links between the oral, the written, and the printed: one of Nayler's works, *A Few Words Occasioned by a Paper Lately Printed, Stiled a Discourse concerning the Quakers, Together With a Call to Magistrates, Ministers, Lawyers and People to Repentence* (1654) used terms like "words," "paper," "discourse," "call" to conjure up oral and literate forms indiscriminately.[42]

In New England the "Antinomian Controversy" shows a similar complexity of forms: it was carried out firstly through oral means, both private and public, in the meetings held at Mrs. Hutchinson's house, the private conferences, the sermons, the public debates at Synod and the trials by church and political authority. The written word was also important as ministers tried to settle their differences by letter or prepared contributions to debates. Others made manuscript records of debates, conferences, sermons, and trials; copies were circulated and much of this material shortly found its way into print. In terms of print culture we are again reminded that old and new England made up one community despite contrasts in religious divisions or notions of orthodoxy: many accounts of New England controversies were printed for their relevance to conflicts in old England in the 1640s. Participants in old England controversies were themselves self-conscious about the forms of debate. There was some dissatisfaction with oral debate and some preference for private discussion or for more predictable printed disputes. Martindale's experiences and Ley's general account both suggest this, as does the narrative of the dispute at Wiveliscombe, "How far truth was distant from a lie; . . . as the eyes from the ears: . . . the eye was a faithful spectator, and authentic witness of things; but the ear was open to lies, and by it fictions and untruths had their entrance into the mind."

---

[42] *The Heads and Substance of a Discourse* (1651); Hughes, "Pulpit Guarded," 47.

This perhaps contradicted the Puritan emphasis on the value of lively preaching as opposed to passive reading, but it has echoes in the increasing preference of seventeenth-century lawyers, historians, and heralds for written over oral evidence.[43]

But, as we have seen oral forms could be part of an educated repertoire while the printed religious literature of the interregnum had an immediacy and an intimate, practical importance that has often been seen as more characteristic of oral discourse. Printed works were dynamic, participatory, open-ended, and at the same time very specific, local, and personal. They defined communities rather than isolating individuals. As *Gangræna* combined local evidence with a general attack on the sects so many disputes were published for local as well as theoretical motives. Intimate local conflicts involving defectors or dissidents from particular congregations were frequently published for provincial booksellers: as the Abergavenny disputants wrote: "we naturally love the transactions of those, whose persons we know; some heard them transiently as they were delivered and would be glad deliberately to read them; some heard them not, but at the second hand as they were variously reported (according to the judgement and affection of the relator) who would be willing to know the business truly stated." John Billingsley, minister of Chesterfield and another of the Presbyterian opponents of Nayler, gave very precise details of when and where he came across Nayler's version of the dispute: "Being lately (viz April 25 1655) at Dronfield in this county, and hearing that a book was come forth written by James Nayler . . . I had an earnest desire to see it, which sight I procured. . . . as I sat at table in a friend's house, in which paper I found many palpable untruths. . . ." Billingsley then resolved on his own version to avoid "hurt to silly souls, who live at a great distance from this place, a lie in print will sound like a truth, when it hath got an hundred miles off from the place where the occasion of its forgery was administered." Here again the intimacy of personal attack is combined with an astute sense of the more generalizing impact of printed works. Pamphlets had as vivid an effect as a verbal argument or even a physical attack. Adam Martindale was "pelted with . . . furious papers

---

[43]Hall, ed., *Antinomian Controversy;* M. Hall, *The Last American Puritan,* 124; in the 1640s Richard Mather published four books in London defending congregational church government, including *A Modest and Brotherly Answer* to the leading Presbyterian Charles Herle. Fullwood, *The Churches and Ministry of England,* sig Cıv; Hughes, "Pulpit Guarded"; D.R. Woolf, "History, Folklore and Oral Traditions in Early Modern England," *Past and Present* 120(1988): 26–52.

from Chester, Stafford, Warrington etc"; Tombes treated his opponents' pamphlet as if it were alive; while the Quaker Edward Burrough in an attack on John Bunyan identified verbal, physical, and printed attacks: "all of you against them called Quakers, the drunkards and swearers they beat them and abuse them, and cast them as for dead into ditches, with stoning in the highways, and in the streets beating down with staves, and the wanton they sing their rhymes in scorn in alehouses, and taverns against them, and thou and thy fellows and generation, appears in open print, slandering and reviling them."[44]

Strategies within the published polemic demanded an active readership. They included questions for opponents and readers in an attempt to compel a direct response and demanded a judgment on controversies. Religious pamphlets conjured up communities of those who had read the various texts under debate, or would study recommended works. Immanuel Bourne refused in his printed account of the Chesterfield debate, to reply to many of the questions posed by Nayler, in some cases because the questions were frivolous, but in others because they had already been answered by "divers religious learned men" such as Baxter and Prynne. The readers are thus referred to these other printed works, and the issues raised by the oral, physical confrontation at Chesterfield are linked to a much wider abstract world of religious controversy, covering both sides of the Atlantic.[45]

Neither in the attitudes to debate nor in the uses of print are there sharp distinctions to be made between orthodox and radical, between educated and popular, or between oral and literate; all these dichotomies become contradictory and blurred on further examination. Disputations indicate the complex and changing nature of religious radicalism as it is usually defined and suggest a new picture of the orthodox Puritans of the Interregnum. Despite some hesitancy and some qualifications in attitudes to learning, to oral forms, and to public debate itself, the willingness of mainstream Puritans to engage in debate with their radical critics suggests that there was more common ground between "orthodox" and "radical" than is sometimes supposed. Interregnum Puritanism took more from the radical Protestantism of the sixteenth century than recent work allows and

---

[44]*A Publicke Dispute,* preface to the reader; John Billingsley, *Strong Comforts for Weak Christians* (1656), 1; *Life of. . . . Martindale,* 117; Tombes, *A Plea,* 1; E. Burrough, *Truth the Strongest of all,* 5–6.

[45]Bourne, *A Defence of the Scriptures,* 50–51.

is not so far distant from Hall's view of the zealous New England Protestants. It had a dynamic, radical and popular edge or potential that may have been blunted but was not destroyed by the attacks of the sects.

Furthermore, public disputations as both direct oral confrontations and as often complex printed texts provide a way into understanding some of the meanings of religious literature in the 1640s and 1650s. In oral debate or in printed polemic there was an urgent need to defend fundamental truth and confute error. The links between pamphlets and face-to-face incidents gave printed works an importance beyond their obvious content. Furthermore, the religious literature of the interregnum was produced at a time when significant groups of people were becoming literate in broad sense for the first time, and moreover in a Protestant culture where as Hall has stressed becoming literate and becoming religious were in effect the same process. The interregnum saw an immense expansion in the circulation of religious literature—again giving the pamphlets a novel and a precious status it is easy for us to forget. Above all religious literature partook of what Goody has called the "magic of the book"; where religious truths are embodied in sacred texts as is preeminently the case in committed Protestantism, books are inevitably more than commodities or academic resources.[46]

[46]Hall, *Worlds of Wonder,* 18; Goody, *Interface Between the Written and the Oral,* 132–133.

Part Four: Contrasting Communities

Conversion Among Puritans

and Amerindians: A Theological

and Cultural Perspective

Charles L. Cohen

O N J U L Y 5, 1 6 5 9, eight Massachusett Amerindians[1] took the final step in becoming Puritan saints by presenting the Roxbury church and "Messengers" from ten neighboring congregations the confessions of religious experience that anyone wishing to enter church fellowship in seventeenth-century Massachusetts had to deliver.[2] Interactions between "the first Americans" and European colonists have especially engaged historians during the past quarter century, with the effort to evangelize the coastal peoples of southern New England attracting significant attention, both because scholars continue to interest themselves in all things Puritan, and because, of all the British colonists, New Englanders mounted the largest mission to the natives.[3] Much of the scholarly literature has commented on the missionaries' inadequacies, Amerindian resistance, and the

This essay was first presented at the conference on "Puritanism in Old and New England" held at Millersville University, April 3–6, 1991. The author has presented subsequent versions to the History colloquium at the University of Chicago, the Early American Studies group at UW-Madison, and the Institute for Early American History and Culture at Williamsburg. He would like to thank the participants at all these meetings for their comments; errors of omission and commission remain his responsibility.

[1] I prefer to contract "American Indians."

[2] To clarify the term. In this essay "conversion" refers to the central Puritan experience of being spiritually regenerated, not to the process of quitting one religion for another faith. On conversion relations see Edmund S. Morgan, *Visible Saints* (Ithaca, N.Y., 1965 ed.), and Patricia Caldwell, *The Puritan Conversion Narrative* (New York, 1983).

[3] The first modern, comprehensive scholarly treatment of relationships between Puritans and Amerindians was Alden T. Vaughan, *New England Frontier: Puritans and Indians*

Saints' ultimate failure, particularly compared to the thousands of converts the hated Jesuits won to the north,[4] but while Puritans probably buried more Amerindians than they saved—at the height of their influence just before Metacom's War, John Eliot's Praying Indian towns contained only 1100 people, most of them not full church members[5]—a few Amerindians did embrace Reformed Protestantism, and we know less about how they negotiated the passage from *manitou* to providence than about how their kin and friends refused. Accepting Jesus Christ as a personal savior obliged natives to undergo a "new birth" alien to their received traditions, a process of transculturation[6] as yet little understood.

What follows attempts to conceptualize and address the issues involved. More tentative about the anthropology of assimilation and the ethnography of aboriginal religion than I could wish, it nevertheless proposes a different perspective on the transculturation of one small group of Amerindians than those usually advanced, using methods of intellectual and ethno-history to explore how the Massachusett appropriated the language of Reformed Christianity and appreciated its meanings. Historians well know the principal materials, a series of works collectively titled the "Eliot tracts" after John Eliot, first teacher of the Roxbury church and the leading seventeenth-century Puritan missionary: most important for this study are *Tears of Repentance,* which records relations delivered at the first attempt to gather an Amerindian church

1620–1675, rev. ed. (New York, 1979 [orig. 1965]). Henry Wayne Bowden, *American Indians and Christian Missions* (Chicago, 1981), 98–128 summarizes seventeenth-century New English efforts. Richard W. Cogley, "John Eliot in Recent Scholarship," *American Indian Culture and Research Journal* 14(1990): 77n.1, lists the relevant literature.

[4]James Ronda, "'We Are Well As We Are': An Indian Critique of Seventeenth-Century Christian Missions," *William and Mary Quarterly,* 3rd ser., 34(1977): 66–82; Neal Salisbury, "Red Puritans: The 'Praying Indians' of Massachusetts Bay and John Eliot," ibid., 31(1974): 27–54; James Axtell, *The Invasion Within* (New York, 1985); Francis Jennings, "Goals and Functions of Puritan Missions to the Indians," *Ethnohistory* 18(1971): 197–212.

[5]Daniel Gookin, *Historical Collections of the Indians in New England,* ed. Jeffrey H. Fiske (n.p., 1970 [1792]), 18. James Axtell reinterprets this figure as an indication of Eliot's success, "Some Thoughts on the Ethnohistory of Missions," Axtell, *After Columbus: Essays on the Ethnohistory of Colonial North America* (New York, 1988), 49–50.

[6]See Alden T. Vaughan and Daniel K. Richter, "Crossing the Cultural Divide: Indians and New Englanders, 1605–1763," *Proceedings of the American Antiquarian Society* 90(1980): 23–99; T. H. Breen, "Creative Adaptations: Peoples and Cultures," in Jack P. Greene and J. R. Pole, eds., *Colonial British America: Essays in the New History of the Early Modern Era* (Baltimore, 1984), 195–232. This essay concentrates on an ideational aspect of cultural change; Harold W. Van Lonkhuyzen, "A Reappraisal of the Praying Indians: Acculturation, Conversion, and Identity at Natick, Massachusetts, 1640–1730," *New England Quarterly* 63(1990): 396–428, examines the social context.

in 1652, and *A further Account of the progress of the Gospel,* which presents the statements of eight successful applicants in 1659.[7] These conversion relations afford the clearest window possible into the religious sensibilities of native converts.

Ministers took down confession statements while applicants for church membership spoke them in public, and the difficulties in interpreting any personal document so produced, nettlesome enough when both testifier and recorder talk the same language and share the same basic cultural assumptions,[8] increase when the candidate speaks a non-cognate tongue and struggles, in an inherently nerve-wracking situation, to articulate complex ideas and novel emotions. One wonders about the translator's ability to understand the speakers and to withstand the temptation, conscious or not, to "improve" their statements. Eliot himself was painfully aware of such concerns and sought to allay them, admitting that at times confessors *"spake not so well to my understanding,"* but contending that *"many things I understood of what they all spake,"* and insisting that *"(according to what I understood) the substance of their Confessions is here truly set down."*[9] He asked other interpreters to monitor his accuracy by attending the confessions, and in at least one instance, Thomas Mayhew, a missionary on Martha's Vineyard as expert in local dialects as Eliot, testified that Eliot's renditions were *"for the substance the same which the* Indians *answered, many times the very words which they spake and alwayes the sense."*[10] Eliot advised the Massachusett to present their statements as plainly and familiarly as possible, "for my more easie and perfect understanding," and he denied having "knowingly, or willingly made them better, than the Lord helped themselves to make them," arguing, if anything, that he had unintentionally weakened the relations by missing words, abbreviating passages, and misrendering native idioms.[11] The case for taking Eliot's transcriptions seriously rests on some debatable propositions: that they give the im-

---

[7]John Eliot and Thomas Mayhew, "Tears of Repentance: Or, a further Narrative of the Progress of our Gospel Amongst the Indians in New England" (originally pub. London, 1653), reprinted in Massachusetts Historical Society, *Collections* [henceforth cited as *MHS Colls.*], ser. 3, 4:197–260; [John Eliot], *A Further Account of the progress of the Gospel Amongst the Indians in New England* (London, 1660).

[8]I have discussed the problem of interpreting narratives produced by English confessors in *God's Caress: The Psychology of Puritan Religious Experience* (New York, 1986), 138–140.

[9][Eliot], *Further Account,* 30; cf. Eliot and Mayhew, "Tears of Repentance," 250.

[10]Eliot and Mayhew, "Tears of Repentance," 220–221; John Eliot, "A Late and Further Manifestation of the Progress of the Gospel Amongst the Indians in New England" [London, 1655], *MHS Colls.,* ser. 3, 4:284.

[11][Eliot], *Further Account,* 45; Eliot and Mayhew, "Tears of Repentance," 245.

pression of historical verisimilitude,[12] that they resemble English confessions in many details, and that, since Puritans valued such exercises so highly, they would have taken all possible measures to set down the narratives as accurately as possible. None of these arguments is incontestable—impressions do not constitute hard evidence, the point about resemblance is tautological (the relations must be true since they look like other true confessions), and there is no necessary reason for historians to believe even Puritans at their word—but there is no compelling basis to discount the confessions, and one to commend them: many of the Amerindians testified twice on the two occasions they were called upon, and in every case the paired versions, while not identical, do not conflict.[13]

Five individuals confessed in both 1652 and 1659, and while historians have discussed the piety of some of Eliot's converts,[14] no one has examined the historical development of these five persons' experiences to analyze their progressive apprehension of Protestant faith. Such a small sample does have its limits. All five are men, and although Amerindian women responded to Puritan preaching too,[15] for whatever reasons Eliot does not seem to have recorded any of their confessions. Moreover, all of the applicants belonged to the Massachusett band from Nonantum, so that other groups, like the Martha's Vineyard Pokanoket proselytized by Mayhew, do not appear. Still, examining their confessions discovers how converts came to Christ and helps explain the successes Puritan missionaries did enjoy. Historians have concentrated primarily on why ministers attracted so few Amerindians, alleging the complicated nature of Reformed Protestant theology, their insistence on civilizing natives before Christianizing them, their inability to adapt evangelistic techniques to native folkways, the bad moral examples set by many colonists, and the attachment of Amerindians to their own beliefs.[16]

---

[12]For instance, when Eliot noted that a confessor responded to an elder's question in "broken English," not in Massachusett dialect, the text renders the answer awkwardly: "When Devil comes, I sometime too much believe him . . . ," [Eliot], *Further Account,* 8–9.

[13]James Axtell argues for the validity of Amerindian conversions in "Were Indian Conversions *Bona Fide?*," *After Columbus,* 100–121.

[14]Notably J. William T. Youngs, Jr., "The Indian Saints of Early New England," *Early American Literature* 10(1981–1982): 241–256.

[15]For example, see Henry Whitfield, "The Light appearing more and more towards the perfect Day" [London, 1651]. *MHS Colls.,* ser. 3, 4:116.

[16]Axtell, *Invasion Within,* esp. chap. 9; Gary B. Nash, *Red, White, and Black: The Peoples of Early America* (Englewood Cliffs, N.J., 1974), 122–123, and see also works listed *supra,* n. 4.

All of these conditions did inhibit evangelization, but we need also examine the religious sensibilities of Amerindians who did join English churches, if only to discover the limits of even their conversions. Their experience suggests that part of the difficulty in becoming a "Red Puritan" stemmed from the cultural background of the Amerindians themselves, and that, even among those most willing to convert, their own cultural legacies threw stumbling blocks on the way to faith.

To understand Massachusett relations requires first reviewing what English Saints expected confessors to recount.[17] Conversion comprised the centerpiece of Puritan spirituality; reading John 3:3 at face value made a new birth prerequisite for salvation. Theologically, conversion marked the irrevocable translation from the estate of sin to salvation; psychologically, it signified an emotional engagement with grace borne by the Spirit. Puritan divines had worked out its "morphology"[18] well before Saints and natives collided along the New England littoral. Before an unregenerate could come to Christ, they taught, the Spirit had to administer a preparatory turning from sin. In its most simply schematized form, preparation required two steps, the first of which, contrition, presumed a knowledge of at least the rudiments of Christian doctrine: God's creation of the world, His sovereignty and omnipotence, the Fall and Original Sin, the divine incarnation in Christ, his crucifixion for human sins, his triumph over death in the resurrection, and salvation through apprehending the Redeemer by faith. By the mid-seventeenth century Puritans might reasonably anticipate that "civilized" people would identify these things, but in Albion's "dark corners," and the even darker forests of North America, no one could take such knowledge for granted. Pondering the truth of Christian doctrine was supposed to illuminate an individual's sins, firing sorrow for them. Pricked by conscience, grieved by iniquity, the person wonders how to reach salvation.

Fearful of damnation and anxious to escape, the sinner resolves to do good works, only to realize, as preparation proceeds, that original sin has tainted all the soul's faculties and vitiated their capacity to perform godly acts. False pride—deceptive self-confidence—dissolves in the terror of confronting the impossibility of doing anything

---

[17]This section derives from Cohen, *God's Caress*, esp. chaps. 3, 4.
[18]The term comes from Morgan, *Visible Saints*, 66 and *passim*.

to save oneself. The sinner tries any stratagem to merit grace but discovers only that Adam's heirs have inherited a fundamental constitutional flaw condemning them to fall short of grace on their own. Humiliation, preparation's second stage, obliterates self-sufficiency and causes unregenerates to throw themselves on Christ, who alone can save them.

From the ashes of false confidence, preachers explained, rises the phoenix of a new self-awareness, the sinner liberated from hell through subordination to God's will. Begging for mercy, the unregenerate receives it, not for merit, but from grace—God's love—alone. In conversion's climactic moment, a person cognizant of one's own complete unworthiness experiences grace as a gift totally free and inspired by the Lord's divine *agape* for His poor creature. Infused with love, the newly redeemed Saint reflects it back to God and humanity, radiating the joy of salvation and the peace "which passeth all understanding" (Phil. 4:7). Buoyed by these sensations, the saint gains assurance of salvation—only to face recurrent fears as sin continues to derange the faculties and Satan questions faith's authenticity. Over time a maturing Saint stares down these dreads and revels more consistently in the knowledge of God's love, and although doubt never entirely disappears—the legacy of sinful flesh—the pious face death confident of eternal life.

Conversion thus produces a predictable affective sequence: the fear and guilt of contrition plunging into terror and holy desperation, yielding love, joy, and peace in turn. Simultaneously, it generates a new perception of power. The emotional signature of grace, conversion also reorders the sources of personal strength. Puritan writings lament humanity's inherent enervation. Unregenerates trust their own energies, despite the Fall's enfeebling corruption, but faith reorders the faculties, enabling regenerates to perform good works. The new birth delivers helpless humans from debility to strength; animated by *agape*, they strive to accomplish God's commands because they love to do His bidding. Saints entrust their powers to the Lord's strength, performing prodigies of godly labor because their potency derives from Him.

To join the company of visible Saints, Amerindians had to rehearse Christian doctrine, but they also had to assimilate the psychodynamics of conversion, and if sovereignty, resurrection, and providence drummed strangely on native ears, so did tales of *agape*. Massachusett religion did not humble sinners to exalt them in grace, and while introducing individuals to spirits of natural power, it did not correlate personal strength with affective cycles. The worship of the coastal tribes, so foreign to Reformed Protestantism, conditioned how natives were born again.

Southern New England Amerindians fashioned a cosmology radically different from monotheistic Christianity centered upon an omnipotent Creator. William Morrell, an Anglican clergyman who settled briefly at Wessagussett in 1623, metered out their universe:

> They now accustom'd are two Gods to serve,
> One good, which gives all good, and doth preserve:
> This they for love adore: the other bad,
> Which hurts and wounds, yet they for feare are glad
> To worship him.

The "good" god, Kitan (Narragansett *Cautàntowwit*), "makes corne growe, trees growe, and all manner of fruits," observed Thomas Morton, the Pilgrims' bane, and in his rendition of the Massachusett creation myth "God made one man and one woman, and bad them live together, and get children, kill deare, beasts, birds, fish, and fowle, and what they would at their pleasure." Kitan dispensed earth's blessings but remained beyond human reach; "Never man saw" him, reported Edward Winslow, one of Plymouth's leaders, "only old men tell them of him, and bid them tell their children. . . ."[19] The "bad" god, Hobbamock (var., *Abbamocho*), "many times smites them with incurable Diseases" and "scares them with his Apparitions and pannick Terrours," the clear and present danger of his presence demanding propitiation: "him they dread and fear, more than they love and honour the former chief good which is God."[20] But the coastal Algonquians did not reduce the universe to a simple Manichean duality, for spiritual powers independent of the two paramount gods suffused the world.[21] Roger Williams, the most perspicacious contemporary student of the Narragansett, remarked

---

[19] "Morell's Poem on New-England," *MHS Colls.*, 1st ser., 1 (1792), 138; Thomas Morton, *New English Canaan* (Amsterdam, 1637; facsimile ed., New York, 1972), 50, 49; Edward Winslow, "Winslow's Relation" [*Good Newes from New England*], in Alexander Young, ed., *Chronicles of the Pilgrim Fathers of the Colony of Plymouth, from 1602 to 1625* (Boston, 1841), 356.

[20] John Josselyn, *An Account of Two Voyages to New-England, Made during the years 1638, 1663* (Boston, 1865), 103; Gookin, *Historical Collections*, 20.

[21] Though cf. William S. Simmons, "Narragansett," in William C. Sturtevant, gen. ed., *Handbook of North American Indians*, vol. 15: *Northeast*, ed. Bruce G. Trigger (Washington, 1978), 192, who suggests Narragansett cosmology constituted "an ordered system in which numerous dualisms . . . are apparent."

upon "a generall Custome amongst them, at the apprehension of any Excellency in Men, Women, Birds, Beasts, Fish, &c. to cry out *Manittoo*, that is it is a God, as thus if they see one man excell others in Wisdome, Valour, strength, Activity &c. they cry out *Manittoo* A God." *Manitou* connoted any exceptional spiritual power, which could reside in animate and inanimate objects alike. "[T]hey had their Men-gods, Women-gods, and Children-gods," Thomas Mayhew complained, "Divine Powers, guiding things amongst men, besides innumerable more feigned [to an English mind] gods belonging to many Creatures, to their Corn, and every Colour of it."[22] Fire and stone, tree and flesh pulsed with *manitous* whose presence affected every human action.

Amerindians attempted to engage spiritual beings collectively through rituals, conducting *Nickómmo*, the principal southern New England "feast," either to cope with sickness, drought, war, and famine, or to celebrate harvest and hunt "when they enjoy a caulme of Peace, Health, Plenty, [and] Prosperity."[23] In pressing circumstances they called upon Hobbamock "to cure their wounds and diseases," while in "plenty" and "victory" they would "sing, dance, feast, give thanks, and hang up garlands" to Kitan "in memory of the same." Narragansetts held a special invocation "to their gods" in which people immolated "almost all the riches they have" in a "great fire," a sacrifice neighboring tribes envied for its putative power to avert the plague.[24] Shamans, called *powwows*, led the ceremonies. "[E]ager and free in speech, fierce in countenance," *powwows* received magical powers from Hobbamock in dreams and exercised them with the assistance of imps "brought forth to hurt their enemies, and heal their friends."[25] Greatly solicited by the "sick and wounded," for whom,

[22] Roger Williams, *A Key into the Language of America*, 2 facsimile vols. in 1 (New York, 1973): 4th edition, ed. J. Hammond Trumbull, [orig. 1866], 150 (this volume also prints the 5th ed., edited by Howard M. Chapin [1936]); Eliot and Mayhew, "Tears of Repentance," 201–202; and see Neal Salisbury, *Manitou and Providence: Indians, Europeans, and the Making of New England, 1500–1643* (New York, 1982), 37–39, and Williams, *Key*, 147 n. 268, and 151 n. 274.
[23] Williams, *Key*, 151.
[24] Winslow, "Relation," 356, 359.
[25] Williams, *Key*, 152; Winslow, "Relation," 357; Henry Whitfield, "Strength out of Weakness; Or a Glorious Manifestation Of the further Progresse of the Gospel Among the Indians in New-England" [London, 1652], *MHS Colls.*, ser. 3, 4:186; [John Wilson], "The Day-Breaking, If Not the Sun-Rising of the Gospel with the Indians in New England" (London, 1647), ibid., 20; Eliot and Mayhew, "Tears of Repentance," 202; and see William Simmons, "Southern New England Shamanism: An Ethnographic Reconstruction," in William Cowan, ed., *Papers of the Seventh Algonquian Conference, 1975* (Ottawa, 1976), 217–256.

Daniel Gookin admitted, "they seem to do wonders," *powwows* were credited with ability to divine if a disease was curable, bring rain and raise storms, pass "shot-free and stick-free" through battle, infuse life into dead skins, and kill humans magically.[26] Amerindians "idolized" *powwows* for their physic while fearing their malefic arts, although John Wilson, Boston's pastor, learned that disgruntled persons might sometimes kill a shaman, who had failed to cure a sick relative.[27] In their role as ceremonial "officiants" imbued with sacred charisma, *powwows* resembled English clergy more than might first appear, but at least one important difference distinguished them: although Puritans demanded ministers transformed by the Spirit, they did not believe that a preacher functioned as anything more than a conduit of grace that God employed as He willed; no clergyman could transmit his own regeneracy. *Powwows,* on the contrary, could use their infused gifts to touch others for good and ill.

While orthodox Puritans believed that the Spirit does not reside corporeally within a Saint, New England shamans "treasured up" their imps "in their bodies," but they were not alone in receiving power from Hobbamock through dreams. *Pnieses,* "commonly men of the greatest stature and strength," prepared from boyhood for visions of the god brought on by ordeals that included induced vomiting, exposure, and beatings designed "to make them hardy and acceptable to the devil [sic], that in time he may appear unto them" and "covenant" to "preserve them from death by wounds with arrows, knives, hatchets, &c.," training that entitled them to sit on the *sachem*'s (band leader's) council and comprise his elite military guard. Even common individuals might communicate with deities in dreams and solicit their aid. Roger Williams related the tale of a dying man invoking Muckquachuckquànd, the "children's god," who had appeared to him in his youth and "bid him when ever he was in distresse call upon him."[28] Like Puritans, who read providential meanings in the world's ebbs and flows, Amerindians believed that all activity affects the relationships between humans and the *manitous*

---

[26] Gookin, *Historical Collections,* 20; "Letters of Samuel Lee and Samuel Sewall Relating to New England and the Indians," *Publications of the Colonial Society of Massachusetts,* 14:151 (no. 90); Williams, *Key,* 94; Winslow, "Relation," 366; Josselyn, *Account of Two Voyages,* 104; Eliot and Mayhew, "Tears of Repentance," 204.

[27] Edward Winslow, "The Glorious Progress of the Gospel, Amongst the Indians In New England" (London, 1649), *MHS Colls.,* ser. 3, 4:90: [Wilson], "Day-Breaking," 20.

[28] Eliot and Mayhew, "Tears of Repentance," 202: Winslow, "Relation," 359–360, and see Isaack de Rasieres to Samuel Blommaert in Sydney V. James, Jr., *Three Visitors to Early Plymouth* (n.p., 1963), 78; Williams, *Key,* 149–150.

connate in nature's veil, taking care, as bands and individuals, to ap-
pease the forces around them. Still, as far as we can tell (and the
evidence does not admit to much), they did not attribute emotions
to their deities as readily as the English, bred in the Bible's vivid
text, projected them onto their Lord, nor did they, encountering the
divine, display the same affective range as did converting Saints.
Scattered references advert to Hobbamock or Kitan visiting disease
on their people out of anger,[29] but otherwise the gods exhibit little
feeling, and human creatures scarce more: no record I know details
a *powwow's* visionary experience as fully, for instance, as the Old Testament relates prophetic trances. In sum, while southern New England Algonquians lived in daily contact with myriad spirits, they possessed no psychological equivalent to the new birth.

Amerindians did not lithify their moral laws as tablets, but they
did develop a comprehensive ethos of behavior governed by notions
of reciprocity, an attitude of mutual dependence among all creatures
requiring each to act in balance with every other.[30] Rituals helped a
band maintain proper relationships with the *manitous*, and dream-
contacts with spirits afforded individuals access to the power they
needed to walk lightly in the world. Prior to contact, Amerindians
could not have developed Christian conceptions of sin, either as an
original transgression corrupting the first couple's heirs[31] or as violation of an omnipotent Lord's decree; instead, they seem to have
viewed "sin" as upsetting the natural equilibrium by, for instance,
killing game unnecessarily.[32] Iniquity meant deranging the natural
order. One can glean a partial notion about native "morality" from
their beliefs about the afterlife. The body dies, but the soul journeys
to the southwest, where "great and good men and Women" enter
Cautàntowwit's house enjoying "hopes (as the Turkes have of carnall
Joyes),", or, as William Wood, a visitor to early Massachusetts Bay,
expanded, "a kind of paradise" where they shall solace themselves

[29]Winslow, "Relation," 357.

[30]Salisbury, *Manitou and Providence*, 10–11, 35–36, and *passim*.

[31]Both Morton, *New English Canaan*, 49, and Josselyn, *Account of Two Voyages*, 105,
report variants of a creation myth alluding to a flood, which may well be early corruptions
of Genesis rather than indigenous tales, and in any case neither account, both of them
brief, contains any native theological reflection that might possibly hint at a doctrine of
Original Sin.

[32]Calvin Martin, *Keepers of the Game: Indian-Animal Relationships and the Fur Trade*
(Berkeley, 1978); Howard S. Russell, *Indian New England Before the Mayflower* (Hanover,
N.H., 1980), 44; Salisbury, *Manitou and Providence*, 35.

"in odoriferous gardens" and reside in "sumptuous palaces."[33] "Murtherers thieves and Lyers" knock there too, Edward Winslow reported, but the god "bids them *quatchet,* that is to say, walk abroad, for there is no place for such; so that they wander in restless want and penury." Williams concurred, with Wood dilating on how "their enemies and loose livers" (he did not expatiate the term) pass on to Hobbamock's "infernal dwellings" and endless torture. However much these descriptions, particularly Wood's, may evidence the early intrusion of European elements, they discriminate behavior along moral lines essentially congruent with Christianity.[34]

While sharing some premises with the Puritans' Reformed Protestantism—e.g.the segregation of the good and the bad to appropriate realms in the afterlife (without, however, a climactic judgment)—native religion developed a fundamentally different worldview premised on a polytheism of greater and lesser deities inhabiting both animate and inanimate objects. Bands participated in collective rituals without distinguishing a spiritual elect chosen for the quality of their religious experience, although becoming either a *powwow* or a *pniese* did require exceptional communication with Hobbamock. Moral behavior linked to the "duty" to establish and maintain one's equilibrium with all creatures, Amerindians agreeing with Europeans about the heinousness of such acts as murder and theft.[35] Eternal life—or the pleasures of "the southwest Elysium"[36] over against an eternity of wandering—depended on "works" (i.e. establishing proper relationships with other creatures) rather than on an infusion of supernatural grace. Christian notions of sin and redemption through apprehending incarnate flesh, a resurrected god-man, were totally alien, as was a detailed arrangement of affective states through which individuals passed as they assumed spiritual power—all of which

---

[33]Williams, *Key,* 154; William Wood, *New England's Prospect,* ed. Alden Vaughan (Amherst, 1977), 115.

[34]Winslow, "Relation," 356; Williams, *Key,* 154; Wood, *New England Prospect,* 116; Simmons, "Narragansett," 192.

[35]Amanda Porterfield's contention that, by accepting "the incipiently modern forms on intention and personal obligation imposed by Puritan notions of sin and conscience, converted Algonquians freed themselves from more primitive, less individualistic conventions of personal identity and moral obligation," *Religion and American Culture* 2(1992):115 somewhat exaggerates the difference between natives' pre- and post-conversion moralities. Whatever "modern," "primitive," and "individualistic" may mean, her formulation diminishes the aboriginal stance of reciprocity with all creatures, a sense of moral responsibility not unlike a Christian ethic.

[36]Wood, *New England Prospect,* 111.

meant that any Algonquian who hoped to wind up a Puritan had to learn not only an entirely new cosmology, encoded in a systematic creed, but a new set of behavioral responses as well, affective patterns about which Massachusett culture had failed to school them.

John Eliot began speaking Massachusett to the natives in 1646, and by 1651 had organized a town of "Praying Indians" at Natick. The ideology of evangelization mandated "civilizing" Amerindians before Christianizing them[37]—only after they had sawed English villages and policed themselves under English laws could an English God transform their hearts—so Eliot waited until the inhabitants "were come up unto Civil Cohabitation, Government, and Labor," and had even constructed a meetinghouse fifty feet by twenty-five before his "argument of delaying them from entering into Church-Estate, was taken away." During the summer of 1652 he called "sundry" of them to "make confession before the Lord of their former sins, and of their present knowledg of Christ, and experience of his Grace," recorded their relations, and advertized them to elders from neighboring churches, asking if the time to settle a church had come. Since the elders "saw nothing to hinder their proceeding," a small knot of men from Natick gathered on October 13 before a larger group of "Magistrates, Elders, and other Christian People" to present their conversion relations.[38] Though the confessors were clearly "daunted"—one of them was so "bashful" that Eliot had followed one of his preliminary recitations only with difficulty—the assembly proceeded. Eliot hoped that all would go well, but in the end the judges advised "refer[ring]" the matter "to a fitter season," albeit in such a way "that the Indians might in no wise be discouraged."[39] Eliot adduced two explanations for their decision: a lack of time—occasioned by lengthy introductory exercises and the task of translating Massachusett into English—that might strand the party in the "remote" woods with "no competent lodgings in the place for such persons"; and the failure of other translators to appear despite his invitations, which left him short one or two people necessary to certify the testimonies' legitimacy. Disappointed, Eliot rationalized the outcome providentially and professed satisfaction that the work "was carried so far as it was."[40]

[37] Axtell, *Invasion Within*, chap. 7, esp. 133–136, and *passim*.
[38] Eliot and Mayhew, "Tears of Repentance," 227–238, 244.
[39] Ibid., 228, 250, 244.
[40] Ibid., 244, 245.

Historians have not made much of this event. Cotton Mather's biography of Eliot in the *Magnalia* omits it completely, and modern scholars tend to gloss it over. One recent interpretation views it as the first stage in a tripartite process for "inchurching" the natives, while the most thorough discussion follows Eliot in explaining the confessors' failure.[41] The confessions themselves, which Eliot, seeking pennies from the pious, published in London, suggest another perspective. The Massachusett relations substantially resemble those of prospective English Saints, at least in form and length.[42] The shortest, John Speene's first confession, takes about one minute to recite, no briefer than the shortest contemporary English ones known, while the longer ones average some two to five minutes, comfortably within the median English range.[43] The differences lie in the content, mainly in emphasis; these relations clearly bear the Puritan stamp. One immediately evident contrast appears in the virtually complete lack of biblical citations, understandable at this time since Eliot had not yet printed any of his scriptural translations. The more important variants, however, are subtle, and if God lies in the details, a clue to the Massachusett's failure to gather a church in 1652 hides in the minutiae of their plaints at having broken His law.

Confessors rehearsed their initial contact with the gospel and their awakening sense of transgression. Shunning discussion of their pre-Christian past, they opened with acknowledgments of their sinfulness or vague references to encountering the Word, as if to admit the circumstances of their escape from a "heathen" past could only emphasize their flaws and void their quest for grace. Ponampam began his first confession by noting that "When God first had mercy on us, when they first prayed at *Noonanetum,* I heard of it," without elaborating on why "they" had started to pray at all or how he had caught wind of the exercise, and John Speene launched his speech,

---

[41] Cotton Mather, *Magnalia Christi Americana* (London, 1702; facsimile ed. New York, 1972), Bk. III. 197; William Kellaway, *The New England Company, 1649–1776* (London, 1961); Neil Salisbury, "Red Puritans," 51–52. Axtell, *Invasion Within,* 238, calls it the first stage, while Vaughan, *New England Frontier,* 267, accepts Eliot. Mather speaks about a day being "set apart" to examine the Natick confessors, but the title he gives it, a "Day of Asking Questions," refers to a doctrinal examination that took place in 1654.

[42] The most important sources for seventeenth-century conversion narratives are three collections printed in *Publications of the Colonial Society of Massachusetts:* "The Diary of Michael Wigglesworth," ed. Edmund S. Morgan, vol. 35, esp. 426–44; *The Notebook of the Reverend John Fiske, 1644–1675;* vol. 47, *passim;* and esp. Thomas Shepard's "Confessions," ed. George Selement and Bruce C. Woolley, vol. 58, *passim.* See also Mary Rhinelander McCarl, "Thomas Shepard's Record of Religious Experience, 1643–1649," in *William & Mary Quarterly,* 3d. ser., 48(1991): 432–466.

[43] Cohen, *God's Caress,* 138–139.

"When I first prayed to God, I did not pray for my soul," implicitly asking listeners to forget whatever had happened beforehand and imagine him as commencing his life breathing out duties to the Lord. What few details confessors gave only tantalize; both Waban and Antony mentioned visiting the English in their houses, but why they had tarried with the colonists goes unremarked.[44] Concourse with "the English" in general exposed Amerindians to their religion, as did discussions with band members already touched by Scripture, but of course evangelists like Eliot played the major role in publicizing Christ, and once started on a course of study, the Massachusett learned doctrine from catechisms as well as sermons.[45] They grasped the message well. Waban knew that, if there was "little good in me," nevertheless "Christ hath kept all Gods Commandements for us" and "doth know all our hearts," while John Speene understood that the souls of believers go to God, those of sinners to hell, and that "when Christ judges the world, our bodies rise again, and then we shall receive the judgment of Christ: the good shal stand at his right hand, the bad at his left."[46] Recognition that God made the world, so obvious to European Christians that the doctrine hardly ever entered their narratives, figured more prominently for recent polytheists; Ponampam remembered hearing "that God made the World, and the first man, and I thought it was true," while Nishohkou understood "That God who made all the World was merciful to sinners."[47]

Familiarity with Christian doctrine startled confessors into seeing, as Ponampam did, that "in every thing I did, I sinned."[48] One measure of Eliot's success, at least with these willing converts, lies in their completely appropriating Christian definitions of iniquity. In the "Eliot tract" immediately preceding *Tears of Repentance,* an unidentified colonial correspondent approvingly wrote the Treasurer of the Society for the Propagation of the Gospel in New England that an anonymous Amerindian "of two yeares profession" had identified sin's "hurt" as *"a continual sicknesse in my heart"* and *"a breach of all Gods Commandments,"* an exposition of Reformed theology's dichotomy of sin into habitual (Original) and particular (actual) that also appears

---

[44]Eliot and Mayhew, "Tears of Repentance," 241, 246, 231, 256.
[45]Learning from other Amerindians: ibid., 241, 256; hearing preachers: Ibid., 240, 249 ("you" refers to Eliot); catechisms: Ibid., 242, 247, 257.
[46]Ibid., 232, 247.
[47]Ibid., 243, 249.
[48]Ibid., 240.

in the answers Amerindian converts gave at a catechetical examination at Roxbury in 1654, and that underlies the 1652 narratives implicitly.[49] Yet if the Massachusett comprehended sin and lamented its effects, they neither explored Original Sin's corruptivity, nor dilated upon their transgressions; no bear-greased Augustine poured out his heart in New England's woods. The announcement of sins are abstract, lacking the dense descriptiveness of individual lives— which is not to say that the confessions are either feigned or formulaic, just formal, since natives related their awakenings to sin idiosyncratically. Ponampam's apprehension grew almost imperceptibly from a series of affirmations and denials. He thought to "cast off all sin" after hearing that Christ was made man only to find he "loved his sins" very much, and he spurned the validity of God's promise to Abraham in Genesis 15:5 "*To increase his Children as the stars for Number*" because the patriarch "had but one Son." This pattern of hearing and discounting continued until he heard that God created the world, "and a little I beleeved that word." Antony's revelation came much more dramatically, precipitated by a construction accident that cracked his skull: when "God brake my head," he "thought that the true God in Heaven is angry with me for my sin, even for al my sins, which every day I live, I do."[50] Typically, however, mere "sight of sin," as Puritan preachers denoted this insight, led not to immediate regeneration but to vacillating. Thinking to pray to God because He made the world, Ponampam "prayed not aright," repented, "prayed only with my mouth," repented again, sinned, rebuked himself, but often "lost all this again, and fell into sin." Nishohkou charged that "my heart plays the hypocrite" because "I yet do not truly beleeve in Jesus Christ."[51]

Their sins dawning upon them, confessors displayed characteristic emotions, especially fear for what they had done and its consequences. Waban dreaded that he might die "before I prayed to God," Ponampan "because every day sin was in my heart, and I thought in vain I looked to Christ," and John Speene "because God hath afflicted me" in "taking away my brother a Ruler" on account of Speene's disbelief.[52] Fear elicited anger "with my self" for erring

---

[49]Whitfield, "Strength out of Weaknesse," 192; William Ames, *The Marrow of Sacred Divinity* (London, 1642), Bk. I., xiii–xiv; Eliot, "Late and Further Manifestation," 279, 281.

[50]Eliot and Mayhew, "Tears of Repentance," 242–243, 257.

[51]Ibid., 243, 251.

[52]Ibid., 231, 240–241, 247.

grief for knowing "so little of Gods Word," and shame for "all my sins."[53] Feeling hastened the lesson home—"I judg that I am a sinner," Waban conceded—and inspired remedial pleas. "Oh Jesus Christ help me," Nishohkou cried, Ponampam implored God "Oh give me Repentance and Faith, freely do it for me," and Antony "beg[ged] faith in Christ," desiring to "live unto God, so long as I live."[54] The most common reaction was prayer. John Speene discerned God's anger towards him for sins committed both before and after he had begun to pray and admitted that he "cannot get pardon for them: but yet my heart saith I will pray to God as long as I live." Converts perceived prayer as more than just a means to grace; as Eliot explained, "their frequent phrase of Praying to God, is not to be understood of that Ordinance and Duty of Prayer only, but of all Religion, and comprehendeth the same meaning with them, as the word [Religion] doth with us." In this light, Speene's locution suggests the desire to engage the Lord fully in every way, what Puritans would call acting "wholeheartedly."[55]

With a few variations in emphasis—an interest in the world's creation, an almost complete absence of information about one's upbringing—these confessions echo the cries of contrition standard in Puritan narrations; the awful recognition of sin, fear of its repercussions, shame at one's malfeasance, and appeals for Christ's forgiveness replicate classic models of preparation's early stages. Contrition initiated the Puritan new birth, and conversion could hardly proceed without it, but sight of sin alone did not suffice for regeneration, and herein lies the key to why the elders demurred at accepting these Massachusett in 1652. Whatever the external circumstances cutting the performance short—the absence of other translators, the forest's darkening shadows—the "Magistrates, Elders, and Grave men present" had heard enough. Nishohkou's remark that "I cannot redeem my self, nor deliver my self, because of all these my many sins," and Antony's concurrence that "I cannot my self get pardon," point to the "holy desperation" that had to succeed contrition, but the statements are isolated, the two men neither elaborate their insight nor discuss it in the context of Original Sin, and they fail to display the

[53]Ibid., 240, 257, 252.
[54]Ibid., 232, 252, 243, 257.
[55]Ibid., 246, 218, and cf. Whitfield, "Light appearing," 139. Robert James Naeher makes this point in "Dialogue in the Wilderness: John Eliot and the Indian Exploration of Puritanism as a Source of Meaning, Comfort, and Ethnic Survival," *New England Quarterly* 62(1989):346–368. On wholeheartedness, see Cohen, *God's Caress*, 34, 37–38, 129.

requisite terror at being damned without any hope via their own strength, humiliation's benchmarks all.[56] None of the other three confessors went even this far. In short, while Eliot's converts displayed good grounds for hope, the "Apostle to the Indians" had showcased them prematurely. Richard Mather, minister at Dorchester, made the point in a prefatory epistle to the published narratives.

> the Spirit of the Lord hath been working thereby in the hearts of many of them such Illumination, such Conviction, &c, as may justly be looked at (if not as a full and through Conversion, yet) as an hopeful beginning and preparation thereto, if the Lord be pleased to go on with what he hath begun, as I hope he will.[57]

The word "Conviction" deepens Mather's observation, for it signifies a technical term in the vocabulary of Reformed soteriology, an element of the contrition process; the Spirit, he maintains, has moved the confessors through preparation's earliest stages. Whatever accidents of the day may have frustrated their hopes, the natives could not yet gather a church at Natick because they lacked the pillars necessary to ground it.

Seven years later Eliot again paraded his charges before a solemn assembly to judge their estates, having taken great care to improve their performance. The five had honed their spiritual (and oratorical) skills in the interim, demonstrating their knowledge of doctrine to an English audience at Roxbury in 1654, and exhorting their people during a fast day service at Natick in 1658.[58] Anxious to avoid the logistical embarrassments of 1652, Eliot welcomed holding the event at Roxbury, and he took care that at least four colonists with capability in Algonquian dialects, plus several native speakers, attended to certify his translations. Once again the confessors gave preliminary statements, to the elders and congregants of the Roxbury church, and then on July 5, before the congregation and "messengers" from surrounding churches, made their public testimonies. This time the messengers agreed that the confessions "were satisfac-

---

[56] Eliot and Mayhew, "Tears of Repentance," 244, 252, 257.

[57] Ibid., 220.

[58] Eliot, "Late and Further Manifestation," prints the examination, [John Eliot], *A further Accompt of the Progress of the Gospel among the Indians In New England* (London, 1659), the exhortations. The account of the examination mentions no individual by name; of the five men here treated, only Ponampam did not speak during the fast day.

tory" and that the candidates "appeared in that respect, to be fit matter for Church estate."[59]

Even a perfunctory look at the 1659 narratives reveals substantial developments over the previous set. For one thing, they are longer, averaging some 6–8 minutes to read aloud, and studded with proof texts, notably Genesis and Matthew.[60] The men elaborated on their earlier experience of contrition, adverting (if only briefly) to their pre-contact lives and family experience. "[W]hen I was a Child, my Parents and I were all wilde." Nishohkou admitted, and Antony seconded that "my Father and Mother were sinners," although Ponampam recalled his father, who seems to have heard John Wilson preach, admonish him while "at play" that "we shall all die shortly."[61] They opened up actual sins in detail, particularly their former polytheism and "lust." His family "prayed to many Gods," Antony remembered, "the Sun, Heavens, Beasts, Trees, and every thing in the world," while all that Nishohkou did "was for the sake of lust, such things as women might like of; if I cut my hair, it was to please women."[62] Confessors also highlighted the importance of the Bible's creation account in raising their consciousness of sin. The Fall taught John Speene that "*Adam* sinned, & fell, and thereby I understood that I became a sinner"; hearing that God had called Eve "the Mother of all living" after having fashioned her from Adam's rib led Antony to believe "that God made us; and therefore I will pray to God as long as I live, and no more cast it off." Occasionally the relations impute emotions to the Lord, almost always ire: man sins against God, Antony said, "and therefore God is angry with me for my sins."[63]

Confessors showed a much keener awareness of Original Sin and expressed their inability to save themselves, two critical signs of humiliation lacking in their earlier narratives. Desiring to pray because

[59] [Eliot], *Further Account*, 1–2, 35–37, 76.

[60] The numerous references to Matthew echo the pattern among English confessors, who cited that book more than any other: see Shepard, *"Confessions,"* 213. The number of references to Genesis is surprising, however: Shepard's 51 applicants cited it only 14 times, while the sample analyzed here also noted specific verses 14 times, making a few other, more diffuse, references as well. The easy explanation for this pattern lies in Eliot's having translated only Genesis, Matthew, and "a few *Psalmes* in Meeter" by 1659 ([Eliot], *Further Accompt*, postscript), but this does not entirely reveal either why confessors should have chosen Genesis, and why they cited the verses they did, invariably from the early part of the book. I suspect that the importance of the creation story for helping further conversion helps account for the popularity of Genesis.

[61] [Eliot], *Further Account*, 37, 47, 54.

[62] Ibid., 47, 38.

[63] Ibid., 59, 50, 49.

he "deserved eternall wrath," Ponampam "knew not what to do, for my sins were many, my heart was full of originall sin." Nishohkou acknowledged his formation in Adam's Image and that when born he "lived in the Image of Satan, and original sin was rooted in my heart, and grew up there." The main force of the Reformed theology of grace thrust towards justification by faith alone, the irrelevance of human works to salvation and the inability of unregenerates to help themselves, doctrine sounded in Waban's realization that "my own righteousness cannot obtain mercy for me," and Ponampam's cry that "nothing that I can do can save me, only Christ," the watchword of Puritan experiential piety.[64] Perhaps the most poignant evocation of humanity's inherent helplessness came from Nishohkou, a reminder of life's parlousness in general, and more particularly on seventeenth-century New England's frontier:

> I am weak, and though I pray, yet I am weak, therefore I desired to be in Christs hand, as in a Fort; in a Fort we are safe from exercise, they cannot easily catch us; out of a Fort we are open to them: So I desire Church-Estate, the Seals of Baptisme, and the Lords Supper, and all Church-Ordinances, as a Fort unto my Soul:[65]

This yearning for grace, echoed in Waban's concluding sigh, "I am almost ready to die; and now I desire to know Christ," signals the proper abject humility: "I do confess before God, and desire to cast off, and forsake my sins, and to go to Christ."[66]

These confessions evidence clear signs of humiliation—and yet, they come somewhat short of evincing its letter and spirit completely. For one thing, they fail to ground the desperate search for Christ within the locus of Original Sin. The orthodox model of conversion held that attempts to do good works by relying on unregenerate capabilities drives sinners into recognizing the extent of their corruption and their inherent incapacity to save themselves, precipitating the despondency leading up to complete submission and faith in Christ.[67] The Massachusett knew the doctrine of Original Sin, and they mourned their failings, but they did not link the two systematically. Beginning his relation, Antony stated that he "was born in iniquity" and "the Image of Satan," but when he later claimed to "have deserved the worst of Gods wrath," the reason, he adduced, was not

---

[64] Ibid., 56, 37, 74, 57.
[65] Ibid., 43.
[66] Ibid., 74, 61.
[67] See Cohen, *God's Caress*, 59–60, 220.

because he finally saw his heinous nature unveiled, but because "I believed not the great works of God," a dire sin, to be sure, but not humiliation's crux.[68] To state the matter theologically, the natives regretted actual, not habitual, sin. Too, the Massachusett did not vilify themselves as did English Saints; their rhetoric of abnegation pales beside the magnificent self-disgust Puritans display.[69] Finally, although the natives craved Christ's mercy, they did not concern themselves overmuch with conversion as a means to accomplish tasks impossible without grace, speaking far more about gaining salvation than about serving God. Comfortably orthodox—the assembly would surely have leapt on any sign these men did not truly exhibit grace—themes of humiliation in Amerindian confessions nevertheless differ from those in English relations in two important ways: they pay less attention to the soul's innate corruption, and they omit the association of despair and helplessness with the strength engendered by the new birth to perform God's will.

The narratives also lack any sense of assurance, which might in itself mean nothing: remembering that God will not break a "bruised reed" nor quench the "smoking flax" (Mat. 12:20), New England churches admitted even applicants unsure of their own standing if, in the congregation's eyes, the individual betrayed the smallest spark of faith. Confessors did not have to relate their grounds for assurance, and a random sample of five English narratives might also fail to include a statement of confident expectancy. One may also surmise that people crossing a prepossessing cultural boundary might hesitate to trumpet their success too smartly. As Nishohkou pointed out, "when I pray, I find hypocrisie in my heart, to do it to be seen of men."[70] But assurance did not just affirm salvation: psychologically, it liberated love to God and the Saints, surpassing peace, and transcendent joy. When Antony believed "that God helped me to receive Christ" and desired to take the Lord's promise to Peter that hell should not prevail against the church, his "heart joyed more and more in Christ," an expression routine among English confessors made remarkable among the Massachusett by its uniqueness: none of the four other Amerindians expressed such a sentiment. The natives do not adore God, thrill to grace, or even rejoice in salvation; if they quiet the negative emotions in the affective cycle of conversion, they hush the positive ones entirely.

[68] [Eliot], *Further Account*, 47, 52.
[69] Cohen, *God's Caress*, 168–169.
[70] [Eliot], *Further Account*, 42.

The Amerindians expressed far more interest in matters of health, understandable given their recent decimation by disease. European-borne pathogens devastated aboriginal peoples throughout the New World, and the Massachusett had probably lost some 90 per cent of their population in two epidemics, the plague in 1616–1618, and smallpox in 1633.[71] Eliot's proselytizing took place within the resulting vacuum, and illness figured repeatedly in the narratives. "I remembred that many of my children are dead," John Speene stated, concluding that "this is Gods punishment on me, because of my sins," a point Speene had applied more generally the previous year when he told a fast day meeting that "God threatneth to kill us, and therefore surely he is angry, and what maketh him angry? we may be sure it is our sins, for we are great sinners." Antony recounted a similar reaction when, having prayed that his sick brothers might live, he heard "that now God tryeth mee whether I will pray or no." Nishohkou responded more bitterly; "sick to death" after his wife and child died, he "put off praying to God," wondering "why should I pray" and "why does God thus punish me[?]"[72] Disease posed a special problem for potential converts, because giving up their old religion diminished the status and influence of the *powwows,* who opposed the evangelists and menaced Amerindians who accepted them.[73] Traducing the *powwows* exposed a native to two deadly threats, magical retaliation, and the loss of the shaman's medical skills. "[A]ll the refuge they have and relie upon in time of sicknesse is their *Powwaws,*" Eliot wrote Thomas Shepard soon after beginning his mission, adding that tutoring them in "Physick" provided a "most effectuall meanes" to break the shamans' hold, but despite the settlers' occasional success in curing native ailments, "if we pray and leave Pauwauing." John Speene rightly asked, "who shall make us well when we are sick?"[74]

In fact, Speene had already answered the question during his preliminary examination when he desired "the Physician of my soul to

[71] Alfred W. Crosby, *Ecological Imperialism: The Biological Expansion of Europe, 900–1900* (New York, 1986), 195–216; Jennings, *Invasion of America,* 15–31; Sherburne F. Cook, *The Indian Population of New England in the Seventeenth Century, University of California Publications in Anthropology,* vol. 12 (Berkeley, 1976), 31–32; Salisbury, *Manitou and Providence,* 101–106, 190–192.
[72] [Eliot], *Further Account,* 18; [Eliot], *Further Accompt,* 15; [Eliot], *Further Account,* 12, 40.
[73] Whitfield, "Light appearing," 139, 142; [Wilson], "Day-Breaking," 22; Shepard, "Clear Sun-Shine," 51.
[74] Shepard, "Clear Sun-Shine," 56; Winslow, "Glorious Progress," 77–78; [Eliot], *Further Account,* 58.

heal mee; and Christ will not in vain heal souls, but such as convert from sin, and believe in Christ."[75] Christ the doctor of sin-sick souls was a staple Puritan credo, but the Massachusett did not limit his therapeutics to the spiritual. In calling Christ "the Phisitian," Waban meant that he "healed mens bodies" as well as their souls, and Antony believed that Christ was the Son of God after hearing "*Mat. 9.* all diseased came to Christ, the blind, halt, &c and he healed them." Similarly, Speene believed that since "Christ healed all manner of diseases," he is "the Son of God, able to heal and pardon all."[76] Christ is both the agent of cure and the cure itself, "a very great life-giving God" who cares for the whole being, spirit and flesh, and whose remedies supersede the *powwows*' "antick, foolish and irrationall conceits." He even delivers the *powwows* themselves from their imps.[77] Craving health, the Massachusett came to Christ through the new birth, pitching themselves on the most powerful shaman of all. Accepting the Redeemer by faith provided Amerindians a far stronger medicine than the *powwows* could procure.

Conversion among the southern New England tribes featured its own dynamic, deriving from but not identical to the experience of English Saints. Amerindians both truncated and muted the affective cycle Puritans underwent, lopping off the joys of sanctification and mitigating the horrors of humiliation.[78] The major benefit of grace (eternal life aside) was less the strength to do good works than mere physical well-being.

The simplest explanation for this phenomenon, the alleged diffi-culties Amerindians bore in appropriating the complexities of Re-formed theology, does not suffice, if only because these tribesmen proved at least as conversant with essential doctrines as did the good-

---

[75] Ibid., 19–20.

[76] [Eliot], *Further Accompt*, 9; [idem], *Further Account*, 52, 19.

[77] Ibid., 73; Shepard, "Clear Sun-Shine," 56; Eliot and Mayhew, "Tears of Repen-tance," 203–204.

[78] The point needs far greater elaboration than possible here, but converts' diminished affectivity presupposed a culturally more generalized suppression of emotionality. "Laughter in them is not common, seldom exceeding a smile," William Wood observed, and although "naturally afraid of death," they bore the "unexpected approach of a mortal wound by a bullet, arrow, or sword" with no more "terror," "exclamation," or "complaint" than "if it had been shot into the body of a tree" (*New England Prospect*, 93). The issue is not whether Amerindians felt happiness or fear—of course they did—but how and under what circumstances they expressed their passions.

men and goodwives of Puritan Massachusetts.[79] A second suggestion raises the possibility that Eliot's converts parroted their teacher's faith, the lacunae in their cycle of feelings mirroring the bias of his sermons. Perhaps, although the point requires more study. Eliot hewed an orthodox soteriology—he participated in the synod that condemned Anne Hutchinson's errors—and Cotton Mather judged his preaching full of Christ and *"well studied* for." Mather further noted Eliot's "special Fervour in the Rebukes which he bestow'd upon *Carnality,"* and one may well imagine the "Apostle" scanting God's love to focus an alien population on His wrath, but this interpretation fails to explain the converts' flattened humiliation.[80] A third argument calls attention to Eastern woodland culture. Regenerative conversion involved Amerindians not only in adapting Christianity to their own preconceptions, but in apprehending it through lenses ground by their own cultural conditioning. Waban and his fellows took Christ in ways guided not only by Puritan standards and expectations, but by the converts' sociopsychological backgrounds.

To be born again, Amerindians had to learn not only the dogmas of creation and Fall, Passion and resurrection, but also the behaviors of grace—piety and godly love. They grasped the former more readily than the latter. Natives understood sin and God's anger, concepts consonant with the morality and experiences of their old faith, yet missed *agape,* a divine emotion pre-contact religion did not conceptualize but Puritanism's psychological payoff. Puritan conversions forged bonds of love from crucibles of despair, but lacking holy desperation, the Massachusett could not apprehend the *agape* in grace, a phenomenon that helps explain why so few natives entered church estate. Historians have stressed how Puritans held Praying Indians at arm's length while enforcing acculturation, despising their bodies while coveting their souls, but we should also insist upon the

[79] See esp. Eliot, "Late and Further Manifestation," 277–284, and cf. John Speene's remarks about the Covenants of Works and Circumcision, [Eliot], *Further Account,* 60, 61.

[80] David D. Hall, ed., *The Antinomian Controversy, 1636–1638: A Documentary History* (Middletown, 1968), *passim;* Mather, *Magnalia,* 3:185–186. Richard W. Cogley has rightly underlined the importance of Eliot's millennialism and his theories of the natives' provenance had on his mission ("John Eliot and the Millennium," *Religion in American Culture* 1(1991): 227–250; "John Eliot and the Origins of the American Indians," *Early American Literature* 21(1986/1987): 210–225, but those beliefs do not seem to have intruded into his proselytizing. On Eliot's millennialism, see Theodore Dwight Bozeman, *To Live Ancient Lives* (Chapel Hill, 1988), 263–286; James Holstun, *A Rational Millennium: Puritan Utopias of Seventeenth-Century England & America* (New York, 1987), 102–165; and Timothy J. Sehr, "John Eliot, Millennialist and Missionary," *Historian* 46(1984): 187–203.

barriers Amerindian culture itself imposed. The gulf between Massachusett and English yawned not only because Saints wanted to civilize the natives before Christianizing them, but also because the Massachusett themselves, unaccustomed to the affective style in which the Puritans communed with their deity, had difficulties conceiving a god of love.

Roger Williams and the

Enclosed Gardens of New England

Keith W. F. Stavely

FOR THE PAST several scholarly generations, two closely related propositions have been widely accepted: first, that England came in the course of the sixteenth century to regard itself as the Elect Nation, the Christian era antitype to Old Testament Israel, and second, that the founders of New England believed that they had transported this identity across the Atlantic with them.[1] Both propositions, but particularly the second one, have recently been called into question. Andrew Delbanco and Theodore Dwight Bozeman have argued that not only was the establishment of an exemplary sacred commonwealth not the dominant motive in the settlement of New England,

Some of the material considered in the present essay is placed in a somewhat different context in Keith W. F. Stavely, "Roger Williams: Bible Politics and Bible Art," *Prose Studies* 14 (3) (1991): 76–91.

[1] The literature on these points is extensive. For England, see William Haller, *The Elect Nation: The Meaning and Relevance of Foxe's* Book of Martyrs (New York, 1963); B. S. Capp, *The Fifth Monarchy Men: A Study in Seventeenth-Century English Millenarianism* (London, 1972), chap. 2; Capp, "The Political Dimension of Apocalyptic Thought," in *The Apocalypse in English Renaissance Thought and Literature: Patterns, Antecedents and Repercussions*, ed. C. R. Patrides and Joseph Wittreich (Ithaca, N. Y., 1984), 93–124; Bryan W. Ball, *A Great Expectation: Eschatological Thought in English Protestantism to 1660* (Leiden, 1975); Richard Bauckham, *Tudor Apocalypse: Sixteenth Century Apocalypticism, Millennialism and the English Reformation: From John Bale to John Foxe and Thomas Brightman* (Oxford, 1978); Paul Christianson, *Reformers and Babylon: English Apocalyptic Visions from the Reformation to the Eve of the Civil War* (Toronto, 1978); and Katherine R. Firth, *The Apocalyptic Tradition in Reformation Britain, 1530–1645* (Oxford, 1979). The scholar who has argued the most strenuously for the centrality of the Elect Nation idea in the culture of early New England is Sacvan Bercovitch; see "Typology in Puritan New England: The Williams-Cotton Controversy Reassessed," *American Quarterly* 19(1967): 166–191; *The Puritan Origins of the American Self* (New Haven, 1975), esp. chaps. 2–3; and *The American Jeremiad* (Madison, 1978).

it was not even a particularly coherent conception in the minds of the founding generation. A sense of itself as the Elect Nation did not become widespread in New England until, at the earliest, the late seventeenth century.[2]

But if apocalyptic nationalism was not a dominant presence in the ideological universe of early- and mid-seventeenth-century Anglo-America, it was nevertheless a definite one, definite enough to elicit from Roger Williams the thoroughgoing critique of it that forms virtually the basis of his thought. Israel had been "selected and separated to the *Lord* . . . from all the *people* and *Nations* of the *World* beside to be his peculiar and onely people," Williams acknowledged. But there was no evidence in the Gospel that some of these European nations were apt to make, that, after the coming of Christ, God had ever intended a corresponding separation of "whole *Nations* or *Kingdomes* (*English, Scotch, Irish, French, Dutch,* &c.) as a peculiar people and *Antitype* of the people of *Israel.*" In response to the claim that the way in which they had "wonderfully come forth of Popery" offered a striking parallel to the miraculous passage of the Chosen People from "*Aegypts bondage*" into the Promised Land, Williams brusquely advised his readers to "bring the *Nations* of *Europe* professing *Protestantisme* to the ballance of the *Sanctuary,* and ponder well whether the *body, bulke,* the generall or one hundreth part of such peoples be truly turned to *God* from *Popery.*"[3]

As for New England itself, Williams made it his business to puncture what he at least regarded as its typologically inflated sense of itself, referring sarcastically to it as "their holy Land of *Canaan*"[4]

[2]Andrew Delbanco, "The Puritan Errand Re-Viewed," *Journal of American Studies* 18(1984): 343–360; Delbanco, *The Puritan Ordeal* (Cambridge, Mass., 1989), 90–117; Theodore Dwight Bozeman, "The Puritans' 'Errand into the Wilderness' Reconsidered," *New England Quarterly* 59(1986): 231–251. The latter article includes a useful summary of the various positions in the debates that have arisen over the Elect Nation idea in the historiography of sixteenth- and seventeenth-century England as well as in that of early America.

[3]*The Bloudy Tenent of Persecution* . . . (1644), in *The Complete Writings of Roger Williams,* ed. Perry Miller, 7 vols. (New York, 1963), 3:324–25. Except for those from his correspondence and *A Key into the Language of America,* all quotations from Williams's writings are taken from this edition. The most important discussions of this aspect of Williams's thought are Perry Miller, *Roger Williams: His Contribution to the American Tradition* (1953; rpt. New York, 1966), 52–54; Edmund S. Morgan, *Roger Williams: The Church and the State* (New York, 1967), 6–10, 64–103, 120–126; Bercovitch, "Typology in Puritan New England," 166–191; Richard Reinitz, "The Separatist Background of Roger Williams' Argument for Religious Toleration," in *Typology in Early American Literature,* ed. Sacvan Bercovitch (Amherst, Mass., 1972), 107–137; and W. Clark Gilpin, *The Millenarian Piety of Roger Williams* (Chicago, 1979), 39–41, 43, 75–81, 109, 122–124.

[4]Williams, *Bloudy Tenent,* 3:284.

and taunting John Cotton with the allegation "that some of the most eminent amongst [the New England clergy] have affirmed, That even the Apostles Churches were not so pure."[5] As Bozeman points out, Cotton hotly denied the charge that New England regarded its ecclesiastical arrangements as "a Rule, and patterne, and precedent to all the Churches of Christ throughout the world."[6] But Williams evidently continued to believe there was rhetorical advantage to be gained by pressing the point, for a decade later he again declared that "*N. England* (in respect of *Spiritual* and *Civil State*) professeth to draw nearer to *Christ Jesus* then other *States* and *Churches*."[7]

In two influential articles, Sacvan Bercovitch and Jesper Rosenmeier have argued that Williams's refusal to countenance the typological/eschatological vision of New England's identity and destiny proceeded from an overall posture of *contemptus mundi*. Williams was concerned almost exclusively with individual grace and salvation, they both maintain. Since the apostasy that began under Constantine, and until the time appointed for the defeat of Antichrist, the realms of society, politics, and history merely constitute the terrain of human depravity and are therefore not worthy of a regenerate Christian's full attention.[8] According to this line of argument, Williams thus devastatingly undermined that concept of ordained exceptionalism which continues to this day—and with renewed firmness since the apparently triumphant resolution of the Cold War—to form the core of the American self-image. Yet he refused to bring forward any alternative basis for national identity. Instead, he implicitly counseled withdrawal from social and political life altogether. I believe this view of Roger Williams's sociopolitical posture is not so much untrue as incomplete. Expressions of a *contemptus mundi* outlook do abound in his writings, and the only social vision he ever succeeded in clearly projecting was the strictly negative one of a state that would not persecute "for cause of conscience." Nevertheless, Williams did not abide in a stoical Calvinist composure with respect to life in this world. A positive alternative to the Elect Nation is latent in his life and thought, and it was his tragedy

---

[5]Roger Williams, *Mr. Cottons Letter Lately Printed, Examined and Answered . . .* [1644], 1:395.

[6]Bozeman, "Puritans' Errand," 249–251; John Cotton, *A Reply to Mr. Williams his Examination . . .* (1647), in Williams, *Complete Writings*, 2:219.

[7]Roger Williams, *The Bloody Tenent Yet More Bloody . . .* [1652], 4:24.

[8]Bercovitch, "Typology in Puritan New England," 175–76; Jesper Rosenmeier, "The Teacher and the Witness: John Cotton and Roger Williams," *William and Mary Quarterly*, 3rd ser., 25(1968): 408–431.

that he was unable or unwilling to make this anti-expansionist emphasis more explicitly available. Perhaps it continues to be our tragedy as well.

In some ways, Williams was more concerned with social definition and vision than were his opponents. It was John Cotton, not Williams, who insisted to the Salem church in 1636 that what ultimately mattered was individual regeneration and salvation, not social order and justice: "Though my house do not flourish with ordinances, not in ruling justly, as the Lord requires; though my house be out of order, And commonwealth out of order, yet . . . God hath laid hold upon Christ, And Christ hath laid hold upon me, and this is his stay and comfort, ..."[9] And the reason Cotton was placing such an emphasis upon the inward Christian life in this particular sermon was that he was offering an antidote to precisely those efforts and interventions by Williams in the outward realm that had led to his banishment. Williams had attempted to make the Salem church conform as closely as possible to the social form of Christianity that was prescribed, as he believed, in Scripture, and the result had been insubordinate behavior on the part of both Williams and the church toward the higher authorities of Massachusetts Bay. At issue had been competing versions of Christian society, and Cotton was simply making use of a time-honored hegemonic strategy when he sought in his subsequent sermon to erase this competition from the discursive map and leave visible on it only a monolithic social order, on the one hand, and a collection of individuals, on the other.

The longing for a purified Christian society runs throughout Williams's writings. He repeatedly draws the sharpest possible distinction between "*Gods* people in their persons, *Heart-waking*, (*Cant.* 5. 2.) in the life of *personall grace*," and those same people remaining nevertheless "fast asleep in respect of *publike Christian Worship*."[10] It was unfortunately true of New Englanders in particular that "though their hearts wake (in respect of personall grace and life of Jesus) yet they sleep, insensible of much concerning the Lords worship."[11] Williams stressed not that personal regeneration was fundamental (this he mostly assumed), but rather that the regenerate played a fundamental role in Christian social life and history: "*Negatively*, wherein

[9]John Cotton, "A Sermon Delivered at Salem, 1636," in *John Cotton on the Churches of New England*, ed. Larzar Ziff (Cambridge, Mass., 1968), 66.
[10]Williams, *Bloudy Tenent*, 3:65.
[11]Williams, *Mr. Cottons Letter*, 1:335.

they *Witnessed* against the *False,* against the *Usurpations* and *Abominations* of *Antichrist,"* and positively, "as they have assumed and pretended to such and such *Ministries,* and *Titles,* and *Churches,* and *Ministrations."* In this positive role, unfortunately, none of the regenerate, "no not *Calvin* himselfe (the greatest *Pretender* to *Church-Order*)," had succeeded in recreating "the first *Patterns* and Institutions of *Christ Jesus."* [12]

But if the visible church remained hidden, this did not make it any less significant to Williams. In addition to the first, saving work of grace in their souls, he anticipated that those who had been personally regenerated would experience "a mighty worke of Gods Spirit to humble and ashame them and to cause them to loath themselves for their Abominations or stincks in Gods nostrils (as it pleaseth Gods Spirit to speak of false Worships:) . . ." So deep-reaching would be this "plucking of . . . souls out from the Abominations of false worships" that it would constitute "a second kind of Regeneration." [13] After one was reborn as an individual Christian, one had to be reborn all over again as a Christian citizen.

In seventeenth-century ecclesiastical discourse, the image most frequently employed to describe the church was drawn from a text in the Song of Songs: "a garden inclosed is my sister, my spouse; a spring shut up, a fountain sealed." [14] In New England this was taken to mean, as John Cotton explained, that in the midst of a world which was "as a wildernesse, or at least a wilde field . . . the Church is Gods garden or orchard . . . as the garden of Paradise was the habitation of *Adam* in the state of innocency, so is the Church of all those who are renewed into innocency." [15] Williams had frequent recourse to such imagery, proclaiming indignantly that to confer ecclesiastical power upon civil rulers was "to turn the *Garden* and *Paradice* of the *Church* and *Saints* into the *Field* of the *Civill State* of the *World,* and to reduce the *World* to the first *chaos* or *confusion."* [16] The manifold disasters of ecclesiastical history had arisen when people had "opened a gap in the hedge or wall of Separation between the Garden of the Church and the Wilderness of the world"; if and when God should choose "to restore his Garden and Paradice again, it

---

[12] Roger Williams, *The Hireling Ministry None of Christs . . .* [1652], 7:161.
[13] Williams, *Mr. Cottons Letter,* 1:350.
[14] Song of Sol. 4:12.
[15] John Cotton, *A Brief Exposition of the whole Book of Canticles, or Song of Solomon . . .* (London, 1642), 130.
[16] Williams, *Bloudy Tenent,* 3:415.

must of necessitie be walled in peculiarly unto himselfe from the world, . . . all that shall be saved out of the world are to be transplanted out of the Wildernes of world [sic], and added unto his Church or Garden."[17] The lines of demarcation were etched just as distinctly near the end of Williams's life, when he found himself engaged in debate with the Quakers. God had made a solemn promise, he reminded them, that "the Garden of his Church & *Saints*" was to be "taken in, inclosed and separate" from "the *howling Desart* of the whole world."[18]

It seems plausible to speculate that at least a few of those who joined in the Great Migration were moved to do so by the opportunities it presented for literal realization of this imagery, for the establishment of pure garden-like churches in the midst of what was frequently described as a wilderness, a howling, savage desert. Assuming that such a group existed, it is more than likely that Roger Williams was among its members, judging from his behavior after he arrived. If so, then the Massachusetts authorities were doing him a favor, in a way, when they banished him from what had become in his eyes just one more figurative wilderness scene of human fallenness and thereby propelled him into a second errand into the still literal wilderness of the Narragansett country, where one might make a fresh start at the fundamental task of gathering churches and planting gardens. Yet either before or not long after his precipitous removal from Massachusetts, Williams came to the conclusion we have already heard him articulating in the 1650s, that it did not matter, ecclesiastically speaking, which kind of wilderness one inhabited. There was simply no way to plant and enclose a true visible church during the Antichristian interim through which the world was still passing.[19] To this extent Bercovitch and Rosenmeier are correct. Williams did for the time being, until the time appointed, give over his quest for the social realization of Christianity.

But he did so only with the utmost reluctance, and it is the ways in which he manifests this reluctance that make him a particularly interesting, appealing, and, in the end, tragic figure. I would like to approach this dimension of Williams's life and thought somewhat circuitously, by looking briefly at how the figure of the enclosed gar-

---

[17] Williams, *Mr. Cottons Letter,* 1:392.

[18] Williams, *George Fox Digg'd Out of His Burrowes* . . . [1676], 5:476.

[19] The fullest discussion of this aspect of Williams's thought is found in Morgan, *Roger Williams,* chap. 2.

den was developed by his friend John Milton.[20] As I have argued
elsewhere, the initial view of Paradise in Book IV of *Paradise Lost*
draws together all the elements of the conventional ecclesiastical imagery that we have seen recurred so frequently in Williams's writings.
The Garden of Eden of the Book of Genesis is also the garden enclosed of the Song of Songs, an "enclosure green" displaying itself,
just as Williams (or indeed John Cotton) would wish, in the starkest
possible contrast to the "steep wilderness" upon which it rests.[21] But
Milton presents this conventional view only to subvert it. Within a
very few lines, the structures by which ecclesiastical purity is enclosed and defined are shown to be ineffectual. Satan easily gains
illegitimate admittance to God's archetypal garden, and Milton then
proceeds to associate the clergy not with the sacred enclosure thus
violated but rather with the demonic violator. In a series of epic sim-
iles, they are transformed from shepherds into "lewd hirelings" who
climb along with the "first grand thief into God's fold."[22]

Before we have even entered Paradise, Milton seems to place us in
the position in which Williams came to find himself. The garden of
the church is overrun by the forces of the wilderness. Enclaves of
divine purity and truth cannot survive the onslaughts of a Satan
whose "one slight bound" here, that "high over leap[s] all bound,"[23]
is merely the most recent of the many successful transgressions of
boundaries that have brought him and the poem to this point. But
beyond this confrontation between the thesis of the bounded, godly
garden and the antithesis of an encroaching Satanic wilderness that
knows no bounds, Milton develops the overall narrative towards the
synthesis that appears at the very end of the poem. The external Paradise is to be destroyed in the Flood, we are told, but in the meantime it has been superseded by the "paradise within"[24] that is instilled
in Adam and Eve prior and preparatory to their exile from the garden
into the fallen wilderness. In some respects, Milton thus leaves Adam

[20]The principal evidence for friendship between Williams and Milton is Williams's
statement that during his stay in London in the 1650s, "The Secretarie of the Councell
(Mr. Milton) for my Dutch I read him read me many more languages"; see Williams to
John Winthrop, Jr., 12 July 1654, in *The Correspondence of Roger Williams*, ed. Glenn W.
LaFantasie, 2 vols. (Hanover, N.H., 1988), 2:393.
[21]John Milton, *Paradise Lost*, in *The Poems of John Milton*, ed. John Carey and Alistair
Fowler (London, 1968), 616 (Book IV, ll. 133, 135).
[22]Ibid., IV, 185, 192–193.
[23]Ibid., IV, 181.
[24]Ibid., XII, 587.

and Eve in the condition attributed by Bercovitch and Rosenmeier to Williams. After the external, institutional forms of godliness have become irredeemably tainted, our first parents learn to cultivate the gardens of inner grace that betoken their personal salvation. But such a view misses altogether the remarkable power of the concluding lines:

> Some natural tears they dropped, but wiped them soon,
> The world was all before them, where to choose
> Their place of rest, and Providence their guide.
> They, hand in hand, with wandering steps and slow,
> Through Eden took their solitary way.[25]

Sobered but not downcast, two people who represent all future human beings set forth hand in hand into a world that is all before them. Modern literature offers no more compelling image of human solidarity and openness to historical experience. Just as the enclosed garden, in losing its static purity, has been made over into a principle of energy and empowerment, so what lies without the garden now appears as less a wasteland than a vista to be explored. The errand into the wilderness is launched in a different spirit.[26]

Many aspects of the banishment of Roger Williams from the enclosed civil and ecclesiastical gardens of Massachusetts Bay in the 1630s strikingly anticipate what Milton was to imagine in the 1660s as the essential configuration of human affairs. In his most explicit and definite way of presenting himself, of course, Williams viewed his exiled situation as a simple adaptation of the conventional confrontation between garden and wilderness. The Narragansett country, he wrote John Winthrop in 1637, was indeed a "remote willdernes." In this barren landscape not a garden was to be seen. But possibly "this materiall desart" would reproduce the "misticall" desert of the Book of Revelation,[27] "where 1200 and 3 score dayes [God's Saints] are hid."[28] Rhode Island might become a uniquely resonant emblem of the state of the entire world during the reign of

---

[25] Ibid., XII, 645–649.
[26] The argument here summarized is developed more fully in Keith W. F. Stavely, "Jonathan Edwards and John Milton: Dominant, Residual, Emergent, Immanent," in *The Critical Response to John Milton's Paradise*, ed. Timothy C. Miller (Westport, Conn., forthcoming).
[27] Rev. 12:6.
[28] Williams, *Correspondence*, 1:133.

Antichrist, given over to depravity but also inhabited by a handful of witnesses to Christian truth.

That Williams also responded to his surroundings in a different spirit, one that closely resembles Milton's representation of the departure of Adam and Eve from Paradise as a merger of garden and wilderness into a horizon of possibility, is clearest in his first published work, *A Key into the Language of America*. The *Key* is best appreciated by contrast with the conventional approach to Native American culture most fully exemplified by John Eliot, who was given to telling his potential converts that so long as they persisted in their traditional way of life, their "souls feed upon nothing but lust, and lying, and stealing, and killing, and pauwauing. And all these are sins which poison, starve, and kill your souls, and expose them to God's wrath that they may be tormented among devils and wicked men in hell fire forever." Eliot followed up on such overbearing rhetoric by gathering his praying Indians into settlements in which they not only worshipped as Christians, but also farmed, dressed, and lived in accordance with English custom and practice. Eliot's form of evangelism is one of the preeminent examples of the "civilization process" described by James Axtell, entailing "the wholesale substitution of a European lifestyle for the natives' own." The peoples indigenous to the North American continent were required by Eliot and others to forsake utterly their shamanistic and nomadic way of life, to become "securely anchored to one plot of ground," encompassed at once within the church and "the encircling web of credit that husbandry entailed." They were to be uprooted from the wilderness and replanted within the garden walls.[29]

There are, to be sure, traces of such ethnocentrism in Williams's *Key*, just as there are in *Paradise Lost*. For example, Williams is unwilling to observe at first hand the efforts of native priests on behalf of the sick, lest he should become a "partaker of Sathans Inventions and Worships."[30] Nevertheless, John J. Teunissen and Evelyn J. Hinz are correct to call attention to the *Key*'s relative freedom from condescending preconception and its disposition to discern signs of dignity

---

[29] *John Eliot's Indian Dialogues: A Study in Cultural Interaction*, ed. Henry W. Bowden and James P. Ronda (Westport, Conn., 1980), 85; James Axtell, *The Invasion Within: The Contest of Cultures in Colonial North America* (New York, 1985), 4, 156. See also James Holstun, *A Rational Millennium: Puritan Utopias of Seventeenth-Century England and America* (New York, 1987), 106–144.

[30] Roger Williams, *A Key into the Language of America* (1643), ed. John J. Teunissen and Evelyn J. Hinz (Detroit, 1973), 192.

and even regeneration in these putative savages.[31] The Narragansetts are "remarkably free and courteous, to invite all Strangers in"; their language reveals how pervasive is this "savour of *civility* and *courtesie*" among them.[32] So prominent a feature of the Narragansett way of life was courtesy and hospitality that Williams was prepared to affirm "that a man shall generally finde more free entertainment amongst these *Barbarians,* then amongst thousands that call themselves *Christians*."[33] This reversal of Eurocentric moral expectations was indeed more generally applicable: "I could never discerne that excesse of scandalous sins amongst them, which *Europe* aboundeth with. Drunkennesse and gluttony, generally they know not what sinnes they be, . . . a man shall never heare of such crimes amongst them of robberies, murthers, adulteries, &c. as amongst the *English*."[34]

Williams had himself experienced the alacrity with which the Narragansetts extended themselves to strangers and wayfarers: "many a time, and at all times of the night (as I have fallen in travell upon their houses) when nothing hath been ready, [they] have themselves and their wives, risen to prepare me some refreshing."[35] In one remarkably lovely chapter, "Of *Travell,*"[36] Williams weaves together both these motifs, Narragansett generosity and literal wayfaring through the wilderness, in a manner that encourages fresh applications of the venerable Christian and Protestant metaphor of life as a pilgrimage.

Each chapter of the *Key* consists of glossaries of Narragansett terms interspersed with observations on Narragansett customs, and, at the end, versified moral/spiritual reflections. As Teunissen and Hinz emphasize, when the English portions of the glossary sections are read vertically, they are apt to cohere as aesthetic units in their own right:[37]

---

[31]*Key,* ed. Teunissen and Hinz, "Introduction," 13–69; "Anti-Colonial Satire in Roger Williams's *A Key into the Language of America*," *Ariel* 7(1976): 5–26; "Roger Williams, St. Paul, and American Primitivism," *Canadian Review of American Studies* 4(1973): 121–36; "Roger Williams, Thomas More, and the Narragansett Utopia," *Early American Literature* 11(1976–77): 281–295. See also Jack L. Davis, "Roger Williams among the Narragansett Indians," *New England Quarterly* 43(1970): 593–604; and Gordon Brotherston, "A Controversial Guide to the Language of America, 1643," in *1642: Literature and Power in the Seventeenth Century,* ed. Francis Barker, et al. (Colchester, Eng., 1981), 84–100.
[32]Williams, *Key,* ed. Teunissen and Hinz, 97, 99.
[33]Ibid., 104.
[34]Ibid., 203.
[35]Ibid., 104.
[36]Ibid., 147–154.
[37]Ibid., "Introduction," 53–55.

A way.
Is there a way?
There is no way.
A great path.
A stone path.

The reader may begin at once to reflect on spiritual as well as physical pathways, especially since by this point he or she has repeatedly seen Williams draw out the "mystical" significance of the material particulars he describes. The subsequent glossary portions of the chapter proceed to depict a lost traveler hiring a guide. As the situation develops, the initial relationship of the purchase and sale of labor (*"Hire him. / I will hire you."*) recedes into the background, in a manner that cannot be appreciated without extensive quotation:

Let us accompany.
I thanke you for your company. . . .
You will lose your way. . . .
I will goe before.
I will stay for you. . . .
I will follow you. . . .
Let us wade.
How deepe?
Thus deep.
I will carry you.
You are heavy.
You are light.
Rise.
Goe.
Run.
Meet him.
Let us meet. . . .
Let us rest here.
Let us sit downe. . . .
I am weary.
I am lame. . . .
I will be here by and by againe.
I will not leave you.
Doe not leave me.
Why doe you forsake me?
A staffe.
Use this staffe. . . .
Lay down your burthen.

The glossary, in short, tells a brief, highly resonant tale of the spontaneous formation of a community of wayfarers, bearing together the many burdens and sharing the few pleasures of a journey through the wilderness.

The accompanying commentary informs us that the Narragansetts manifest not only skill but also charity in their capacity as pathmakers and guides: "It is admirable to see, what paths their naked hardened feet have made in the wildernesse in most stony and rockie places. . . . I have heard of many *English* lost, and have oft been lost my selfe, and my selfe and others have often been found, and succoured by the *Indians*." The idea that the Narragansetts, just as they are, manifest their own particular dignity is not quite explicitly expressed, but it hardly needs to be, so delicate is Williams's touch, so calm his tone. Narragansett travels, both among themselves and together with Englishmen, are viewed with an attentiveness comparable to that which Bunyan would later lavish on the community of the faithful in *The Pilgrim's Progress*.

If Narragansett material experience trembles on the brink of being Christian experience, this is hardly surprising in view of what Williams tells us about Narragansett spiritual experience. Native piety earns from him the compliment of being likened to that of one of the central figures in the unfolding of Judaeo-Christian sacred history: "When they have a bad Dreame, which they conceive to be a threatning from God, they fall to prayer at all times of the night, especially early before day: So *Davids* zealous heart to the true and living God: *At midnight will I rise* &c. *I prevented the dawning of the day,* &c. Psal. 119 &c."[38] When Williams later relates how he presented the concept of monotheism to the Narragansetts—by simply saying, *"There is onely one God. / You are mistaken. / You are out of the way,"*[39]—his words thus have behind them the genuine respect for Narragansett wayfaring and Narragansett religiosity he has already demonstrated. In the context formed by such respect, conversion does not require a violent transformation of Narragansett paganism, merely a slight, subtle change in focus within existing Narragansett culture. Williams remarks in the last section of the chapter on travel that "the same Sun shines on the Wildernesse that doth on a Garden,"[40] but even this amounts to a retreat from the most far-reaching implications of the presentation he has been making. As Narragansett nightmares converge with the Book of Psalms, Narragansett nomads with English

[38] Ibid., 107.
[39] Ibid., 195.
[40] Ibid., 153.

spiritual seekers, the opposition between wilderness and garden begins to be erased altogether.

Only one other document from Williams's pen, a letter sent to the Massachusetts General Court in 1654, manifests to anywhere near the same degree this wayfaring, exploratory sensibility. In the course of an effort to dissuade the Massachusetts authorities from making war on the Narragansetts, Williams notes that such a war might call into question the legitimacy of the evangelical efforts by John Eliot and others that Massachusetts was officially sponsoring: "I beseech You consider how the name of the most holy and jealous God may be preserved betweene the clashings of these Two: Viz: The Glor [Glorious] Conversion of the Indians in N. Engl. and the Unnecessary Warrs and cruel Destruction of the Indians in New Engl."[41] But earlier in the letter, Williams had already subjected Eliot's evangelistic methods to a more searching critique, suggesting that they amounted not to an alternative to war, but rather to the waging of it by other means. Before his recent trip to England, the Narragansetts had asked him to petition the English authorities "that they might not be forced from their Religion, and for not changing their Religion be invaded by War. For they said they were dayly visited with Threatnings by Indians that came from about the Massachusets, that if they would not pray they should be destroyed by War."[42]

At the close of the letter, Williams invokes the standard formula used in all discussions of conversion of the Native Americans, "that Civilitie may be a leading step to Christianitie."[43] It was in the name of this formula that Eliot linked conversion to Christianity with living in such places as the English-style settlement he had created at Natick, Massachusetts. Williams claims here that he joins "prudent and pious Mr Wintrop deceased" in advocacy of the inseparability of civilizing and evangelizing. But the alert reader may suspect that Williams has something rather different in mind than does Eliot, for Williams has earlier drawn a parallel between "prudent and pious Mr Wintrop deceased" and the Narragansett sachem Canonicus: "Their late famous longliv'd Caunounicus . . . liv'd and died [inclined to peace and Love with the English Nation] and in the same most honble [honorable] manner and sollemnitie (in their way) as You laid to sleepe Your Prudent Peacemaker Mr Wintrop, did they honour this their Prudent and Peaceable Prince. His Son Meiksah inherites his

[41] Williams, *Correspondence*, 2:410.
[42] Ibid., 2:409.
[43] Ibid., 2:413.

Spirit. Yea through all their Townes and Countries, how frequently doe many and ofttimes one English man travell alone with safetie and loving kindnes?"[44] In the eyes of Williams and Winthrop, the implicit argument runs, civilizing and converting must proceed from a willingness to set aside the assumption that all that meets the eye of the Englishman, as he gazes out from his garden wall, is untracked, unimproved wilderness. Those who "travell alone" through the unenclosed Native American territory will, if they have eyes to see, find abundance of good seed and healthy growth.

Although Williams always remained on good terms with the Narragansetts, he never articulated his uniquely open and respectful perceptions of them in a manner that would have been direct and forceful enough to constitute an alternative vision of English-Native American relations. Like most Puritans, Williams's thought was grounded in stark antithetical contrasts: between regeneracy and fallenness, the Bible and human invention, the New Testament and the Old, the garden of the true visible church and the wilderness of virtually all other human phenomena. His originality lay in his sharpening of such antitheses, his application of them in unexpected directions, so that the New Testament is seen to annul the Old Testament's legitimation of civil power in ecclesiastical affairs, or the necessity of spiritual rebirth is shown to point, in strict Calvinist logic, to the spiritual equality of all the unregenerate, be they Protestant or Catholic, Christian or Pagan. This latter consequence of an orthodox antithesis ruthlessly pursued constitutes the moral that is most insistently drawn in the *Key*. The more radical affirmation that I am arguing hovers just beneath the surface of the *Key*—that Narragansett culture contains within itself the seeds of genuine regeneracy —would have required for its full and open articulation a synthesizing power, an ability to break through to the terrain of redefined categories, that nothing in the corpus of Williams's writings indicates he possessed.

In the 1654 letter, the critique of cultural imperialism and the intimations of a different view of the Narragansetts are buried even further beneath the surface than in the *Key*. The letter's more overt argument does not hesitate to characterize the peoples indigenous to the continent as "Pagans and Beasts wallowing in Idlenes, stealing, lying, whoring, Treacherie[,] Witchcrafts, Blasphemies and Idol-

[44]Ibid., 2:412.

atries," and to warn that the effort to attack such savagery head on might result not in the preservation but rather the destruction of "all that the gracious hand of the Lo. [Lord] hath so wonderfully planted in this Wildernes."[45] Missing from rhetoric of this sort is not merely the Miltonic synthesis, but even Williams's own special variation on the garden/wilderness antithesis. He propounds instead that cruder confrontation of civilized English garden with grotesque native and New World wilderness which informed the consciousness of virtually everyone in New England besides himself.

No doubt Williams was in part fulfilling his rhetorical intentions here, now saying what he thought the recipients of his letter wanted to hear, and now, in masterly fashion, slyly unsaying it. But there is reason to believe that he was also, precisely because he was unable to reconcile his intuitions of Native American dignity with his formally maintained perspective, simply setting aside those intuitions and articulating a New England conventionality to which, with a part of himself, he sincerely subscribed. In *Experiments of Spiritual Life and Health*, published two years before this letter, he speaks in a less strident but otherwise similar vein about how the local tribes "see the *excellency* of the *English industry*, joyned with *plenty*, and a better *condition* then their own, but endure not that *life* of *labour* and *indeavour*, wherein that *plenty* and better *state* is found."[46]

In the end, what governed Williams's understanding of ordinary social affairs was neither the generous, unenclosed Miltonism towards which some of his writings partially stir, nor the rigorously enclosed, separatistic Calvinism on which his formal discourses avowedly rest. It was, rather, a quirky variation on this standard New England fortress mentality, one that brought his career of stubborn, isolated radicalism to a fitting conclusion. In the last two decades of his life, Williams became embroiled with one of his fellow townsmen, William Harris, in a protracted controversy over Providence land policy.[47] Harris claimed that Providence had a legal right to take over Narragansett territory and, as one of the founding English/Narragansett agreements of the 1630s seemed to say, expand to the west "upstream without limits."[48] Thus confronted with Harris's crude early version of Manifest Destiny, Williams was in effect confronted

[45]Ibid., 2:413.
[46]Roger Williams, *Experiments* [1652], 7:69.
[47]For the context and details of this controversy, see Sidney V. James, *Colonial Rhode Island: A History* (New York, 1975), 88–93; and Williams, *Correspondence*, 2:556–570.
[48]See Williams, *Correspondence*, 2:741–742.

with the need to translate his long-standing opposition to the Elect
Nation into more practical, tangible terms.

Unfortunately, the terms—enclosed garden over against damnable
wilderness—lay ready to hand, ready-made. Williams presented
himself throughout the dispute as the defender of a vision of New
England as a scattering of bounded enclaves of civility and godliness
across the raw New World landscape. At the time he had founded
Providence, he insisted, his intent had been that the town should be
"of as large a Plantation and Accomodation as any Towne in this
Countrey of N. Engl."[49] As large, but no larger. In letter after letter
during the 1660s and 1670s, Williams entered into Scholastic disqui-
sitions on the history of the boundaries of Providence. He felt he had
painstakingly to redraw the boundaries of Providence rhetorically,
because in Harris he was faced with the spirit of boundlessness itself,
threatening to obscure and engulf the enclosures that defined both
the civil and the sacred. To argue as Harris did for the unchecked
upstream expansion of Providence was to create something "monstrous and terrible because without Bounds or Lymits," comparable
to the Antichristian beast in the Book of Daniel. Such "a terrible
Beast" not only tears "our Peace and Neighbourhood in pieces, but
it spits fire and spreads fire, and sets the Townes on Fire, and the
Whole Colony allso." In the spiritual realm, Harris's monstrous land
greed dares "to lift up his head and hornes in blaspheamy agnst the
God of Heaven. What God can that be, Say the Indians, that is followed by such Extortioners, Cheatours and Lyers, as his Servants
and Worshippers?"[50]

In the course of the controversy, Williams broadened his indictment of Harris until it became boundless itself, taking in every aspect
of his conduct. During the Interregnum, Harris had written in favor
of what amounted to anarchy, in a book that "traiterously vomits out
his filth agst all Govrnmnts and Governors (of what Rank soever) all
Lords and Masters, agst all Lawes, and Lawmaking Assemblies, agst
all Courts, all Punishments, prisons, Rates and all Records, as
Thievs, Robbers, Hypocrites, Satyrs, Owles (courts of Owles) Dragons and Devills, and Souldiers, Legions of Devills."[51] As for Harris's
religious views, his interpretation of the "upstream without limits"
clause was similar to the Antichristian scriptural hermeneutics of papists, universalists, and Quakers, wresting texts into "Nonsensicall

[49]Ibid., 2:743; see also 587, 596.
[50]Ibid., 2:599.
[51]Ibid., 2:581.

Whimsies without any Bounds or Order."[52] But any religion Harris might profess, however absurd in itself, was in any case but a cover for the atheism and self-seeking of this "Prodigie of Pride and Scorning . . . who being an impudent Morris dancer in Kent under the Cloake of (scurrilous) jeasts agnst the Bp [Bishop] got into a flight to N. Engl and under a Cloake of Seperacion got in with my selfe Till his Selfe Ends and restles strife and at last his Atheisticall denying of Heaven and Hell made honest souls to fly from him."[53]

We have returned full circle to Milton. Just at the time that this more imaginative Puritan radical was introducing to the world his literary examplar of self-aggrandizement, Williams was, with considerably less artistry but with comparable intensity, conceiving of Harris in precisely the same terms. In portraying his fellow townsman as Satan, Williams joined Milton in disapprobation of the expansive, secularizing energies of the seventeenth century. There is a broad consensus among historians of early Rhode Island that, as the heretic colony discarded or eroded traditional structures of authority in both church and state, it moved more rapidly than the rest of New England, in such areas as ecclesiology, town government, farming, and trade, toward democracy, secularism, urbanism, and capitalism.[54] The founder of Rhode Island had helped to bring about this emergence of the modern world, and he was neither the first nor would he be the last historical protagonist to recoil in horror from the ironical results of his own actions.

But Williams had painted himself into a corner. He was unable or unwilling to do as Milton did at the end of *Paradise Lost,* take the energy and mobility that Satan was deforming and reform it in a way that could redefine the entire situation. In attacking Harris, he was protecting the Narragansetts against the local Satan's proto-capitalistic worship of "God Land,"[55] but he was at the same time conspicuously overlooking a method of doing so that he above any-

---

[52]Ibid., 2:597.

[53]Ibid., 2:769.

[54]See Carl Bridenbaugh, *Fat Mutton and Liberty of Conscience: Society in Rhode Island, 1636–1690* (Providence, R.I., 1974); James, *Colonial Rhode Island;* William G. McLoughlin, *Rhode Island: A Bicentennial History* (New York, 1978), chaps. 1–2; Bruce C. Daniels, *Dissent and Conformity on Narragansett Bay: The Colonial Rhode Island Town* (Middletown, Conn., 1983); and Sidney V. James, "Ecclesiastical Authority in the Land of Roger Williams," *New England Quarterly* 57(1984): 323–346. For an argument that the representation of Satan in *Paradise Lost* constitutes Milton's response to emergent capitalism and modernism, see Keith W. F. Stavely, *Puritan Legacies:* Paradise Lost *and the New England Tradition, 1630–1890* (Ithaca, N. Y., 1987), chap. 3.

[55]Williams, *Correspondence,* 2:528.

one else in New England was qualified to bring forward, that of teaching the energetic English settlers some other mode and manner of stepping forth and making contact with their alien neighbors. Instead, he merely told them to stay put behind the boundaries that he had set for them. He had retained the rhetoric of enclosure while dispensing with most of its institutional reality, with the inevitable result that the rhetoric grew at once more and more strident and less and less effective.

Williams claimed in 1677 that Harris's expansionist schemes had been one of the major causes of King Philip's War, in the course of which Williams's own house had been burned to the ground, along with the rest of Providence, by a party of Narragansett and other warriors.[56] But Williams must himself bear some of the responsibility for this early American *götterdämerung* of enclosing, gardening palefaces and marauding, Satanic redmen. For in the pattern of his life in New England, he traced the narrative of *Paradise Lost* in reverse, beginning where Milton's epic ends in recognition and relishing of the world all before him, and ending where the poem begins, with gardens of order and dignity maintained in vigilance against the menace of the demonic wilderness. No matter that to him it was not native peoples but rather piratical Englishmen that were the real redmen, the true genii of the forest. The most original mind of the founding generation had nevertheless been unable to break beyond the conceptual impasse which the palefaces and redmen of New England proceeded to bring to tragic realization. It is not known whether Williams ever read *Paradise Lost*. If he owned a copy, it may have been consumed along with many of his other papers and effects in the sacking of Providence in 1676. Such an erasure of the Miltonic synthesis from American history would, alas, have been all too appropriate.

[56]Ibid., 2:744.

Part Five: The Legacy

The Spirit of the Old Writers:

The Great Awakening and the

Persistence of Puritan Piety

Charles E. Hambrick-Stowe

SCORES OF Congregational pastors from throughout New England responded to Thomas Prince's 1743 invitation to submit accounts of local manifestations of the "happy revival of religion" for publication in America's first religious periodical, *The Christian History*. Prince's correspondents not only reported on the numbers of souls converted and the circumstances surrounding the awakening, they offered a reassuring, conservative interpretation of what to the more genteel and rationalist of the day seemed an unruly outburst of "enthusiasm, delusion, and disorder." To New Light clergy, the Great Awakening at its best vindicated what we could call "old time religion," basic seventeenth-century Puritan principles and spirituality. In issue after issue of the weekly magazine, they concluded that the work of revival "was essentially the same" as that put forth in "the writings of Messirs. Shepard, Willard, Stoddard, and numberless other Divines of that Stamp and Principle" who had "rightly understood the Way of Salvation." This analysis was solidly in line with Prince's objectives in publishing *The Christian History*. The journal was an unwieldy collection of (a) extracts from the devotional-theological writings of "the most famous Old Writers" of Puritan England, Scotland, and "the first Settlers of new-England and their Children"; (b) "Manuscript original Letters now in the Hands of the Rev. Mr. Prince," written by ministers and other observers of mini-revivals "in almost all Parts of the Land" between 1660 and 1720; and (c) reports from Scotland and the British North American colonies concerning the Great Awakening of the 1730s and 1740s. By printing these types of materials, Prince sought to illustrate the traditionalism of the Awakening. Specifically, he wished to demonstrate that "the pious Principles and Spirit" of the "Old Writers" were "at this Day revived," and "also [to] guard against all extremes."[1]

This conservative and print-oriented approach to pro-revival clergy casts a different light on our general understanding of the Great Awakening as an oral and present- or future-oriented phenomenon. According to such historical scholarship, the revival brought something entirely new to colonial American society. Words such as "crucial turning point," "watershed," "final break with the Middle Ages," "crisis," sprinkle the writings of historians who have effectively described the changes wrought by this pre-Revolutionary spiritual upheaval. As Richard Bushman interpreted it, in what has become a classic description, "The converted were new men, with new attitudes towards themselves, their religion, their neighbors, and their rulers in church and state. A psychological earthquake had reshaped the human landscape." These changes have to do with individualism and democracy (over against, in Perry Miller's words, Puritanism's "basically medieval" static worldview), with the rise of an emotion-laden heart-religion (as opposed to Puritan scholasticism), and with the rise of a distinctly American identity. The innovation of extemporaneous sermon delivery, according to Harry S. Stout, was linked with the ministry's need to win the loyalty of the laity in an increasingly competitive market. Richard D. Brown, in his recent study of how information was diffused within American society from the colonial to the early national period, states that "in the Great Awakening the notion of individual choice was forcefully asserted, together with the exercise of personal preference by ordinary people who announced that they would henceforth decide what religious information they would choose to hear." Martin Marty astutely summarizes: "The Awakening can be seen as an event or a process in the course of which the religion of the colonial way of life was supplanted by a second way—the evangelical route through which, ever since, a

[1] Thomas Prince, Jr., *The Christian History, Containing Accounts of the Revival and Propagation of Religion in Great-Britain and America for the Year 1743* (Boston, 1744), 1–2, 113, 155, 162, 185. The weekly was edited by the younger Prince, who nevertheless asked contributors to send manuscripts to his father, pastor of Boston's Third Church.

person might become a fervent American believer." Many evangelical preachers themselves promoted the impression that God was now doing a new thing. Jonathan Edwards himself referred to the Northampton revival of 1734 as "the Surprising Work of God."[2]

Jon Butler has recently taken a radically different view of the Great Awakening, which corresponds at certain points with the conservative agenda apparent in Thomas Prince's *The Christian History*. Prince's inclusion of accounts of spiritual awakening from the generations between 1660 and 1720 demonstrates his own sense of, or desire for, continuity. Butler, arguing that the notion of a single event called the "Great Awakening" is artificial, similarly observes that "revivals linked to it started in New England long before 1730 yet did not appear with force in Virginia until the 1760s." Further, the revivals of the 1730s and 1740s were neither as geographically pervasive nor as enduring in influence as is commonly portrayed. Revivals were spawned not so much in an environment of spiritual depression, or the failure of traditional religion, as within the context of a gradual renaissance of "the state church tradition" of Anglicanism and Congregationalism and of ecclesiastical and clerical authority even among dissenting revival-born groups over an extended period from about 1680 to 1760. "In general, revivalism embraced conservative rather than radical or egalitarian approaches to the question of authority." For Butler the idea of the "Great Awakening" is the construct of nineteenth-century religious historians trying to promote revivals in their own day—that is, using the events of the 1730s and 1740s much as Thomas Prince and other New Light clergy used seventeenth-century Puritanism. Butler thus thinks of the Great Awakening as "an interpretive fiction . . . an American equivalent of

Richard L. Bushman, *From Puritan to Yankee: Character and the Social Order in Connecticut, 1690–1765* (Cambridge, Mass., 1967), 207; Perry Miller, "Jonathan Edwards and the Great Awakening," *Errand into the Wilderness* (Cambridge, Mass., 1956), 153–166; Edwin Scott Gaustad, *The Great Awakening in New England* (New York, 1957), 1–15, 102–140; Alan Heimert, *Religion and the American Mind: From the Great Awakening to the Revolution* (Cambridge, Mass., 1966), esp. 27–94; Wesley M. Gewehr, *The Great Awakening in Virginia, 1740–1790* (Gloucester, Mass., 1965; orig. 1930), 3–18; David S. Lovejoy, *Religious Enthusiasm in the New World: Heresy to Revolution* (Cambridge, Mass., 1985), 178–214; William G. McLoughlin, "'Enthusiasm for Liberty': The Great Awakening as a Key to the Revolution," *Preachers and Politicians* (Worcester, Mass., 1977), 47–73; Harry S. Stout, *The New England Soul: Preaching and Religious Culture in Colonial New England* (New York, 1986), 185–211; Richard D. Brown, *Knowledge is Power: The Diffusion of Information in Early America, 1700–1865* (New York, 1989), 273; Martin E. Marty, *Religion, Awakening, and Revolution* (n.p., 1977), 79–80, 93; Jonathan Edwards, *A Faithful Narrative of the Surprising Work of God* (London, 1737).

the Roman Empire's Donation of Constantine." Whether or not this conclusion is too extreme, it has become evident that the revivals of the 1730s and 1740s embodied tradition as well as innovation.[3]

Several other scholars have specifically identified themes of continuity in the Great Awakening with earlier Presbyterian-Congregational experience. Marilyn J. Westerkamp has shown that middle colony revivalism was a traditional, not an innovative, form of religious expression rooted in seventeenth-century Old World Scots-Irish piety. Leigh Eric Schmidt demonstrates that a particular Scottish tradition of "sacramental seasons," large outdoor protracted gatherings (typically eight days in duration) for preaching and the celebration of Holy Communion, shaped some of the major contours of American revivalism and gave birth to the supposedly uniquely "frontier" camp meeting. "From at least the 1730s," Schmidt shows, "though far removed from Ulster or Scotland," the "holy faires" of the communion seasons "provided a notable portion" of the force that invigorated the evangelical revivals in the middle colonies. Since at least one high-profile New Englander, David Brainerd, was mightily affected by his experience of these ritual exercises in 1745, the practice may well have influenced the revivalist spirit subsequently in New England.[4]

Proponents of the revival in New England similarly drew upon long established English and seventeenth-century American Puritan devotional practices and patterns of spiritual experience both to fuel and to guide the Great Awakening in their region.[5] These efforts took place locally in the pulpit and in the context of pastoral work. On a broader, regional scale, New Light leaders specifically promoted the revivals of the 1730s and 1740s through their use of print media. The types of material included by Prince in *The Christian History* are mirrored in the lists of books published in Boston during this period. Although the mass publication of books and the advent of the reli-

[3]Jon Butler, *Awash in a Sea of Faith: Christianizing the American People* (Cambridge, Mass., 1990), 128, 164–166, 170–174, 179–181. See also Gregory H. Nobles, *Divisions Throughout the Whole: Politics and Society in Hampshire County, Mass., 1740–1775* (New York, 1983). Noble demonstrates the presence of a conservative impulse among Connecticut Valley clergy eager for "a stable ecclesiastical and social order" (37).

[4]Marilyn J. Westerkamp, *Triumph of the Laity: Scots-Irish Piety and the Great Awakening, 1625–1760* (New York, 1988); Leigh Eric Schmidt, *Holy Fairs: Scottish Communions and American Revivals in the Early Modern Period* (Princeton, 1989), 54–56.

[5]I have analyzed these foundational Puritan devotional practices and spiritual experience in *The Practice of Piety: Puritan Devotional Disciplines in Seventeenth-Century New England* (Chapel Hill, N.C., 1982) and *Early New England Meditative Poetry: Anne Bradstreet and Edward Taylor* (New York and Mahwah, N.J., 1988).

gious periodical were technologically innovative, the strong presence of traditional themes and old titles raises questions about how such underlying continuity accompanied the undeniable changes wrought in the Great Awakening decades. The motives behind this publishing effort included those identified by Prince in *The Christian History*: to re-establish a spiritual foundation and to guard against the excesses of enthusiasm.

Among the books published during this period one finds an astonishing number of reprints of seventeenth-century devotional tracts and manuals. Many of these were old favorites by English Nonconformist giants, such as John Owen, John Flavel, John Bunyan, James Janeway, Benjamin Keach, Thomas Gouge, Thomas Doolittle, William Burkitt, Thomas Vincent, Mordecai Matthews, Richard Baxter, Richard Standfast, and many others, all of whom died before 1710. William Dyer's *Christ's Famous Titles, and A Believer's Golden Chain, The Black Book of Conscience* by the pseudonymous Andrew Jones, Joseph Alleine's *Alarm to Unconverted Sinners,* and John Rawlet's *The Christian Monitor* are just a few of the genuine blockbusters from the mid-seventeenth century (they enjoyed ten, twenty and even more printings) that still commanded a large market when they appeared in the 1730s and 1740s. The influence of English Dissenter John Corbet, who died in 1680, was likewise not limited to his own century. Fresh reprints of *Self-Imployment in Secret* (orig. London, 1681; Boston, 1684), a record of his devotional practices, persisted through the 1740s. Similarly popular was Thomas Wilcox's *A Choice Drop of Honey, From the Rock Christ,* an early-seventeenth-century chestnut first published in Massachusetts in 1667, which saw several new editions during the Great Awakening. Jeremiah Burroughs's *The Rare Jewel of Christian Contentment,* first published in London in 1648, was also circulating again.[6] These "steady-sellers," as David Hall has described them in his study of seventeenth-century popular religion, thrived in the mid-eighteenth-century marketplace, some of them even into the early 1800s (and in the cases of Bunyan and Baxter until our own time). Although their publication both pre- and (with some) post-dated the Great Awakening, it is also the case that the appearance of editions of Puritan devotional classics during the

[6]William Dyer, *Christ's Famous Titles, and A Believer's Golden Chain* (Boston, 1731); Andrew Jones, *The Black Book of Conscience* (Boston, 1732); [Joshua Scottow], *Old Men's Tears* (Boston, 1691; reprinted 1733); John Corbet, *Enquiry into the State of his own Soul* (Boston, 1743); [Thomas Wilcox], *A Choice Drop of Honey, From the Rock Christ* (Boston, 1734, 1741); Jeremiah Burroughs, *The Rare Jewel of Christian Contentment* (Boston, 1731).

1730s and 1740s was part of a New Light strategy to guide the Awakening.[7]

Spiritual autobiography was also a staple of the religious book trade spanning the Puritan and Great Awakening eras. Elizabeth White's *The Experiences of God's Gracious Dealing*, for example, had appeared in numerous London and Glasgow editions from 1671 on and into the new century before being published in Boston in 1741. This work was mistaken as a product of colonial New England by Daniel Shea in his study of *Spiritual Autobiography in Early America* (1968). In his "Preface and Retrospect" in a 1988 reprinting of his monograph Shea acknowledges the error and defers to Patricia Caldwell's "suggestive explorations" of how different White's Old World spirituality really was from the distinctively American forms of "national autobiographical expression" she sees developing almost immediately after immigration. Yet Mrs. White's *Experiences* was republished in America almost a century after and an ocean away from its time and place of origin, Shea notes, "as part of the promotional literature associated with the Great Awakening." The historical question of why this work was still so popular and/or useful in the New England of the 1740s is at least as significant as that, raised by literary scholarship, of its stylistic differences from indigenous New World autobiographies. Whatever the differences that made the Great Awakening uniquely "American," the phenomenon was also part of an international transatlantic evangelical revival. The influence of George Whitefield in America, the near-simultaneous publication of *The Christian History* in Edinburgh and Boston, and the republication of so many older English devotional manuals and tracts in America attest to this fact. The way New Light leaders used the print media strengthened their Old World links and the traditionalism of their movement.[8]

The devotional classics published in New England during the decades of the Great Awakening represented the major themes of Puritan spirituality, including the essentially medieval techniques of med-

---

[7]David D. Hall, *Worlds of Wonder, Days of Judgment* (New York, 1989), 21–70. See also, Margaret Spufford, *Small Books and Pleasant Histories: Popular Fiction and its Readership in Seventeenth-Century England* (Athens, Ga., 1981), esp. the chapter "Small Godly Books: Popular Religion," 194–218; William L. Joyce, et. al., eds., *Printing and Society in Early America* (Worcester, Mass., 1983), 1–173; and David D. Hall, *On Native Ground: From the History of Printing to the History of the Book* (Worcester, Mass., 1984).

[8]Daniel B. Shea, *Spiritual Autobiography in Early America* (Madison, Wisc., 1988; orig. Princeton, 1968), x, 183–187; Patricia Caldwell, *The Puritan Conversion Narrative* (New York, 1983), 1–8, 34–41; Hambrick-Stowe, *Practice of Piety*, 5n.

itation. This was a spirituality of the heart and not merely of rational understanding or proper behavior. Thomas Doolittle's seventeenth-century devotional treatise, *Captives Bound in Chains,* which appeared again in a 1742 Boston edition, included a crescendo of arguments in order "yet more to affect your heart." These included acts of meditation: "Consider, that Christ did ransom you from your Captivity when you were an enemy unto him." The underlying spirituality of self-abasement preparatory to receiving the grace of God was once more set before the people. Thomas Wilcox in his *Choice Drop of Honey* wrote: "Thou who hast seen Christ all, and self nothing, who makes Christ thy life, and art dead to all righteousness besides, thou art the Christian who hath found favor with God." Mordecai Matthews's *The Christian's Daily Exercise* (Boston, 1730) and John Corbet's *Self-Imployment in Secret,* among others, outlined the familiar regimen of reading, meditation, and prayer in private and family settings, morning and night. Matthews followed the convention of including meditative poetry with prose sections of exhortation and sample meditations. In the morning, for example: "Rouze up thy sluggish Soul, O men / When first awake thou art; / And then let God and his concerns / be next unto thy heart." And at the start of the workday: "Imagine this same day to be / Thy last and dying day; / And God this night for ought thou knowest / Should take thy breath away. . . ." The medieval tradition of preparation for death was thus represented to the Great Awakening generation. Matthews exhorted: "Write in thy Book, or rather Heart, Against a Dying day." Richard Standfast's *A New-Years-Gift for Fainting Souls* (seventh edition, Boston, 1733) instructed its readers on traditional methods of self-examination, a fundamental exercise in Puritan preparationist spirituality. Cotton Mather augmented James Janeway's manual for children, *A Token for Children* (orig. London, 1671–1672) with case material from the deaths of pious New England children. This 1700 Boston edition was reprinted in 1728 and several times more in the 1740s and later. Its successful combination of the traditions of *ars moriendi* (meditative preparation for death) and the exemplar (meditative use of the lives of exemplary believers) demonstrates the continued vitality of age-old devotional conventions in the pre-Revolutionary "age of reason."[9]

[9]Thomas Doolittle, *Captives Bound in Chains, Made Free by Christ their Surety* (Boston, 1742), 211; [Thomas Wilcox], *A Choice Drop of Honey, From the Rock Christ,* eighth ed. (Boston, 1741), 23; Mordecai Matthews, *The Christian's Daily Exercise* (Boston, 1730), 2, 11.

Reprinted seventeenth-century books on sacramental meditation, such as Samuel Willard's *Some Brief Sacramental Meditations* (second edition, Boston, 1743), Thomas Vincent's *A Companion for Communicants* (Boston, 1730), and John Quick's *The Young Man's Claim Unto the Sacrament of the Lord's Supper* (Boston, 1741) put forth the well worn disciplines for preparation to receive the sacrament in familiar manual or catechetical form. William Burkitt's *The Poor Man's Help, and Young Man's Guide,* for example, advised: "The Consideration of our Baptismal Vows, renewed and ratified by many Sacramental Engagements at the Holy Table, is certainly one of the strongest ties that Christianity lays upon us to oblige us to the Love and Practice of Universal Holiness." Vincent provided sample meditations for daily preparations during the week prior to the Supper and for minute-by-minute contemplation during Communion itself. The republication in Boston of the eucharistic manual by John Quick, a seventeenth-century minister in London, addressed issues that divided some New Englanders in the 1740s. Against the position associated with Solomon Stoddard, Quick asserted: "All that are baptized, have no more a right to the blessed Sacrament of the Eucharist" than did unclean but circumcised Israelites to the Passover. He called for believers to be "refreshed and revived" and set forth rigorous spiritual self-examination as the means of such revival.[10]

Works by the old Congregational authors also cautioned against some of the dangers of the revival's excesses. As one late-seventeenth-century manual, reprinted in a 1731 Boston edition, put it, "it is hard to say, from which Religion suffers most, whether from the want of Zeal in some, or from the Mistakes of Zeal in others." Some specific problems of the Great Awakening, such as the splintering of congregations, had been addressed authoritatively in the earlier period. John Owen, for example, wrote that "It is convenient that all Believers of one Place should joyne themselves in one Congregation . . . Which Order cannot be disturbed without Danger, Strife, Emulation, and Breach of Love." His "Rules of Walking in Fellowship, with Reference to the Pastor or Minister that watcheth for our Souls" stressed the need for respect for and submission to clerical authority. As reprinted in 1744, this argument for a homogenous, village-based congregationalism can only be read as a response to the tendency

---

[10]William Burkitt, *The Poor Man's Help, and Young Man's Guide,* eighth ed. (Boston, 1731), 134; Thomas Vincent's *A Companion for Communicants* (Boston, 1730), 8; John Quick's *The Young Man's Claim Unto the Sacrament of the Lord's Supper* (Boston, 1741), iv, vi.

for Separate congregations and itinerant preachers to splinter New England society. The word "rule," derived from medieval monastic spirituality, took on new meaning as settled ministers struggled to retain control in a freer society. Jeremiah Burroughs's classic, *The Rare Jewel of Christian Contentment* (originally published in London in 1648, reprinted Boston 1731) consisted of "eighteen rules for the obtaining of [the] excellent grace" of assurance. In an age of enthusiasm such talk of rules bespoke a desire among clergy for order. Daniel Burgess's *Rules for Hearing the Word of God* (reprinted Boston, 1742) urged that "when these Rules shall be observed, Ministers shall be joyful (both) Fathers and Nurses." Another manual advised believers to "have frequent recourse to your Minister, your Spiritual Guide, desire his Advice, and follow his Instructions." The message could also be couched in fearful terms. *The Black Book of Conscience*, an extraordinary piece whose 26th edition was reprinted in Boston in 1732, warned against the "dreadful Terror" that will befall "all those that live and die in their Sins" as they "go to Hell without controul." New Light clergy thus hoped to guard against emotional excess and loss of clerical authority in the very Awakening they otherwise promoted.[11]

At the same time, the old works gave voice to the central theme of the Great Awakening, the rebirth of the soul from sin. Thomas Gouge (1609–1681) whose *The Young Man's Guide* was republished in 1742, argued: "It is necessary to be converted, that so thou mayest live. Thou dyest without Remedy, thou dyest without Mercy, if thou turn not." The directness associated with New Light preaching could readily be found in the classics. Thus, James Janeway (1636–1674): "What say you to all this? . . . If you will not be acquainted with God, you shall be acquainted with the Devil, and know whose Company is best by woful Experience." Richard Baxter (1615–1691), known for his irenic temperament, nevertheless brought a message of immediacy and ultimacy, and of both warning and promise. The very title of one of his devotional works reprinted (the 32nd edition!) in Boston in 1731 has a distinctively Great Awakening tone: *A Call to the Unconverted to Turn and Live.* The words on the page can be imagined from a New England pulpit: "I beseech thee, I charge thee, to hear

---

[11]Burkitt, *Poor Man's Help*, 1, 137; John Owen, *Eschol: A Cluster of the Fruit of Canaan* (seventh edition, Boston, 1744), 4, 7; Jeremiah Burroughs, *The rare Jewel of Christian Contentment* (Boston, 1731), 18; Daniell Burgess, *Rules for Hearing the Word of God* (Boston, 1742), 18; Andrew Jones, *The Black Book of Conscience, or God's High Court of Justice in the Soul*, 26th edition (Boston, 1732), 13, 15.

and obey the Call of God, and resolvedly to turn, that thou mayst live. But if thou wilt not . . . I summon thee answer for it before the Lord." In a prayer for use in family devotions Baxter humbles the reader: "O woe to us that ever we were born, if thou forgive not our sins, and make us not holy before this short uncertain Life be at an end." His "Prayer for a Penitent Sinner" contains the language of the later revivalism: "Thou knowest my secret sins . . . My sins, O Lord, have found me out. Fears and Sorrows overwhelm me! . . . O God, be merciful to me a Sinner. . . ." Janeway challenged all "that as yet are Strangers to God" whether they have "such a Friend as he is, that will always be at your Elbow . . . ? And if not, why then will *you* not *now accept* of his Acquaintance, who will be such a friend to all who love him?" (emphasis added). The directness of Janeway's personal, evangelical address to the reader is identical with that put forth by the New Light preacher. "Come away, poor Soul, for all this it is not yet quite too late . . . Once more I make such an offer to thee, as I am sure none but a mad Man will refuse." And finally, he paints salvation in vivid colors borrowed from the Song of Solomon: "O the sweet Pleasures of Divine Love, infinitely transcending all carnal Affections."[12]

These devotional classics did not stint on the traditional "use of terror" nor shrink from proclaiming the urgent need for a personal conversion experience. Their republication reinforced a shift back in this direction in New Light pulpits. Between 1690 and 1730 Congregationalist preachers had typically adopted a kinder, gentler evangelistic style. Jon Butler, building on the work of Harry Stout, states that the presentation of the biblical promise of salvation from sin by God's grace through faith was reduced to a "commonplace exposition" of the message. "Preachers did not terrorize. Nor did they ignore. They simply assumed that their listeners should hear about the necessity of salvation and proceeded to tell them in thoroughly mundane ways."[13] Preachers seeking to promote the revival through their own revival of evangelistic preaching, with renewed emphasis on the "use of terror" and the immediate call for repentance and faith, found support for their "innovations" in the writings of their Puritan forebears.

Ministers like Thomas Prince, continuing an editorial tradition es-

---

[12]Thomas Gouge, *The Young Man's Guide* (Boston, 1742), 52; James Janeway, *Heaven upon Earth* (Boston, 1730), 125, 133, 144, 205, 260; Richard Baxter, *Call to the Unconverted to Turn and Live*, 32nd ed. (Boston, 1731), sig. D4, 149, 158.
[13]Butler, *Awash in a Sea of Faith*, 172; Stout, *New England Soul*, chap. 8.

tablished by Cotton Mather, likewise dedicated much energy to reprinting old works of reliable New Englanders and to publishing exemplary personal devotional manuscripts in danger of being lost. In the first category, the works of Thomas Shepard were always both influential in the thinking of preachers like Jonathan Edwards and popular among New England readers. John E. Smith showed how Edwards built his *Treatise Concerning Religious Affections* (1746) on the foundation of Shepard's theology of conversion, especially as enunciated in *The Parable of the Ten Virgins*. Edwards cites "Mr. Shepard's principles" with greater frequency than he does any other author, though not uncritically, often including lengthy quotations from his works. Moreover, new editions of Shepard's *The Sound Beleever: Or, A Treatise of Evangelical Conversion* (1736, 1742), *The Sincere Convert* (1735, 1742, 1743), *The Saints Jewel* (1743), and *Three Valuable Pieces* (1747) were published in Boston during the period associated with the Great Awakening. A reprinting of Thomas Hooker's *The Poor Doubting Christian Drawn to Christ*, which had enjoyed a powerful influence upon the founding generation in New England, appeared again in 1743. Samuel Willard's writings, such as the monumental *Compleat Body of Divinity* (1726) and his *Brief Directions to a Young Scholar Designing the Ministry for the Study of Divinity* (1735), were limited in their direct influence to the clergy, though a collection of sermons, *Spiritual Desertions Discovered and Remedied* (1741), and *Some Brief Sacramental Meditations* (1743) because of their content probably found a wider audience. These books may have seemed old-fashioned to some, but for others they provided theological and spiritual moorings during a time of rapid change, increasing diversity, and secularization. To those who saw New England's only hope in spiritual awakening, Joshua Scottow's popular jeremiad, *Old Men's Tears For their own Declensions*, carried the same message when reissued in the 1730s as on its first appearance in 1691: "It is time for our churches to remember from whence they are fallen, repent and do their first works."[14]

A prime example of newly published devotional writing is Thomas Prince's edition of *The Memoirs of Capt. Roger Clap* (Boston, 1731). Clap, who had come to Boston as a pious youth in 1630, recalled how in those early years, "The Lord Jesus Christ was so plainly held out in the Preaching of the Gospel unto poor lost Sinners, and the

---

[14]Jonathan Edwards, *Religious Affections*, John E. Smith ed. (New Haven, 1959), 53–57, 475, index under "Shepard, Thomas"; Joshua Scottow, *Old Men's Tears* (Boston, 1733), 11.

absolute Necessity of the new Birth, and God's holy Spirit in those Days was pleased to accompany the Word with such Efficacy upon the Hearts of many," that many souls were converted. The language of "poor lost sinners," "new birth," and heart religion resonates strikingly with the spiritual tenor of the 1730s and 1740s. That the narrative was written by an elderly Clap in the late seventeenth century as he looked back on the earliest years of the Founding served Prince's purpose to a tee. Here he could show that the emotional conversion of individuals within the context of general revival was in continuity with early New England experience, and that excess could be controlled by theological orthodoxy.[15]

Jonathan Edwards, Prince, and others were similarly intent on gathering and publishing first-hand narratives of contemporary spiritual experience, in part to demonstrate that the soul-searching and spiritual ecstasy of the Awakening were not new but something very old. Edwards edited and published *The Life of David Brainerd,* the famous missionary to the Indians who died at age thirty, wishing it to serve as a model of piety for the mid-eighteenth century. The value for Edwards lay in its correlation with Puritan prototypes of journals and spiritual autobiographies. Brainerd himself overtly strove to replicate this traditional devotionalism in his own life and diaries and to advance it for others. Since the practice of journal-keeping was a living part of the Puritan legacy in Brainerd's day, he was familiar with the personal writings of the earlier generations and certainly conscious of their format. Cotton Mather had preserved many samples for just this purpose in his *Magnalia Christi Americana* (1702). Toward the end of Brainerd's life he was specifically aware of the journal of Thomas Shepard as a model not only for his own interior life but for others as well. "While I was confined at Boston," he recorded, "I read with care and attention some papers of old Mr. Shepard's, lately come to light and designed for the press." Brainerd helped with the editorial work on this diary of Thomas Shepard and later, at Edwards's Northampton parsonage, wrote a preface. Thomas Prince published the volume, along with Brainerd's preface, as *Meditations and Spiritual Experiences of Mr. Thomas Shepard* in 1747, at the very time that Edwards was editing the just-deceased Mr. Brainerd's own journals. The message could not be more clear, that the piety of David Brainerd, whom Edwards viewed as an exemplar

[15] *Memoirs of Capt. Roger Clap* (Dorchester Antiquarian and Historical Society, *Collections* [Boston, 1854], orig. Boston, 1731), 1:17–20; Hambrick-Stowe, *Practice of Piety,* 5–7; Shea, *Spiritual Autobiography in Early America,* 118–126.

of the Great Awakening at its best, was of a piece with that of Thomas Shepard, one of the greatest representatives of the old Puritan spirituality. This is the viewpoint consistently put forth by New Light clergy through their entire use of print media.[16]

The dynamics of the colonial publishing and bookselling business are only gradually coming to light. Stephen Botein has shown in reference to book importation that until the Revolutionary War "the Anglo-America book trade took form within networks of religious affiliation." Likewise, the seventeenth century's "shifting coalition of ministers, printers, and booksellers" no doubt continued though the period of the Awakening, in spite of increasing secularization of the business. Richard D. Brown observes that while in the seventeenth and early eighteenth centuries "public speech and printing" were fairly tightly controlled by "the right sort of people"—namely the ministers, magistrates, and leading merchants—by the 1720s this "closed and confined" communications system could no longer be so fully monopolized by the elite; "the union of class and culture was dissolving." Nevertheless, Brown expresses doubt that "a single movement, even one so profound and so extensive as the Great Awakening, could shatter the common culture and information system that sustained it, since both were closely attached to the actual circumstances and customary social functions of so many people." Although with the Awakening "the information system could never again be quite so unitary and deferential as before . . . the common culture and its restricted information system survived." Compared with the far more extensive social changes of the early nineteenth century, Brown states, "the Great Awakening, which might seem to have changed so much theoretically, made little practical difference."[17]

On the one hand, decisions concerning publication were market-

[16]Jonathan Edwards, *The Life of David Brainerd,* ed. Norman Petit (New Haven, 1985), 451, 460, 513; *An Account of the Life of the late Reverend Mr. David Brainerd* was originally published in Boston, 1749. Prince published the portions of Shepard's "Private Diary" which had been edited as part of his collection of *Three Valuable Pieces* by Shepard (Boston, 1747). Shepard's journal and autobiography are available in a modern edition, *God's Plot: The Paradoxes of Puritan Piety,* ed. Michael McGiffert (Amherst, Mass., 1972).

[17]Stephen Botein, "The Anglo-American Book Trade Before 1776: Personnel and Strategies," in Joyce, et al. eds., *Printing and Society in Early America,* 51; Hall, *Worlds of Wonder,* 49, 244. Michael G. Hall sheds light on the matter as he describes Increase Mather's life-long relationship with the publishing business in *The Last American Puritan: The Life of Increase Mather* (Middletown, Conn., 1988), passim. For Anglican and Quaker books, see, for example, the "List of Books Sold by T. Cox at the Lamb on the Southside of the Town House in Boston," printed at the end of John Rawlet, *The Christian Monitor,* 25th edition (Boston, 1733), 69–70; Brown, *Knowledge is Power,* 40, 272–273. See

driven throughout the colonial period and cannot simply be chalked up to authoritarian motives of clerical or political elites. On the other hand, the clergy's role in determining what got published did not vanish with the rise of secular-minded printers like the Franklins. By the 1730s and 1740s Boston publishers were freely coming out with Anglican and Quaker works, so it is not that the Congregational clergy, much less the New Light faction, maintained control over the press. Clerical involvement in publishing was of necessity exercised within the context of multivalent market forces. During the Great Awakening the worlds of publishing and religious life were both becoming increasingly competitive; that is, colonial society itself, of which religion and publishing were manifestations, was becoming more free and competitive. It was natural, then, that when theological lines were drawn, battles were fought through the printed word, as revealed by the famous exchange between Jonathan Edwards (*Some Thoughts Concerning the Present Revival of Religion* [Boston, 1742]) and Charles Chauncy (*Seasonable Thoughts on the State of Religion* [Boston, 1743]).

New Light leaders responded to this challenge of modernity by aggressively employing print media in their strategy to promote and guide the revival. Their effort was a direct appeal for popular support. The use of traditional materials—republication of devotional classics by English and American Puritan "Old Writers" and the printing of personal spiritual writings from both seventeenth-century and contemporary believers—in fact played to certain strengths in the popular marketplace. David Hall and Jon Butler suggest that as society was becoming more secular during the period of the Great Awakening the old "mentality of wonders, the story line of deliverance and confession, and the moral allegory of a land swept clean of sin . . . flourished once more among ordinary people." Hall explains that "for them printers continued to publish . . . books like Alleine's *Alarm to Unconverted Sinners.*" The persistence of a popular market, for example, helps to explain why in 1749 Benjamin Franklin would come out with yet another edition of Janeway's *Token for Children* with Cotton Mather's by-then-traditional *Token for the Children of New England.* Printers were not simply responding to economic opportunity, however. The books were published at the urging, under the

---

also, Edwin Wolf II, *The Book Culture of a Colonial American City: Philadelphia Books, Bookmen, and Booksellers* (Oxford, 1988).

editorship, and sometimes with the financial sponsorship of New Light clergy and their friends.[18]

What New England Congregationalist promoters of the Great Awakening sought, therefore, was truly a "*revival* of religion." Along with all that was undeniably "new" in the 1730s and 1740s—including a freer use of print media by spokespersons of every religious persuasion—New Light leaders played to the persistent market appeal of old devotional works and newer works displaying old themes. They prayed specifically, in Prince's words, that "the pious Principles and Spirit" of the "Old Writers" might be renewed in their time. Their goal was to encourage the spiritual awakening and to channel it along lines congruent with basic tenets of seventeenth-century Puritanism. In that evangelical Christianity did secure an authoritative and traditional role in American society during these decades leading up to the Revolution, New Light prayers—and efforts—were rewarded with success in the popular marketplace.

[18]Hall, *Worlds of Wonder,* 244; Butler, *Awash in a Sea of Faith,* 182–185; James Janeway, *A Token for Children. . . . To Which is added, A Token for the Children of New England* (Philadelphia, 1749).

Index